WEBSTER'S
NEW
INTERNATIONAL
ATLAS

Created in Cooperation with the Editors of

MERRIAM-WEBSTER

Bounty
Books

Originally published in the United States as *Webster's
International Atlas* by Federal Street Press.

This updated edition published 2004 by Bounty Books,
a division of Octopus Publishing Group Ltd,
2-4 Heron Quays, London E14 4JP

ISBN 0 7537 0903 1

Printed and bound in Hong Kong

Contents

Abbreviations

Ala.	Alabama	Mt.	Mount
Ark.	Arkansas	Mtn.	Mountain
Arm.	Armenia	Mts.	Mountains
ASEAN	Association of Southeast Asian Nations	N	north(ern)
		Nat'l	National
Azer.	Azerbaijan	N.C.	North Carolina
Belg.	Belgium	NE	northeast(ern)
Calif.	California	N.H.	New Hampshire
C.A.R	Central African Republic	N.J.	New Jersey
		N.P.	National Park
Caricom	Caribbean Community	NW	northwest(ern)
CFA	Communauté Financière Africaine (African Financial Community)	N.Y.	New York
		N.Z.	New Zealand
		Okla.	Oklahoma
		Penin.	Peninsula
Conn.	Connecticut	Penn.	Pennsylvania
D.C.	District of Columbia	Pk.	Peak
Del.	Delaware	Port.	Portugal
Dem.	Democratic	Pt.	Point
Den.	Denmark	Rep.	Republic
E	east(ern)	R.I.	Rhode Island
Fla.	Florida	S	south(ern)
Fr.	France	S.C.	South Carolina
ft.	foot (feet)	SE	southeast(ern)
GNP	gross national product	sq.	square
		St.	Saint
I.	Island	SW	southwest(ern)
Ill.	Illinois	Switz.	Switzerland
Ind.	Indiana	Tenn.	Tennessee
Indon.	Indonesia	Turkmen.	Turkmenistan
Is.	Islands	U.A.E.	United Arab Emirates
km.	kilometer(s)	U.K.	United Kingdom
La.	Louisiana	U.S.	United States
Mass.	Massachusetts	Va.	Virginia
Md.	Maryland	Vt.	Vermont
mi.	mile(s)	W	west(ern)
Mich.	Michigan	Wash.	Washington
Minn.	Minnesota	Wis.	Wisconsin
Miss.	Mississippi	W.Va.	West Virginia

Map Legend

Cities and Towns

Ottawa ⊛   National Capital

Edinburgh ◉   Second level
political capital

São Paulo •   City symbol

Boundaries

▬▬▬▬   International

▬▬ ▬▬   Disputed

― ― ―   Defacto

········   Line of control

▬▬▬▬   Political subdivisions

Other Features

SERENGETI
NATIONAL PARK ▪   National park

Mount Everest
29,028 ft. ▲   Mountain Peak

∿⬭   Dam

∿ᵥ   Falls

∿ᵥ   Rapids

―――   River

― ― ―   Intermittent river

▬▬▬   Canal

•••••   Aqueduct

∿∿∿∿   Reef

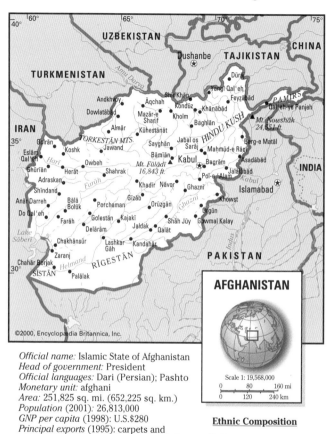

Official name: Islamic State of Afghanistan
Head of government: President
Official languages: Dari (Persian); Pashto
Monetary unit: afghani
Area: 251,825 sq. mi. (652,225 sq. km.)
Population (2001): 26,813,000
GNP per capita (1998): U.S.$280
Principal exports (1995): carpets and
rugs 54.3%; dried fruits and nuts 15.6%
to: Pakistan 20.1%; Belgium-
Luxembourg 8.7%; France 7.4%; U.S.
6.7%; Japan 6.0%

Scale 1: 19,568,000

0   80   160 mi
0   120   240 km

Ethnic Composition

Hazāra 19%
Other 18%
Tadzhik 25%
Pashtun 38%

After the fall of the Taliban in 2001, the newly established
Afghan Interim Authority restored, in a modified form,
the national flag first introduced in 1928. Black represents
the dark ages of the past; red, the blood shed in the
struggle for independence; and green, hope and prosperity
for the future.

©2000, Encyclopædia Britannica, Inc.

Official name: Republic of Albania
Head of government: Prime Minister
Official language: Albanian
Monetary unit: lek
Area: 11,082 sq. mi. (28,703 sq. km.)
Population (2001): 3,091,000
GNP per capita (1999): U.S.$930
Principal exports (2000): misc. manufactured articles 68.0%; manufactured goods 12.1%; crude materials 8.7%; food and beverages 6.6%) *to:* Italy 70.3%; Greece 12.9%; Germany 6.6%

ALBANIA

Scale 1: 5,731,000

0   20   40 mi
0 30   60 km

Religious Affiliation

Roman Catholic 10%
Muslim 70%
Albanian Orthodox 20%

On Nov. 28, 1443, the flag was first raised by Skanderbeg, the national hero. After independence from Turkish rule was proclaimed on Nov. 28, 1912, the flag was flown by various regimes, each of which identified itself by adding a symbol above the double-headed eagle. The current flag, which features only the eagle, was adopted on May 22, 1993.

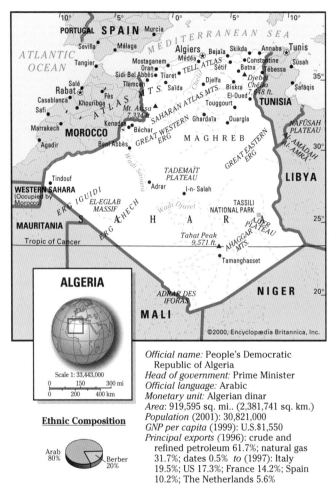

@2000, Encyclopædia Britannica, Inc.

ALGERIA

Scale 1: 33,443,000

0   150   300 mi
0   200   400 km

Ethnic Composition

Arab 80%

Berber 20%

Official name: People's Democratic Republic of Algeria
Head of government: Prime Minister
Official language: Arabic
Monetary unit: Algerian dinar
Area: 919,595 sq. mi.. (2,381,741 sq. km.)
Population (2001): 30,821,000
GNP per capita (1999): U.S.$1,550
Principal exports (1996): crude and refined petroleum 61.7%; natural gas 31.7%; dates 0.5% *to* (1997): Italy 19.5%; US 17.3%; France 14.2%; Spain 10.2%; The Netherlands 5.6%

In the early 19th century, during the French conquest of North Africa, Algerian resistance fighters led by Emir Abdelkader supposedly raised the current flag. Its colors and symbols are associated with Islam and the Arab dynasties of the region. The flag was raised over an independent Algeria on July 2, 1962.

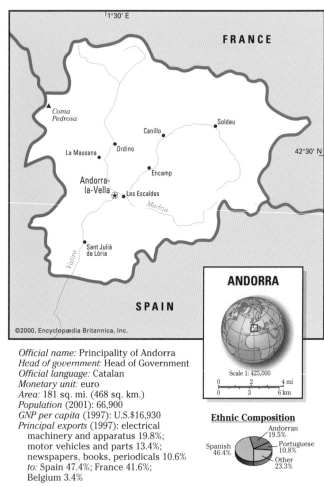

FRANCE

▲ *Coma Pedrosa*

Soldeu

Canillo

La Massana Ordino

Encamp

Andorra-la-Vella

Les Escaldes

Madriu

Sant Julià de Lòria

Valira

SPAIN

©2000, Encyclopædia Britannica, Inc.

ANDORRA

Scale 1: 425,000

0 — 2 — 4 mi
0 — 3 — 6 km

Official name: Principality of Andorra
Head of government: Head of Government
Official language: Catalan
Monetary unit: euro
Area: 181 sq. mi. (468 sq. km.)
Population (2001): 66,900
GNP per capita (1997): U.S.$16,930
Principal exports (1997): electrical machinery and apparatus 19.8%; motor vehicles and parts 13.4%; newspapers, books, periodicals 10.6% *to:* Spain 47.4%; France 41.6%; Belgium 3.4%

Ethnic Composition

Andorran 19.5%
Spanish 46.4%
Portuguese 10.8%
Other 23.3%

The flag may date to 1866, but the first legal authority for it is unknown. The design was standardized in July 1993. Possible sources for its colors are the flags of neighboring Spain (red-yellow-red) and France (blue-white-red). The coat of arms incorporates both French and Spanish elements dating to the 13th century or earlier.

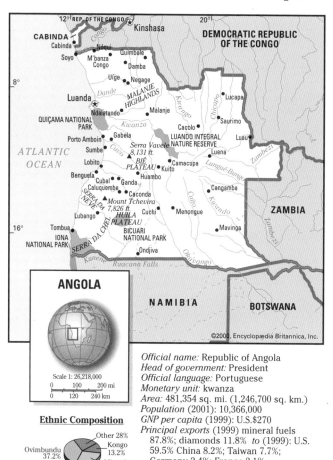

Official name: Republic of Angola
Head of government: President
Official language: Portuguese
Monetary unit: kwanza
Area: 481,354 sq. mi. (1,246,700 sq. km.)
Population (2001): 10,366,000
GNP per capita (1999): U.S.$270
Principal exports (1999) mineral fuels
87.8%; diamonds 11.8% *to* (1999): U.S.
59.5% China 8.2%; Taiwan 7.7%;
Germany 2.4%; France 2.1%

ANGOLA

Scale 1: 26,218,000

0   100   200 mi

0   120   240 km

Ethnic Composition

Other 28%
Ovimbundu 37.2%
Kongo 13.2%
Mbundu 21.6%

After Portugal withdrew from Angola on Nov. 11, 1975, the flag of the leading rebel group gained recognition. Inspired by designs of the Viet Cong and the former Soviet Union, it includes a star for internationalism and progress, a cogwheel for industrial workers, and a machete for agricultural workers. The black stripe is for the African people.

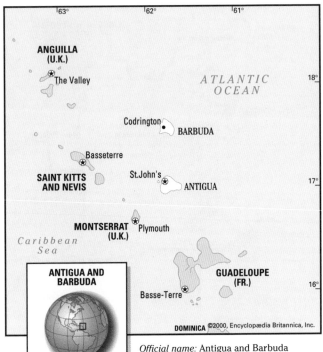

Official name: Antigua and Barbuda
Head of government: Prime Minister
Official language: English
Monetary unit: Eastern Caribbean dollar
Area: 170.5 sq. mi. (441.6 sq. km.)
Population (2001): 71,500
GNP per capita (1999): U.S.$8,990
Principal exports (1998): reexports
(significantly, petroleum products
reexported to neighboring islands)
59.1%; domestic exports 40.9%
to (1994): U.S. 40.0%; also United
Kingdom; Canada; and Caricom

Scale 1: 4,945,000

| 0 | 20 | 40 mi |
| 0 | 30 | 60 km |

Religious Affiliation

Other 15.5%
Roman Catholic 10.8%
Protestant 73.7%

When "associated statehood" was granted by Britain on Feb. 27, 1967, the flag was introduced, and it remained after independence (Nov. 1, 1981). Red is for the dynamism of the people, the V-shape is for victory, and the sun is for the climate. Black is for the majority population and the soil, blue is for the sea, and white is for the beaches.

BOLIVIA
GRAN CHACO
PARAGUAY
BRAZIL

Tropic of Capricorn
Mount Palermo
20,073 ft.
Salta
San Miguel
de Tucumán
Asunción
Formosa
Posadas
Resistencia
Corrientes
Mt. Pissis
22,235 ft.
Santiago
del Estero
Avellaneda
La Rioja
Concordia
San
Juan
Mount Aconcagua
22,825 ft.
Córdoba
Santa Fe
Villa María
Paraná
URUGUAY
Santiago
Mercedes
Luján
Montevideo
San Rafael
Tigre
Buenos Aires
La Plata

PACIFIC
OCEAN

Santa Rosa
Tandil
Neuquén
Colorado
Mar del Plata
Negro
Bahía
Blanca
Viedma

ATLANTIC
OCEAN

Rawson

Comodoro
Rivadavia

FALKLAND ISLANDS
(ISLAS MALVINAS)
(Administered by U.K.;
claimed by Argentina)

Río Gallegos
Stanley

TIERRA DEL
FUEGO
Ushuaia

©2000, Encyclopædia Britannica, Inc.

ARGENTINA

Scale 1: 57,746,000
0   250   500 mi
0   400   800 km

Official name: Argentine Republic
Head of government: President
Official language: Spanish
Monetary unit: peso
Area: 1,073,400 sq. mi. (2,780,092 sq. km.)
Population (2001): 37,487,000
GNP per capita (1999): U.S.$7,550
Principal exports (1999): food products
   and live animals 35.1%; petroleum and
   petroleum products 12.1%; machinery
   and transport equipment 12.0%;
   manufactured products 10.8%;
   to: Brazil 24.4%; U.S. 11.4%; Chile 8.0%

Ethnic Composition

European
85%
Mestizo and
Amerindian
15%

The uniforms worn by Argentines when the British attacked
Buenos Aires (1806) and the blue ribbons worn by patriots in
1810 may have been the origin of the celeste-white-celeste
flag hoisted on Feb. 12,1812. The flag's golden "sun of May"
was added on Feb. 25,1818, to commemorate the yielding of
the Spanish viceroy in 1810.

ARMENIA

Scale 1: 4,429,000

0 20	40 mi
0 30	60 km

Ethnic Composition

Azerbaijani 2.6%
Other 4.1%
Armenian 93.3%

Official name: Republic of Armenia
Head of government: Prime Minister
Official language: Armenian
Monetary unit: dram
Area: 11,484 sq. mi. (29,800 sq. km.)
Population (2001): 3,807,000
GNP per capita (1999): U.S.$490
Principal exports (2000): jewelry 39.4%;
  machinery and equipment 14.3%;
  mineral products 12.4%; agricultural
  products 9.8%; *to:* Belgium 24.5%;
  Russia 14.7%; Iran 9.1%

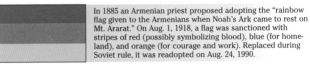

In 1885 an Armenian priest proposed adopting the "rainbow flag given to the Armenians when Noah's Ark came to rest on Mt. Ararat." On Aug. 1, 1918, a flag was sanctioned with stripes of red (possibly symbolizing blood), blue (for homeland), and orange (for courage and work). Replaced during Soviet rule, it was readopted on Aug. 24, 1990.

©2000, Encyclopædia Britannica, Inc.

AUSTRALIA

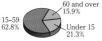

Scale 1: 70,500,000

| 0 | 300 | 600 mi |
| 0 | 400 | 800 km |

Official name: Commonwealth of
Australia
Head of government: Prime Minister
Official language: English
Monetary unit: Australian dollar
Area: 2,969,910 sq. mi. (7,692,030 sq. km.)
Population (2001): 19,358,000
GNP per capita (1999): U.S.$20,950
Principal exports (1999–2000): crude
materials excluding fuels 18.9%;
mineral fuels and lubricants 18.6%;
food and live animals 17.3% *to:* Japan
19.3%; U.S. 9.8%

Age Breakdown

60 and over
15.9%

15–59
62.8%

Under 15
21.3%

After Australian confederation was achieved on Jan. 1, 1901,
the flag was chosen in a competition. Like the blue flags of
British colonies, it displays the Union Jack in the canton. Also
shown are the Southern Cross and a "Commonwealth Star."
The design became official on May 22, 1909, and it was recognized as the national flag on Feb. 14, 1954.

©2000, Encyclopædia Britannica, Inc.

AUSTRIA

Scale 1: 8,842,000

Official name: Republic of Austria
Head of government: Chancellor
Official language: German
Monetary unit: euro
Area: 32,378 sq. mi. (83,858 sq. km.)
Population (2001): 8,069,000
GNP per capita (1999): U.S.$25,430
Principal exports (1999): machinery and
transport equipment 43.1%; chemical
products 9.4%; fabricated metals 4.9%;
paper and paper products 4.7%
to: Germany 34.9%; Italy 8.4%

Religious Affiliation

Nonreligious and atheist 8.6%
Other 8.6%
Lutheran 4.8%
Roman Catholic 78%

The colors of the Austrian coat of arms date from the seal of Duke Frederick II in 1230. With the fall of the Austro-Hungarian Empire in 1918, the new Austrian republic adopted the red-white-red flag. The white is sometimes said to represent the Danube River. The imperial eagle, with one or two heads, has been an Austrian symbol for centuries.

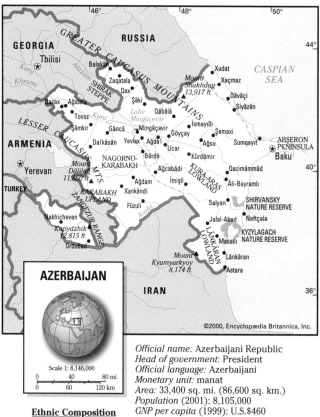

©2000, Encyclopædia Britannica, Inc.

Scale 1: 8,146,000

0   40   80 mi
0   60   120 km

Ethnic Composition

Azerbaijani 82.7%
Armenian 5.6%
Russian 5.7%
Other 6%

Official name: Azerbaijani Republic
Head of government: President
Official language: Azerbaijani
Monetary unit: manat
Area: 33,400 sq. mi. (86,600 sq. km.)
Population (2001): 8,105,000
GNP per capita (1999): U.S.$460
Principal exports (1998): petroleum products 69.1%; textiles 9.2%; food 7.7%; machinery and equipment 6.0% *to:* Turkey 22.4%; Russia 17.4%; Georgia 12.7%

In the early 20th century anti-Russian nationalists exhorted the Azerbaijanis to "Turkify, Islamicize, and Europeanize," and the 1917 flag was associated with Turkey and Islam. In 1918 the crescent and star (also symbols of Turkic peoples) were introduced. Suppressed under Soviet rule, the flag was re-adopted on Feb. 5, 1991.

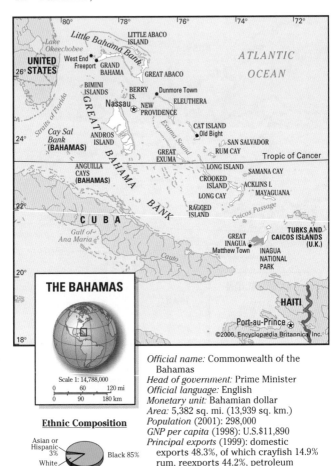

THE BAHAMAS

Scale 1: 14,788,000

0   60   120 mi
0   90   180 km

Ethnic Composition

Asian or Hispanic 3%
Black 85%
White 12%

Official name: Commonwealth of the Bahamas
Head of government: Prime Minister
Official language: English
Monetary unit: Bahamian dollar
Area: 5,382 sq. mi. (13,939 sq. km.)
Population (2001): 298,000
GNP per capita (1998): U.S.$11,890
Principal exports (1999): domestic exports 48.3%, of which crayfish 14.9% rum, reexports 44.2%, petroleum exports 7.5% *to* (1998): U.S. 56.5%; EC 31.4%; Canada 2.1%

The flag of The Bahamas was adopted on July 10, 1973, the date of independence from Britain. Several entries from a competition were combined to create the design. The two aquamarine stripes are for the surrounding waters, the gold stripe is for the sand and other rich land resources, and the black triangle is for the people and their strength.

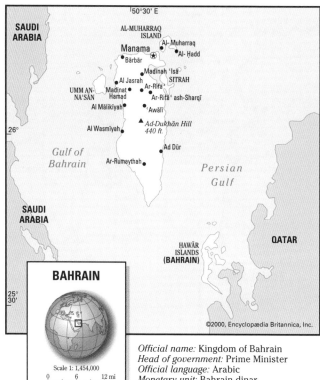

Official name: Kingdom of Bahrain
Head of government: Prime Minister
Official language: Arabic
Monetary unit: Bahrain dinar
Area: 268.0 sq. mi. (694.2 sq. km.)
Population (2001): 701,000
GNP per capita (1998): U.S.$7,640
Principal exports (1998): petroleum
products 51.8%; metal and metal
products 29.5% to: Saudi Arabia 8.2%;
U.S. 6.0%; Japan 4.4%; India 2.8%;
Taiwan 2.6%

Religious Affiliation

Other 9.7%
Christian 8.5%
Sunni Muslim 24.5%
Shi'ite Muslim 57.3%

Red was the color of the Kharijite Muslims of Bahrain about
1820, and white was chosen to show amity with the British.
The flag was recognized in 1933 but was used long before.
The current flag law was adopted on Aug. 19, 1972. Between
the white and red there may be a straight or serrated line,
but the latter is most common.

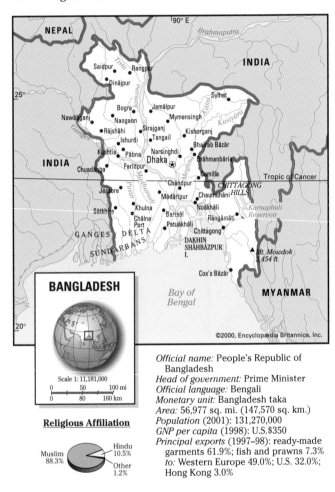

©2000, Encyclopædia Britannica, Inc.

BANGLADESH

Scale 1: 11,181,000

0   50   100 mi

0   80   160 km

Religious Affiliation

Muslim 88.3%

Hindu 10.5%

Other 1.2%

Official name: People's Republic of Bangladesh
Head of government: Prime Minister
Official language: Bengali
Monetary unit: Bangladesh taka
Area: 56,977 sq. mi. (147,570 sq. km.)
Population (2001): 131,270,000
GNP per capita (1998): U.S.$350
Principal exports (1997–98): ready-made garments 61.9%; fish and prawns 7.3% *to:* Western Europe 49.0%; U.S. 32.0%; Hong Kong 3.0%

The flag is dark green to symbolize Islam, plant life, and the hope placed in Bengali youth. Its original design included a red disk and a silhouette of the country. On Jan. 13, 1972, the silhouette was removed and the disk shifted off-center. The disk is the "rising sun of a new country" colored by the blood of those who fought for independence.

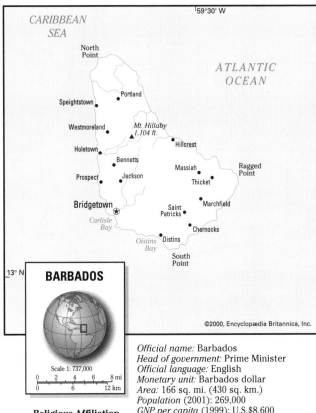

CARIBBEAN SEA

59°30' W

North Point

ATLANTIC OCEAN

Portland
Speightstown
Westmoreland
Mt. Hillaby
1,104 ft.
Holetown
Hillcrest
Bennetts
Massiah
Ragged Point
Prospect
Jackson
Thicket
Bridgetown ✪
Saint Patricks
Marchfield
Carlisle Bay
Charnocks
Oistins Bay
Oistins
South Point

13° N

©2000, Encyclopædia Britannica, Inc.

BARBADOS

Scale 1: 737,000

0   2   4   6   8 mi
0   6   12 km

Religious Affiliation

Roman Catholic 4.4%
Anglican 33%
Other 12.6%
Nonreligious 20.2%
Other Protestant 29.8%

Official name: Barbados
Head of government: Prime Minister
Official language: English
Monetary unit: Barbados dollar
Area: 166 sq. mi. (430 sq. km.)
Population (2001): 269,000
GNP per capita (1999): U.S.$8,600
Principal exports (1997): domestic exports 74.4%, of which sugar 12.7%; reexports 25.6% *to* (1997): United Kingdom 17.1%; U.S. 14.7%; Jamaica 6.6%

The flag was designed by Grantley Prescod, a Barbadian art teacher. Its stripes of blue-yellow-blue are for sea, sand, and sky. The black trident head was inspired by the colonial flag of Barbados, which featured a trident-wielding Poseidon, or Neptune, figure. The flag was first hoisted on Nov. 30, 1966, the date of independence from Britain.

©2000, Encyclopædia Britannica, Inc.

BELARUS

Scale 1: 9,358,000

| 0 | 40 | 80 mi |
| 0 | 60 | 120 km |

Ethnic Composition

Other 5.6%
Ukrainian 3%
Russian 13.5%
Belarusian 77.9%

Official name: Republic of Belarus
Head of government: President
Official languages: Belarusian; Russian
Monetary unit: rubel
Area: 80,153 sq. mi. (207,595 sq. km.)
Population (2001): 9,986,000
GNP per capita (1998): U.S.$2,620
Principal exports (1997): industrial products 98.3%, of which machinery and metalworking 32.9%, chemical and petroleum products 20.9% *to:* Russia 64.8%; Ukraine 5.8%

In 1951 the former Soviet republic created a striped flag in red (for communism) and green (for fields and forests), with the hammer, sickle, and star of communism. In 1991–95 an older design was used, but the Soviet-era flag was then altered and readopted without communist symbols. The vertical stripe is typical of embroidery on peasant clothing.

NORTH SEA

THE NETHERLANDS

FRANCE

GERMANY

LUXEMBOURG

©2000, Encyclopædia Britannica, Inc.

BELGIUM

Scale 1: 4,176,000

| 0 | 20 | 40 mi |
| 0 | 30 | 60 km |

Language Composition

Other 8%

Dutch 59%

French 33%

Official name: Kingdom of Belgium
Head of government: Prime Minister
Official languages: Dutch; French;
   German
Monetary unit: euro
Area: 11,787 sq. mi. (30,528 sq. km.)
Population (2001): 10,268,000
GNP per capita (1999): U.S.$24,650
Principal exports (1999): machinery and
   transport equipment 30.0%; chemicals
   20.3%; food 8.7% *to:* Germany 17.9%;
   France 17.7%; The Netherlands 12.8%;
   United Kingdom 10.0%

A gold shield and a black lion appeared in the seal of Count Philip of Flanders as early as 1162, and in 1787 cockades of black-yellow-red were used in a Brussels revolt against Austria. After a war for independence, the flag was recognized on Jan. 23, 1831. By 1838 the design, which was influenced by the French tricolor, became standard.

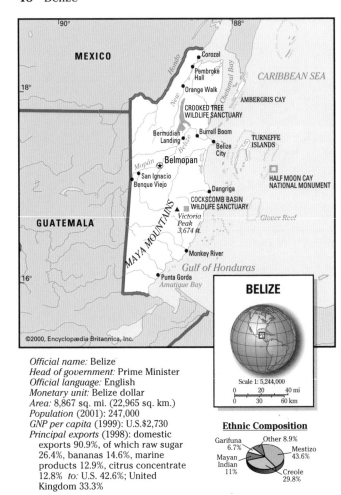

Official name: Belize
Head of government: Prime Minister
Official language: English
Monetary unit: Belize dollar
Area: 8,867 sq. mi. (22,965 sq. km.)
Population (2001): 247,000
GNP per capita (1999): U.S.$2,730
Principal exports (1998): domestic
  exports 90.9%, of which raw sugar
  26.4%, bananas 14.6%, marine
  products 12.9%, citrus concentrate
  12.8% *to:* U.S. 42.6%; United
  Kingdom 33.3%

Scale 1: 5,244,000

0   20   40 mi
0 30   60 km

Ethnic Composition

Garifuna 6.7%
Other 8.9%
Mayan Indian 11%
Mestizo 43.6%
Creole 29.8%

The flag of Belize (former British Honduras) was based on the flag of the nationalist People's United Party. Its coat of arms shows a mahogany tree, a shield, and a Creole and a Mestizo. The red stripes, symbolic of the United Democratic Party, were added on independence day (Sept. 21, 1981), when the flag was first officially hoisted.

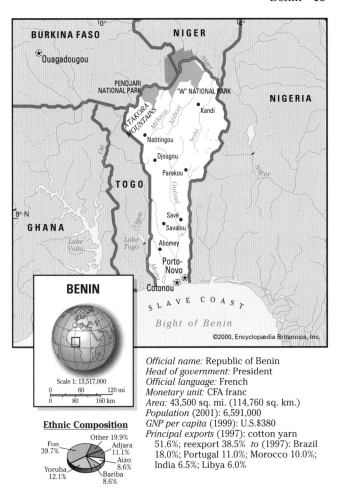

©2000, Encyclopædia Britannica, Inc.

BENIN

Scale 1: 13,517,000

| 0 | 60 | 120 mi |
| 0 | 80 | 160 km |

Ethnic Composition

Fon 39.7%
Other 19.9%
Adjara 11.1%
Aizo 8.6%
Bariba 8.6%
Yoruba 12.1%

Official name: Republic of Benin
Head of government: President
Official language: French
Monetary unit: CFA franc
Area: 43,500 sq. mi. (114,760 sq. km.)
Population (2001): 6,591,000
GNP per capita (1999): U.S.$380
Principal exports (1997): cotton yarn
51.6%; reexport 38.5% *to* (1997): Brazil
18.0%; Portugal 11.0%; Morocco 10.0%;
India 6.5%; Libya 6.0%

Adopted on Nov. 16, 1959, the flag of the former French colony used the Pan-African colors. Yellow was for the savannas in the north and green was for the palm groves in the south. Red stood for the blood of patriots. In 1975 a Marxist-oriented government replaced the flag, but after the demise of Communism it was restored on Aug. 1, 1990.

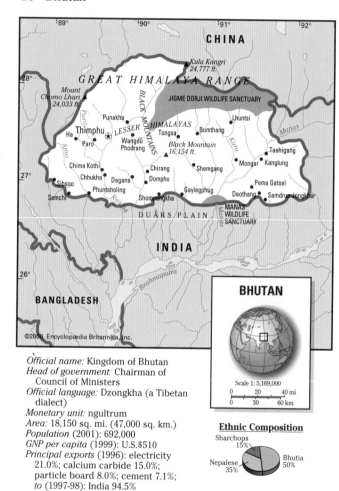

Official name: Kingdom of Bhutan
Head of government: Chairman of
Council of Ministers
Official language: Dzongkha (a Tibetan
dialect)
Monetary unit: ngultrum
Area: 18,150 sq. mi. (47,000 sq. km.)
Population (2001): 692,000
GNP per capita (1999): U.S.$510
Principal exports (1996): electricity
21.0%; calcium carbide 15.0%;
particle board 8.0%; cement 7.1%;
to (1997-98): India 94.5%

Ethnic Composition

Sharchops 15%
Nepalese 35%
Bhutia 50%

The flag of Bhutan ("Land of the Dragon") features a dragon
grasping jewels; this represents natural wealth and perfec-
tion. The white color is for purity and loyalty, the gold is for
regal power, and the orange-red is for Buddhist sects and religious commitment. The flag may have been introduced as
recently as 1971.

©2000, Encyclopædia Britannica, Inc.

Official name: Republic of Bolivia
Head of government: President
Official languages: Spanish, Aymara,
   Quechua
Monetary unit: boliviano
Area: 424,164 sq. mi. (1,098,581 sq. km.)
Population (2001): 8,516,000
GNP per capita (1999): U.S.$990
Principal exports (1998): zinc 14.1%;
   soybeans 13.6%; gold 10.1%; silver
   6.6% *to:* U.S. 18.4%; United Kingdom
   17.8%; Peru 11.9%

BOLIVIA

Scale 1: 23,517,000
0   100   200 mi
0   100   200   300 km

Ethnic Composition

White
14.5%
Aymara
16.9%
Other
12%
Quechua
25.4%
Mestizo
31.2%

A version of the flag was first adopted on July 25, 1826, but
on Nov. 5, 1851, the order of the stripes was changed to red-
yellow-green. The colors were often used by the Aymara and
Quechua peoples; in addition, red is for the valor of the army,
yellow for mineral resources, and green for the land. The current flag law dates from July 14, 1888.

BOSNIA AND HERZEGOVINA

Scale 1: 6,252,000

0 — 30 — 60 mi
0 — 40 — 80 km

Ethnic Composition

Muslim 49.2%

Serb 31.3%

Croat 17.3%

Other 2.2%

Official name: Bosnia and Herzegovina
Head of government: Prime Minister
Official languages: Bosnian (Serbo-Croatian)
Monetary unit: marka
Area: 19,741 sq. mi. (51,129 sq. km.)
Population (2001): 3,922,000. (excludes nearly 300,000 refugees in adjacent countries and Western Europe)
GNP per capita (1999): U.S.$1,210
Principal exports (2000): *to:* Italy 23.4%; Yugoslavia 21.6%; Switzerland 11.9%; Germany 9.2%; Croatia 7.9%

Upon independence from Yugoslavia on March 3, 1992, the Bosnian-led government chose a neutral flag in order to appease the Serb and Croat populations. The flag was adopted on May 4, 1992, and although civil war caused the administrative division of the country in 1995, the white flag is recognized internationally.

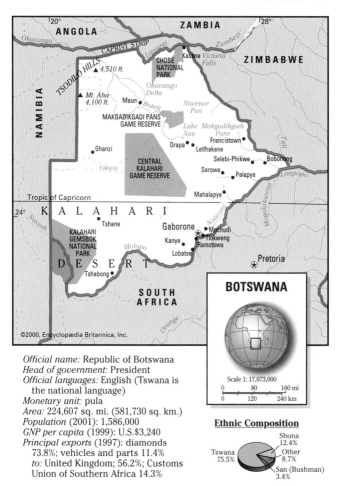

©2000, Encyclopædia Britannica, Inc.

Official name: Republic of Botswana
Head of government: President
Official languages: English (Tswana is the national language)
Monetary unit: pula
Area: 224,607 sq. mi. (581,730 sq. km.)
Population (2001): 1,586,000
GNP per capita (1999): U.S.$3,240
Principal exports (1997): diamonds 73.8%; vehicles and parts 11.4%
to: United Kingdom; 56.2%; Customs Union of Southern Africa 14.3%

BOTSWANA

Scale 1: 17,673,000

| 0 | 80 | 160 mi |
| 0 | 120 | 240 km |

Ethnic Composition

Shona 12.4%
Other 8.7%
San (Bushman) 3.4%
Tswana 75.5%

Adopted in 1966, the flag was designed to contrast symbolically with that of neighboring South Africa, where apartheid was then in effect. The black and white stripes in Botswana's flag are for racial cooperation and equality. The background symbolizes water, a scarce resource in the expansive Kalahari Desert.

©2000, Encyclopædia Britannica, Inc.

BRAZIL

Scale 1: 69,689,000

0 — 300 — 600 mi
0 — 400 — 800 km

Racial Composition

White 54%

Mulatto and Mestizo 39%

Other 7%

Official name: Federative Republic of Brazil
Head of government: President
Official language: Portuguese
Monetary unit: real
Area: 3,300,171 sq. mi. (8,547,404 sq. km.)
Population (2001): 172,118,000
GNP per capita (1999): U.S.$4,350
Principal exports (1998): food products 20.3%; road vehicles 9.4%; non-electrical machinery and apparatus 8.5%; iron and steel 7.2% *to:* U.S. 19.3%; Argentina 13.2%

The original flag was introduced on Sept. 7, 1822, when Dom Pedro declared independence from Portugal. In 1889 the blue disk and the motto Ordem e Progresso ("Order and Progress") were added. The Brazilian states and territories are symbolized by the constellations of stars. Green is for the land, while yellow is for gold and other mineral wealth.

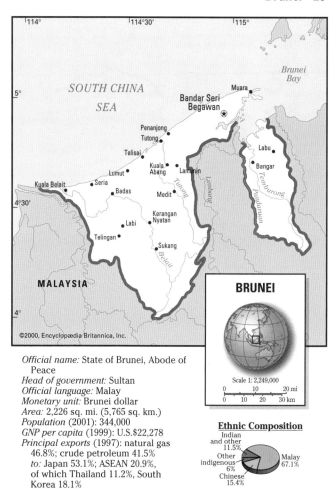

Official name: State of Brunei, Abode of Peace
Head of government: Sultan
Official language: Malay
Monetary unit: Brunei dollar
Area: 2,226 sq. mi. (5,765 sq. km.)
Population (2001): 344,000
GNP per capita (1999): U.S.$22,278
Principal exports (1997): natural gas 46.8%; crude petroleum 41.5%
to: Japan 53.1%; ASEAN 20.9%, of which Thailand 11.2%, South Korea 18.1%

Scale 1: 2,249,000

0   10   20 mi
0 10 20 30 km

Ethnic Composition

Indian and other 11.5%
Other indigenous 6%
Chinese 15.4%
Malay 67.1%

When Brunei became a British protectorate in 1906, diagonal stripes were added to its yellow flag. The yellow stood for the sultan, while white and black were for his two chief ministers. Introduced in September 1959, the coat of arms has a parasol as a symbol of royalty and a crescent and inscription for the state religion, Islam.

Official name: Republic of Bulgaria
Head of government: Prime Minister
Official language: Bulgarian
Monetary unit: lev
Area: 110,971.4 sq. mi. (8,190,876 sq. km.)
Population (2001): 7,953,000
GNP per capita (1999): U.S.$1,410
Principal exports (1997): chemicals and
plastics 22.3%; food, beverages and
tobacco 13.5%; machinery and
metalworking equipment 9.6%
to: Italy 11.7%; Germany 9.5%;
Turkey 9.0%

BULGARIA

Scale 1: 8,710,000

| 0 | 40 | 80 mi |
| 0 | 60 | 120 km |

Ethnic Composition

Bulgarian 85.7%

Turkish 9.4%
Other 4.9%

The flag was based on the Russian flag of 1699, but with green substituted for blue. Under communist rule, a red star and other symbols were added, but the old tricolor was reestablished on Nov. 27, 1990. The white is for peace, love, and freedom; green is for agriculture; and red is for the independence struggle and military courage.

Official name: Burkina Faso
Head of government: Prime Minister
Official language: French
Monetary unit: CFA franc
Area: 105,946 sq. mi. (274,400 sq. km.)
Population (2001): 12,272,000
GNP per capita (1999): U.S.$240
Principal exports (1999): raw cotton
53.4%; live animals 10.1%; hides and
skins 7.5% *to* (1998): France 23.1%;
Belgium; 10.8%; Cote d'lvoire 9.8%

Scale 1: 14,037,000

| 0 | 60 | 120 mi |
| 0 | 90 | 180 km |

Ethnic Composition

Fulani
8.3%

Other
35%

Mande
8.8%

Mossi
47.9%

On Aug. 4, 1984, Upper Volta was renamed Burkina Faso by
the revolutionary government of Thomas Sankara, and the
current flag was adopted with Pan-African colors. The yellow
star symbolizes leadership and revolutionary principles. The
red stripe is said to stand for the revolutionary struggle,
while the green stripe represents hope and abundance.

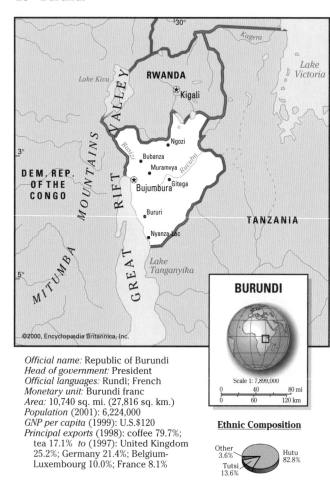

Official name: Republic of Burundi
Head of government: President
Official languages: Rundi; French
Monetary unit: Burundi franc
Area: 10,740 sq. mi. (27,816 sq. km.)
Population (2001): 6,224,000
GNP per capita (1999): U.S.$120
Principal exports (1998): coffee 79.7%;
tea 17.1% *to* (1997): United Kingdom
25.2%; Germany 21.4%; Belgium-
Luxembourg 10.0%; France 8.1%

Ethnic Composition

Other
3.6%

Hutu
82.8%

Tutsi
13.6%

The flag became official on June 28, 1967. Its white saltire
(diagonal cross) and central disk symbolize peace. The red
color is for the independence struggle, and green is for hope.
The stars correspond to the national motto, "Unity, Work,
Progress." They also recall the Tutsi, Hutu, and Twa peoples
and the pledge to God, king, and country.

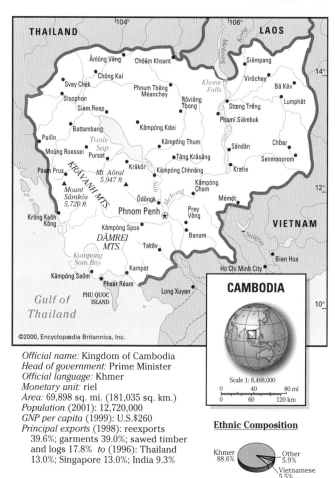

THAILAND 104° 106° LAOS

Ânlóng Vêng
Chôăm Khsant
Siĕmpang
Chóng Kal
Virôchey
Svay Chék
Bă Kêv
Phnum Tbêng Méanchey
Rôviĕng Tbong
Lumphăt
Sisophon
Stœng Trêng
Siem Reap
Phumĭ Siĕmbok
Battambang
Kâmpóng Kdei
Sândăn
Chbar
Pailĭn
Kâmpóng Thum
Moŭng Roessei
Pursat
Tăng Krâsăng
Senmonorom
Péam Prus
Krâkôr
Kâmpóng Chhnăng
Kratie
Mt. Aôral 5,947 ft.
Kâmpóng Cham
Mémót
Mount Sâmkôs 5,720 ft.
Ŏdôngk
Prey Vêng
Krŏng Kaôh Kŏng
Phnom Penh
Kâmpóng Spoe
Banam
VIETNAM
Takêv
Bien Hoa
Kâmpóng Saôm
Kampot
Ho Chi Minh City
Phsar Réam
Long Xuyen
PHU QUOC ISLAND

Tonle Sap
Khone Falls
KRÂVANH MTS.
DÂMREI MTS.
Kompong Som Bay
Gulf of Thailand
Mekong
Kong
Saigon

14°
12°
10°

©2000, Encyclopædia Britannica, Inc.

Official name: Kingdom of Cambodia
Head of government: Prime Minister
Official language: Khmer
Monetary unit: riel
Area: 69,898 sq. mi. (181,035 sq. km.)
Population (2001): 12,720,000
GNP per capita (1999): U.S.$260
Principal exports (1998): reexports 39.6%; garments 39.0%; sawed timber and logs 17.8% *to* (1996): Thailand 13.0%; Singapore 13.0%; India 9.3%

CAMBODIA

Scale 1: 8,468,000

0   40   80 mi
0   60   120 km

Ethnic Composition

Khmer 88.6%
Other 5.9%
Vietnamese 5.5%

Artistic representations of the central ruined temple of Angkor Wat, a 12th-century temple complex, have appeared on Khmer flags since the 19th century. The current flag design dates to 1948. It was replaced in 1970 under the Khmer Republic and in 1976 under communist leadership, but it was again hoisted on June 29, 1993.

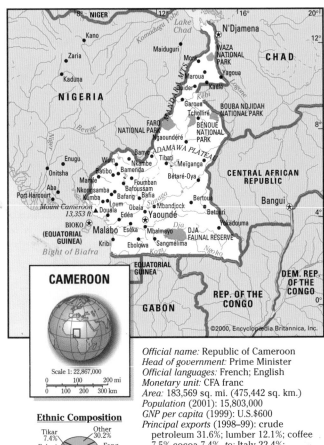

Official name: Republic of Cameroon
Head of government: Prime Minister
Official languages: French; English
Monetary unit: CFA franc
Area: 183,569 sq. mi. (475,442 sq. km.)
Population (2001): 15,803,000
GNP per capita (1999): U.S.$600
Principal exports (1998–99): crude
   petroleum 31.6%; lumber 12.1%; coffee
   7.5% cocoa 7.4% *to:* Italy 22.4%;
   France 12.6%; Spain 9.4%

Scale 1: 22,867,000

| 0 | 100 | 200 mi |
| 0 | 100 | 200 | 300 km |

Ethnic Composition

Tikar 7.4%
Fulani 9.6%
Duala, Luanda, and Basa 14.7%
Bamileke and Bamum 18.5%
Fang 19.6%
Other 30.2%

The flag was officially hoisted on Oct. 29, 1957, prior to independence (Jan. 1, 1960). Green is for the vegetation of the
south, yellow for the savannas of the north, and red for union
and sovereignty. Two yellow stars were added (for the British
Cameroons) in 1961, but these were replaced in 1975 by a sin-
gle star symbolizing national unity.

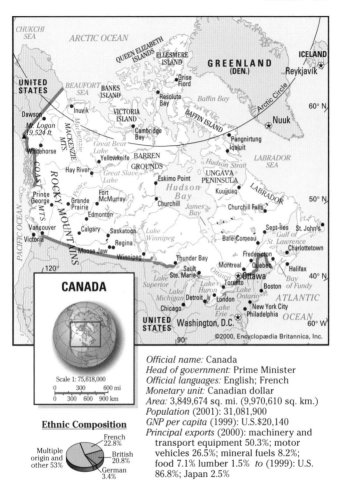

Official name: Canada
Head of government: Prime Minister
Official languages: English; French
Monetary unit: Canadian dollar
Area: 3,849,674 sq. mi. (9,970,610 sq. km.)
Population (2001): 31,081,900
GNP per capita (1999): U.S.$20,140
Principal exports (2000): machinery and
transport equipment 50.3%; motor
vehicles 26.5%; mineral fuels 8.2%;
food 7.1% lumber 1.5% *to* (1999): U.S.
86.8%; Japan 2.5%

Scale 1: 75,618,000

| 0 | 300 | | 600 mi |
| 0 | 300 | 600 | 900 km |

Ethnic Composition

French 22.8%
British 20.8%
German 3.4%
Multiple origin and other 53%

During Canada's first century of independence the Union Jack was still flown, but with a Canadian coat of arms. The maple leaf design, with the national colors, became official on Feb. 15, 1965. Since 1868 the maple leaf has been a national symbol, and in 1921 a red leaf in the coat of arms stood for Canadian sacrifice during World War I.

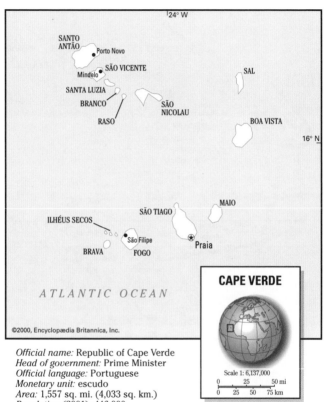

24° W

SANTO ANTÃO
Porto Novo

Mindelo • SÃO VICENTE

SANTA LUZIA
BRANCO
RASO

SÃO NICOLAU

SAL

BOA VISTA

16° N

MAIO

SÃO TIAGO

ILHÉUS SECOS

São Filipe
BRAVA FOGO
★ Praia

ATLANTIC OCEAN

©2000, Encyclopædia Britannica, Inc.

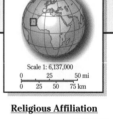

CAPE VERDE

Scale 1: 6,137,000

0   25   50 mi
0 25 50 75 km

Official name: Republic of Cape Verde
Head of government: Prime Minister
Official language: Portuguese
Monetary unit: escudo
Area: 1,557 sq. mi. (4,033 sq. km.)
Population (2001): 446,000
GNP per capita (1999): U.S.$1,330
Principal exports (1998): shoes 22.5%;
    clothing 7.1%; fish and fish
    preparations 6.7%; reexports 62.1%
    to: Portugal 89.3%; Spain 7.9%

Religious Affiliation

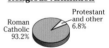

Protestant and other 6.8%

Roman Catholic 93.2%

After the elections of 1991, the flag was established with a
blue field bearing a ring of 10 yellow stars to symbolize the
10 main islands of Cape Verde. The stripes of white-red-white
suggest peace and national resolve. Red, white, and blue also
are a symbolic link to Portugal and the United States. The
new flag became official on Sept. 25, 1992.

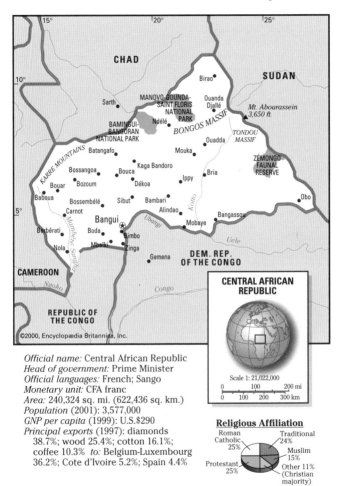

Official name: Central African Republic
Head of government: Prime Minister
Official languages: French; Sango
Monetary unit: CFA franc
Area: 240,324 sq. mi. (622,436 sq. km.)
Population (2001): 3,577,000
GNP per capita (1999): U.S.$290
Principal exports (1997): diamonds
  38.7%; wood 25.4%; cotton 16.1%;
  coffee 10.3% *to:* Belgium-Luxembourg
  36.2%; Cote d'Ivoire 5.2%; Spain 4.4%

Scale 1: 21,022,000

0   100   200 mi
0 100 200 300 km

Religious Affiliation

Roman
Catholic
25%
Traditional
24%
Muslim
15%
Protestant
25%
Other 11%
(Christian
majority)

Barthélemy Boganda designed the flag in 1958. It combines
French and Pan-African colors. The star is a guide for
progress and an emblem of unity. The blue stripe is for liberty, grandeur, and the sky; the white is for purity, equality, and
candor; the green and yellow are for forests and savannas;
and the red is for the blood of humankind.

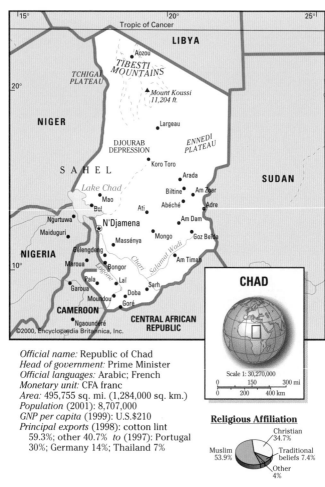

Official name: Republic of Chad
Head of government: Prime Minister
Official languages: Arabic; French
Monetary unit: CFA franc
Area: 495,755 sq. mi. (1,284,000 sq. km.)
Population (2001): 8,707,000
GNP per capita (1999): U.S.$210
Principal exports (1998): cotton lint
  59.3%; other 40.7% *to* (1997): Portugal
  30%; Germany 14%; Thailand 7%

Religious Affiliation

Christian
34.7%

Muslim
53.9%

Traditional
beliefs 7.4%

Other
4%

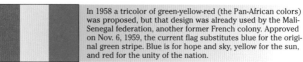

In 1958 a tricolor of green-yellow-red (the Pan-African colors)
was proposed, but that design was already used by the Mali-
Senegal federation, another former French colony. Approved
on Nov. 6, 1959, the current flag substitutes blue for the original green stripe. Blue is for hope and sky, yellow for the sun,
and red for the unity of the nation.

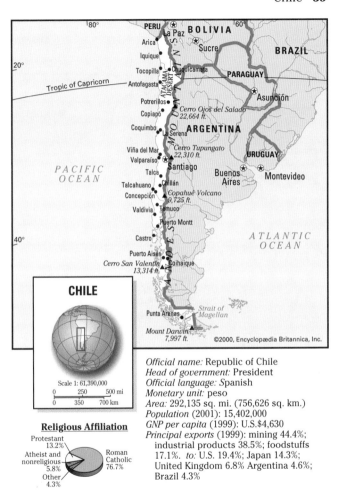

Official name: Republic of Chile
Head of government: President
Official language: Spanish
Monetary unit: peso
Area: 292,135 sq. mi. (756,626 sq. km.)
Population (2001): 15,402,000
GNP per capita (1999): U.S.$4,630
Principal exports (1999): mining 44.4%;
industrial products 38.5%; foodstuffs
17.1%. *to:* U.S. 19.4%; Japan 14.3%;
United Kingdom 6.8% Argentina 4.6%;
Brazil 4.3%

Religious Affiliation

Protestant 13.2%
Atheist and nonreligious 5.8%
Other 4.3%
Roman Catholic 76.7%

On Oct. 18, 1817, the flag was established for the new republic. The blue is for the sky, and the star is "a guide on the
path of progress and honor." The white is for the snow of the
Andes Mountains while the red recalls the blood of patriots.
In the 15th century the Araucanian Indians gave red-white-
blue sashes to their warriors.

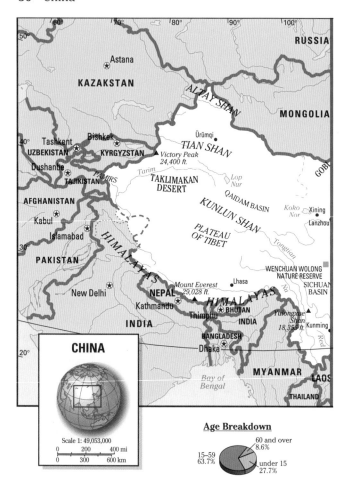

Age Breakdown

60 and over
8.6%

15–59
63.7%

under 15
27.7%

Scale 1: 49,053,000

| 0 | 200 | 400 mi |
| 0 | 300 | 600 km |

The flag was hoisted on Oct. 1, 1949. The red is for communism and the Han Chinese. The large star was originally for the Communist Party, and the smaller stars were for the proletariat, the peasants, the petty bourgeoisie, and the "patriotic capitalists." The large star was later said to stand for China, the smaller stars for minorities.

Official name: People's Republic of China
Head of government: Premier
Official language: Mandarin Chinese
Monetary unit: Renminbi (yuan)
Area: 3,696,100 sq. mi. (9,572,900 sq. km.)
Population (2001): 1,274,915,000
GNP per capita (1999): U.S.$750
Principal exports (1998): machinery and transport equipment 27.3%;
   products of the textile industries, rubber and metal products 17.6%
   to: Hong Kong 21.1%; U.S. 20.7%; Japan 16.2%

Official name: Republic of Colombia
Head of government: President
Official language: Spanish
Monetary unit: peso
Area: 440,762 sq. mi. (1,141,568 sq. km.)
Population (2001): 43,071,000
GNP per capita (1999): U.S.$2,170
Principal exports (1998): petroleum
products 23.5%; coffee 19.6%;
chemicals 9.4% *to* (1997): U.S. 37.8%;
Venezuela 8.9%; Germany 6.3%

Racial Composition

White 20%
Mestizo 58%
Mulatto 14%
Other 8%

In the early 19th century "the Liberator" Simon Bolivar created a yellow-blue-red flag for New Granada (which included
Colombia, Venezuela, Panama, and Ecuador). The flag symbolized the yellow gold of the New World separated by the
blue ocean from the red of "bloody Spain." The present
Colombian flag was established on Nov. 26, 1861.

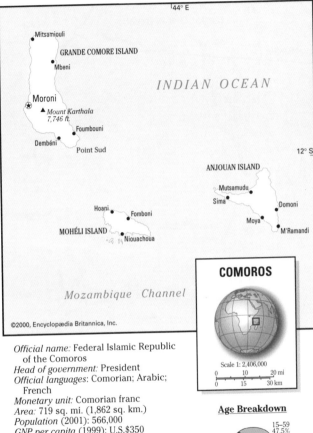

Official name: Federal Islamic Republic
of the Comoros
Head of government: President
Official languages: Comorian; Arabic;
French
Monetary unit: Comorian franc
Area: 719 sq. mi. (1,862 sq. km.)
Population (2001): 566,000
GNP per capita (1999): U.S.$350
Principal exports (1999): vanilla 43.2%;
cloves 27.7%; ylang-ylang 13.3%
to: U.S. 26.8%; France 25.4%;
Germany 12.2%

Scale 1: 2,406,000

| 0 | 10 | 20 mi |
| 0 | 15 | 30 km |

Age Breakdown

15–59
47.5%

Under 15
48.5%

60 and over
4%

The flag was adopted on Oct. 3, 1996. Its green background
and white crescent are symbols of Islam, and the Arabic
words for Allah and Muhammad are inscribed in the corners.
The four stars are for the islands of Njazidja (formerly
Grande-Comore), Mwali (Mohéli), Nzwani (Anjouan), and
Mayotte (a French territory that is claimed by Comoros).

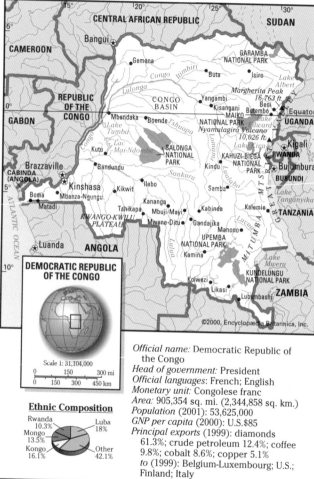

CENTRAL AFRICAN REPUBLIC · SUDAN
CAMEROON
Bangui
GARAMBA NATIONAL PARK
Gemena · Buta · Isiro · Lake Albert
Congo · Itimbiri
Lulonga · Yangambi · Margherita Peak 16,763 ft.
REPUBLIC OF THE CONGO · CONGO BASIN · Kisangani · Beni · Butembo · Equator
GABON · Mbandaka · Boende · Tshuapa · MAIKO NATIONAL PARK · UGANDA
Lake Tumba · Nyamulagira Volcano 10,026 ft. · Lake Edward
Lac Mai-Ndombe · SALONGA NATIONAL PARK · Lake Kivu
Kutu · Lomami · KAHUZI-BIEGA NATIONAL PARK · Kigali
Brazzaville · Bandundu · Sankuru · Kindu · RWANDA · Bujumbura
CABINDA (ANGOLA) · Kinshasa · Kiwit · Ilebo · Luabala · BURUNDI
Boma · Mbanza-Ngungu · Samba · Kalemie · Lake Tanganyika
Matadi · Tshikapa · Kananga · Kabinda · GREAT RIFT MTS. · TANZANIA
KWANGO-KWILU PLATEAU · Mbuji-Mayi · Mwene-Ditu · Gandajika · Manono · MATUMBA
Luanda · Kwango · Lulua · UPEMBA NATIONAL PARK · Lake Mweru
ANGOLA · Kamina · Kolwezi · KUNDELUNGU NATIONAL PARK · ZAMBIA
ATLANTIC OCEAN · Likasi · Lubumbashi
©2000, Encyclopædia Britannica, Inc.

DEMOCRATIC REPUBLIC OF THE CONGO

Scale 1: 31,104,000

0 — 150 — 300 mi
0 — 150 — 300 — 450 km

Ethnic Composition

Rwanda 10.3%
Mongo 13.5%
Kongo 16.1%
Luba 18%
Other 42.1%

Official name: Democratic Republic of the Congo
Head of government: President
Official languages: French; English
Monetary unit: Congolese franc
Area: 905,354 sq. mi. (2,344,858 sq. km.)
Population (2001): 53,625,000
GNP per capita (2000): U.S.$85
Principal exports (1999): diamonds 61.3%; crude petroleum 12.4%; coffee 9.8%; cobalt 8.6%; copper 5.1%
  to (1999): Belgium-Luxembourg; U.S.; Finland; Italy

In 1877 the flag of the Congo Free State was blue with a gold star, for a shining light in the "Dark Continent." At independence (June 30, 1962) six stars were added for the existing six provinces, but in 1971 the flag was replaced with a green flag depicting an arm and a torch. The regime led by Laurent Kabila restored the old flag on May 17, 1997.

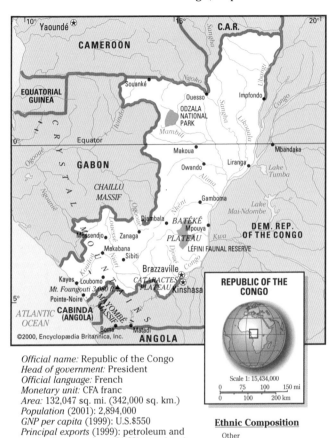

REPUBLIC OF THE CONGO

Scale 1: 15,434,000

| 0 | 75 | 100 | 150 mi |

| 0 | 100 | 200 km |

Official name: Republic of the Congo
Head of government: President
Official language: French
Monetary unit: CFA franc
Area: 132,047 sq. mi. (342,000 sq. km.)
Population (2001): 2,894,000
GNP per capita (1999): U.S.$550
Principal exports (1999): petroleum and
petroleum products 91.9%; wood and
wood products 4.3% *to:* Taiwan 31.5%;
U.S. 22.8%; South Korea 15.3%

Ethnic Composition

Other 19.7%
Teke 17.3%
Mboshi 11.5%
Kongo 51.5%

First adopted on Sept. 15, 1959, the flag uses the Pan-African colors. Green was originally said to stand for Congo's agriculture and forests, and yellow for friendship and the nobility of the people, but the red was unexplained. Altered in 1969 by a Marxist government, the flag was restored to its initial form on June 10, 1991.

Scale 1: 5,424,000

| 0 | 25 | | 50 mi |
| 0 | 40 | 80 km |

Ethnic Composition

White 87%

Mestizo 7%

Other 6%

Official name: Republic of Costa Rica
Head of government: President
Official language: Spanish
Monetary unit: Costa Rican colon
Area: 19,730 sq. mi. (51,100 sq. km.)
Population (2001): 3,936,000
GNP per capita (1999): U.S.$3,570
Principal exports (1998): bananas 21.8%;
coffee 13.3%; processed food and
tobacco products 9.3%; fish and
shrimp 7.6% *to:* U.S. 42%; United
Kingdom 7%; Germany 7%

The blue and white stripes originated in the flag colors of the United Provinces of Central America (1823–40). On Sept. 29, 1848, the red stripe was added to symbolize sunlight, civilization, and "true independence." The current design of the coat of arms, which is included on government flags, was established in 1964.

Official name: Republic of Croatia
Head of government: Prime Mlnister
Official language: Croatian (Serbo-
    Croatian)
Monetary unit: kuna
Area: 21,359 sq. mi. (56,542 sq. km.)
Population (2001): 4,393,000
GNP per capita (1999): U.S.$4,530
Principal exports (1998): machinery and
    transport equipment 30.4%; clothing
    12.2% *to:* Italy 17.7%; Germany 16.9%;
    Bosnia and Herzegovina 14.4%

During the European uprisings of 1848, Croatians designed a flag based on that of Russia. In April 1941 the fascistic Ustasa used this flag, adding the checkered shield of Croatia. A communist star soon replaced the shield, but the current flag was adopted on Dec. 22, 1990. Atop the shield is a "crown" inlaid with historic coats of arms.

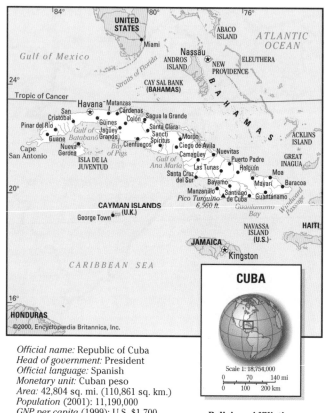

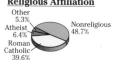

CUBA

Scale 1: 18,754,000

0   70   140 mi
0   100   200 km

@2000, Encyclopædia Britannica, Inc.

Official name: Republic of Cuba
Head of government: President
Official language: Spanish
Monetary unit: Cuban peso
Area: 42,804 sq. mi. (110,861 sq. km.)
Population (2001): 11,190,000
GNP per capita (1999): U.S. $1,700
Principal exports (1996): sugar 52.8%;
  minerals and concentrates 23.7%; fish
  products 6.8%; raw tobacco products
  5.9% *to* (1999): Russia 23.3%; Canada
  14.5%; The Netherlands 12.9%

Religious Affiliation

Other 5.3%
Atheist 6.4%
Roman Catholic 39.6%
Nonreligious 48.7%

In the mid-19th century Cuban exiles designed the flag, which was later carried into battle against Spanish forces. It was adopted on May 20, 1902. The stripes were for the three military districts of Cuba and the purity of the patriotic cause. The red triangle was for strength, constancy, and equality, and the white star symbolized independence.

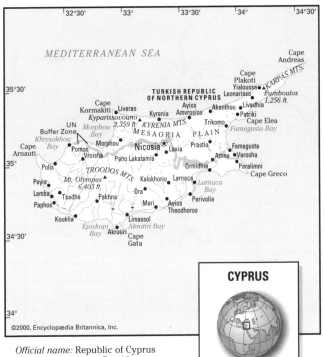

MEDITERRANEAN SEA

©2000, Encyclopædia Britannica, Inc.

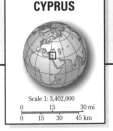

CYPRUS

Scale 1: 3,402,000

0   15   30 mi

0   15   30   45 km

Official name: Republic of Cyprus
Head of government: President
Official languages: Greek; Turkish
Monetary unit: Cyprus pound
Area: 2,276 sq. mi. (5,896 sq. km.)
Population (2001): 675,000
GNP per capita (1999): U.S.$11,950
Principal exports (1998): reexports
  55.6%; domestic exports 38.7%, of
  which clothing 5.3%, chemicals 5.2%
  to: United Kingdom 14.6%; Russia
  10.3%; Greece 9.8%

<u>Age Breakdown</u>

60 and over
14.9%
15–59
59.8%
Under 15
25.3%

On Aug. 7, 1960, the Republic of Cyprus was proclaimed with
a national flag of a neutral design. It bears the island in silhouette and a green olive wreath, for peace. In 1974 there was
a Turkish invasion of the island. A puppet government, which
adopted a flag based on the Turkish model, was set up on the
northern third of Cyprus.

Official name: Ceska Republika
Head of government: Prime Minister
Official language: Czech
Monetary unit: koruna
Area: 30,450 sq. mi. (78,864 sq. km.)
Population (2001): 10,269,000
GNP per capita (1999): U.S.$5,020
Principal exports (1998): machinery and
  apparatus 32.7%; transport equipment
  9.8%; chemicals and chemical
  products 6.9% *to* (1999): Germany
  42.1%; Slovakia 8.2%; Austria 6.4%

CZECH REPUBLIC

Scale 1: 6,810,000

| 0 | 20 | 40 mi |
| 0 | 40 | 60 km |

Ethnic Composition

Czech 81.2%
Moravian 13.2%
Other 5.6%

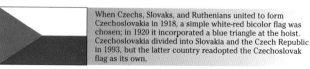

When Czechs, Slovaks, and Ruthenians united to form
Czechoslovakia in 1918, a simple white-red bicolor flag was
chosen; in 1920 it incorporated a blue triangle at the hoist.
Czechoslovakia divided into Slovakia and the Czech Republic
in 1993, but the latter country readopted the Czechoslovak
flag as its own.

Official name: Kingdom of Denmark
Head of government: Prime Minister
Official language: Danish
Monetary unit: Danish krone
Area: 16,639 sq. mi. (43,096 sq. km.)
Population (2001): 5,358,000
GNP per capita (1999): U.S.$32,050
Principal exports (2000): machinery and
  apparatus 23.5%; food and live
  animals 18.4%; pharmaceuticals 5.1%
  to: Germany 18.9%; Sweden 13.0%;
  United Kingdom 9.8%

DENMARK

Scale 1: 6,930,000

0   20   40 mi

0 30   60 km

Age Breakdown

Under 15
17.3%

15–59
62.9%

60 and over
19.8%

A traditional story claims that the Danish flag fell from
heaven on June 15, 1219, but the previously existing war flag
of the Holy Roman Empire was of a similar design, with its
red field symbolizing battle and its white cross suggesting
divine favor. In 1849 the state and military flag was altered
and adopted as a symbol of the Danish people.

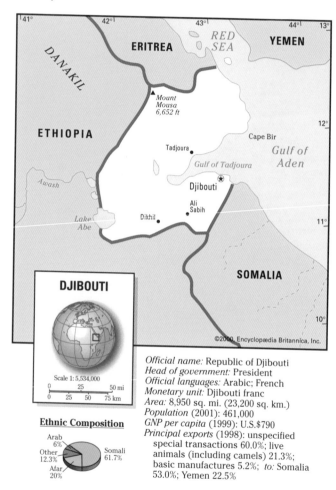

Official name: Republic of Djibouti
Head of government: President
Official languages: Arabic; French
Monetary unit: Djibouti franc
Area: 8,950 sq. mi. (23,200 sq. km.)
Population (2001): 461,000
GNP per capita (1999): U.S.$790
Principal exports (1998): unspecified
special transactions 60.0%; live
animals (including camels) 21.3%;
basic manufactures 5.2%; to: Somalia
53.0%; Yemen 22.5%

Ethnic Composition

Arab 6%
Other 12.3%
Afar 20%
Somali 61.7%

First raised by anti-French separatists, the flag was officially
hoisted on June 27, 1977. The color of the Afar people, green,
stands for prosperity. The color of the Issa people, light blue,
symbolizes sea and sky, and recalls the flag of Somalia.
The white triangle is for equality and peace; the red star is for
unity and independence.

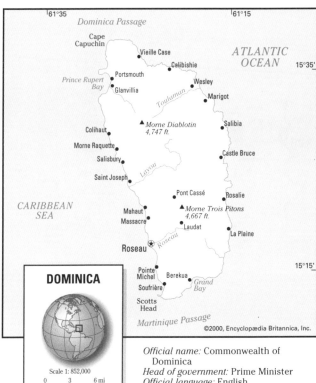

Dominica Passage

Cape Capuchin
Vieille Case
Calibishie
ATLANTIC OCEAN
15°35'
Portsmouth
Prince Rupert Bay
Glanvillia
Wesley
Touluman
Marigot
▲ *Morne Diablotin 4,747 ft.*
Salibia
Colihaut
Morne Raquette
Castle Bruce
Salisbury
Layou
Saint Joseph
Pont Cassé
Rosalie
CARIBBEAN SEA
Mahaut
Massacre
▲ *Morne Trois Pitons 4,667 ft.*
Roseau
Laudat
La Plaine
★ Roseau
15°15'
Pointe Michel
Berekua
Grand Bay
Soufrière
Scotts Head
Martinique Passage
©2000, Encyclopædia Britannica, Inc.

DOMINICA

Scale 1: 852,000

| 0 | 3 | 6 mi |
| 0 | 5 | 10 km |

Religious Affiliation

Other 12.7%
Roman Catholic 70.1%
Protestant 17.2%

Official name: Commonwealth of Dominica
Head of government: Prime Minister
Official language: English
Monetary unit: East Caribbean dollar
Area: 285.3 sq. mi. (739.0 sq. km.)
Population (2001): 71,700
GNP per capita (1999): U.S.$3,260
Principal exports (1999): manufactured exports 61.7%; coconut-based soaps 26.7%; agricultural exports 38.3% *to:* Caricom 55.3%; United Kingdom 27.5%

The flag was hoisted on Nov. 3, 1978, at independence from Britain. Its background symbolizes forests; its central disk is red for socialism and bears a sisserou (a rare local bird). The stars are for the parishes of the island. The cross of yellow, white, and black is for the Carib, Caucasian, and African peoples and for fruit, water, and soil.

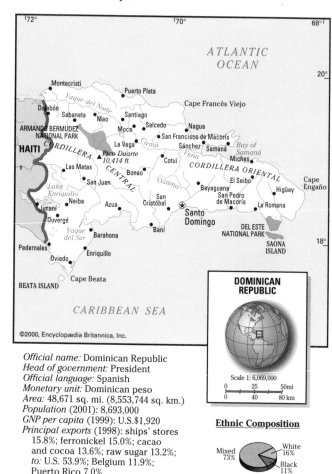

72° 70° 68°

ATLANTIC
OCEAN

20°

Montecristi • Puerto Plata • Cape Francés Viejo

Dajabón • Sabaneta • Mao • Santiago • Salcedo • Nagua

ARMANDO BERMUDEZ NATIONAL PARK • Moca • San Francisco de Macorís

Yaque del Norte

HAITI • CORDILLERA • La Vega • *Camú* • Sánchez • Samaná • Bay of Samaná

Pico Duarte ▲ 10,414 ft. • *Yuna* • Miches

Las Matas • CENTRAL • Cotuí • CORDILLERA ORIENTAL

San Juan • Bonao • *Ozama* • El Seibo • Cape Engaño

Lake Enriquillo • Neiba • Bayaguana • Higüey

Jimaní • Azua • San Cristóbal • San Pedro de Macorís • La Romana

Duvergé • *Yaque del Sur* • Baní • ★ Santo Domingo

Pedernales • Barahona • DEL ESTE NATIONAL PARK • SAONA ISLAND

18°

Oviedo • Enriquillo

Cape Beata

BEATA ISLAND

CARIBBEAN SEA

©2000, Encyclopædia Britannica, Inc.

DOMINICAN REPUBLIC

Scale 1: 6,069,000

0   25   50mi
0   40   80 km

Official name: Dominican Republic
Head of government: President
Official language: Spanish
Monetary unit: Dominican peso
Area: 48,671 sq. mi. (8,553,744 sq. km.)
Population (2001): 8,693,000
GNP per capita (1999): U.S.$1,920
Principal exports (1998): ships' stores
15.8%; ferronickel 15.0%; cacao
and cocoa 13.6%; raw sugar 13.2%;
to: U.S. 53.9%; Belgium 11.9%;
Puerto Rico 7.0%

Ethnic Composition

Mixed 73%
White 16%
Black 11%

On Feb. 28, 1844, Spanish-speaking Dominican revolutionaries
added a white cross to the simple blue-red flag of eastern
Hispaniola, in order to emphasize their Christian heritage. On
November 6 of that same year the new constitution established the flag, but with the colors at the fly end reversed so
that the blue and red would alternate.

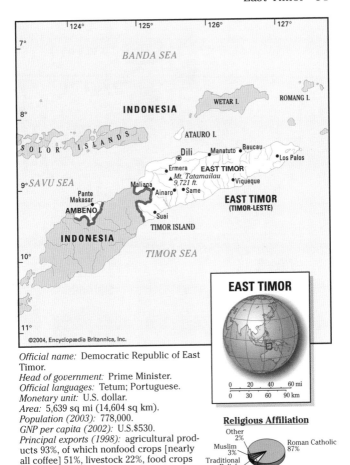

Official name: Democratic Republic of East Timor.
Head of government: Prime Minister.
Official languages: Tetum; Portuguese.
Monetary unit: U.S. dollar.
Area: 5,639 sq mi (14,604 sq km).
Population (2003): 778,000.
GNP per capita (2002): U.S.$530.
Principal exports (1998): agricultural products 93%, of which nonfood crops [nearly all coffee] 51%, livestock 22%, food crops 15%; garments, bottled water, handicrafts, and other manufactured goods 5% to: Indonesia 96%.

Religious Affiliation

Roman Catholic 87%
Protestant 5%
Traditional Beliefs 3%
Muslim 3%
Other 2%

Based on the flag of the Revolutionary Front of Independent East Timor, this design became the country's official flag at independence on May 20, 2002. The black represents four centuries of colonial oppression, the arrowhead the struggle for independence, and the red the suffering of the East Timorese people. The white star symbolizes hope for the future.

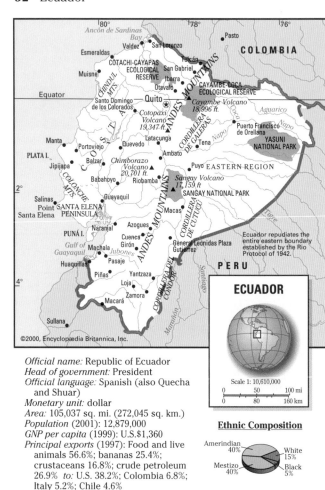

©2000, Encyclopædia Britannica, Inc.

Official name: Republic of Ecuador
Head of government: President
Official language: Spanish (also Quecha and Shuar)
Monetary unit: dollar
Area: 105,037 sq. mi. (272,045 sq. km.)
Population (2001): 12,879,000
GNP per capita (1999): U.S.$1,360
Principal exports (1997): Food and live animals 56.6%; bananas 25.4%; crustaceans 16.8%; crude petroleum 26.9% *to:* U.S. 38.2%; Colombia 6.8%; Italy 5.2%; Chile 4.6%

Scale 1: 10,610,000

| 0 | 50 | 100 mi |
| 0 | 80 | 160 km |

Ethnic Composition

Amerindian 40%
White 15%
Mestizo 40%
Black 5%

Victorious against the Spanish on May 24, 1822, Antonio José de Sucre hoisted a yellow-blue-red flag. Other flags were later used, but on Sept. 26, 1860, the current flag design was adopted. The coat of arms is displayed on the flag when it is used abroad or for official purposes, to distinguish it from the flag of Colombia.

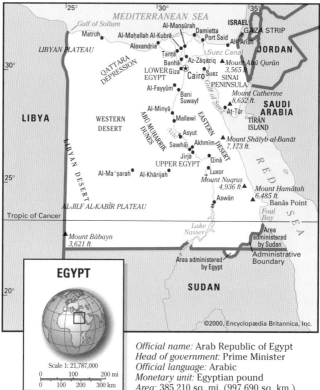

Official name: Arab Republic of Egypt
Head of government: Prime Minister
Official language: Arabic
Monetary unit: Egyptian pound
Area: 385,210 sq. mi. (997,690 sq. km.)
Population (2001): 65,239,000
GNP per capita (1999): U.S.$1,380
Principal exports (1999): petroleum and
  petroleum products 22.9%; cotton,
  yarn, textiles, and clothing 9.7%;
  bunkers and ships' stores 10.3%
  to: U.S. 12.4%; Italy 10.1%; The
  Netherlands 7.1%

Religious Affiliation

Sunni Muslim 90%

Christian 10%

The 1952 revolt against British rule established the red-white-black flag with a central gold eagle. Two stars replaced the eagle in 1958, and in 1972 a federation with Syria and Libya was formed, adding instead the hawk of Quraysh (the tribe of Muhammad). On Oct. 9, 1984, the eagle of Saladin (a major 12th-century ruler) was substituted.

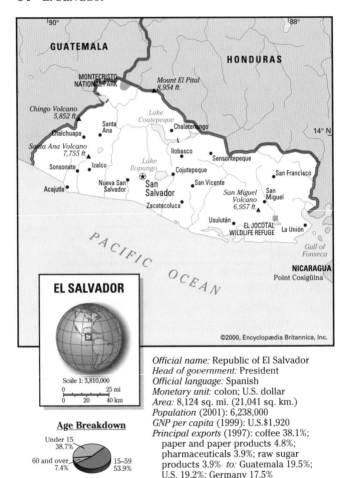

Official name: Republic of El Salvador
Head of government: President
Official language: Spanish
Monetary unit: colon; U.S. dollar
Area: 8,124 sq. mi. (21,041 sq. km.)
Population (2001): 6,238,000
GNP per capita (1999): U.S.$1,920
Principal exports (1997): coffee 38.1%;
  paper and paper products 4.8%;
  pharmaceuticals 3.9%; raw sugar
  products 3.9% *to:* Guatemala 19.5%;
  U.S. 19.2%; Germany 17.5%

Age Breakdown

Under 15
38.7%

60 and over
7.4%

15–59
53.9%

In the early 19th century a blue-white-blue flag was designed
for the short-lived United Provinces of Central America, in
which El Salvador was a member. On Sept. 15, 1912, the flag
was reintroduced in El Salvador. The coat of arms in the center resembles that used by the former federation and
includes the national motto, "God, Union, Liberty."

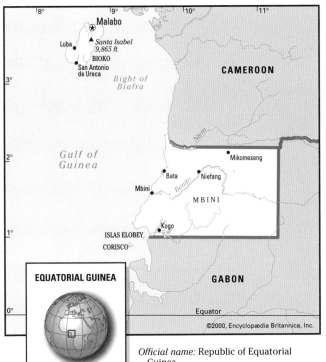

Official name: Republic of Equatorial Guinea
Head of government: Prime Minister
Official language: Spanish; French
Monetary unit: CFA franc
Area: 10,831 sq. mi. (28,051 sq. km.)
Population (2001): 486,000
GNP per capita (1999): U.S.$1,170
Principal exports (1998): petroleum 87.6%; wood 9.2%; cocoa 1.5%
  to: U.S. 62.0%; Spain 17.3%

Scale 1: 6,500,000

0   20   40 mi
0   30   60 km

Ethnic Composition

Fang 82.9%
Bubi 9.6%
Other 7.5%

The flag was first hoisted at independence (Oct. 12, 1968). Its coat of arms shows the silk-cotton tree, or god tree, which recalls early Spanish influence in the area. The sea, which links parts of the country, is reflected in the blue triangle. The green is for vegetation, white is for peace, and red is for the blood of martyrs in the liberation struggle.

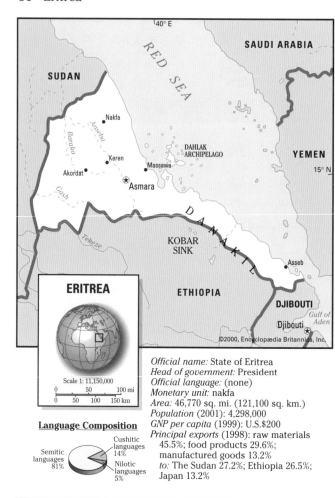

Official name: State of Eritrea
Head of government: President
Official language: (none)
Monetary unit: nakfa
Area: 46,770 sq. mi. (121,100 sq. km.)
Population (2001): 4,298,000
GNP per capita (1999): U.S.$200
Principal exports (1998): raw materials
45.5%; food products 29.6%;
manufactured goods 13.2%
to: The Sudan 27.2%; Ethiopia 26.5%;
Japan 13.2%

Language Composition

Semitic
languages
81%

Cushitic
languages
14%

Nilotic
languages
5%

Officially hoisted at the proclamation of independence on
May 24, 1993, the national flag was based on that of the
Eritrean People's Liberation Front. The red triangle is for the
blood of patriots, the green is for agriculture, and the blue is
for maritime resources. Around a central branch is a circle of
olive branches with 30 leaves.

ESTONIA

Scale 1: 4,840,000

| 0 | 20 | 40 mi |
| 0 | 30 | 60 km |

Ethnic Composition

Estonian 63.9%

Russian 29%

Other 7.1%

Official name: Republic of Estonia
Head of government: Prime Minister
Official language: Estonian
Monetary unit: kroon
Area: 16,769 sq. mi. (43,431 sq. km.)
Population (2001): 1,363,000
GNP per capita (1999): U.S.$3,400
Principal exports (2000): electrical and
non-electrical machinery 37.5%; wood
and wood products 13.4%; textiles and
clothing 11.3% *to:* Finland 32.3%;
Sweden 20.5%; Germany 8.5%

In the late 19th century an Estonian students' association
adopted the blue-black-white flag. Blue was said to stand for
the sky, black for the soil, and white for aspirations to freedom and homeland. The flag was officially recognized on July
4, 1920. It was replaced under Soviet rule, and readopted on
Oct. 20, 1988.

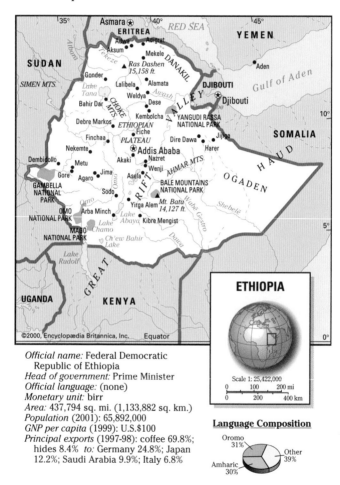

Official name: Federal Democratic
  Republic of Ethiopia
Head of government: Prime Minister
Official language: (none)
Monetary unit: birr
Area: 437,794 sq. mi. (1,133,882 sq. km.)
Population (2001): 65,892,000
GNP per capita (1999): U.S.$100
Principal exports (1997-98): coffee 69.8%;
  hides 8.4% *to:* Germany 24.8%; Japan
  12.2%; Saudi Arabia 9.9%; Italy 6.8%

ETHIOPIA

Scale 1: 25,422,000

| 0 | 100 | 200 mi |
| 0 | 200 | 400 km |

Language Composition

Oromo
31%

Other
39%

Amharic
30%

The flag is red (for sacrifice), green (for labor, development,
and fertility), and yellow (for hope, justice, and equality).
Tricolor pennants were used prior to the official flag of Oct. 6,
1897, and a tricolor was flown by antigovernment forces in
1991. On Feb. 6, 1996, the disk (for peace) and star (for unity
and the future) were added.

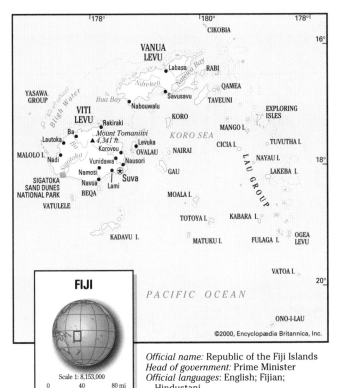

©2000, Encyclopædia Britannica, Inc.

FIJI

Scale 1: 8,153,000

0   40   80 mi
0   60   120 km

Ethnic Composition

Indian 43.5%
Fijian 50.7%
Other 5.8%

Official name: Republic of the Fiji Islands
Head of government: Prime Minister
Official languages: English; Fijian;
    Hindustani
Monetary unit: Fiji dollar
Area: 7,055 sq. mi. (18,272 sq. km.)
Population (2001): 827,000
GNP per capita (1999): U.S.$2,310
Principal exports (1997): sugar 24.4%;
    clothing 23.5%; gold 8.7%; fish 5.3%;
    timber 3.5% *to:* Australia 40.5%;
    United Kingdom 21.4%; Japan 13.4%;
    U.S. 10.2%

The national flag, introduced on Oct. 10, 1970, is a modified version of Fiji's colonial flag. It includes the Union Jack on a light blue field. The shield has the red cross of St. George on a white background, below a yellow lion, which holds a cocoa pod. Local symbols (sugar cane, coconuts, bananas, and the Fiji dove) are also shown.

Official name: Republic of Finland
Head of government: Prime Minister
Official language: (none)
Monetary unit: euro
Area: 130,559 sq. mi. (338,145 sq. km.)
Population (2001): 5,185,000
GNP per capita (1999): U.S.$24,730
Principal exports (1999): electrical
  machinery and apparatus 23.7%;
  paper and paper products 20.5%
  to: Germany 13.1%; Sweden 9.9%;
  United Kingdom 9.1%; U.S. 7.9%;
  France 5.3%

Scale 1: 18,656,000

0   25   50   150 mi

0   120   240 km

Religious Affiliation

Nonreligious 12%

Other 2.1%

Evangelical Lutheran 85.9%

In 1862, while Finland was under Russian control, a flag was proposed that would have a white background for the snows of Finland and blue for its lakes. The blue was in the form of a "Nordic cross" similar to those used by other Scandinavian countries. The flag was officially adopted by the newly independent country on May 29, 1918.

©2000, Encyclopædia Britannica, Inc.

Official name: French Republic
Head of government: Prime Minister
Official language: French
Monetary unit: euro
Area: 210,026 sq. mi. (543,965 sq. km.)
Population (2001): 59,090,000
GNP per capita (1999): U.S.$24,170
Principal exports (1998): machinery and apparatus 26.1%; transport equipment 17.7%; chemicals and chemical products 12.7%; agricultural products 12.0% *to:* Germany 16.1%; United Kingdom 10.0%; Italy 9.2%; Spain 8.7%

Scale 1: 18,620,000

| 0 | 80 | 160 mi |
| 0 | 80 | 160 | 240 km |

Religious Affiliation

Roman Catholic 76.4%

Other 23.6%

From 1789 blue and red, the traditional colors of Paris, were included in flags with Bourbon royal white. In 1794 the tricolor was made official. It embodied liberty, equality, fraternity, democracy, secularism, and modernization, but there is no symbolism attached to the individual colors. It has been the sole national flag since March 5, 1848.

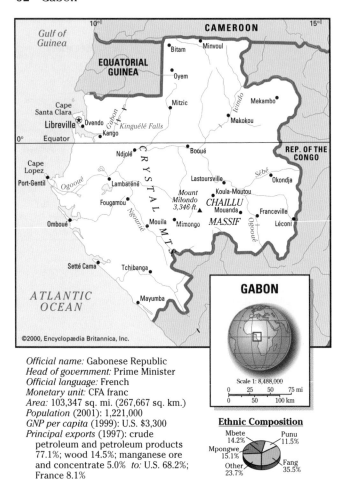

Official name: Gabonese Republic
Head of government: Prime Minister
Official language: French
Monetary unit: CFA franc
Area: 103,347 sq. mi. (267,667 sq. km.)
Population (2001): 1,221,000
GNP per capita (1999): U.S. $3,300
Principal exports (1997): crude petroleum and petroleum products 77.1%; wood 14.5%; manganese ore and concentrate 5.0% *to:* U.S. 68.2%; France 8.1%

Scale 1: 8,488,000

0   25   50   75 mi
0   50   100 km

Ethnic Composition

Mbete 14.2%
Punu 11.5%
Mpongwe 15.1%
Fang 35.5%
Other 23.7%

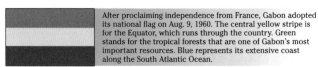

After proclaiming independence from France, Gabon adopted its national flag on Aug. 9, 1960. The central yellow stripe is for the Equator, which runs through the country. Green stands for the tropical forests that are one of Gabon's most important resources. Blue represents its extensive coast along the South Atlantic Ocean.

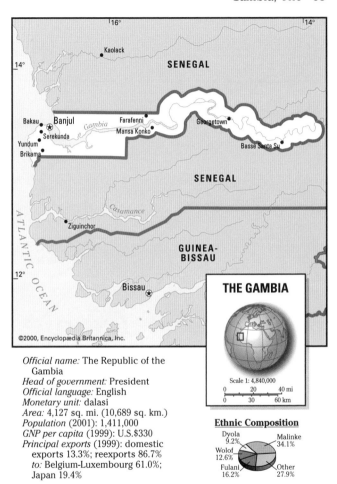

©2000, Encyclopædia Britannica, Inc.

THE GAMBIA

Scale 1: 4,840,000

| 0 | 20 | 40 mi |
| 0 | 30 | 60 km |

Official name: The Republic of the Gambia
Head of government: President
Official language: English
Monetary unit: dalasi
Area: 4,127 sq. mi. (10,689 sq. km.)
Population (2001): 1,411,000
GNP per capita (1999): U.S.$330
Principal exports (1999): domestic exports 13.3%; reexports 86.7% *to:* Belgium-Luxembourg 61.0%; Japan 19.4%

Ethnic Composition

Dyola 9.2%
Wolof 12.6%
Fulani 16.2%
Malinke 34.1%
Other 27.9%

The Gambia achieved independence from Britain on Feb. 18, 1965, under the current flag. The center stripe is blue to symbolize the Gambia River. The red stripe is for the sun and the equator. The green stripe is for agricultural produce (peanuts, grains, and citrus fruits), while the white stripes are said to stand for peace and unity.

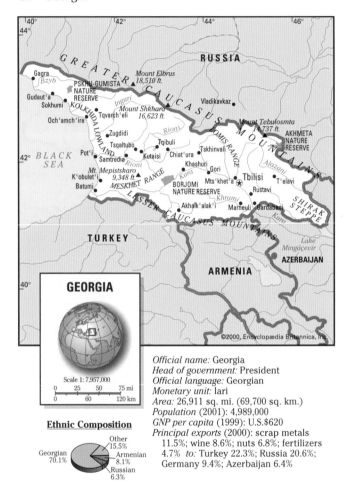

Official name: Georgia
Head of government: President
Official language: Georgian
Monetary unit: lari
Area: 26,911 sq. mi. (69,700 sq. km.)
Population (2001): 4,989,000
GNP per capita (1999): U.S.$620
Principal exports (2000): scrap metals
11.5%; wine 8.6%; nuts 6.8%; fertilizers
4.7% *to:* Turkey 22.3%; Russia 20.6%;
Germany 9.4%; Azerbaijan 6.4%

Ethnic Composition

Georgian 70.1%
Other 15.5%
Armenian 8.1%
Russian 6.3%

According to tradition, Queen Tamara (1184–1213) and other rulers used white, black, and cherry red for their flags. The current flag was first hoisted on March 25, 1917. It was replaced under Soviet rule, but readopted on Nov. 14, 1990. Cherry red is the national color, black stands for past tragedies, and white is for hope.

Official name: Federal Republic of Germany
Head of government: Chancellor
Official language: German
Monetary unit: euro
Area: 137,846 sq. mi. (357,021 sq. km.)
Population (2001): 82,386,000
GNP per capita (1999): U.S.$25,620
Principal exports (2000): machinery and transport equipment 51.2%; chemicals and chemical products 12.7%
to: France 11.4%; U.S. 10.2%

GERMANY

Scale 1: 15,019,000

| 0 | 40 | 80 | 120 mi |
| 0 | 60 | 120 | 180 km |

Age Breakdown

60 and over
20.7%
15–59
63%
Under 15
16.3%

In the early 19th century German nationalists displayed black, gold, and red on their uniforms and tricolor flags. The current flag was used officially from 1848 to 1852 and re-adopted by West Germany on May 9, 1949. East Germany flew a similar flag but only the flag of West Germany was maintained upon reunification in 1990.

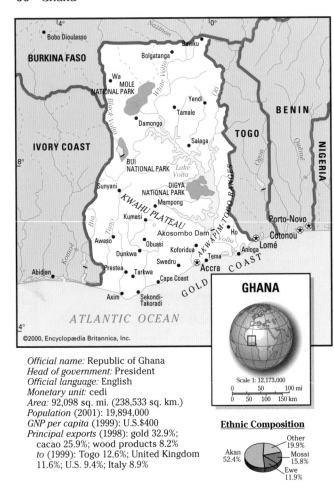

©2000, Encyclopædia Britannica, Inc.

Official name: Republic of Ghana
Head of government: President
Official language: English
Monetary unit: cedi
Area: 92,098 sq. mi. (238,533 sq. km.)
Population (2001): 19,894,000
GNP per capita (1999): U.S.$400
Principal exports (1998): gold 32.9%;
cacao 25.9%; wood products 8.2%;
to (1999): Togo 12.6%; United Kingdom
11.6%; U.S. 9.4%; Italy 8.9%

GHANA

Scale 1: 12,173,000

0   50   100 mi
0   50   100   150 km

Ethnic Composition

Akan 52.4%
Other 19.9%
Mossi 15.8%
Ewe 11.9%

On March 6, 1957, independence from Britain was granted and a flag, based on the red-white-green tricolor of a nationalist organization, was hoisted. A black "lodestar of African freedom" was added and the white stripe was changed to yellow, symbolizing wealth. Green is for forests and farms, red for the independence struggle.

MACEDONIA BULGARIA THRACE

Tirane

ALBANIA Flórina
Kastoria Edessa
Mount Thessaloníki Thásos Samothrace
Olympus Katerini Kariaí
9,568 ft. Gulf of Mount Athos LEMNOS
Thérmai 6,667 ft. ISLAND

Kérkira Ioánnina Tríkala Larissa
CORFU Igoumenitsa Volos Mount Pelion Mytilene TURKEY
Karditsa 5,089 ft. AEGEAN LESBOS
Préveza Lamía SEA ISLAND
Árta Karpenision EUBOEA SKÝROS Khíos İzmir
LEUCAS Mount ISLAND ISLAND CHIOS
ISLAND Parnassus Néa Ionía ISLAND
Mesolóngion 8,061 ft. Thebes Khalkís Ándros Sámos
CEPHALONIA Pátrai Mégara Athens MÍKONOS
ISLAND PELOPONNESE Piraeus ISLAND
Zákinthos Árgos Laurium Kéa SÝROS Náxos I.
Pyrgos Nauplia ISLAND Ermoúpolis
Megalópolis Sparta Melos Náxos Kálimnos
Kalámata CYCLADES
Pylos Ýithion Monemvasía Rhodes
RHODES

SEA OF CRETE KÁRPATHOS
ISLAND

Khaniá Iráklion
Réthimnon CRETE Áyios
Nikólaos

MEDITERRANEAN
SEA ©2000, Encyclopædia Britannica, Inc.

GREECE

Scale 1: 11,646,000

0   50   100 mi
0   80   160 km

Age Breakdown

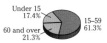

Under 15
17.4%
60 and over
21.3%
15–59
61.3%

Official name: Hellenic Republic
Head of government: Prime Minister
Official language: Greek
Monetary unit: euro
Area: 50,949 sq. mi. (131,957 sq. km.)
Population (2001): 10,975,000
GNP per capita (1999): U.S.$12,110
Principal exports (1998): food 18.4%;
   clothing and apparel 16.8%; petroleum
   6.4%; aluminum 4.2%; tobacco
   products 4.1% *to:* Germany 18.3%;
   Italy 11.9%; United Kingdom 7.9%;
   U.S. 4.7%

In March 1822, during the revolt against Ottoman rule, the first Greek national flags were adopted; the most recent revision to the flag was made on Dec. 22, 1978. The colors symbolize Greek Orthodoxy while the cross stands for "the wisdom of God, freedom and country." The stripes are for the battle cry for independence: "Freedom or Death."

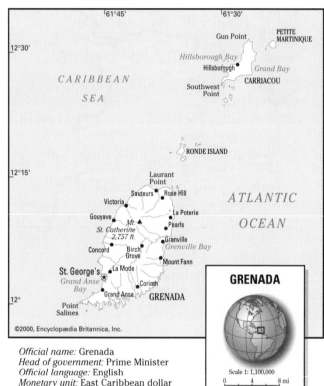

61°45' 61°30'

12°30'

Gun Point PETITE MARTINIQUE

Hillsborough Bay
Hillsborough *Grand Bay*

CARIBBEAN CARRIACOU

Southwest
Point

SEA

RONDE ISLAND

12°15'

Laurant
Point

Sauteurs Rose Hill ATLANTIC

Victoria

La Poterie OCEAN

Gouyave

Mt. Pearls
St. Catherine
2,757 ft.

Grenville
Birch *Grenville Bay*
Concord Grove

Mount Fann

La Mode
St. George's

Grand Anse Corinth
Bay
Grand Anse GRENADA

12°

Point
Salines

©2000, Encyclopædia Britannica, Inc.

Official name: Grenada
Head of government: Prime Minister
Official language: English
Monetary unit: East Caribbean dollar
Area: 133 sq. mi. (344 sq. km.)
Population (2001): 102,000
GNP per capita (1999): U.S.$3,440
Principal exports (1997): domestic
 exports 91.5%, of which nutmeg 26.3%,
 fish 14.3%, cocoa beans 7.3%;
 reexports 8.5% *to:* Germany 46.9%;
 U.S. 12.2%; St. Lucia 6.1%

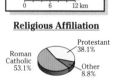

GRENADA

Scale 1: 1,100,000

0   4   8 mi
0   6   12 km

Religious Affiliation

Protestant
38.1%

Roman
Catholic
53.1%

Other
8.8%

Grenada's flag was officially hoisted on Feb. 3, 1974. Its background is green for vegetation and yellow for the sun, and its
red border is symbolic of harmony and unity. The seven stars
are for the original administrative subdivisions of Grenada.
Nutmeg, a crop for which the "Isle of Spice" is internationally
known, is represented as well.

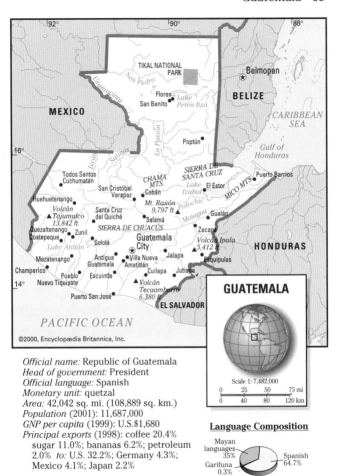

©2000, Encyclopædia Britannica, Inc.

Official name: Republic of Guatemala
Head of government: President
Official language: Spanish
Monetary unit: quetzal
Area: 42,042 sq. mi. (108,889 sq. km.)
Population (2001): 11,687,000
GNP per capita (1999): U.S.$1,680
Principal exports (1998): coffee 20.4%
sugar 11.0%; bananas 6.2%; petroleum
2.0% *to:* U.S. 32.2%; Germany 4.3%;
Mexico 4.1%; Japan 2.2%

Language Composition

Mayan
languages
35%

Garifuna
0.3%

Spanish
64.7%

The flag was introduced in 1871. It has blue and white stripes
(colors of the former United Provinces of Central America)
and a coat of arms with the quetzal (the national bird), a
scroll, a wreath, and crossed rifles and sabres. Different
artistic variations have been used but on Sept. 12, 1968, the
present pattern was established.

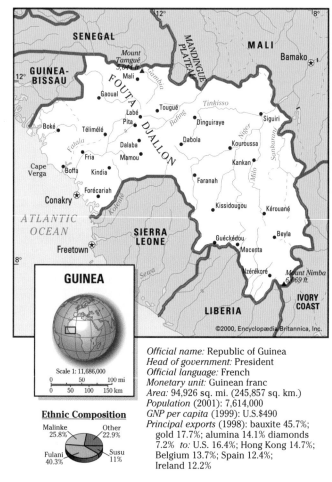

SENEGAL

GUINEA-BISSAU

MALI

Bamako

Mount Tamgué 5,046 ft.

Mali

FOUTA DJALLON

MANDINGUE PLATEAU

Gaoual

Gambia

Boké

Télimélé

Labé

Pita

Tougué

Tinkisso

Dinguiraye

Siguiri

Bafing

Niger

Dabola

Kouroussa

Fatala

Fria

Dalaba

Mamou

Kankan

Sankarani

Cape Verga

Boffa

Kindia

Forécariah

Faranah

Milo

Conakry

Kolente

Kissidougou

Kérouané

ATLANTIC OCEAN

SIERRA LEONE

Beyla

Freetown

Guéckédou

Macenta

Sewa

Nzérékoré

Mount Nimba 6,069 ft.

IVORY COAST

LIBERIA

©2000, Encyclopædia Britannica, Inc.

GUINEA

Scale 1: 11,686,000

0   50   100 mi

0   50   100   150 km

Official name: Republic of Guinea
Head of government: President
Official language: French
Monetary unit: Guinean franc
Area: 94,926 sq. mi. (245,857 sq. km.)
Population (2001): 7,614,000
GNP per capita (1999): U.S.$490
Principal exports (1998): bauxite 45.7%; gold 17.7%; alumina 14.1% diamonds 7.2% *to:* U.S. 16.4%; Hong Kong 14.7%; Belgium 13.7%; Spain 12.4%; Ireland 12.2%

Ethnic Composition

Malinke 25.8%
Other 22.9%
Fulani 40.3%
Susu 11%

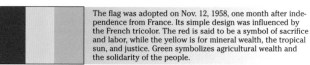

The flag was adopted on Nov. 12, 1958, one month after independence from France. Its simple design was influenced by the French tricolor. The red is said to be a symbol of sacrifice and labor, while the yellow is for mineral wealth, the tropical sun, and justice. Green symbolizes agricultural wealth and the solidarity of the people.

Official name: Republic of Guinea-Bissau
Head of government: Prime Minister
Official language: Portuguese
Monetary unit: CFA franc
Area: 13,948 sq. mi. (36,125 sq. km.)
Population (2001): 1,316,000
GNP per capita (1999): U.S.$160
Principal exports (1997): cashews 94.0%;
  sawn wood 1.6% *to:* India 85.2%;
  other/unspecified 13.1%

Ethnic Composition

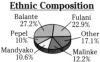

Balante 27.2%
Fulani 22.9%
Pepel 10%
Other 17.1%
Mandyako 10.6%
Malinke 12.2%

The flag has been used since the declaration of independence from Portugal on Sept. 24, 1973. The black star on the red stripe was for African Party leadership, the people, and their will to live in dignity, freedom, and peace. Yellow was for the harvest and other rewards of work, and green was for the nation's vast jungles and agricultural lands.

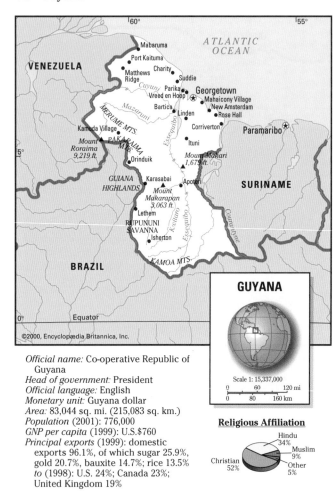

©2000, Encyclopædia Britannica, Inc.

Official name: Co-operative Republic of Guyana
Head of government: President
Official language: English
Monetary unit: Guyana dollar
Area: 83,044 sq. mi. (215,083 sq. km.)
Population (2001): 776,000
GNP per capita (1999): U.S.$760
Principal exports (1999): domestic exports 96.1%, of which sugar 25.9%, gold 20.7%, bauxite 14.7%; rice 13.5% *to* (1998): U.S. 24%; Canada 23%; United Kingdom 19%

Scale 1: 15,337,000

0   60   120 mi
0   80   160 km

Religious Affiliation

Hindu 34%
Muslim 9%
Other 5%
Christian 52%

Upon independence from Britain on May 26, 1966, the flag was first hoisted. The green stands for jungles and fields, white suggests the rivers which are the basis for the Indian word guiana ("land of waters"), red is for zeal and sacrifice in nation-building, and black is for perseverance. The flag is nicknamed "The Golden Arrowhead."

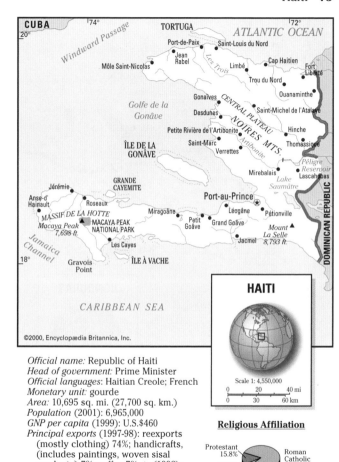

CUBA | 74° | TORTUGA | ATLANTIC OCEAN | 72°
20°

Windward Passage

Port-de-Paix · Saint-Louis du Nord
Môle Saint-Nicolas · Jean Rabel · Limbé · Cap Haïtien · Fort Liberté
Les Trois · Trou du Nord · Ouanaminthe

Gonaïves · CENTRAL PLATEAU · Saint-Michel de l'Atalaye
Golfe de la Gonâve
Desdunes · NOIRES MTS. · Hinche
Petite Rivière de l'Artibonite · Thomassique
ÎLE DE LA GONÂVE · Saint-Marc · *Artibonite*
Verrettes

Mirebalais · *Péligre Reservoir* · Lascahobas
Lake Saumâtre

GRANDE CAYEMITE
Jérémie
Anse-d'Hainault · Roseaux · Miragoâne · Port-au-Prince · Pétionville
MASSIF DE LA HOTTE · Léogâne
Macaya Peak 7,698 ft. · MACAYA PEAK NATIONAL PARK · Petit Goâve · Grand Goâve
Jamaica Channel · Les Cayes · Jacmel · Mount La Selle 8,793 ft.

18° · Gravois Point · ÎLE À VACHE

CARIBBEAN SEA

DOMINICAN REPUBLIC

©2000, Encyclopædia Britannica, Inc.

HAITI

Scale 1: 4,550,000
0   20   40 mi
0   30   60 km

Official name: Republic of Haiti
Head of government: Prime Minister
Official languages: Haitian Creole; French
Monetary unit: gourde
Area: 10,695 sq. mi. (27,700 sq. km.)
Population (2001): 6,965,000
GNP per capita (1999): U.S.$460
Principal exports (1997-98): reexports (mostly clothing) 74%; handicrafts, (includes paintings, woven sisal products) 7%; coffee 7% *to* (1998): U.S. 88%; Belgium 3%; France 3%

Religious Affiliation

Protestant 15.8%
Other 3.9%
Roman Catholic 80.3%

After the French Revolution of 1789 Haiti underwent a slave revolt, but the French tricolor continued in use until 1803. The new blue-red flag represented the black and mulatto populations only. A black-red flag was used by various dictators, including François "Papa Doc" Duvalier and his son, but on Feb. 25, 1986, the old flag was reestablished.

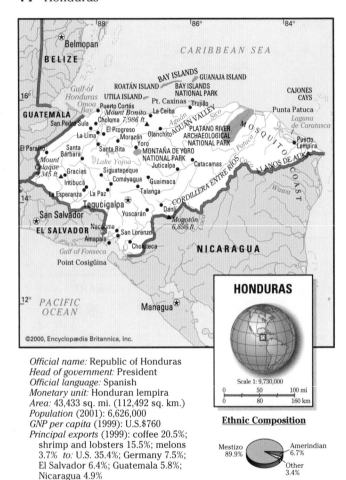

Official name: Republic of Honduras
Head of government: President
Official language: Spanish
Monetary unit: Honduran lempira
Area: 43,433 sq. mi. (112,492 sq. km.)
Population (2001): 6,626,000
GNP per capita (1999): U.S.$760
Principal exports (1999): coffee 20.5%;
  shrimp and lobsters 15.5%; melons
  3.7% *to:* U.S. 35.4%; Germany 7.5%;
  El Salvador 6.4%; Guatemala 5.8%;
  Nicaragua 4.9%

HONDURAS

Scale 1: 9,730,000

0   50   100 mi

0   80   160 km

Ethnic Composition

Mestizo 89.9%
Amerindian 6.7%
Other 3.4%

Since Feb. 16, 1866, the Honduran flag has retained the blue-white-blue design of the flag of the former United Provinces of Central America, but with five central stars symbolizing the states of Honduras, El Salvador, Nicaragua, Costa Rica, and Guatemala. The flag design has often been associated with Central American reunification attempts.

Official name: Republic of Hungary
Head of government: Prime Minister
Official language: Hungarian
Monetary unit: forint
Area: 35,919 sq. mi. (93,030 sq. km.)
Population (2001): 10,190,000
GNP per capita (1999): U.S.$4,640
Principal exports (1999): non-electrical
  machinery 16.8%; office machines and
  computers 13.4%; electrical machinery
  11.0% *to:* Germany 38.4%; Austria
  9.6%; Italy 5.9%

Scale 1: 8,147,000

| 0 | 30 | 60 | 90 mi |
| 0 | 40 | 80 | 120 km |

Religious Affiliation

Protestant 25.1%
Roman Catholic 67.8%
Other 7.1%

The colors of the Hungarian flag were mentioned in a 1608
coronation ceremony, but they may have been used since the
13th century. The tricolor was adopted on Oct. 12, 1957, after
the abortive revolution of 1956. The white is said to symbolize Hungary's rivers, the green its mountains, and the red the
blood shed in its many battles.

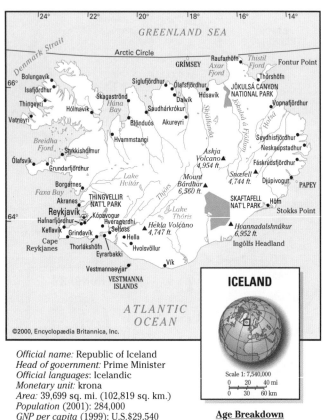

GREENLAND SEA

Arctic Circle

Denmark Strait

Bolungavík
Ísafjördhur
Thingeyri
Vatneyri
Hólmavík
Skagaströnd
Siglufjördhur
Ólafsfjördhur
Dalvík
Húsavík
Grímsey
Raufarhöfn
Thistil Fjord
Thórshöfn
Fontur Point
Axar Fjord
JÖKULSÁ CANYON NATIONAL PARK
Vopnafjördhur
Húna Bay
Saudhárkrókur
Akureyri
Blönduós
Hvammstangi
Skjálfanda
Jökulsá á Fjöllum
Holsá
Seydhisfjördhur
Neskaupstadhur
Breidha Fjord
Stykkishólmur
Askja Volcano ▲ 4,954 ft.
Fáskrúdhsfjördhur
Djúpivogur
PAPEY
Ólafsvík
Grundarfjördhur
Borgarnes
Lake Hvítár
Snæfell ▲ 4,744 ft.
Faxa Bay
Akranes
THINGVELLIR NAT'L PARK
Mount Bárdhar ▲ 6,560 ft.
Thórs
SKAFTAFELL NAT'L PARK
Höfn
Stokks Point
Reykjavík
Kópavogur
Hafnarfjördhur
Hveragerdhi
Selfoss
Lake Thóris
Hekla Volcano 4,747 ft.
Keflavík
Grindavík
Hella
▲ *Hvannadalshnúkur* 6,952 ft.
Cape Reykjanes
Thorlákshöfn
Hvolsvöllur
Ingólfs Headland
Eyrarbakki
Vestmannaeyjar
Vík
VESTMANNA ISLANDS

ATLANTIC OCEAN

©2000, Encyclopædia Britannica, Inc.

ICELAND

Scale 1: 7,540,000

0   20   40 mi
0   30   60 km

Official name: Republic of Iceland
Head of government: Prime Minister
Official languages: Icelandic
Monetary unit: krona
Area: 39,699 sq. mi. (102,819 sq. km.)
Population (2001): 284,000
GNP per capita (1999): U.S.$29,540
Principal exports (1999): marine products 61.2%; frozen fish 36.3%; aluminum 15.6%; transportation equipment 4.5% *to:* United Kingdom 19.6%; U.S. 14.7%; The Netherlands 6.0%

Age Breakdown

Under 15
24.6%

15–59
60.4%

60 and over
15%

Approval for an Icelandic flag was given by the king of Denmark on June 19, 1915; it became a national flag on Dec. 1, 1918, when the separate kingdom of Iceland was proclaimed. The flag was retained upon the creation of a republic on June 17, 1944. The design has a typical "Scandinavian cross".

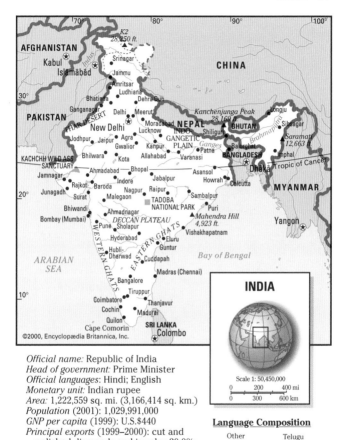

Official name: Republic of India
Head of government: Prime Minister
Official languages: Hindi; English
Monetary unit: Indian rupee
Area: 1,222,559 sq. mi. (3,166,414 sq. km.)
Population (2001): 1,029,991,000
GNP per capita (1999): U.S.$440
Principal exports (1999–2000): cut and
polished diamonds and jewelry 20.0%;
cotton ready-made garments 9.2%;
cotton yarn, fabrics and thread 7.9%
to: U.S. 22.2%; Hong Kong 6.7%; United
Kingdom 5.6%

INDIA

Scale 1 : 50,450,000

| 0 | 200 | 400 mi |
| 0 | 300 | 600 km |

Language Composition

Other 38%
Telugu 8%
Bengali 7.6%
Marathi 7.4%
Hindi 39%

Earlier versions of the flag were used from the 1920s, but the
current flag was hoisted officially on July 22, 1947. The
orange was said to stand for courage and sacrifice, white for
peace and truth, and green for faith and chivalry. The blue
wheel is a chakra, associated with Emperor Asoka's attempts
to unite India in the 3rd century BC.

©2000, Encyclopædia Britannica, Inc.

Official name: Republic of Indonesia
Head of government: President
Official language: Indonesian (Bahasa Indonesia)
Monetary unit: Indonesian rupiah
Area: 741,052 sq. mi. (1,922,570 sq. km.)
Population (2001): 212,195,000
GNP per capita (1999): U.S.$600
Principal exports (1998): crude petroleum 8.3%; natural gas 7.8%; garments 5.4% *to:* Japan 18.7%; U.S. 14.4%; Singapore 10.6%

INDONESIA

Scale 1: 88,292,000

| 0 | 400 | 800 mi |
| 0 | 600 | 1200 km |

Language Composition

Indonesian (Malay) 12.1%
Javanese 39.4%
Sundanese 15.8%
Other 32.7%

Indonesia's red and white flag was associated with the Majapahit empire which existed from the 13th to the 16th century. It was adopted on Aug. 17, 1945, and it remained after Indonesia won its independence from The Netherlands in 1949. Red is for courage and white for honesty. The flag is identical, except in dimensions, to the flag of Monaco.

Official name: Islamic Republic of Iran
Head of government: President
Official language: Farsi (Persian)
Monetary unit: rial
Area: 629,315 sq. mi. (1,629,918 sq. km.)
Population (2001): 63,442,000
GNP per capita (1999): U.S.$1,810
Principal exports (1998–99): petroleum
and natural gas 75.7%; fruit 4.5%;
carpets 4.3% *to:* United Kingdom
16.8%; Japan 15.7%; Italy 8.6%; UAE
6.7%; South Korea 5.0%

Ethnic Composition

Other 28.5%
Azerbaijani 16.8%
Persian 45.6%
Kurd 9.1%

The tricolor flag was recognized in 1906 but altered after the revolution of 1979. Along the central stripe are the Arabic words Allahu akbar ("God is great"), repeated 22 times. The coat of arms can be read as a rendition of the word Allah, as a globe, or as two crescents. The green is for Islam, white is for peace, and red is for valor.

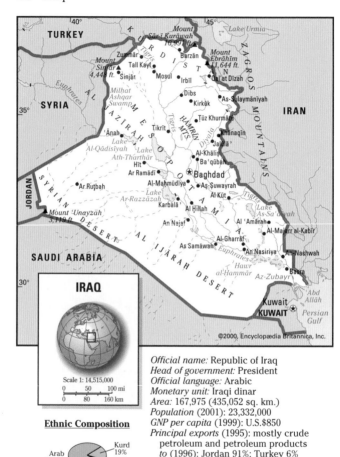

Official name: Republic of Iraq
Head of government: President
Official language: Arabic
Monetary unit: Iraqi dinar
Area: 167,975 (435,052 sq. km.)
Population (2001): 23,332,000
GNP per capita (1999): U.S.$850
Principal exports (1995): mostly crude
petroleum and petroleum products
to (1996): Jordan 91%; Turkey 6%

Ethnic Composition

Arab 77.1%
Kurd 19%
Other 3.9%

Adopted on July 30, 1963, the Iraqi flag is based on the liberation flag first flown in Egypt in 1952. The stars express a
desire to unite with Egypt and Syria. Red is for the willingness
to shed blood, green is for Arab lands, black is for past suffering, and white is for purity. On Jan. 14, 1991, the Arabic
inscription "God is Great" was added.

Official name: Ireland
Head of government: Prime Minister
Official languages: Irish; English
Monetary unit: euro
Area: 27,133 sq. mi. (70,273 sq. km.)
Population (2001): 3,823,000
GNP per capita (1999): U.S.$21,470
Principal exports (1999): machinery and
transport equipment 38.8%; chemical
products 31.6%; manufactured goods
11.1% *to:* United Kingdom 22.0%; U.S.
15.4%; Germany 11.9%

Age Breakdown

Under 15
26.7%

15–59
58.1%

60 and over
15.2%

In the 19th century various tricolor flags and ribbons became
symbolic of Irish opposition to British rule. Many of them
included the colors green (for the Catholics), orange (for the
Protestants), and white (for the peace between the two
groups). The tricolor in its modern form was recognized by
the constitution on Dec. 29, 1937.

©2000, Encyclopædia Britannica, Inc.

Official name: State of Israel
Head of government: Prime Minister
Official languages: Hebrew; Arabic
Monetary unit: New (Israeli) shekel
Area: 7,886 sq. mi. (20,425 sq. km.)
Population (2001): 6,258,000
GNP per capita (1999): U.S.$16,310
Principal exports (2000): machinery and
  transport equipment 39.7%; diamonds
  23.7%; chemicals 13.4%; apparel 4.9%
  to: U.S. 35.5%; United Kingdom 5.5%;
  Belgium 5.4%

Scale 1: 6,301,000

| 0 | 25 | 50 mi |
| 0 | 40 | 80 km |

Religious Affiliation

Jewish 81%

Muslim 14.5%

Other 4.5%

Symbolic of the traditional *tallit*, or Jewish prayer shawl, and
including the Star of David, the flag was used from the late
19th century. It was raised when Israel proclaimed independence on May 14, 1948, and the banner was legally recognized on Nov. 12, 1948. A dark blue was also substituted for
the traditional lighter shade of blue.

Official name: Italian Republic
Head of government: Prime Minister
Official language: Italian
Monetary unit: euro
Area: 116,324 sq. mi. (301,277 sq. km.)
Population (2001): 57,892,000
GNP per capita (1999): U.S.$20,170
Principal exports (1999): machinery and
    transport equipment 41.7%; electrical
    machinery 9.8%; textiles and wearing
    apparel 10.7% *to:* Germany 16.5%;
    France 13.0%; U.S. 9.5%; United
    Kingdom 7.1%; Spain 6.3%

Age Breakdown

Under 15
16.4%

15–59
63%

60 and over
20.6%

The first Italian national flag was adopted on Feb. 25, 1797, by
the Cispadane Republic. Its stripes were vertically positioned
on May 11, 1798, and thereafter it was honored by all Italian
nationalists. The design was guaranteed by a decree (March
23, 1848) of King Charles Albert of Sardinia, ordering troops
to carry the flag into battle.

MALI

BURKINA FASO

GUINEA

Tengrela

Odienné
Ferkéssédougou

Boundiali
Korhogo
Kong
Bouna

Tortiya
KOMOÉ NATIONAL PARK

Séguéla
Katiola
Bondoukou

Biankouma
Lake Kossou
Bouaké

Mount Nimba 6,069 ft. • Man
Bouaflé
Daoukro

GHANA

Duékoué
Daloa
Yamoussoukro

Guiglo
Sinfra
Dimbokro
Abengourou

LIBERIA

Gagnoa
Oumé
Arrah

Lakota
Adzopé

TAÏ NATIONAL PARK
Divo
Agboville

Anyama

Abidjan
Aboisso

Sassandra
Grand-Bassam

San-Pedro

Cape Palmas
Tabou

ATLANTIC OCEAN

©2000, Encyclopædia Britannica, Inc.

IVORY COAST

Scale 1: 12,565,000

| 0 | 60 | 120 mi |
| 0 | 80 | 160 km |

Official name: Republic of Cote d'Ivoire
Head of government: President
Official language: French
Monetary unit: CFA franc
Area: 124,504 sq. mi. (322,463 sq. km.)
Population (2001): 16,393,000
GNP per capita (1999): U.S.$670
Principal exports (1997): cocoa beans and products 33.5%; petroleum products 16.8%; coffee and coffee products 7.3% *to:* France 17.3%; The Netherlands 13.2%; U.S. 7.5%

Religious Affiliation

Catholic 20.8%
Animist 17%
Atheist 13.4%
Muslim 38.7%
Other 10.1%

Adopted on Aug. 7, 1959, the flag of the former French colony has three stripes corresponding to the national motto (Unity, Discipline, Labor). The orange is for growth, the white is for peace emerging from purity and unity, and the green is for hope and the future. Unofficially the green is for forests and the orange is for savannas.

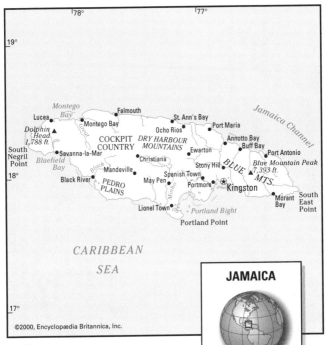

Montego Bay

Jamaica Channel

Lucea • Falmouth • St. Ann's Bay • Port Maria
• Montego Bay • Ocho Rios • Annotto Bay
Dolphin Head 1,788 ft. ▲ COCKPIT COUNTRY *DRY HARBOUR MOUNTAINS* Buff Bay • Port Antonio
South Negril Point *Bluefield Bay* • Savanna-la-Mar Ewarton • Blue Mountain Peak 7,393 ft. ▲
• Christiana Stony Hill • *BLUE*
• Mandeville Spanish Town • *MTS.*
Black River • May Pen Portmore • ⊛ Kingston
PEDRO PLAINS Morant Bay South East Point
Lionel Town • *Portland Bight*
Portland Point

CARIBBEAN

SEA

©2000, Encyclopædia Britannica, Inc.

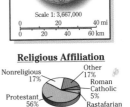

JAMAICA

Scale 1: 3,667,000

| 0 | 20 | 40 mi |
| 0 | 20 | 40 | 60 km |

Official name: Jamaica
Head of government: Prime Minister
Official language: English
Monetary unit: Jamaica dollar
Area: 4,244 sq. mi. (10,991 sq. km.)
Population (2001): 2,624,000
GNP per capita (1999): U.S.$2,430
Principal exports (1999): crude materials 55.7%; food 19.1%; beverages and tobacco 4.8%. *to:* U.S. 33.4%; Canada 14.1%; United Kingdom 13.4%; The Netherlands 10.2%

Religious Affiliation

Nonreligious 17%
Other 17%
Roman Catholic 5%
Rastafarian 5%
Protestant 56%

The flag was designed prior to independence from Britain (Aug. 6, 1962). The black color stood for hardships faced by the nation, green for agriculture and hope, and yellow for the natural wealth of Jamaica. This was summed up in the phrase, "Hardships there are, but the land is green and the sun shineth."

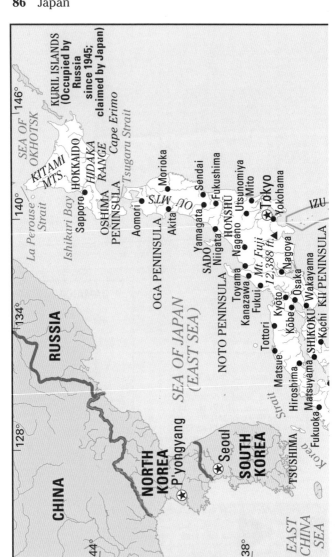

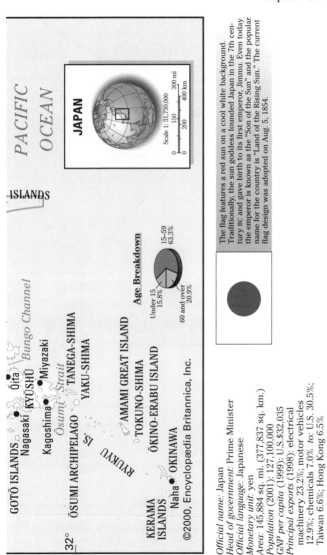

PACIFIC OCEAN

ISLANDS

JAPAN

Scale 1: 31,730,000

0   150   300 mi
0   200   400 km

The flag features a red sun on a cool white background. Traditionally, the sun goddess founded Japan in the 7th century BC and gave birth to its first emperor, Jimmu. Even today the emperor is known as the "Son of the Sun" and the popular name for the country is "Land of the Rising Sun." The current flag design was adopted on Aug. 5, 1854.

Age Breakdown

Under 15
15.8%

15–59
63.3%

60 and over
20.9%

GOTŌ ISLANDS
Nagasaki   KYŪSHŪ   Ōita   *Bungo Channel*
Kagoshima   Miyazaki
Ōsumi Strait   TANEGA-SHIMA
YAKU-SHIMA
ŌSUMI ARCHIPELAGO
AMAMI GREAT ISLAND
RYUKYU IS
TOKUNO-SHIMA
ŌKINO-ERABU ISLAND
KERAMA
ISLANDS   OKINAWA
Naha

32°

©2000, Encyclopædia Britannica, Inc.

Official name: Japan
Head of government: Prime Minister
Official language: Japanese
Monetary unit: yen
Area: 145,884 sq. mi. (377,837 sq. km.)
Population (2001): 127,100,000
GNP per capita (1999): U.S.$32,035
Principal exports (1998): electrical machinery 23.2%; motor vehicles 12.9%; chemicals 7.0% *to:* U.S. 30.5%; Taiwan 6.6%; Hong Kong 6.5%

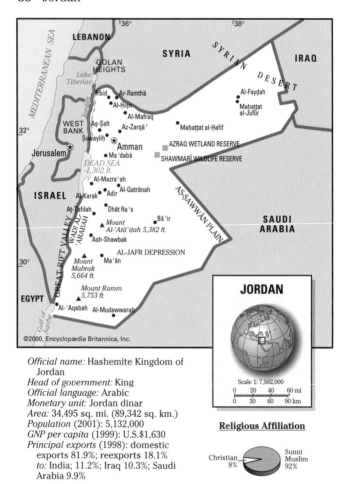

Official name: Hashemite Kingdom of Jordan

Head of government: King

Official language: Arabic

Monetary unit: Jordan dinar

Area: 34,495 sq. mi. (89,342 sq. km.)

Population (2001): 5,132,000

GNP per capita (1999): U.S.$1,630

Principal exports (1998): domestic exports 81.9%; reexports 18.1% *to:* India; 11.2%; Iraq 10.3%; Saudi Arabia 9.9%

Scale 1: 7,562,000

0 20 40 60 mi
0 30 60 90 km

Religious Affiliation

Christian 8%

Sunni Muslim 92%

In 1917 Husayn ibn Ali raised the Arab Revolt flag. With the addition of a white seven-pointed star, this flag was adopted by Transjordan on April 16, 1928, and retained upon the independence of Jordan on March 22, 1946. White is for purity, black for struggle and suffering, red for bloodshed, and green for Arab lands.

Official name: Republic of Kazakhstan
Head of government: President
Official language: Kazakh
Monetary unit: tenge
Area: 1,052,100 sq. mi. (2,724,900 sq. km.)
Population (2001): 14,868,000
GNP per capita (1999): U.S.$1,250
Principal exports (1998): oil and gas
condensate 28.6%; rolled ferrous metal
8.9%; refined copper 8.8% *to:* Russia
28.9%; United Kingdom 9.0%; China
7.2%; Switzerland 6.1%

KAZAKSTAN

Scale 1: 43,241,000

0   200   400 mi

0   200   400   600 km

Ethnic Composition

Russian 34.8%
Other 14.3%
Ukrainian 4.9%
Kazak 46%

The flag was adopted in June 1992. Light blue is a traditional
color of the nomads of Central Asia; it symbolizes peace and
well-being. The golden sun and eagle represent freedom and
the high ideals of the Kazaks. Along the edge is a band of traditional Kazak ornamentation; the band was originally in red
but is now in golden yellow.

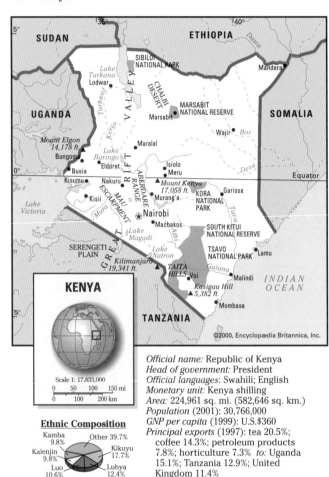

Official name: Republic of Kenya
Head of government: President
Official languages: Swahili; English
Monetary unit: Kenya shilling
Area: 224,961 sq. mi. (582,646 sq. km.)
Population (2001): 30,766,000
GNP per capita (1999): U.S.$360
Principal exports (1997): tea 20.5%;
   coffee 14.3%; petroleum products
   7.8%; horticulture 7.3% *to:* Uganda
   15.1%; Tanzania 12.9%; United
   Kingdom 11.4%

Ethnic Composition

Kamba 9.8%
Kalenjin 9.8%
Luo 10.6%
Luhya 12.4%
Kikuyu 17.7%
Other 39.7%

Upon independence from Britain (Dec. 12, 1963), the Kenyan flag became official. It was based on the flag of the Kenya African National Union. Black is for the people, red for humanity and the struggle for freedom, green for the fertile land, and white for unity and peace. The shield and spears are traditional weapons of the Masai people.

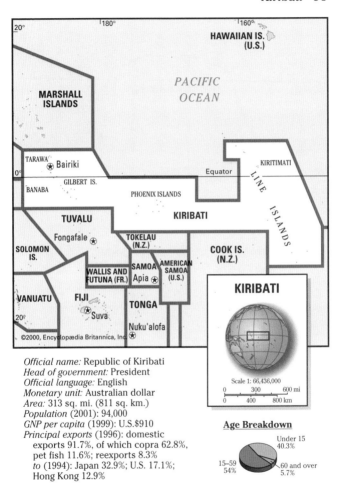

HAWAIIAN IS.
(U.S.)

*PACIFIC
OCEAN*

MARSHALL
ISLANDS

TARAWA
★ Bairiki
KIRITIMATI

Equator

BANABA
GILBERT IS.

PHOENIX ISLANDS

LINE ISLANDS

TUVALU
KIRIBATI

Fongafale ★
TOKELAU
(N.Z.)

SOLOMON
IS.
COOK IS.
(N.Z.)

WALLIS AND
FUTUNA (FR.)
SAMOA
AMERICAN
SAMOA
(U.S.)
Apia ★

VANUATU
FIJI
TONGA

★ Suva
Nuku'alofa ★

©2000, Encyclopædia Britannica, Inc.

KIRIBATI

Scale 1: 66,436,000

0   300   600 mi
0   400   800 km

Official name: Republic of Kiribati
Head of government: President
Official language: English
Monetary unit: Australian dollar
Area: 313 sq. mi. (811 sq. km.)
Population (2001): 94,000
GNP per capita (1999): U.S.$910
Principal exports (1996): domestic
exports 91.7%, of which copra 62.8%,
pet fish 11.6%; reexports 8.3%
to (1994): Japan 32.9%; U.S. 17.1%;
Hong Kong 12.9%

Age Breakdown

Under 15
40.3%

15–59
54%

60 and over
5.7%

Great Britain acquired the Gilbert and Ellice Islands in the
19th century. In 1975 the Gilbert Islands separated from the
Ellice Islands to form Kiribati, and a new flag was adopted
based on the coat of arms granted to the islands in 1937. It
has waves of white and blue, for the Pacific Ocean, as well as
a yellow sun and a local frigate bird.

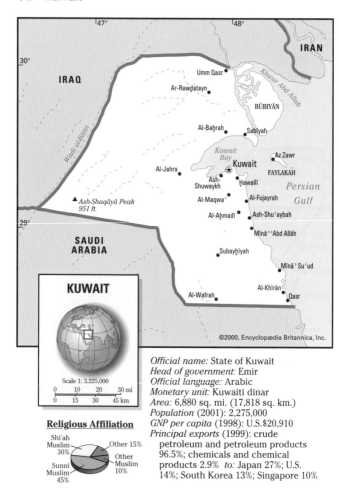

©2000, Encyclopædia Britannica, Inc.

Official name: State of Kuwait
Head of government: Emir
Official language: Arabic
Monetary unit: Kuwaiti dinar
Area: 6,880 sq. mi. (17,818 sq. km.)
Population (2001): 2,275,000
GNP per capita (1998): U.S.$20,910
Principal exports (1999): crude
petroleum and petroleum products
96.5%; chemicals and chemical
products 2.9% *to:* Japan 27%; U.S.
14%; South Korea 13%; Singapore 10%

Scale 1: 3,225,000

| 0 | 10 | 20 | 30 mi |
| 0 | 15 | 30 | 45 km |

Religious Affiliation

Shi'ah Muslim 30%
Other 15%
Sunni Muslim 45%
Other Muslim 10%

The red flag of Kuwait, in use since World War I, was replaced
by the current flag on Oct. 24, 1961, shortly after independence from Britain. The symbolism is from a poem written
over six centuries ago. The green stands for Arab lands, black
is for battles, white is for the purity of the fighters, and red is
for the blood on their swords.

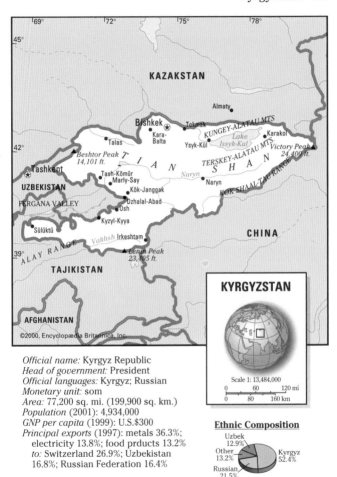

Official name: Kyrgyz Republic
Head of government: President
Official languages: Kyrgyz; Russian
Monetary unit: som
Area: 77,200 sq. mi. (199,900 sq. km.)
Population (2001): 4,934,000
GNP per capita (1999): U.S.$300
Principal exports (1997): metals 36.3%;
  electricity 13.8%; food prducts 13.2%
  to: Switzerland 26.9%; Uzbekistan
  16.8%; Russian Federation 16.4%

Ethnic Composition

Uzbek 12.9%
Other 13.2%
Russian 21.5%
Kyrgyz 52.4%

The Kyrgyz flag replaced a Soviet-era design on March 3, 1992. The red recalls the flag of the national hero Mansas the Noble. The central yellow sun has 40 rays, corresponding to the followers of Mansas and the tribes he united. On the sun is the stylized view of the roof of a yurt, a traditional nomadic home that is now seldom used.

Official name: Lao People's Democratic
  Republic
Head of government: Prime Minister
Official language: Lao
Monetary unit: kip
Area: 91,429 sq. mi. (236,800 sq. km.)
Population (2001): 5,636,000
GNP per capita (1999): U.S.$290
Principal exports (1998): wood products
  34.3%; garments 20.8%; electricity
  18.0% coffee 14.3% *to* (1997): Viet
  Nam 42.7%; Thailand 22.1%; France
  6.3%; Belgium 5.6%

Ethnic Composition

Lao-Lum
67%

Lao-Theung
16.5%

Other
8.7%

Lao-Tai
7.8%

The Lao flag was first used by anticolonialist forces from the
mid-20th century. The white disk honored the Japanese who
had supported the Lao independence movement, but it also
symbolized a bright future. Red was said to stand for the
blood of patriots and blue was for the promise of future prosperity. The flag was adopted on Dec. 2, 1975.

Official name: Republic of Latvia
Head of government: Prime Minister
Official language: Latvian
Monetary unit: lats
Area: 24,938 sq. mi. (64,589 sq. km.)
Population (2001): 2,358,000
GNP per capita (1999): U.S.$2,420
Principal exports (1998): wood and paper
  products 33.5%; textiles and clothing
  16.1% *to:* Germany 15.6%; United
  Kingdom 13.5%; Russia 12.1%;
  Sweden 10.3%

Ethnic Composition

Latvian 54.8%
Russian 32.8%
Other 8.4%
Belarusian 4%

The basic flag design was used by a militia unit in 1279,
according to a 14th century source. Popularized in the 19th
century among anti-Russian nationalists, the flag flew in 1918
and was legally adopted on Jan. 20, 1923. Under Soviet control the flag was suppressed, but it was again legalized in
1988 and flown officially from Feb. 27, 1990.

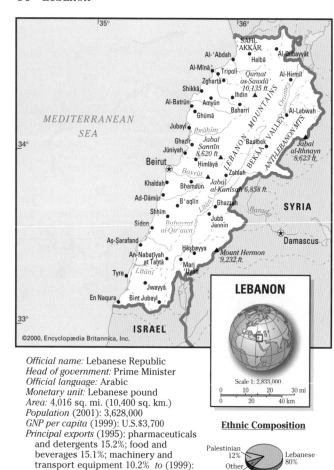

Official name: Lebanese Republic
Head of government: Prime Minister
Official language: Arabic
Monetary unit: Lebanese pound
Area: 4,016 sq. mi. (10,400 sq. km.)
Population (2001): 3,628,000
GNP per capita (1999): U.S.$3,700
Principal exports (1995): pharmaceuticals
  and detergents 15.2%; food and
  beverages 15.1%; machinery and
  transport equipment 10.2% *to* (1999):
  Saudi Arabia 10.5%; UAE 8.0%;
  France 7.7%

LEBANON

Scale 1: 2,833,000

0   10   20   30 mi
0   20   40 km

Ethnic Composition

Palestinian 12%
Lebanese 80%
Other 8%

On Sept. 1, 1920, French-administered Lebanon adopted a flag
based on the French tricolor. The current red-white flag was
established by the constitution of 1943, which divided power
among the Muslim and Christian sects. On the central stripe
is a cedar tree, which is a biblical symbol for holiness, peace,
and eternity.

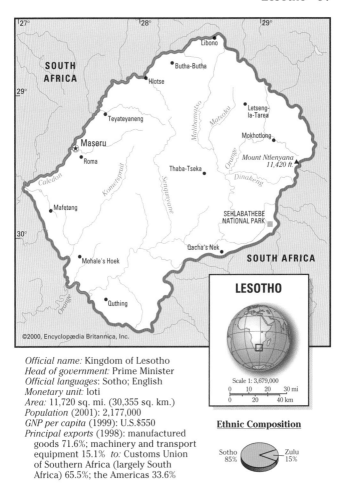

Official name: Kingdom of Lesotho
Head of government: Prime Minister
Official languages: Sotho; English
Monetary unit: loti
Area: 11,720 sq. mi. (30,355 sq. km.)
Population (2001): 2,177,000
GNP per capita (1999): U.S.$550
Principal exports (1998): manufactured
goods 71.6%; machinery and transport
equipment 15.1% *to:* Customs Union
of Southern Africa (largely South
Africa) 65.5%; the Americas 33.6%

Scale 1: 3,679,000

0   10   20   30 mi
0   20   40 km

Ethnic Composition

Sotho
85%

Zulu
15%

The flag was hoisted on Jan. 20, 1987, after the military over-
threw the government of prime minister Leabua Jonathan.
It contains a white triangle (for peace) on which are an
animal-skin shield and traditional weapons used in battles
to preserve Sotho independence. The green triangle is for
prosperity, and the blue stripe is for rain.

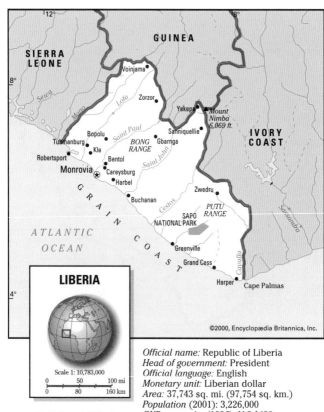

Official name: Republic of Liberia
Head of government: President
Official language: English
Monetary unit: Liberian dollar
Area: 37,743 sq. mi. (97,754 sq. km.)
Population (2001): 3,226,000
GNP per capita (1996): U.S.$490
Principal exports (1999): rubber 56.9%; logs and timber 39.1% to (1999): U.S. 54.3%; France 24.3%; Singapore 5.2%; Belgium 4.4%

Religious Affiliation

Traditional beliefs and other 18.5%
Christian 67.7%
Muslim 13.8%

In the 19th century land was purchased on the African coast by the American Colonization Society, in order to return freed slaves to Africa. On April 9, 1827, a flag based on that of the United States was adopted, featuring a white cross. On Aug. 24, 1847, after independence, the cross was replaced by a star and the number of stripes was reduced.

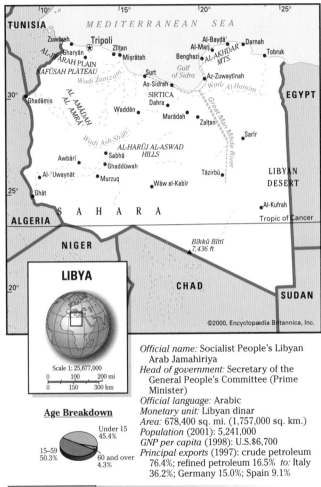

Official name: Socialist People's Libyan Arab Jamahiriya

Head of government: Secretary of the General People's Committee (Prime Minister)

Official language: Arabic

Monetary unit: Libyan dinar

Area: 678,400 sq. mi. (1,757,000 sq. km.)

Population (2001): 5,241,000

GNP per capita (1998): U.S.$6,700

Principal exports (1997): crude petroleum 76.4%; refined petroleum 16.5% *to:* Italy 36.2%; Germany 15.0%; Spain 9.1%

Age Breakdown

Under 15
45.4%

15–59
50.3%

60 and over
4.3%

After the coup d'état of 1969, Muammar al-Qaddafi adopted a flag based on the Egyptian flag. When the Egyptian president Anwar el-Sadat made peace with Israel, however, Qaddafi broke diplomatic relations and replaced the flag. In November 1977 he established a plain green banner, symbolizing promises of agricultural wealth.

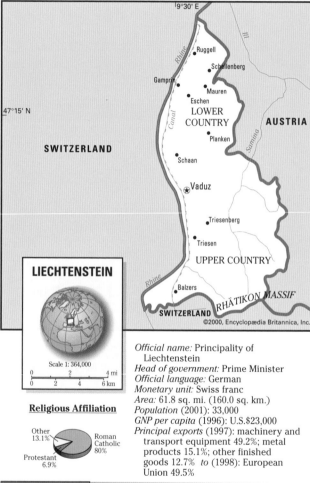

47°15' N

9°30' E

SWITZERLAND

Rhine

Canal

Ruggell

Schellenberg

Gamprin

Mauren

Eschen

LOWER
COUNTRY

AUSTRIA

Samina

Planken

Schaan

⊛ Vaduz

Triesenberg

Triesen

UPPER COUNTRY

Rhine

Balzers

SWITZERLAND

RHÄTIKON MASSIF

©2000, Encyclopædia Britannica, Inc.

LIECHTENSTEIN

Scale 1: 364,000

| 0 | | 2 | | 4 mi |
| 0 | 2 | 4 | | 6 km |

Religious Affiliation

Other
13.1%

Roman
Catholic
80%

Protestant
6.9%

Official name: Principality of
    Liechtenstein
Head of government: Prime Minister
Official language: German
Monetary unit: Swiss franc
Area: 61.8 sq. mi. (160.0 sq. km.)
Population (2001): 33,000
GNP per capita (1996): U.S.$23,000
Principal exports (1997): machinery and
    transport equipment 49.2%; metal
    products 15.1%; other finished
    goods 12.7% *to* (1998): European
    Union 49.5%

The blue-red flag was given official status in October 1921. At
the 1936 Olympics it was learned that this same flag was used
by Haiti; thus, in 1937 a yellow crown was added, which symbolizes the unity of the people and their prince. Blue stands
for the sky, red for the evening fires in homes. The flag was
last modified on Sept. 18, 1982.

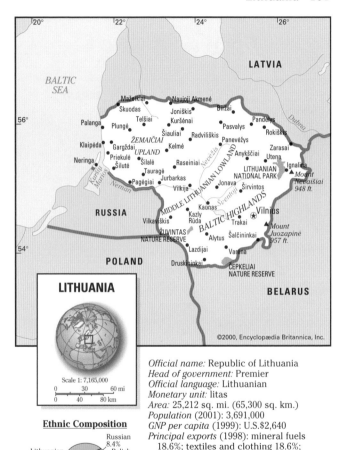

©2000, Encyclopædia Britannica, Inc.

LITHUANIA

Scale 1: 7,165,000

0   30   60 mi
0   40   80 km

Ethnic Composition

Russian 8.4%
Polish 7%
Lithuanian 81.3%
Other 3.3%

Official name: Republic of Lithuania
Head of government: Premier
Official language: Lithuanian
Monetary unit: litas
Area: 25,212 sq. mi. (65,300 sq. km.)
Population (2001): 3,691,000
GNP per capita (1999): U.S.$2,640
Principal exports (1998): mineral fuels
   18.6%; textiles and clothing 18.6%;
   food products 12.3%; machinery and
   apparatus 10.8% *to:* Russia 16.5%;
   Germany 13.1%; Latvia 11.1%

The tricolor flag of Lithuania was adopted on Aug. 1, 1922. It was long suppressed under Soviet rule until its reestablishment on March 20, 1989. The yellow color suggests ripening wheat and freedom from want. Green is for hope and the forests of the nation, while red stands for love of country, sovereignty, and valor in defense of liberty.

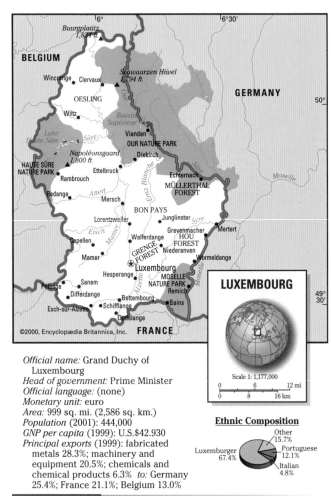

Official name: Grand Duchy of Luxembourg
Head of government: Prime Minister
Official language: (none)
Monetary unit: euro
Area: 999 sq. mi. (2,586 sq. km.)
Population (2001): 444,000
GNP per capita (1999): U.S.$42.930
Principal exports (1999): fabricated metals 28.3%; machinery and equipment 20.5%; chemicals and chemical products 6.3% *to:* Germany 25.4%; France 21.1%; Belgium 13.0%

Scale 1: 1,177,000

| 0 | | 6 | | 12 mi |
| 0 | | 8 | | 16 km |

Ethnic Composition

Luxembourger 67.4%
Other 15.7%
Portuguese 12.1%
Italian 4.8%

In the 19th century the national colors, from the coat of arms of the dukes of Luxembourg, came to be used in a tricolor of red-white-blue, coincidentally the same as the flag of The Netherlands. To distinguish it from the Dutch flag, the proportions were altered and the shade of blue was made lighter. It was recognized by law on Aug. 16, 1972.

YUGOSLAVIA

Sofia ⊛

BULGARIA

ŠAR MTS.

SKOPSKA CRNA GORA

Kumanovo

OSOGOVSKE MTS.

42° N

Tetovo

▲ Mount Titov
9,010 ft.

⊛ Skopje

Kočani

Mount Korab
9,030 ft.

Gostivar

Vardar

Bregalnica

Štip

MALEŠEVSKE MTS.

KORAB MTS.

Crna Drim

MAVROVO
NATIONAL PARK

Titov Veles

Strumica

Kičevo

Kruševo

Kavadarci

Strumica

BELASITSA MOUNTAINS

Prilep

GALIČICA
NATIONAL PARK

Lake
Dojran

Ohrid

Lake
Ohrid

Mount ▲ Bitola
Pelister
8,531 ft.

Crna

NIDŽE MTN.

KOŽUF MTS.

Lake
Prespa

PELISTER
NATIONAL
PARK

▲ Mount
Kajmakčalan
8,269 ft.

Vardar

ALBANIA

GREECE

©2000, Encyclopædia Britannica, Inc.

MACEDONIA

Scale 1: 4,190,000

0   20   40 mi
0   30   60 km

Official name: Republic of Macedonia
Head of government: Prime Minister
Official language: Macedonian
Monetary unit: denar
Area: 9,928 sq. mi. (25,713 sq. km.)
Population (2001): 2,046,000
GNP per capita (1999): U.S.$1,160
Principal exports (1998): manufactured
  products 34.2%; machinery and
  transport equipment 7.5%; food
  products 5.0% *to:* Germany 21.4%;
  Yugoslavia 18.3%; U.S. 13.3%

Ethnic Composition

Albanian
23.1%

Other
10.5%

Macedonian
66.4%

A "starburst" flag replaced the communist banner on Aug. 11,
1992. The starburst was a symbol of Alexander the Great and
his father, Philip of Macedon, but its use by Macedonia was
opposed by Greece. Thus on Oct. 6, 1995, the similar "golden
sun" flag was chosen instead. The gold and red colors originated in an early Macedonian coat of arms.

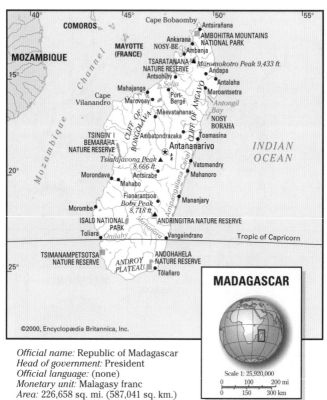

©2000, Encyclopædia Britannica, Inc.

Official name: Republic of Madagascar
Head of government: President
Official language: (none)
Monetary unit: Malagasy franc
Area: 226,658 sq. mi. (587,041 sq. km.)
Population (2001): 15,983,000
GNP per capita (1999): U.S.$250
Principal exports (1998): coffee 17.2%;
  cotton fabrics 14.1%; minerals 11.3%;
  shrimp 6.0% *to* (1998): France 39.4%;
  Mauritius 6.8%; U.S. 5.5%

MADAGASCAR

Scale 1: 25,920,000

| 0 | 100 | 200 mi |

| 0 | 150 | 300 km |

Religious Affiliation

Roman Catholic 26%
Protestant 22.8%
Traditional beliefs 47%
Other 4.2%

The Madagascar flag was adopted on Oct. 16, 1958, by the newly proclaimed Malagasy Republic, formerly a French colony. The flag combines the traditional Malagasy colors of white and red with a stripe of green. The white and red are said to stand for purity and sovereignty, while the green represents the coastal regions and symbolizes hope.

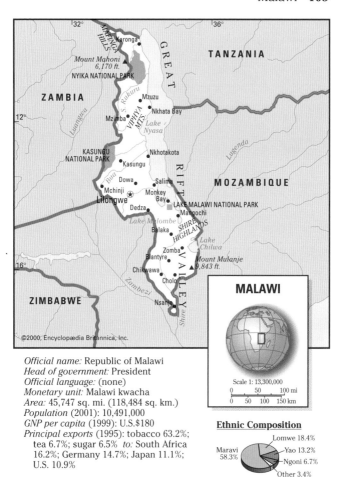

Official name: Republic of Malawi
Head of government: President
Official language: (none)
Monetary unit: Malawi kwacha
Area: 45,747 sq. mi. (118,484 sq. km.)
Population (2001): 10,491,000
GNP per capita (1999): U.S.$180
Principal exports (1995): tobacco 63.2%; tea 6.7%; sugar 6.5% *to:* South Africa 16.2%; Germany 14.7%; Japan 11.1%; U.S. 10.9%

Scale 1: 13,300,000

0   50   100 mi
0   50   100   150 km

Ethnic Composition

Lomwe 18.4%
Yao 13.2%
Ngoni 6.7%
Other 3.4%
Maravi 58.3%

The flag of the Malawi Congress Party was striped black for the African people, red for the blood of martyrs, and green for the vegetation and climate. The country's name means "flaming waters," referring to the setting sun on Lake Malawi. With independence on July 6, 1964, a new flag was created by adding the sun symbol to the party flag.

Official name: Malaysia
Head of government: Prime Minister
Official language: Malay
Monetary unit: ringgit
Area: 127,354 sq. mi. (329,845 sq. km.)
Population (2001): 22,602,000
GNP per capita (1999): U.S.$3,390
Principal exports (1998): machinery and
  transport equipment 59.2%; basic
  manufactures 8.3%; animal and
  vegetable oils 7.5% to: U.S. 21.9%;
  Singapore 16.5%; Japan 11.6%

MALAYSIA

Scale 1: 32,013,000

| 0 | 150 | 300 mi |
| 0 | 200 | 400 km |

Ethnic Composition

Malay
and other
indigenous
59.9%

Chinese
29.9%

Indian
and other
10.2%

The flag hoisted on May 26, 1950, had 11 stripes, a crescent,
and an 11-pointed star. The number of stripes and star points
was increased to 14 on Sept. 16, 1963. Yellow is a royal color
in Malaysia while red, white, and blue indicate connections
with the Commonwealth. The crescent is a reminder that the
population is mainly Muslim.

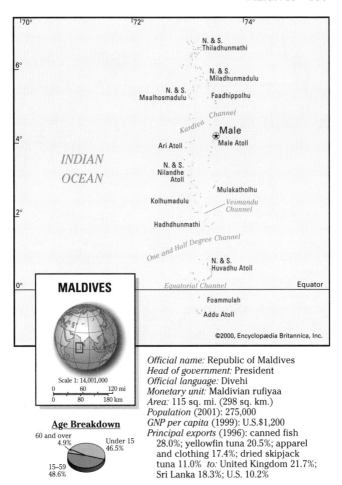

70° 72° 74°

6°

N. & S.
Thiladhunmathi

N. & S.
Miladhunmadulu

N. & S.
Maalhosmadulu

Faadhippolhu

Kardiva Channel

4° ⊛ **Male**
Male Atoll

Ari Atoll

N. & S.
Nilandhe
Atoll

INDIAN

OCEAN

Mulakatholhu

Kolhumadulu *Veimandu Channel*

2°

Hadhdhunmathi

One and Half Degree Channel

N. & S.
Huvadhu Atoll

0° *Equatorial Channel* Equator

Foammulah

Addu Atoll

©2000, Encyclopædia Britannica, Inc.

MALDIVES

Scale 1: 14,001,000
0   60   120 mi
0   80   180 km

Age Breakdown

60 and over
4.9%

Under 15
46.5%

15–59
48.6%

Official name: Republic of Maldives
Head of government: President
Official language: Divehi
Monetary unit: Maldivian rufiyaa
Area: 115 sq. mi. (298 sq. km.)
Population (2001): 275,000
GNP per capita (1999): U.S.$1,200
Principal exports (1996): canned fish
   28.0%; yellowfin tuna 20.5%; apparel
   and clothing 17.4%; dried skipjack
   tuna 11.0% *to:* United Kingdom 21.7%;
   Sri Lanka 18.3%; U.S. 10.2%

Maldivian ships long used a plain red ensign like those flown
by Arabian and African nations. While a British protectorate
in the early 20th century, the Maldives adopted a flag which
was only slightly altered upon independence (July 26, 1965).
The green panel and white crescent are symbolic of Islam,
progress, prosperity, and peace.

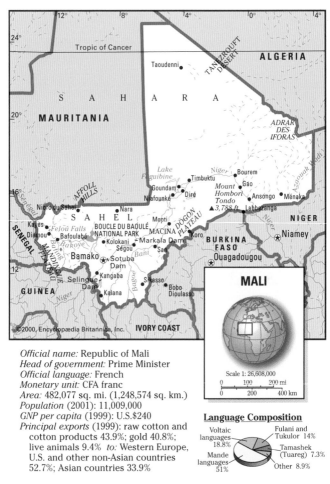

Official name: Republic of Mali
Head of government: Prime Minister
Official language: French
Monetary unit: CFA franc
Area: 482,077 sq. mi. (1,248,574 sq. km.)
Population (2001): 11,009,000
GNP per capita (1999): U.S.$240
Principal exports (1999): raw cotton and
    cotton products 43.9%; gold 40.8%;
    live animals 9.4% *to:* Western Europe,
    U.S. and other non-Asian countries
    52.7%; Asian countries 33.9%

MALI

Scale 1: 26,608,000

0   100   200 mi
0   200   400 km

Language Composition

Voltaic languages 18.8%
Fulani and Tukulor 14%
Mande languages 51%
Tamashek (Tuareg) 7.3%
Other 8.9%

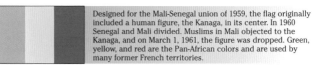

Designed for the Mali-Senegal union of 1959, the flag originally
included a human figure, the Kanaga, in its center. In 1960
Senegal and Mali divided. Muslims in Mali objected to the
Kanaga, and on March 1, 1961, the figure was dropped. Green,
yellow, and red are the Pan-African colors and are used by
many former French territories.

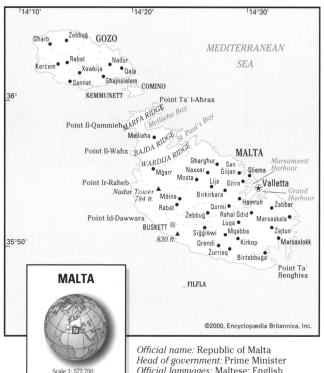

©2000, Encyclopædia Britannica, Inc.

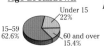

MALTA

Scale 1: 572,700

0   2   4 mi
0   3   6 km

Age Breakdown

Under 15
22%

15–59
62.6%

60 and over
15.4%

Official name: Republic of Malta
Head of government: Prime Minister
Official languages: Maltese; English
Monetary unit: Maltese lira
Area: 122 sq. mi. (316 sq. km.)
Population (2001): 381,000
GNP per capita (1999): U.S.$9,210
Principal exports (1998): machinery and
  transport equipment 64.6%;
  manufactured goods 27.7% *to:* France
  20.5%; U.S. 19.0%; Singapore 14.3%

The Maltese flag was supposedly based on an 11th-century
coat of arms, and a red flag with a white cross was used by
the Knights of Malta from the Middle Ages. The current flag
dates from independence within the Commonwealth (Sept.
21, 1964). The George Cross was granted by the British for
the heroic defense of the island in World War II.

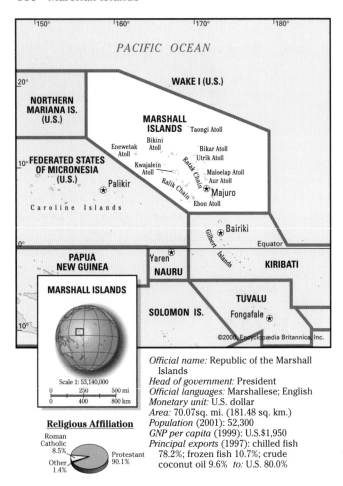

PACIFIC OCEAN

WAKE I (U.S.)

NORTHERN MARIANA IS. (U.S.)

MARSHALL ISLANDS

Taongi Atoll

Enewetak Atoll

Bikini Atoll

Bikar Atoll

Utrik Atoll

FEDERATED STATES OF MICRONESIA (U.S.)

Kwajalein Atoll

Ralik Chain

Rakik Chain

Maloelap Atoll

Aur Atoll

Palikir

Majuro

Caroline Islands

Ebon Atoll

Bairiki

Equator

PAPUA NEW GUINEA

Yaren

NAURU

Gilbert Islands

KIRIBATI

MARSHALL ISLANDS

TUVALU

SOLOMON IS.

Fongafale

©2000 Encyclopædia Britannica, Inc.

Scale 1: 53,140,000

0 250 500 mi
0 400 800 km

Religious Affiliation

Roman Catholic 8.5%

Other 1.4%

Protestant 90.1%

Official name: Republic of the Marshall Islands
Head of government: President
Official languages: Marshallese; English
Monetary unit: U.S. dollar
Area: 70.07sq. mi. (181.48 sq. km.)
Population (2001): 52,300
GNP per capita (1999): U.S.$1,950
Principal exports (1997): chilled fish 78.2%; frozen fish 10.7%; crude coconut oil 9.6% *to:* U.S. 80.0%

The island nation hoisted its flag on May 1, 1979. The blue stands for the ocean. The white is for brightness while the orange is for bravery and wealth. The two stripes joined symbolize the Equator, and they increase in width to show growth and vitality. The rays of the star are for the municipalities; its four long rays recall a Christian cross.

Official name: Islamic Republic of
  Mauritania
Head of government: President
Official language: Arabic
Monetary unit: ouguiya
Area: 398,000 sq. mi. (1,030,700 sq. km.)
Population (2001): 2,591,000
GNP per capita (1999): U.S.$390
Principal exports (1997): iron ore 52.4%;
  fish 47.6% *to:* Japan 23.3%; Italy 16.7%;
  France 13.9%; Spain 8.3%

MAURITANIA

Scale 1: 26,914,000

| 0 | 100 | 200 mi |
| 0 | 200 | 400 km |

Age Breakdown

Under 15
43.1%

15–59
51.7%

60 and over
5.2%

In 1958 Mauritania was granted autonomous status within the
French Community. The current flag replaced the French tricolor on April 1, 1959, and no changes were made to the
design at independence (Nov. 28, 1960). The green background of the flag and its star and crescent are traditional
Muslim symbols that have been in use for centuries.

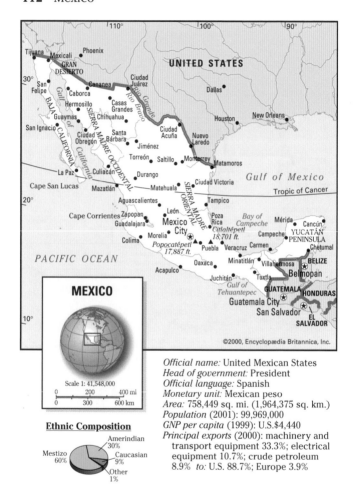

©2000, Encyclopædia Britannica, Inc.

MEXICO

Scale 1: 41,548,000

0   200   400 mi
0   300   600 km

Ethnic Composition

Amerindian 30%
Mestizo 60%
Caucasian 9%
Other 1%

Official name: United Mexican States
Head of government: President
Official language: Spanish
Monetary unit: Mexican peso
Area: 758,449 sq. mi. (1,964,375 sq. km.)
Population (2001): 99,969,000
GNP per capita (1999): U.S.$4,440
Principal exports (2000): machinery and
  transport equipment 33.3%; electrical
  equipment 10.7%; crude petroleum
  8.9% *to:* U.S. 88.7%; Europe 3.9%

The green-white-red tricolor was officially established in 1821.
Green is for independence, white for Roman Catholicism, and
red for union. The emblem depicts the scene supposedly wit-
nessed by the Aztecs in 1325: an eagle with a snake in its
beak standing upon a cactus growing out of rocks in the
water. The flag was modified on Sept. 17, 1968.

Map labels:
20°
140° 150° 160° 170°
WAKE I. (U.S.)
NORTHERN MARIANA IS. (U.S.)
GUAM (U.S.)
PACIFIC OCEAN
MARSHALL ISLANDS
10°
Colonia • YAP
CAROLINE ISLANDS
NGULU ISLANDS
CHUUK
Weno •
Palikir
⊛ POHNPEI
KOSRAE
PALAU
MORTLOCK ISLANDS
FEDERATED STATES OF MICRONESIA
0°
Equator
PAPUA NEW GUINEA
Yaren ⊛
NAURU
INDONESIA
Bismarck Sea
Solomon Sea
SOLOMON IS.
10°
Port Moresby ⊛
AUSTRALIA
Coral Sea
©2000, Encyclopædia Britannica, Inc.

FEDERATED STATES OF MICRONESIA

Scale 1: 59,373,000
0   250   500 mi
0   400   800 km

Official name: Federated States of Micronesia
Head of government: President
Official language: (none)
Monetary unit: U.S. dollar
Area: 270.8 sq. mi. (701.4 sq. km.)
Population (2001): 118,000
GNP per capita (1999): U.S.$1,980
Principal exports (1998): marine products 89.2%; agricultural products 4.4% *to:* Japan 80.0%; U.S. 9.3%; Guam 8.3%

Ethnic Composition

Pohnpeian 25.9%
Other 17.3%
Mortlockese 8.3%
Kosraean 7.4%
Trukese 41.1%

On Nov. 30, 1978, the flag of the former United States trust territory was approved by an interim congress. Based on the symbolism of the territory, the flag has stars for the four states of Micronesia. After sovereignty was granted in 1986, a dark blue background (for the Pacific Ocean) was substituted for the original "United Nations blue."

Official name: Republic of Moldova
Head of government: Prime Minister
Official language: Romanian
Monetary unit: Moldovan leu
Area: 13,000 sq. mi. (33,700 sq. km.)
Population (2001): 4,431,000
GNP per capita (1999): U.S.$410
Principal exports (1996): food and
   agricultural goods 72.8%; textile
   products 6.2%; machinery 5.3%
   to: Russia 53.6%; Romania 9.4%,
   Ukraine 5.9%

Ethnic Composition

Moldovan 64.5%
Ukrainian 13.8%
Russian 13%
Gagauz 3.5%
Other 5.2%

By 1989, Moldovans protested against communist rule, and
the traditional tricolor of blue-yellow-red, which had flown
briefly in 1917–18, became a popular symbol. It replaced the
communist flag in May 1990 and remained after independence
in 1991. The shield has an eagle on whose breast are an
aurochs head, a crescent, a star, and a flower.

©2000, Encyclopædia Britannica, Inc.

Official name: Mongolia
Head of government: Prime Minister
Official language: Khalkha Mongolian
Monetary unit: tugrik
Area: 603,930 sq. mi. (1,564,160 sq. km.)
Population (2001): 2,435,000
GNP per capita (1999): U.S.$390
Principal exports (1998): mineral
    products 59.0; textile and cashmere
    products 13.5% *to:* China 29.3%;
    Switzerland 20.4%; Russia 11.8%

MONGOLIA

Scale 1: 36,059,000
0   150   300 mi
0   200   400 km

Ethnic Composition

Khalkha
Mongol
78.8%

Other
15.3%

Kazak
5.9%

In 1945, the flag symbolizing communism (red) and Mongol
nationalism (blue) was established. Near the hoist is a *soyon-
ba,* a grouping of philosophical symbols (flame, sun, moon,
yin-yang, triangles, and bars). Yellow traditionally stood for
Lamaist Buddhism. On Jan. 12, 1992, a five-pointed star (for
Communism) was removed from the flag.

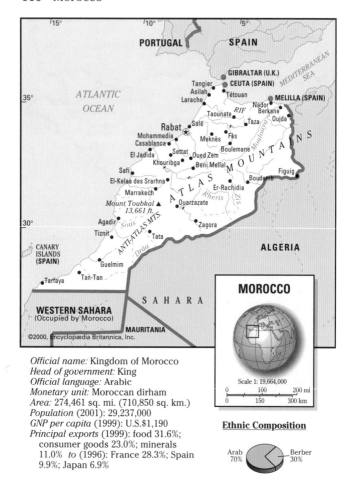

PORTUGAL
SPAIN
GIBRALTAR (U.K.)
CEUTA (SPAIN)
MEDITERRANEAN SEA
Tangier
Asilah
Tétouan
MELILLA (SPAIN)
Larache
Nador
ATLANTIC
OCEAN
Taounate
Berkane
RIF
Oujda
35°
Taza
Rabat
Salé
Mohammedia
Meknès
Fès
Casablanca
Boulemane
Moulouya
El Jadida
Settat
Oued Zem
Khouribga
Beni Mellal
Safi
Figuig
El-Kelaa des Srarhna
Boudenib
Marrakech
Er-Rachidia
Mount Toubkal ▲
13,661 ft.
Ouarzazate
Rheris
30°
Agadir
Sous
Zagora
Tiznit
ANTI-ATLAS MTS.
ATLAS MOUNTAINS
CANARY
ISLANDS
(SPAIN)
Tata
Draa
ALGERIA
Guelmim
Tan-Tan
Tarfaya
SAHARA
WESTERN SAHARA
(Occupied by Morocco)
MAURITANIA
©2000, Encyclopædia Britannica, Inc.

MOROCCO

Scale 1: 19,664,000

| 0 | 100 | 200 mi |
| 0 | 150 | 300 km |

Official name: Kingdom of Morocco
Head of government: King
Official language: Arabic
Monetary unit: Moroccan dirham
Area: 274,461 sq. mi. (710,850 sq. km.)
Population (2001): 29,237,000
GNP per capita (1999): U.S.$1,190
Principal exports (1999): food 31.6%;
  consumer goods 23.0%; minerals
  11.0% *to* (1996): France 28.3%; Spain
  9.9%; Japan 6.9%

Ethnic Composition

Arab
70%
Berber
30%

After Morocco was subjected to the rule of France and Spain in the 20th century, the plain red flag, which had been displayed on its ships, was modified on Nov. 17, 1915. To its center was added the ancient pentagram known as the "Seal of Solomon." The flag continued in use even after the French granted independence in 1956.

©1998, Encyclopædia Britannica, Inc.

Official name: Republic of Mozambique
Head of government: President
Official language: Portuguese
Monetary unit: metical
Area: 313,661 sq. mi. (812,379 sq. km.)
Population (2001): 19,371,000
GNP per capita (1999): U.S.$220
Principal exports (1996): food and
beverages 66.4%, of which shellfish
38.1%; machinery and transport
equipment 11.5% *to:* European Union
34.7%; South Africa 19.4%; India 11.8%;
U.S. 11.4%

MOZAMBIQUE

Scale 1: 26,326,000
0   75   150   225 mi
0   100   200   300 km

Language Composition

Other 36.1%
Makua 27.8%
Tsonga 12.4%
Sena 9.4%
Lomwe 7.8%
Shona 6.5%

In the early 1960s, anti-Portuguese groups adopted flags of
green (for forests), black (for the majority population), white
(for rivers and the ocean), gold (for peace and mineral
wealth), and red (for the blood of liberation). The current flag
was readopted in 1983; on its star are a book, a hoe, and an
assault rifle.

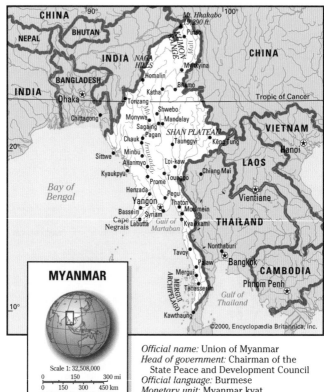

@2000, Encyclopædia Britannica, Inc.

MYANMAR

Scale 1: 32,508,000

0   150   300 mi
0   150   300   450 km

Ethnic Composition

Other 11.8%
Shan 8.5%
Burman 69%
Karen 6.2%
Rakhine 4.5%

Official name: Union of Myanmar
Head of government: Chairman of the
  State Peace and Development Council
Official language: Burmese
Monetary unit: Myanmar kyat
Area: 261,228 sq. mi. (676,577 sq. km.)
Population (2001): 41,995,000
GNP per capita (1996): U.S.$2,610
Principal exports (1997–98): pulses and
  beans 22.3%; teak 11.1%; fish and fish
  products 4.6% *to:* India 22.6%;
  Singapore 13.2%; Thailand 11.9%

The current flag design dates to Jan. 4, 1974. Its 14 stars, for
the states and divisions of Myanmar, form a circle around a
cogwheel, for industrial workers, and ears and leaves of rice,
symbolizing the peasantry. Blue is for truthfulness and
strength; red for bravery, unity, and determination; and white
for truth, purity, and steadfastness.

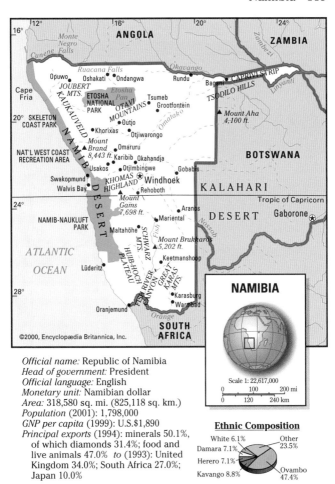

Official name: Republic of Namibia
Head of government: President
Official language: English
Monetary unit: Namibian dollar
Area: 318,580 sq. mi. (825,118 sq. km.)
Population (2001): 1,798,000
GNP per capita (1999): U.S.$1,890
Principal exports (1994): minerals 50.1%,
   of which diamonds 31.4%; food and
   live animals 47.0% *to* (1993): United
   Kingdom 34.0%; South Africa 27.0%;
   Japan 10.0%

NAMIBIA

Scale 1: 22,617,000

0   100   200 mi
0   120   240 km

Ethnic Composition

White 6.1%   Other
Damara 7.1%   23.5%
Herero 7.1%
                        Ovambo
Kavango 8.8%   47.4%

The flag was adopted on Feb. 2, 1990, and hoisted on independence from South Africa, March 21, 1990. Its colors are
those of the South West Africa People's Organization: blue
(for sky and ocean), red (for heroism and determination), and
green (for agriculture). The gold sun represents life and energy while the white stripes are for water resources.

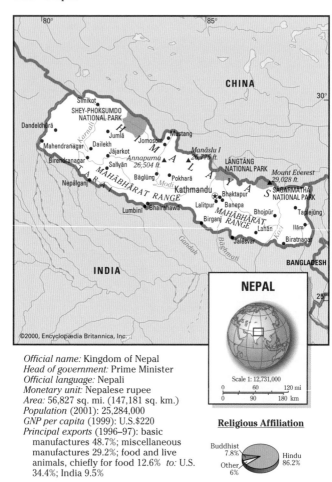

CHINA

Simikot

SHEY-PHOKSUMDO
NATIONAL PARK

Dandeldhūrā

Jumlā

Mustang

Mahendranagar

Dailekh

Jomoson

Jājarkot

Manāslu I
26,775 ft.

LĀNGTĀNG
NATIONAL PARK

Birendranagar

Annapurna
26,504 ft.

Mount Everest
29,028 ft.

Sallyān

Bāglūng

Pokharā

Nepālganj

Modi

Kathmandu

SAGARMĀTHA
NATIONAL PARK

MAHĀBHĀRAT RANGE

Bhaktapur

Lumbinī

Lalitpur

Banepa

Bhairahawa

Birganj

MAHĀBHĀRAT
RANGE

Bhojpūr

Taplejūng

Lahān

Ilām

Jalesvar

Biratnagar

INDIA

Gandak

Bāgmati

BANGLADESH

©2000, Encyclopædia Britannica, Inc.

NEPAL

Scale 1: 12,731,000

0   60   120 mi

0   90   180 km

Official name: Kingdom of Nepal
Head of government: Prime Minister
Official language: Nepali
Monetary unit: Nepalese rupee
Area: 56,827 sq. mi. (147,181 sq. km.)
Population (2001): 25,284,000
GNP per capita (1999): U.S.$220
Principal exports (1996–97): basic
  manufactures 48.7%; miscellaneous
  manufactures 29.2%; food and live
  animals, chiefly for food 12.6% *to:* U.S.
  34.4%; India 9.5%

Religious Affiliation

Buddhist
7.8%

Hindu
86.2%

Other
6%

Established on Dec. 16, 1962, Nepal's flag consists of two united pennant shapes; it is the only non-rectangular national flag in the world. In the upper segment is a moon with a crescent attached below; in the bottom segment appears a stylized sun. The symbols are for different dynasties and express a hope for the immortality of the nation. The crimson and blue colors are common in Nepali art.

Scale 1: 5,169,000

0   20   40 mi
0   30   60 km

Religious Affiliation

Roman
Catholic
31%

Protestant
22%

Muslim
4%

No religion
39%

Other
4%

Official name: Kingdom of The Netherlands
Head of government: Prime Minister
Official language: Dutch
Monetary unit: euro
Area: 16,033 sq. mi. (41,526 sq. km.)
Population (2001): 15,968,000
GNP per capita (1999): U.S.$25,140
Principal exports (1999): machinery 27.8%; chemical products 15.3%; food 13.4% *to:* Germany 26.1%; Belgium-Luxembourg 12.2%; France 10.8%; United Kingdom 10.8%

The history of the Dutch flag dates to the use of orange, white, and blue as the livery colors of William, Prince of Orange, and the use of the tricolor at sea in 1577. By 1660 the color red was substituted for orange. The flag was legalized by pro-French "patriots" on Feb. 14, 1796, and reaffirmed by royal decree on Feb. 19, 1937.

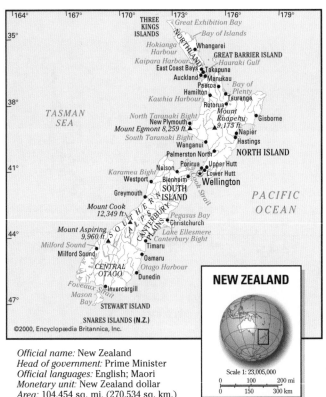

Official name: New Zealand
Head of government: Prime Minister
Official languages: English; Maori
Monetary unit: New Zealand dollar
Area: 104,454 sq. mi. (270,534 sq. km.)
Population (2001): 3,861,000
GNP per capita (1999): U.S.$13,990
Principal exports (1998–99): food 47.2%;
wood and wood products 10.6%;
machinery 7.7% *to:* Australia 21.4%;
U.S. 13.3%; Japan 12.7%

NEW ZEALAND

Scale 1: 23,005,000
0   100   200 mi
0   150   300 km

Ethnic Composition

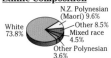

White 73.8%
N.Z. Polynesian (Maori) 9.6%
Other 8.5%
Mixed race 4.5%
Other Polynesian 3.6%

The Maori of New Zealand accepted British control in 1840, and a colonial flag was adopted on Jan. 15, 1867. It included the Union Jack in the canton and the letters "NZ" at the fly end. Later versions used the Southern Cross. Dominion status was granted on Sept. 26, 1907, and independence on Nov. 25, 1947, but the flag was unchanged.

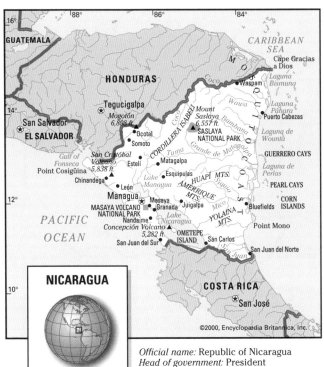

NICARAGUA

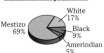

Scale 1: 11,073,000

| 0 | 50 | 100 mi |
| 0 | 80 | 160 km |

Ethnic Composition

White 17%
Mestizo 69%
Black 9%
Amerindian 5%

Official name: Republic of Nicaragua
Head of government: President
Official language: Spanish
Monetary unit: cordoba oro
Area: 50,337 sq. mi. (130,373 sq. km.)
Population (2001): 4,918,000
GNP per capita (1999): U.S.$410
Principal exports (1999): coffee 24.9%;
 manufactured products 19.9%;
 crustaceans 15.4%; beef 7.7%
 to: U.S. 37.7%; El Salvador 12.5%;
 Germany 9.8%

On Aug. 21, 1823, a blue-white-blue flag was adopted by the five member states of the United Provinces of Central America, which included Nicaragua. From the mid-19th century various flag designs were used in Nicaragua, but the old flag was readopted in 1908, with a modified coat of arms, and reaffirmed by law on Aug. 27, 1971.

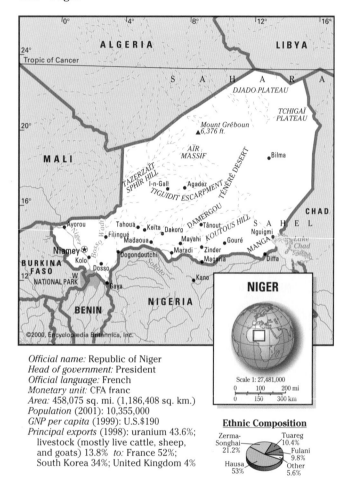

Official name: Republic of Niger
Head of government: President
Official language: French
Monetary unit: CFA franc
Area: 458,075 sq. mi. (1,186,408 sq. km.)
Population (2001): 10,355,000
GNP per capita (1999): U.S.$190
Principal exports (1998): uranium 43.6%;
   livestock (mostly live cattle, sheep,
   and goats) 13.8% *to:* France 52%;
   South Korea 34%; United Kingdom 4%

Ethnic Composition

Zerma-Songhai 21.2%
Tuareg 10.4%
Fulani 9.8%
Hausa 53%
Other 5.6%

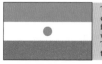

The flag of Niger was chosen on Nov. 23, 1959. The white color is for purity, innocence, and civic spirit. The orange is for the Sahara Desert and the heroic efforts of citizens to live within it, while the orange central disk represents the sun. The green color stands for agriculture and hope; it is suggestive of the Niger River valley.

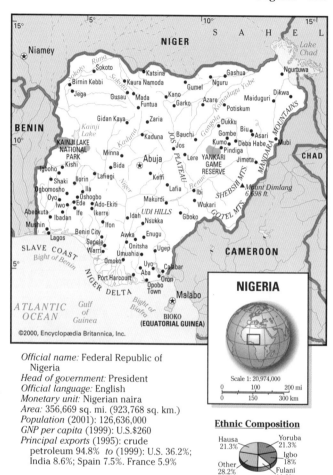

©2000, Encyclopædia Britannica, Inc.

Official name: Federal Republic of
  Nigeria
Head of government: President
Official language: English
Monetary unit: Nigerian naira
Area: 356,669 sq. mi. (923,768 sq. km.)
Population (2001): 126,636,000
GNP per capita (1999): U.S.$260
Principal exports (1995): crude
  petroleum 94.8% *to* (1999): U.S. 36.2%;
  India 8.6%; Spain 7.5%. France 5.9%

NIGERIA

Scale 1: 20,974,000

| 0 | 100 | 200 mi |
| 0 | 150 | 300 km |

Ethnic Composition

Hausa 21.3%
Yoruba 21.3%
Igbo 18%
Fulani 11.2%
Other 28.2%

The Nigerian flag became official upon independence from
Britain on Oct. 1, 1960. The flag design is purposefully simple
in order not to favor the symbolism of any particular ethnic
or religious group. Agriculture is represented by the green
stripes while unity and peace are symbolized by the white
stripe.

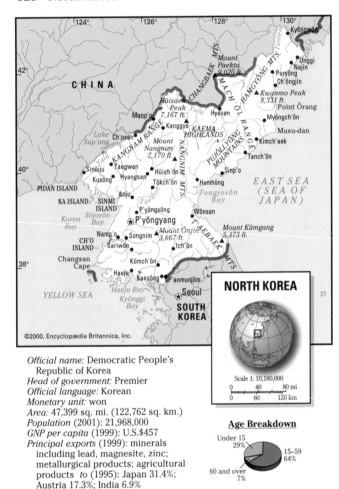

Kyŏngwŏn · Unggi · Najin · Puryŏng · Ch'ŏngjin
Mount Paektu 9,020 ft. · CHANGBAEK MTS. · MACH'ŎL RANGE · HAMGYŎNG MTS. · Tumen

CHINA

Hŭisaek Peak 7,167 ft. · Manp'o · Hyesan · Point Ŏrang · Myŏngch'ŏn · Musu-dan
Ch'osan · Kanggye · KAEMA HIGHLANDS · Kimch'aek
Sinŭiju · Taegwan · Hyangsan · Hŭich'ŏn · Tŏkch'ŏn · Sinp'o · Tanch'ŏn
PIDAN ISLAND · Kusŏng · Anju · Taedong · Hamhŭng
KA ISLAND · SINMI ISLAND · Sŏjosŏn Bay · P'yŏngsŏng · Tongjosŏn Bay
Korea Bay · ⊛P'yŏngyang · Wŏnsan
Namp'o · Songnim · Mount Ŏnjin 3,667 ft. · Ich'ŏn · Mount Kŭmgang 5,373 ft.
CH'O ISLAND · Sariwŏn
Changsan Cape · Kŭmch'ŏn · T'AEBAEK MTS.
Haeju · Kaesŏng · P'anmunjŏm
YELLOW SEA · Haeju Bay · Kyŏnggi Bay · ⊛Seoul · SOUTH KOREA

Yalu · Lake Sup'ung · KANGNAM RANGE · Mount Nangnim 7,170 ft. · NANGNIM MTS. · PUJŎLLYŎNG MOUNTAINS

EAST SEA (SEA OF JAPAN)

©2000, Encyclopædia Britannica, Inc.

Official name: Democratic People's Republic of Korea
Head of government: Premier
Official language: Korean
Monetary unit: won
Area: 47,399 sq. mi. (122,762 sq. km.)
Population (2001): 21,968,000
GNP per capita (1999): U.S.$457
Principal exports (1999): minerals including lead, magnesite, zinc; metallurgical products; agricultural products *to* (1995): Japan 31.4%; Austria 17.3%; India 6.9%

NORTH KOREA

Scale 1: 10,160,000
0   40   80 mi
0   60   120 km

Age Breakdown

Under 15 29%
15–59 64%
60 and over 7%

The traditional Korean Taeguk flag (still used by South Korea) was official in North Korea until July 10, 1948, when the current flag was introduced. Its red stripe and star are for the country's commitment to communism, while blue is said to stand for a commitment to peace. The white stripes stand for purity, strength, and dignity.

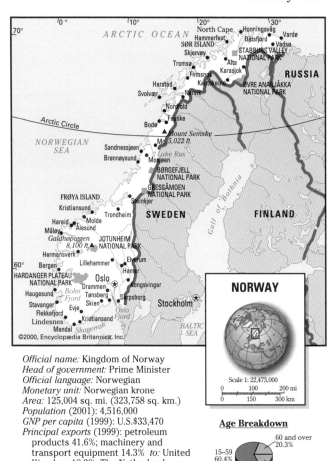

Official name: Kingdom of Norway
Head of government: Prime Minister
Official language: Norwegian
Monetary unit: Norwegian krone
Area: 125,004 sq. mi. (323,758 sq. km.)
Population (2001): 4,516,000
GNP per capita (1999): U.S.$33,470
Principal exports (1999): petroleum
products 41.6%; machinery and
transport equipment 14.3% *to:* United
Kingdom 18.2%; The Netherlands
10.5%; Germany 10%; Sweden 9.4%

NORWAY

Scale 1: 22,473,000

| 0 | 100 | 200 mi |
| 0 | 150 | 300 km |

Age Breakdown

- 60 and over 20.3%
- 15–59 60.4%
- Under 15 19.3%

The first distinctive Norwegian flag was created in 1814 while
the country was under Swedish rule. It was based on the red
Danish flag with its white cross. In 1821 the Norwegian parlia-
ment developed the current flag design. From 1844 to 1899,
six years before independence, the official flag included a
symbol of Swedish-Norwegian union.

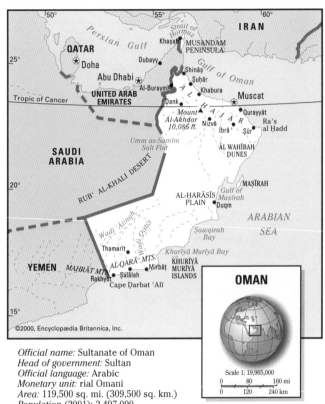

Official name: Sultanate of Oman
Head of government: Sultan
Official language: Arabic
Monetary unit: rial Omani
Area: 119,500 sq. mi. (309,500 sq. km.)
Population (2001): 2,497,000
GNP per capita (1998): U.S.$5,950
Principal exports (2000): domestic
  exports 88.5%, of which petroleum
  82.8%; reexports 11.5% *to:* (non-oil)
  United Arab Emirates 40.1%; Saudi
  Arabia 8.4%; Iran 7.8%

OMAN

Scale 1: 19,965,000

0   80   160 mi
0   120   240 km

Religious Affiliation

Hindu 25%

Ibadiyah Muslim 56.3%

Sunni Muslim 18.7%

The flag dates to Dec. 17, 1970, and it was altered on Nov. 18, 1995. The white is for peace and prosperity, red is for battles, and green is for the fertility of the land. Unofficially, white recalls the imamate, red the sultanate, and green Al-Jabal Al-Akhdar ("The Green Mountain"). The coat of arms has two swords, a dagger, and a belt.

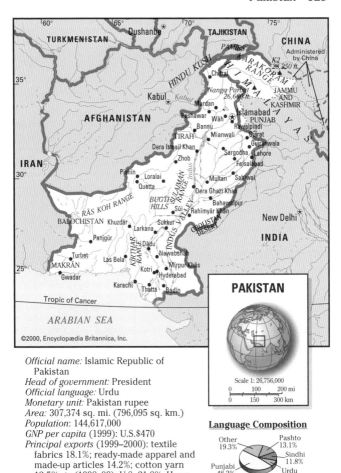

Official name: Islamic Republic of Pakistan
Head of government: President
Official language: Urdu
Monetary unit: Pakistan rupee
Area: 307,374 sq. mi. (796,095 sq. km.)
Population: 144,617,000
GNP per capita (1999): U.S.$470
Principal exports (1999–2000): textile fabrics 18.1%; ready-made apparel and made-up articles 14.2%; cotton yarn 12.5% *to* (1998–99): U.S. 21.8%; Hong Kong 7.1%

Language Composition

Other 19.3%
Pashto 13.1%
Sindhi 11.8%
Urdu 7.6%
Punjabi 48.2%

On Dec. 30, 1906, the All India Muslim League approved this typically Muslim flag, with its star and crescent. At independence (Aug. 14, 1947) a white stripe was added for minority religious groups. Also symbolized are prosperity and peace by the green and white colors, progress by the crescent, and knowledge and light by the star.

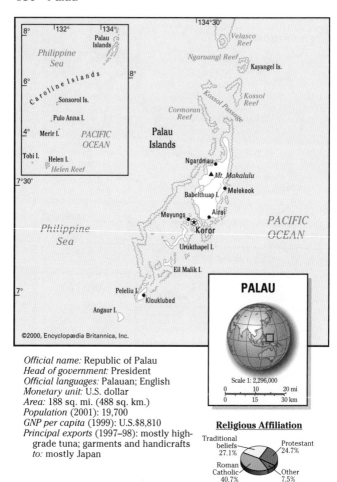

©2000, Encyclopædia Britannica, Inc.

Official name: Republic of Palau
Head of government: President
Official languages: Palauan; English
Monetary unit: U.S. dollar
Area: 188 sq. mi. (488 sq. km.)
Population (2001): 19,700
GNP per capita (1999): U.S.$8,810
Principal exports (1997–98): mostly high-
grade tuna; garments and handicrafts
to: mostly Japan

PALAU

Scale 1: 2,296,000
0   10   20 mi
0   15   30 km

Religious Affiliation

Traditional
beliefs
27.1%

Protestant
24.7%

Roman
Catholic
40.7%

Other
7.5%

Approved on Oct. 22, 1980, and hoisted on Jan. 1, 1981, the
Palauan flag was left unaltered at independence in 1994. The
golden disk represents the full moon, which is said on Palau
to be propitious for fishing, planting, and other activities and
gives the people "a feeling of warmth, tranquillity, peace,
love, and domestic unity."

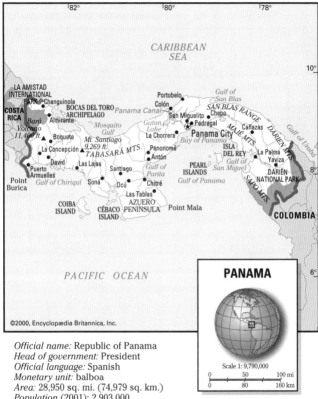

©2000, Encyclopædia Britannica, Inc.

Official name: Republic of Panama
Head of government: President
Official language: Spanish
Monetary unit: balboa
Area: 28,950 sq. mi. (74,979 sq. km.)
Population (2001): 2,903,000
GNP per capita (1999): U.S.$3,080
Principal exports (1998): bananas 19.7%;
   shrimps 19.4%; fish 7.9%; sugar 3.6%;
   clothing 3.6% *to:* U.S. 40.0%; Sweden
   7.2%; Costa Rica 6.6%; Spain 5.4%

Scale 1: 9,790,000

0   50   100 mi
0   80   160 km

Ethnic Composition

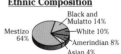

Mestizo 64%
Black and Mulatto 14%
White 10%
Amerindian 8%
Asian 4%

The Panamanian flag became official on July 4, 1904, after
independence from Colombia was won through the interven-
tion of the United States, which was determined to construct
the Panama Canal. The flag was influenced by the United
States, and its quartered design was said to symbolize the
power sharing of Panama's two main political parties.

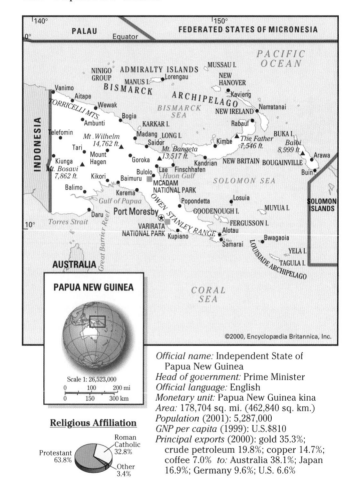

©2000, Encyclopædia Britannica, Inc.

PAPUA NEW GUINEA

Scale 1: 26,523,000

| 0 | 100 | 200 mi |
| 0 | 150 | 300 km |

Religious Affiliation

Roman Catholic 32.8%

Protestant 63.8%

Other 3.4%

Official name: Independent State of
  Papua New Guinea
Head of government: Prime Minister
Official language: English
Monetary unit: Papua New Guinea kina
Area: 178,704 sq. mi. (462,840 sq. km.)
Population (2001): 5,287,000
GNP per capita (1999): U.S.$810
Principal exports (2000): gold 35.3%;
  crude petroleum 19.8%; copper 14.7%;
  coffee 7.0% *to:* Australia 38.1%; Japan
  16.9%; Germany 9.6%; U.S. 6.6%

The formerly German-, British-, and Australian-controlled territory officially recognized its flag on March 11, 1971, and flag
usage was extended to ships at independence (Sept. 16,
1975). The colors red and black are shown extensively in
local art and clothing. Featured emblems are a bird of par-
adise and the Southern Cross constellation.

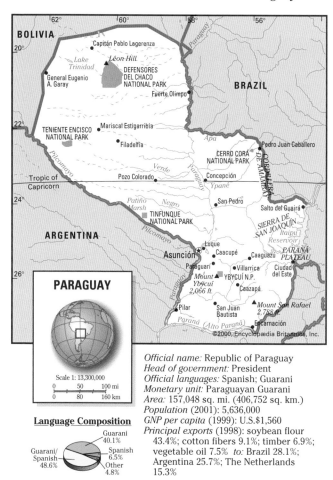

©2000, Encyclopædia Britannica, Inc.

Official name: Republic of Paraguay
Head of government: President
Official languages: Spanish; Guarani
Monetary unit: Paraguayan Guarani
Area: 157,048 sq. mi. (406,752 sq. km.)
Population (2001): 5,636,000
GNP per capita (1999): U.S.$1,560
Principal exports (1998): soybean flour
43.4%; cotton fibers 9.1%; timber 6.9%;
vegetable oil 7.5% *to:* Brazil 28.1%;
Argentina 25.7%; The Netherlands
15.3%

PARAGUAY

Scale 1: 13,300,000

| 0 | 50 | 100 mi |
| 0 | 80 | 160 km |

Language Composition

Guarani
40.1%
Guarani/
Spanish
48.6%
Spanish
6.5%
Other
4.8%

Under the dictator José Gaspar Rodríguez de Francia
(1814–40) the French colors were adopted for the flag. The
coat of arms (a golden star surrounded by a wreath) is on the
obverse side, but the seal of the treasury (a lion, staff, and
liberty cap, with the motto "Peace and Justice") is on the
reverse; the flag is unique in this respect.

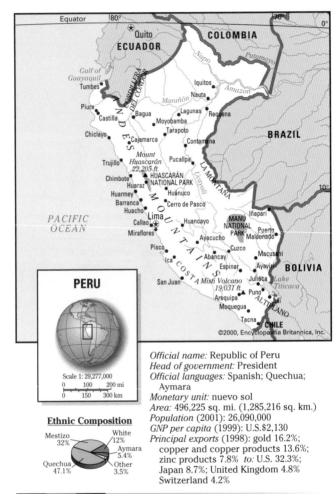

PERU

Scale 1: 29,277,000

| 0 | 100 | 200 mi |
| 0 | 150 | 300 km |

Ethnic Composition

Mestizo 32%
White 12%
Aymara 5.4%
Quechua 47.1%
Other 3.5%

Official name: Republic of Peru
Head of government: President
Official languages: Spanish; Quechua; Aymara
Monetary unit: nuevo sol
Area: 496,225 sq. mi. (1,285,216 sq. km.)
Population (2001): 26,090,000
GNP per capita (1999): U.S.$2,130
Principal exports (1998): gold 16.2%; copper and copper products 13.6%; zinc products 7.8% *to:* U.S. 32.3%; Japan 8.7%; United Kingdom 4.8%; Switzerland 4.2%

Partisans in the early 19th century adopted a red-white-red flag resembling that of Spain, but they soon made its stripes vertical. In 1825 the current design was established. The shield includes figures symbolic of national wealth—the vicuña (a relative of the alpaca), a cinchona tree, and a cornucopia with gold and silver coins.

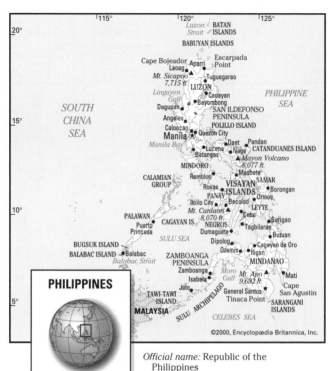

Official name: Republic of the Philippines
Head of government: President
Official languages: Pilipino; English
Monetary unit: Philippine peso
Area: 115,860 sq. mi. (300,076 sq. km.)
Population (2001): 78,609,000
GNP per capita (1999): U.S.$1,050
Principal exports (1999): electronics 56.2%; garments 6.5%; ignition wiring sets 1.5% *to:* U.S. 29.6%; Japan 13.3%; Taiwan 8.5%; The Netherlands 8.2%

Language Composition

Tagalog 27.9%
Cebuano 24.3%
Ilocano 9.8%
Hiligaynon 9.3%
Ilongo 9.3%
Other 28.7%

In 1898, during the Spanish-American War, Filipinos established the basic flag in use today; it was officially adopted in 1936. The white triangle is for liberty. The golden sun and stars are for the three main areas of the Philippines: Luzon, the Visayan Islands, and Mindanao. The red color is for courage and the blue color is for sacrifice.

Official name: Republic of Poland
Head of government: Prime Minister
Official language: Polish
Monetary unit: zloty
Area: 120,728 sq. mi. (312,685 sq. km.)
Population (2001): 38,647,000
GNP per capita (1999): U.S.$4,070
Principal exports (1999): machinery and transport equipment 30.3%; food 8.5%; chemicals and chemical products 6.2% *to:* Germany 36.1%; Italy 6.5%; The Netherlands 5.3%

Age Breakdown

Under 15
22.8%
15–59
61.4%
60 and over
15.8%

The colors of the Polish flag originated in its coat of arms, a white eagle on a red shield, dating from 1295. The precise symbolism of the colors is not known, however. Poland's simple flag of white-red horizontal stripes was adopted on Aug. 1, 1919. The flag was left unaltered under the Soviet-allied communist regime (1944 to 1990).

Official name: Portuguese Republic
Head of government: Prime Minister
Official language: Portuguese
Monetary unit: euro
Area: 35,662 sq. mi. (92,365 sq. km.)
Population (2001): 10,328,000
GNP per capita (1999): U.S.$11,030
Principal exports (1998): machinery and
transport equipment 32.9%; textiles
and wearing apparel 25.5%; footwear
6.6% *to* (1999): Germany 19.8%; Spain
18.1%; France 13.9%

PORTUGAL

Scale 1: 8,756,000

| 0 | 40 | 80 mi |
| 0 | 60 | 120 km |

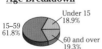

Age Breakdown

Under 15
18.9%
15–59
61.8%
60 and over
19.3%

The central shield includes five smaller shields for a victory
over the Moors in 1139, and a red border with gold castles.
Behind the shield is an armillary sphere (an astronomical
device) recalling world explorations and the kingdom of
Brazil. Red and green were used in many early Portuguese
flags. The current flag dates to June 30, 1911.

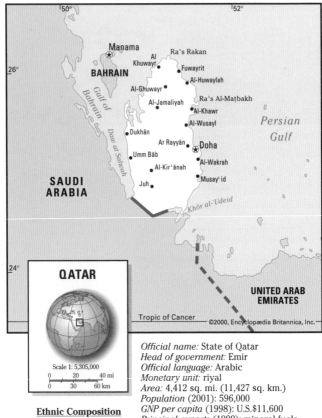

50° 52°

26°

Manama Ra's Rakan
Al
Khuwayr Fuwayrit
BAHRAIN Al-Huwaylah

Al-Ghuwayr

Al-Jamaliyah Ra's Al-Maṭbakh

Al-Khawr
Al-Wusayl *Persian*
Dukhān *Gulf*

Ar Rayyān Doha
Umm Bāb

Al-Wakrah
Al-Kirʿānah

SAUDI Juh Musayʾ id
ARABIA

Khōr al-ʾUdeid

24°

**UNITED ARAB
EMIRATES**

Tropic of Cancer ©2000, Encyclopædia Britannica, Inc.

QATAR

Scale 1: 5,305,000
0   20   40 mi
0   30   60 km

Ethnic Composition

Arab
40%

Other
(Pakistani,
Indian, and
Iranian)
60%

Official name: State of Qatar
Head of government: Emir
Official language: Arabic
Monetary unit: riyal
Area: 4,412 sq. mi. (11,427 sq. km.)
Population (2001): 596,000
GNP per capita (1998): U.S.$11,600
Principal exports (1999): mineral fuels
   and lubricants 81.2%; chemicals and
   chemical products 10.4%;
   manufactured goods 5.9% *to* (1999):
   Japan 51.0%; South Korea 12.9%;
   Singapore 9.1%

The 1868 treaty between Great Britain and Qatar may have
inspired the creation of the flag. Qataris chose mauve or
maroon instead of red (a more typical color among Arab
countries) perhaps to distinguish it from the flag used in
Bahrain. Passages from the Quran, in Arabic script, have
sometimes been added to the flag.

ROMANIA

Scale 1: 10,966,000

0 ___ 50 ___ 100 mi
0 ___ 80 ___ 160 km

Official name: Romania
Head of government: Prime Minister
Official language: Romanian
Monetary unit: Romanian leu
Area: 91,699 sq. mi. (237,500 sq. km.)
Population (2001): 22,413,000
GNP per capita (1999): U.S.$2,250
Principal exports (1996): textiles 20.8%;
   mineral products 9.2%; chemicals
   9.0%; machinery 8.0% *to:* Germany
   18.2%; Italy 16.6%; France 5.6%; United
   Kingdom 2.9%

Ethnic Composition

Romanian 89.4%
Hungarian 7.1%
Other 3.5%

In 1834 Walachia, an ancient region of Romania, chose a naval ensign with stripes of red, blue, and yellow. The modern Romanian tricolor was created in 1848 and flown for a brief time. In 1867 Romania reestablished the vertical tricolor, and with the fall of the 20th-century communist regime, it was defined on Dec. 27, 1989.

0° 30° 60° 90°

U.K.

NORWEGIAN SEA

SVALBARD (NORWAY)

ARCTIC

NORWAY

DENMARK

SWEDEN

FRANZ JOSEF LAND

Stockholm

Helsinki

FINLAND

Murmansk

Kirovsk

KOLA PEN.

BARENTS SEA

KARA SEA

NOVAYA ZEMLYA

YAMAL PEN.

NORTH

GYDAN PEN.

Dudinka

BALTIC SEA

LATVIA

POLAND

ESTONIA

LITHUANIA

Petersburg

Petrozavodsk

WHITE SEA

KANIN PEN.

Nar'yan-Mar

Minsk

BELARUS

Novgorod

Lake Ladoga

Lake Onega

Cherepovets

Vologda

TIMAN RIDGE

Salekhard

Gulf of Ob

Moscow

Smolensk

Tver'

Yaroslavl'

Syktyvkar

Ob

Kiev

Kaluga

Vladimir

Nizhny Novgorod

RUSSIAN

Kudymkar

URAL MOUNTAINS

Khanty-Mansiysk

UKRAINE

Voronezh

Cheboksary

Yoshkar-Ola

PLAIN

Perm'

WEST

S

Yenisey

Saransk

Kazan

Izhevsk

Yekaterinburg

Nizhnevartovsk

SEA OF AZOV

Penza

Saratov

Samara

Ufa

Tyumen'

SIBERIAN

Don

Rostov-na-Donu

Volga

Salavat

Chelyabinsk

Tobol

PLAIN

Ket'

BLACK SEA

Maykop

Volgograd

Orenburg

Orsk

Kurgan

Omsk

Tomsk

Mount Elbrus 18,510 ft.

Ural

GEORGIA

Grozny

CAUCASUS

Nal'chik

Makhachkala

CASPIAN SEA

ARM.

AZER.

Novosibirsk

Krasnoyarsk

Abakan

KULUNDA STEPPE

Novokuznetsk

Biysk

Gorno-Altaysk

ALTAY NATURE RESERVE

KAZAKSTAN

Belukha 15,157 ft.

IRAN

TURKMEN.

CHINA

RUSSIA

Scale 1: 55,746,000

0   300   600 mi

0   400   800 km

Ethnic Composition

Other 14.7%

Russian 81.5%

Tatar 3.8%

Tsar Peter the Great visited the Netherlands in order to modernize the Russian navy, and in 1699 he chose a Dutch-influenced flag for Russian ships. The flag soon became popular on land as well. After the Russian Revolution it was replaced by the communist red banner, but the tricolor again became official on Aug. 21, 1991.

Official name: Russian Federation
Head of government: Prime Minister
Official language: Russian
Monetary unit: ruble
Area: 6,592,800 sq. mi. (17,075,400 sq. km.)
Population (2001): 144,417,000
GNP per capita (1999): U.S.$2,250
Principal exports (1999): fuels and lubricants 43.8%; ferrous and non-ferrous metals 20.5% *to:* U.S. 8.9%; Germany 8.5%; Ukraine 6.6%; Belarus 5.2%

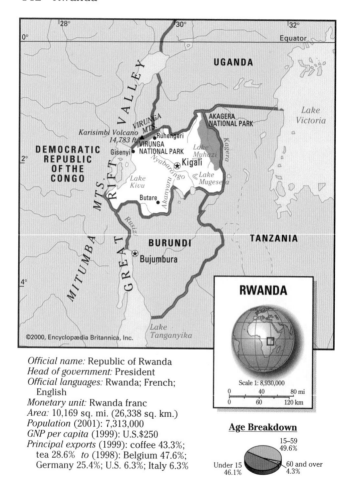

©2000, Encyclopædia Britannica, Inc.

Official name: Republic of Rwanda
Head of government: President
Official languages: Rwanda; French;
  English
Monetary unit: Rwanda franc
Area: 10,169 sq. mi. (26,338 sq. km.)
Population (2001): 7,313,000
GNP per capita (1999): U.S.$250
Principal exports (1999): coffee 43.3%;
  tea 28.6% *to* (1998): Belgium 47.6%;
  Germany 25.4%; U.S. 6.3%; Italy 6.3%

RWANDA

Scale 1: 8,930,000
0   40   80 mi
0   60   120 km

Age Breakdown

15–59
49.6%

Under 15
46.1%

60 and over
4.3%

R

On Jan. 28, 1961, the republic was proclaimed under a tricolor of red, yellow, and green—the Pan African colors. In Rwanda these symbolize the blood shed for liberation, peace and tranquility, and hope and optimism. In 1961 a black "R" was added to distinguish the flag from that of Guinea and to stand for Rwanda, revolution, and referendum.

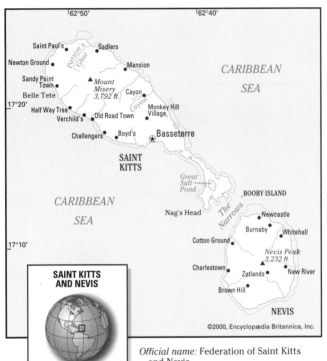

Official name: Federation of Saint Kitts
and Nevis
Head of government: Prime Minister
Official language: English
Monetary unit: Eastern Caribbean dollar
Area: 104.0 sq. mi. (269.4 sq. km.)
Population (2001): 38,800
GNP per capita (1999): U.S.$6,330
Principal exports (1997): food 56.0%;
   machinery and transportation
   equipment (mostly electronic goods)
   31.7% *to* (1997): U.S. 55.0%; United
   Kingdom 32.6%

Religious Affiliation

Protestant
76.4%

Other
12.9%

Roman
Catholic
10.7%

On Sept. 18, 1983, at the time of its independence from
Britain, St. Kitts and Nevis hoisted the current flag. It has
green (for fertility), red (for the struggle against slavery and
colonialism), and black (for African heritage). The yellow
flanking stripes are for sunshine, and the two stars, one for
each island, are for hope and liberty.

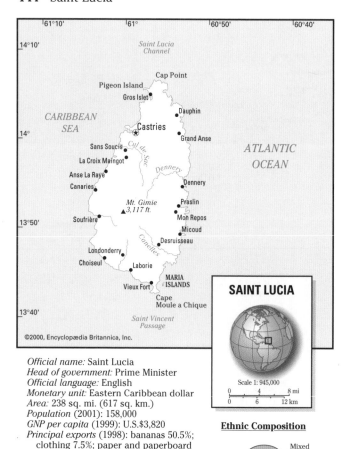

Official name: Saint Lucia
Head of government: Prime Minister
Official language: English
Monetary unit: Eastern Caribbean dollar
Area: 238 sq. mi. (617 sq. km.)
Population (2001): 158,000
GNP per capita (1999): U.S.$3,820
Principal exports (1998): bananas 50.5%;
clothing 7.5%; paper and paperboard
5.9% *to:* United Kingdom 60.0%; U.S.
21.0%; Caricom countries 16.3%

SAINT LUCIA

Scale 1: 945,000

0   4   8 mi
0   6   12 km

Ethnic Composition

Black 90.5%
Mixed 5.5%
Other 4%

The flag was hoisted on March 1, 1967, when the former colony assumed a status of association with the United Kingdom; it was slightly altered in 1979. The blue represents Atlantic and Caribbean waters. The white and black colors are for racial harmony, while the black triangle also represents volcanoes. The yellow triangle is for sunshine.

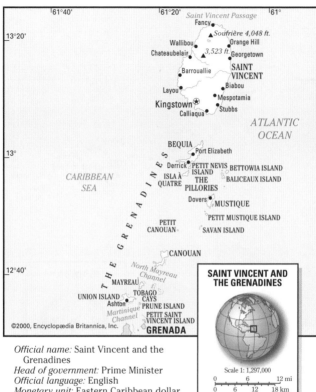

Official name: Saint Vincent and the
  Grenadines
Head of government: Prime Minister
Official language: English
Monetary unit: Eastern Caribbean dollar
Area: 150.3 sq. mi. (389.3 sq. km.)
Population (2001): 113,000
GNP per capita (1999): U.S.$2,640
Principal exports (1998): domestic
  exports 94.1%, of which
  bananas 41.5%; reexports 5.9%
  to: Caricom countries 49.1%; United
  Kingdom 42.2%

Scale 1: 1,297,000

0   6   12 mi
0   6   12   18 km

Ethnic Composition

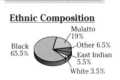

Mulatto
19%
Other 6.5%
Black
65.5%
East Indian
5.5%
White 3.5%

At independence from Britain in 1979 a national flag was
designed, but it was replaced by the current flag on Oct. 22,
1985. The three green diamonds are arranged in the form of
a V. Green is for the rich vegetation and the vitality of the
people, yellow is for sand and personal warmth, and blue is
for sea and sky.

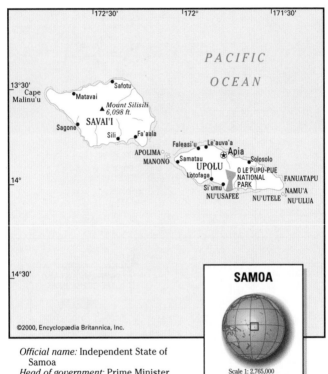

PACIFIC OCEAN

SAVAI'I
Mount Silisili 6,098 ft.
Cape Malinu'u
Safotu
Matavai
Sagone
Sili
Fa'aala
APOLIMA
MANONO
Faleasi'u
Le'auva'a
Samatau
UPOLU
Apia
Solosolo
Lotofaga
O LE PUPU-PUE NATIONAL PARK
FANUATAPU
Si'umu
NU'USAFEE
NU'UTELE
NAMU'A
NU'ULUA

©2000, Encyclopædia Britannica, Inc.

Official name: Independent State of Samoa
Head of government: Prime Minister
Official languages: Samoan; English
Monetary unit: tala
Area: 1,093 sq. mi. (2,831 sq. km.)
Population (2001): 179,000
GNP per capita (1999): U.S.$1,070
Principal exports (1997): fresh fish 33.0%;
  copra 21.1%; coconut oil 18.1%;
  coconut cream 12.8% *to:* New Zealand
  48.1%; American Samoa (dependency)
  15.3%; Australia 9.2%

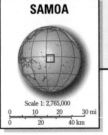

SAMOA

Scale 1: 2,765,000
0   10   20   30 mi
0   20   40 km

Religious Affiliation

Protestant 63%
Roman Catholic 21%
Mormon 10%
Other 11%

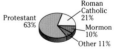

The first national flag of Samoa may date to 1873. Under British administration, a version of the current flag was introduced on May 26, 1948. On Feb. 2, 1949, a fifth star was added to the Southern Cross. White in the flag is said to stand for purity, blue for freedom, and red for courage. The flag was left unaltered upon independence in 1962.

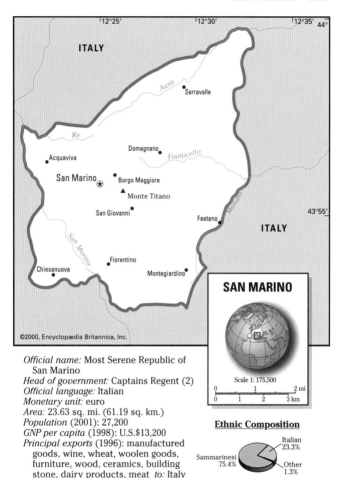

©2000, Encyclopædia Britannica, Inc.

Official name: Most Serene Republic of San Marino
Head of government: Captains Regent (2)
Official language: Italian
Monetary unit: euro
Area: 23.63 sq. mi. (61.19 sq. km.)
Population (2001): 27,200
GNP per capita (1998): U.S.$13,200
Principal exports (1996): manufactured goods, wine, wheat, woolen goods, furniture, wood, ceramics, building stone, dairy products, meat *to:* Italy

SAN MARINO

Scale 1: 175,500

Ethnic Composition

Italian 23.3%
Sammarinesi 75.4%
Other 1.3%

The colors of the flag, blue and white, were first used in the national cockade in 1797. The coat of arms in its present form was adopted on April 6, 1862, when the crown was added as a symbol of national sovereignty. Also in the coat of arms are three towers (Guaita, Cesta, and Montale) from the fortifications on Mount Titano.

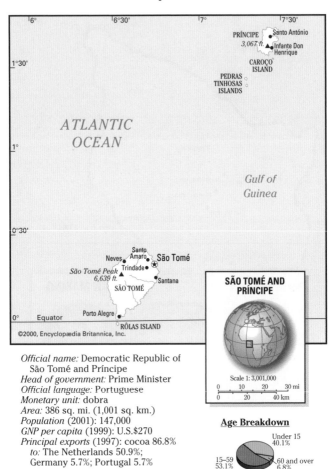

Official name: Democratic Republic of
São Tomé and Príncipe
Head of government: Prime Minister
Official language: Portuguese
Monetary unit: dobra
Area: 386 sq. mi. (1,001 sq. km.)
Population (2001): 147,000
GNP per capita (1999): U.S.$270
Principal exports (1997): cocoa 86.8%
   to: The Netherlands 50.9%;
   Germany 5.7%; Portugal 5.7%

Scale 1: 3,001,000

| 0 | 10 | 20 | 30 mi |
| 0 | 20 | 40 km | |

Age Breakdown

Under 15
40.1%

15–59
53.1%

60 and over
6.8%

The national flag was adopted upon independence from
Portugal on July 12, 1975. Its colors are associated with Pan-
African independence. The red triangle stands for equality
and the nationalist movement. The stars are for the African
population living on the nation's two main islands. Green is
for vegetation and yellow is for the tropical sun.

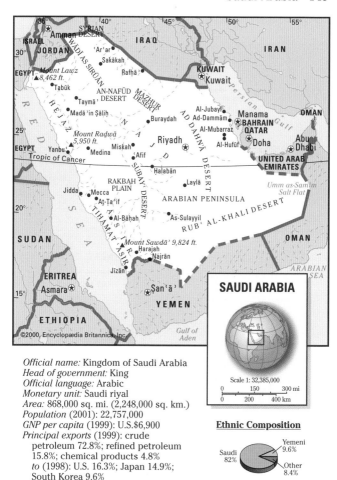

Official name: Kingdom of Saudi Arabia
Head of government: King
Official language: Arabic
Monetary unit: Saudi riyal
Area: 868,000 sq. mi. (2,248,000 sq. km.)
Population (2001): 22,757,000
GNP per capita (1999): U.S.$6,900
Principal exports (1999): crude
petroleum 72.8%; refined petroleum
15.8%; chemical products 4.8%
to (1998): U.S. 16.3%; Japan 14.9%;
South Korea 9.6%

SAUDI ARABIA

Scale 1: 32,385,000

0   150   300 mi

0   200   400 km

Ethnic Composition

Saudi
82%

Yemeni
9.6%

Other
8.4%

The Saudi flag, made official in 1932 but altered in 1968, originated in the military campaigns of Muhammad. The color
green is associated with Fatima, the Prophet's daughter, and
the Arabic inscription is translated as "There is no God but
Allah and Muhammad is the Prophet of Allah." The saber
symbolizes the militancy of the faith.

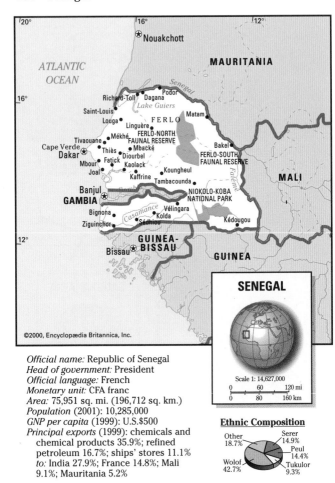

©2000, Encyclopædia Britannica, Inc.

SENEGAL

Scale 1: 14,627,000

| 0 | 60 | 120 mi |
| 0 | 80 | 160 km |

Official name: Republic of Senegal
Head of government: President
Official language: French
Monetary unit: CFA franc
Area: 75,951 sq. mi. (196,712 sq. km.)
Population (2001): 10,285,000
GNP per capita (1999): U.S.$500
Principal exports (1999): chemicals and
  chemical products 35.9%; refined
  petroleum 16.7%; ships' stores 11.1%
  to: India 27.9%; France 14.8%; Mali
  9.1%; Mauritania 5.2%

Ethnic Composition

Wolof 42.7%
Serer 14.9%
Peul 14.4%
Tukulor 9.3%
Other 18.7%

In a federation with French Sudan (now Mali) on April 4, 1959,
Senegal used a flag with a human figure in the center. After
the federation broke up in August 1960, Senegal substituted a
green star for the central figure. Green is for hope and religion, yellow is for natural riches and labor, and red is for
independence, life, and socialism.

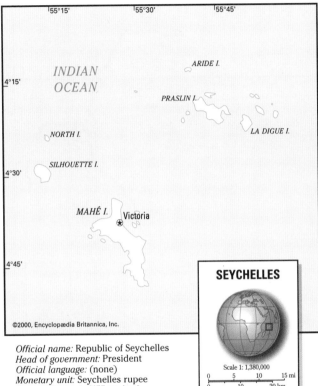

INDIAN OCEAN

ARIDE I.

PRASLIN I.

NORTH I.

LA DIGUE I.

SILHOUETTE I.

MAHÉ I. Victoria

©2000, Encyclopædia Britannica, Inc.

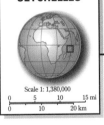

SEYCHELLES

Scale 1: 1,380,000

0 5 10 15 mi

0 10 20 km

Official name: Republic of Seychelles
Head of government: President
Official language: (none)
Monetary unit: Seychelles rupee
Area: 176 sq. mi. (455 sq. km.)
Population (2001): 80,600
GNP per capita (1999): U.S.$6,500
Principal exports (1999): canned tuna
70.2%; petroleum products 21.9%;
other fish, including dried shark fins
1.9%; *to* (1997): France 29.2%;
Germany 27.3%; Italy 24.0

Age Breakdown

Under 15
31.2%

15–59
60.3%

60 and over
8.3%

The former British colony underwent a revolution in 1977.
The government was democratized in 1993, and on Jan. 8,
1996, a new flag was designed. The blue color is for sky and
sea, yellow is for the sun, red is for the people and their work
for unity and love, white is for social justice and harmony,
and green is for the land and natural environment.

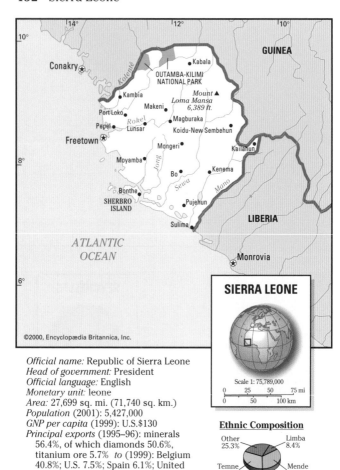

GUINEA

Conakry

Kabala

OUTAMBA-KILIMI
NATIONAL PARK

Kolenté

Kambia

*Mount ▲
Loma Mansa
6,389 ft.*

Port Loko
Makeni

Pepel
Lunsar
Magburaka

Rokel

Koidu-New Sembehun

Freetown

Mongeri

Kailahun

Moyamba

Jong

Kenema

Bo

Sewa

Bonthe
SHERBRO
ISLAND

Pujehun

Mano

LIBERIA

Sulima

*ATLANTIC
OCEAN*

Monrovia

©2000, Encyclopædia Britannica, Inc.

SIERRA LEONE

Scale 1: 75,789,000

| 0 | 25 | 50 | 75 mi |
| 0 | 50 | 100 km |

Official name: Republic of Sierra Leone
Head of government: President
Official language: English
Monetary unit: leone
Area: 27,699 sq. mi. (71,740 sq. km.)
Population (2001): 5,427,000
GNP per capita (1999): U.S.$130
Principal exports (1995–96): minerals
56.4%, of which diamonds 50.6%,
titanium ore 5.7% *to* (1999): Belgium
40.8%; U.S. 7.5%; Spain 6.1%; United
Kingdom 4.1%

Ethnic Composition

Other
25.3%

Limba
8.4%

Temne
31.7%

Mende
34.6%

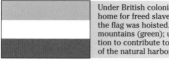

Under British colonial control Sierra Leone was founded as a
home for freed slaves. With independence on April 27, 1961,
the flag was hoisted. Its stripes stand for agriculture and the
mountains (green); unity and justice (white); and the aspira-
tion to contribute to world peace, especially through the use
of the natural harbor at Freetown (blue).

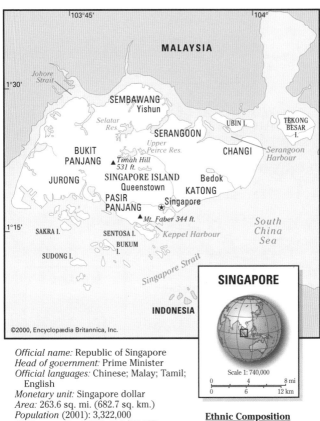

©2000, Encyclopædia Britannica, Inc.

Official name: Republic of Singapore
Head of government: Prime Minister
Official languages: Chinese; Malay; Tamil; English
Monetary unit: Singapore dollar
Area: 263.6 sq. mi. (682.7 sq. km.)
Population (2001): 3,322,000
GNP per capita (1999): U.S.$29,660
Principal exports (2000): office machines 22.6%; petroleum products 7.2%; telecommunications apparatus 5.5% *to* (1999): U.S. 19.2%; Malaysia 16.6%; Hong Kong 7.7%; Japan 7.4%

Scale 1: 740,000

Ethnic Composition

Malay 14.2%
Chinese 77.4%
Indian 7.2%
Other 1.2%

On Dec. 3, 1959, the flag was acquired, and it was retained after separation from Malaysia on Aug. 9, 1965. The red and white stripes stand for universal brotherhood, equality, purity, and virtue. The crescent symbolizes the growth of a young country, while the five stars are for democracy, peace, progress, justice, and equality.

Official name: Slovak Republic
Head of government: Prime Minister
Official language: Slovak
Monetary unit: Slovak koruna
Area: 18,933 sq. mi. (49,035 sq. km.)
Population (2001): 5,410,000
GNP per capita (1999): U.S.$3,770
Principal exports (2000): machinery and
transport equipment 39.5%;
manufactured goods 27.3% to (2000):
Germany 26.7%; Czech Republic
20.0%; Italy 9.1%

Scale 1: 6,249,000

| 0 | 30 | 60 mi |
| 0 | 40 | 80 km |

Ethnic Composition

Slovak 85.7%
Hungarian 10.6%
Other 3.7%

In 1189 the kingdom of Hungary (including Slovakia) introduced a double-barred cross in its coat of arms; this symbol was altered in 1848-49 by Slovak nationalists. After a period of communist rule, the tricolor was made official in 1989. On Sept. 3, 1992, the shield was added to the white-blue-red flag to differentiate it from the flag of Russia.

©2000, Encyclopædia Britannica, Inc.

Official name: Republic of Slovenia
Head of government: Prime Minister
Official language: Slovene
Monetary unit: Slovene tolar
Area: 7,827 sq. mi. (20,273 sq. km.)
Population (2001): 1,991,000
GNP per capita (1999): U.S.$10,000
Principal exports (2000): machinery and
  transport equipment 36.0%;
  manufactured goods 27.3%
  to: Germany 27.2%; Italy 13.6%;
  Croatia 7.9%; Austria 7.5%;
  France 7.1%

SLOVENIA

Scale 1: 4,314,000

0   20   40 mi
0   30   60 km

Age Breakdown

60 and over
18.3%

15–59
63.9%

Under 15
17.8%

Under the current flag Slovenia proclaimed independence on
June 25, 1991, but it was opposed for a time by the Yugoslav
army. The flag is the same as that of Russia and Slovakia
except for the coat of arms. It depicts the peaks of Triglav
(the nation's highest mountain), the waves of the Adriatic
coast, and three stars on a blue background.

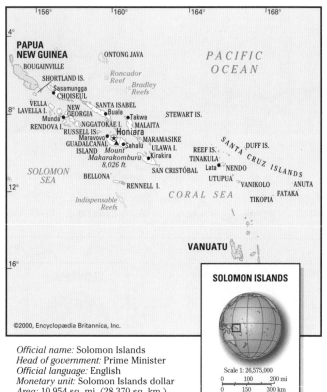

Official name: Solomon Islands
Head of government: Prime Minister
Official language: English
Monetary unit: Solomon Islands dollar
Area: 10,954 sq. mi. (28,370 sq. km.)
Population (2001): 480,000
GNP per capita (1999): U.S.$750
Principal exports (1996): timber products 60.6%; fish products 18.3%; palm oil products 10.9% *to:* Japan 40.1%; South Korea 19.4%; United Kingdom 18.4%; Thailand 3.8%

SOLOMON ISLANDS

Scale 1: 26,575,000

| 0 | 100 | 200 mi |
| 0 | 150 | 300 km |

Age Breakdown

Under 15
43.7%

15–59
52%

60 and over
4.3%

The flag was introduced on Nov. 18, 1977, eight months before independence from Britain. The yellow stripe stands for the sun. The green triangle is for the trees and crops of the fertile land, while the blue triangle symbolizes rivers, rain, and the ocean. The five stars represented the original five districts of the island.

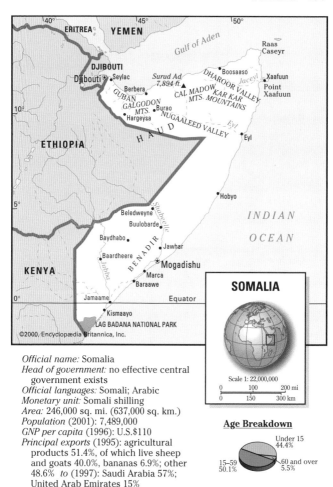

©2000, Encyclopædia Britannica, Inc.

Official name: Somalia
Head of government: no effective central
  government exists
Official languages: Somali; Arabic
Monetary unit: Somali shilling
Area: 246,000 sq. mi. (637,000 sq. km.)
Population (2001): 7,489,000
GNP per capita (1996): U.S.$110
Principal exports (1995): agricultural
  products 51.4%, of which live sheep
  and goats 40.0%, bananas 6.9%; other
  48.6% *to* (1997): Saudi Arabia 57%;
  United Arab Emirates 15%

SOMALIA

Scale 1: 22,000,000

| 0 | 100 | 200 mi |
| 0 | 150 | 300 km |

Age Breakdown

Under 15
44.4%

15–59
50.1%

60 and over
5.5%

From the mid-19th century, areas in the Horn of Africa with
Somali populations were divided between Ethiopia, France,
Britain, and Italy. On Oct. 12, 1954, with the partial unifica-
tion of these areas, the flag was adopted with a white star,
each point referring to a Somali homeland. The colors were
influenced by the colors of the United Nations.

15° 20° 25° 30°

ZIMBABWE

20° Windhoek ⊛

Tropic of Capricorn

BOTSWANA

MOZAMBIQUE

Limpopo

LEBOMBO MTS.

KALAHARI

NAMIBIA

KALAHARI GEMSBOK NATIONAL PARK

Gaborone ⊛

WITWATERSRAND MTS.

Seshego

KRUGER NATIONAL PARK

25° Rustenburg

Pretoria ⊛

Maputo

DESERT

Krugersdorp

Johannesburg

Mbabane ⊛

Kuruman

Soweto

Germiston

SWAZILAND

Klerksdorp

Vanderbijlpark

UMFOLOZI GAME RESERVE

Upington

Newcastle

Kimberley

Welkom

Vaal

Mont-Aux-Sources 10,822 ft.

Port Nolloth

Orange

Bloemfontein ⊛

Maseru ⊛

Pietermaritzburg

30° Mount Kamies 5,599 ft.

Mount Hexrivier ▲ 5,648 ft.

LESOTHO

Caledon

Durban

ATLANTIC OCEAN

Mount Bokkeveld ▲ 2,765 ft.

Orange

STORMBERG RANGE

Margate

INDIAN OCEAN

Calvinia

SNEEUBERG

GREAT ESCARPMENT

Queenstown

St. Helena Bay

Bisho

Hopefield

Worcester

Oudtshoorn

Uitenhage

East London

Bellville

Stellenbosch

George

Port Elizabeth

Cape Town ⊛

Cape of Good Hope

False Bay

Cape Agulhas

35°

©2000, Encyclopædia Britannica, Inc.

SOUTH AFRICA

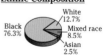

Scale 1: 29,306,000

0 — 100 — 200 mi
0 — 150 — 300 km

Official name: Republic of South Africa
Head of government: President
Official languages: Afrikaans; English;
  Ndebele; Pedi; Sotho; Swazi; Tsonga;
  Tswana; Venda; Xhosa; Zulu
Monetary unit: rand
Area: 470,693 sq. mi. (1,219,090 sq. km.)
Population (2001): 43,586,000
GNP per capita (1999): U.S.$3,170
Principal exports (1995): gold 19.9%;
  metal products 15.4%; gem diamonds
  9.8% *to* (1999): United Kingdom 8.3%;
  U.S. 8.2%; Germany 7.0%

Ethnic Composition

White 12.7%
Black 76.3%
Mixed race 8.5%
Asian 2.5%

With the decline of apartheid, the flag was hoisted on April 27, 1994, and confirmed in 1996. Its six colors collectively represent Zulus, English or Afrikaners, Muslims, supporters of the African National Congress, and other groups. The Y-symbol stands for "merging history and present political realities" into a united and prosperous future.

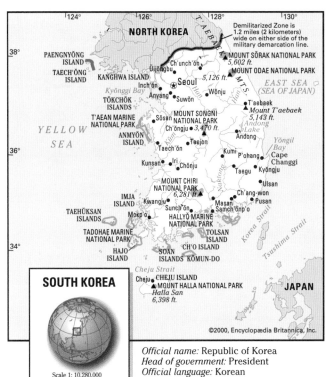

NORTH KOREA

Demilitarized Zone is 1.2 miles (2 kilometers) wide on either side of the military demarcation line.

PAENGNYŎNG ISLAND
TAECH'ŎNG ISLAND
KANGHWA ISLAND
Ch'unch'ŏn
Ŭijŏngbu
MOUNT SŎRAK NATIONAL PARK 5,602 ft.
MOUNT ODAE NATIONAL PARK

Inch'ŏn
⊛ Seoul
5,126 ft.
EAST SEA (SEA OF JAPAN)

Kyŏnggi Bay
Anyang
Suwŏn
Wŏnju

TŎKCHŎK ISLANDS
T'aebaek
Mount T'aebaek 5,143 ft.
Andong Lake

T'AEAN MARINE NATIONAL PARK
Sŏsan
MOUNT SONGNI NATIONAL PARK
Ch'ŏngju ● 3,470 ft.
Andong
Yŏngil Bay

YELLOW SEA

ANMYŎN ISLAND
Taech'ŏn
Taejŏn
Kumi
P'ohang
Cape Changgi

Kunsan
Iri
Chŏnju
Taegu
Kyŏngju

IMJA ISLAND
MOUNT CHIRI NATIONAL PARK
6,281 ft. ▲
Ulsan
Ch'ang-won

TAEHŬKSAN ISLANDS
Kwangju
Masan
Samch'ŏnp'o
Pusan

Mokp'o
Sunch'ŏn
HALLYŎ MARINE NATIONAL PARK

TADOHAE MARINE NATIONAL PARK
TOLSAN ISLAND
Korea Strait

HAJO ISLAND
SOAN ISLANDS KŎMUN-DO
CH'O ISLAND
Tsushima Strait

Cheju Strait
Cheju ▲ CHEJU ISLAND
▲ MOUNT HALLA NATIONAL PARK
Halla San 6,398 ft.

JAPAN

©2000, Encyclopædia Britannica, Inc.

SOUTH KOREA

Scale 1: 10,280,000
0   40   80 mi
0   60   120 km

Age Breakdown

Under 15 23.2%
15–59 67.8%
60 and over 9%

Official name: Republic of Korea
Head of government: President
Official language: Korean
Monetary unit: won
Area: 38,402 sq. mi. (99,461 sq. km.)
Population (2001): 47,676,000
GNP per capita (1999): U.S.$8,490
Principal exports (2000): electric and electronic products 36.0%; machinery and transport equipment 18.2%; chemicals 7.0% *to:* U.S. 21.8%; Japan 11.9%; China 10.7%

The flag was adopted in August 1882. Its white background is for peace, while the central emblem represents yin-yang (Korean: *um-yang*), the duality of the universe. The black bars recall sun, moon, earth, heaven and other Confucian principles. Outlawed under Japanese rule, the flag was revived in 1945 and slightly modified in 1950 and 1984.

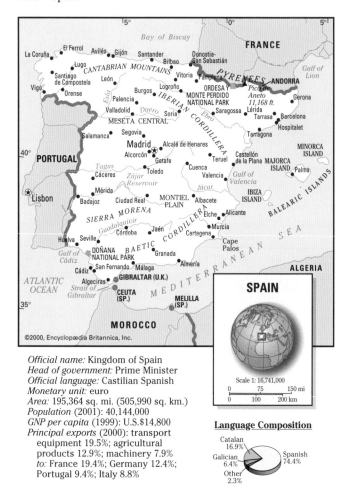

Official name: Kingdom of Spain
Head of government: Prime Minister
Official language: Castilian Spanish
Monetary unit: euro
Area: 195,364 sq. mi. (505,990 sq. km.)
Population (2001): 40,144,000
GNP per capita (1999): U.S.$14,800
Principal exports (2000): transport
equipment 19.5%; agricultural
products 12.9%; machinery 7.9%
to: France 19.4%; Germany 12.4%;
Portugal 9.4%; Italy 8.8%

Scale 1: 16,741,000

0	75		150 mi
0	100	200 km	

Language Composition

Catalan 16.9%
Galician 6.4%
Other 2.3%
Spanish 74.4%

The colors of the flag have no official symbolic meaning.
Introduced in 1785 by King Charles III, the flag was changed
only under the Spanish Republic (1931–39). Under different
regimes, however, the coat of arms has been altered. The current design dates from Dec. 18, 1981, with the death of
Francisco Franco and the resurgence of democracy.

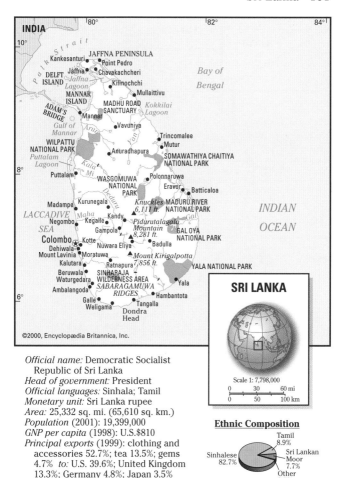

©2000, Encyclopædia Britannica, Inc.

Official name: Democratic Socialist
  Republic of Sri Lanka
Head of government: President
Official languages: Sinhala; Tamil
Monetary unit: Sri Lanka rupee
Area: 25,332 sq. mi. (65,610 sq. km.)
Population (2001): 19,399,000
GNP per capita (1998): U.S.$810
Principal exports (1999): clothing and
  accessories 52.7%; tea 13.5%; gems
  4.7% *to:* U.S. 39.6%; United Kingdom
  13.3%; Germany 4.8%; Japan 3.5%

SRI LANKA

Scale 1: 7,798,000

0   30   60 mi
0   50   100 km

Ethnic Composition

Sinhalese 82.7%
Tamil 8.9%
Sri Lankan Moor 7.7%
Other 0.7%

From the 5th century BC the Lion flag was a symbol of the
Sinhalese people. The flag was replaced by the Union Jack in
1815 but readopted upon independence in 1948. The stripes
of green (for Muslims) and orange (for Hindus) were added in
1951. In 1972 four leaves of the Bo tree were added as a symbol of Buddhism; the leaves were altered in 1978.

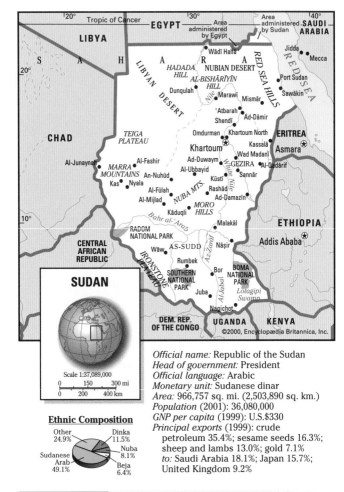

Official name: Republic of the Sudan
Head of government: President
Official language: Arabic
Monetary unit: Sudanese dinar
Area: 966,757 sq. mi. (2,503,890 sq. km.)
Population (2001): 36,080,000
GNP per capita (1999): U.S.$330
Principal exports (1999): crude
  petroleum 35.4%; sesame seeds 16.3%;
  sheep and lambs 13.0%; gold 7.1%
  to: Saudi Arabia 18.1%; Japan 15.7%;
  United Kingdom 9.2%

Ethnic Composition

Other 24.9%
Dinka 11.5%
Nuba 8.1%
Beja 6.4%
Sudanese Arab 49.1%

Scale 1:37,089,000
0   150   300 mi
0   200   400 km

The flag was first hoisted on May 20, 1970. It uses Pan-Arab colors. Black is for al-Mahdi (a leader in the 1800s) and the name of the country (sudan in Arabic means black); white recalls the revolutionary flag of 1924 and suggests peace and optimism; red is for patriotic martyrs, socialism, and progress; and green is for prosperity and Islam.

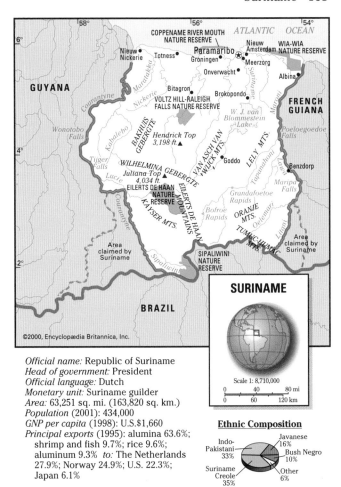

©2000, Encyclopædia Britannica, Inc.

SURINAME

Scale 1: 8,710,000

0   40   80 mi
0   60   120 km

Official name: Republic of Suriname
Head of government: President
Official language: Dutch
Monetary unit: Suriname guilder
Area: 63,251 sq. mi. (163,820 sq. km.)
Population (2001): 434,000
GNP per capita (1998): U.S.$1,660
Principal exports (1995): alumina 63.6%;
   shrimp and fish 9.7%; rice 9.6%;
   aluminum 9.3% *to:* The Netherlands
   27.9%; Norway 24.9%; U.S. 22.3%;
   Japan 6.1%

Ethnic Composition

Indo-Pakistani 33%
Suriname Creole 35%
Javanese 16%
Bush Negro 10%
Other 6%

Adopted on Nov. 21, 1975, four days before independence from the Dutch, the flag of Suriname features green stripes for jungles and agriculture, white for justice and freedom, and red for the progressive spirit of a young nation. The yellow star is symbolic of the unity of the country, its golden future, and the people's spirit of sacrifice.

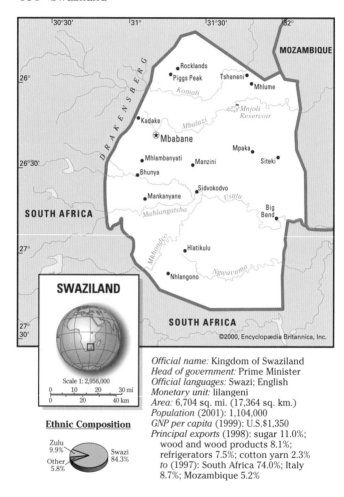

MOZAMBIQUE

Rocklands
Piggs Peak
Tshaneni
Mhlume
Komati
Mnjoli Reservoir
Kadake
Mbuluzi
⊛ Mbabane
Mpaka
Siteki
Mhlambanyati
Manzini
Bhunya
Mankanyane
Sidvokodvo
Usutu
Big Bend
Mahlangatsha
Mkhondvo
Hlatikulu
Ngwavuma
Nhlangono

SOUTH AFRICA

DRAKENSBERG

SOUTH AFRICA

©2000, Encyclopædia Britannica, Inc.

SWAZILAND

Scale 1: 2,956,000
0   10   20   30 mi
0   20   40 km

Ethnic Composition

Zulu 9.9%
Other 5.8%
Swazi 84.3%

Official name: Kingdom of Swaziland
Head of government: Prime Minister
Official languages: Swazi; English
Monetary unit: lilangeni
Area: 6,704 sq. mi. (17,364 sq. km.)
Population (2001): 1,104,000
GNP per capita (1999): U.S.$1,350
Principal exports (1998): sugar 11.0%;
  wood and wood products 8.1%;
  refrigerators 7.5%; cotton yarn 2.3%
  to (1997): South Africa 74.0%; Italy
  8.7%; Mozambique 5.2%

The flag dates to the creation of a military banner in 1941,
when Swazi troops were preparing for the Allied invasion of
Italy. On April 25, 1967, it was hoisted as the national flag.
The crimson stripe stands for past battles, yellow for mineral
wealth, and blue for peace. Featured are a Swazi war shield,
two spears, and a "fighting stick."

@2000, Encyclopædia Britannica, Inc.

Official name: Kingdom of Sweden
Head of government: Prime Minister
Official language: Swedish
Monetary unit: Swedish krona
Area: 173,732 sq. mi. (449,964 sq. km.)
Population (2001): 8,888,000
GNP per capita (1998): U.S.$26,750
Principal exports (1999): machinery and
   transport equipment 50.8%; paper
   products 8.1% *to* (1998): Germany
   11.2%; United Kingdom 9.1%;
   Norway 8.8%

SWEDEN

Scale 1: 23,567,000
0   100   200 mi
0 100 200 300 km

Age Breakdown

60 and over
22.1%

15–59
59.1%

Under 15
18.8%

From the 14th century the coat of arms of Sweden had a blue
field with three golden crowns, and the earlier Folkung
dynasty used a shield of blue and white wavy stripes with a
gold lion. The off-center "Scandinavian cross" was influenced
by the flag of the rival kingdom of Denmark. The current flag
law was adopted on July 1, 1906.

©2000, Encyclopædia Britannica, Inc.

SWITZERLAND

Scale 1: 5,214,000

0   20   40 mi
0   30   60 km

Language Composition

German 64%
French 19%
Other 9%
Italian 8%

Official name: Swiss Confederation
Head of government: President
Official languages: French; German;
   Italian; Romansh
Monetary unit: Swiss franc
Area: 15,940 sq. mi. (41,284 sq. km.)
Population (2001): 7,222,000
GNP per capita (1999): U.S.$38,380
Principal exports (2000): machinery
   29.3%; chemical products 28.4%;
   precision instruments, watches, and
   jewelry 16.2% *to:* Germany 22.2%; U.S.
   11.6%; France 9.0%

The Swiss flag is ultimately based on the war flag of the Holy Roman
Empire. Schwyz, one of the original three cantons of the Swiss
Confederation, placed a narrow white cross in the corner of its flag in
1240. This was also used in 1339 at the Battle of Laupen. Following the
1848 constitution, the flag was recognized by the army, and it was
established as the national flag on land on Dec. 12, 1889.

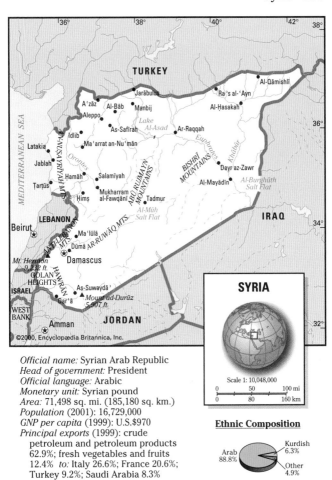

Official name: Syrian Arab Republic
Head of government: President
Official language: Arabic
Monetary unit: Syrian pound
Area: 71,498 sq. mi. (185,180 sq. km.)
Population (2001): 16,729,000
GNP per capita (1999): U.S.$970
Principal exports (1999): crude
  petroleum and petroleum products
  62.9%; fresh vegetables and fruits
  12.4% *to:* Italy 26.6%; France 20.6%;
  Turkey 9.2%; Saudi Arabia 8.3%

Ethnic Composition

Arab 88.8%

Kurdish 6.3%

Other 4.9%

In 1918 the Arab Revolt flag flew over Syria, which joined Egypt in the United Arab Republic in 1958 and based its new flag on that of the Egyptian revolution of 1952; its stripes were red-white-black, with two green stars for the constituent states. In 1961 Syria broke from the union, but it readopted the flag on March 29, 1980.

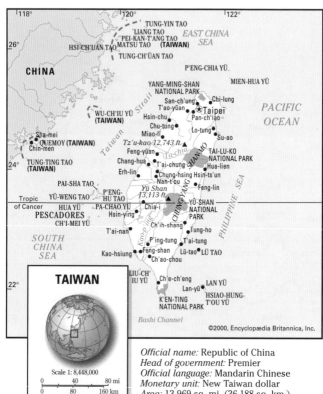

©2000, Encyclopædia Britannica, Inc.

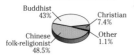

TAIWAN

Scale 1: 8,448,000

| 0 | 40 | 80 mi |
| 0 | 80 | 160 km |

Religious Affiliation

Buddhist 43%
Christian 7.4%
Chinese folk-religionist 48.5%
Other 1.1%

Official name: Republic of China
Head of government: Premier
Official language: Mandarin Chinese
Monetary unit: New Taiwan dollar
Area: 13,969 sq. mi. (36,188 sq. km.)
Population (2001): 22,340,000
GNP per capita (2000): U.S.$14,220
Principal exports (2000): electronics and
   other machinery 55.7%; textile
   products 10.3%; plastic articles 6.1%
   to: U.S. 23.5%; Hong Kong 21.1%; Japan
   11.2%; Singapore 3.7%

Under Chiang Kai-shek, a new Chinese national flag was
adopted on Oct. 28, 1928, and it was carried to Taiwan in
1949–50 when the Nationalists fled the mainland. The three
colors stand for the "Three Principles of the People" of the
Nationalist (Kuomintang) Party—nationalism, democracy, and
socialism.

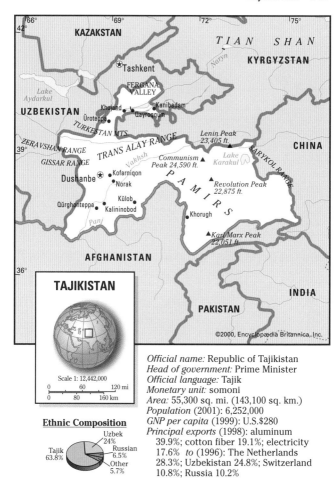

Official name: Republic of Tajikistan
Head of government: Prime Minister
Official language: Tajik
Monetary unit: somoni
Area: 55,300 sq. mi. (143,100 sq. km.)
Population (2001): 6,252,000
GNP per capita (1999): U.S.$280
Principal exports (1998): aluminum
39.9%; cotton fiber 19.1%; electricity
17.6% *to* (1996): The Netherlands
28.3%; Uzbekistan 24.8%; Switzerland
10.8%; Russia 10.2%

Ethnic Composition

Tajik 63.8%
Uzbek 24%
Russian 6.5%
Other 5.7%

Following independence from the Soviet Union in 1991, Tajikistan developed a new flag on Nov. 24, 1992. The green stripe is for agriculture, while red is for sovereignty. White is for the main crop—cotton. The central crown contains seven stars representing unity among workers, peasants, intellectuals, and other social classes.

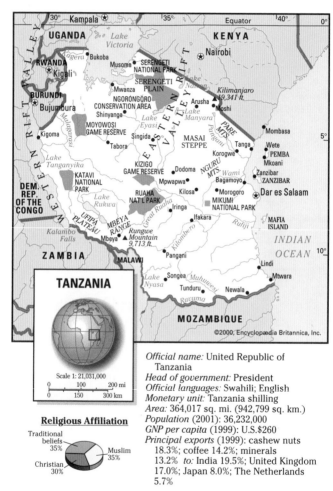

©2000, Encyclopædia Britannica, Inc.

TANZANIA

Scale 1: 21,031,000

| 0 | 100 | 200 mi |
| 0 | 150 | 300 km |

Religious Affiliation

Traditional beliefs 35%

Muslim 35%

Christian 30%

Official name: United Republic of Tanzania
Head of government: President
Official languages: Swahili; English
Monetary unit: Tanzania shilling
Area: 364,017 sq. mi. (942,799 sq. km.)
Population (2001): 36,232,000
GNP per capita (1999): U.S.$260
Principal exports (1999): cashew nuts 18.3%; coffee 14.2%; minerals 13.2% *to:* India 19.5%; United Kingdom 17.0%; Japan 8.0%; The Netherlands 5.7%

In April 1964 Tanganyika and Zanzibar united, and in July their flag traditions melded to create the current design. The black stripe is for the majority population, while green is for the rich agricultural resources of the land. Mineral wealth is reflected in the yellow fimbriations (narrow borders), while the Indian Ocean is symbolized by blue.

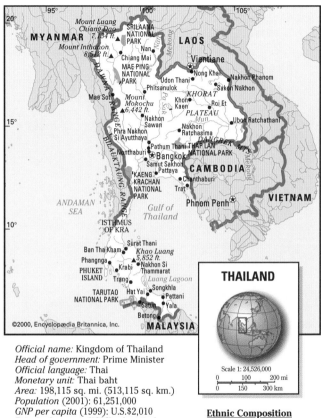

Official name: Kingdom of Thailand
Head of government: Prime Minister
Official language: Thai
Monetary unit: Thai baht
Area: 198,115 sq. mi. (513,115 sq. km.)
Population (2001): 61,251,000
GNP per capita (1999): U.S.$2,010
Principal exports (1998): electrical
   machinery 18.9%; power generating
   equipment 18.6%; garments 6.1%
   to: U.S. 22.3%; Japan 13.7%;
   Singapore 8.6%

Scale 1: 24,526,000

| 0 | 100 | 200 mi |
| 0 | 150 | 300 km |

Ethnic Composition

Chinese 12.1%
Malay 3.7%
Other 4.7%
Thai 79.5%

In the 17th century, the flag of Thailand was plain red, and Thai ships in 1855 displayed a flag with a central white elephant as a symbol of good fortune. The Thai king replaced the elephant with two white stripes in 1916 and added the blue stripe on Sept. 28, 1917. Red symbolizes the blood of patriots, white is for Buddhism, and blue is for royal guidance.

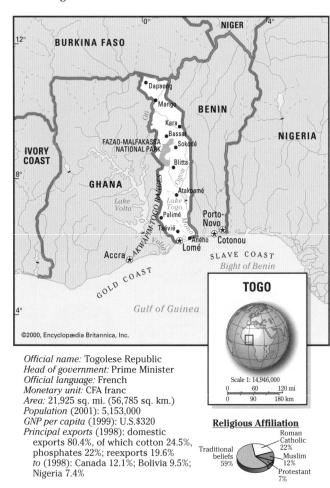

©2000, Encyclopædia Britannica, Inc.

Official name: Togolese Republic
Head of government: Prime Minister
Official language: French
Monetary unit: CFA franc
Area: 21,925 sq. mi. (56,785 sq. km.)
Population (2001): 5,153,000
GNP per capita (1999): U.S.$320
Principal exports (1998): domestic
exports 80.4%, of which cotton 24.5%,
phosphates 22%; reexports 19.6%
to (1998): Canada 12.1%; Bolivia 9.5%;
Nigeria 7.4%

TOGO

Scale 1: 14,946,000

| 0 | 60 | 120 mi |
| 0 | 90 | 180 km |

Religious Affiliation

Roman
Catholic
22%

Muslim
12%

Protestant
7%

Traditional
beliefs
59%

On April 27, 1960, Togo became independent from France under the current flag. Its stripes correspond to the administrative regions and symbolize that the population depends on the land for its sustenance (green) and its own labor for development (yellow). The red is for love, fidelity, and charity, while the white star is for purity and unity.

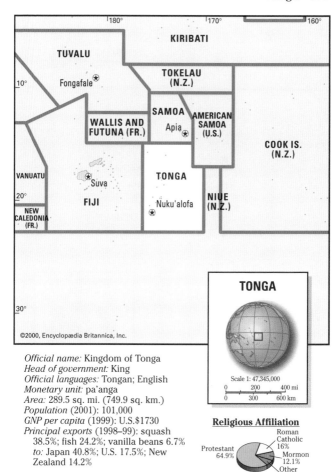

KIRIBATI

TUVALU

Fongafale ⊛

TOKELAU
(N.Z.)

SAMOA

WALLIS AND
FUTUNA (FR.)

Apia ⊛

AMERICAN
SAMOA
(U.S.)

COOK IS.
(N.Z.)

VANUATU

Suva ⊛

TONGA

FIJI

Nuku'alofa
⊛

NIUE
(N.Z.)

NEW
CALEDONIA
(FR.)

©2000, Encyclopædia Britannica, Inc.

TONGA

Scale 1: 47,345,000

| 0 | 200 | 400 mi |
| 0 | 300 | 600 km |

Official name: Kingdom of Tonga
Head of government: King
Official languages: Tongan; English
Monetary unit: pa'anga
Area: 289.5 sq. mi. (749.9 sq. km.)
Population (2001): 101,000
GNP per capita (1999): U.S.$1730
Principal exports (1998–99): squash
  38.5%; fish 24.2%; vanilla beans 6.7%
  to: Japan 40.8%; U.S. 17.5%; New
  Zealand 14.2%

Religious Affiliation

Roman
Catholic
16%

Protestant
64.9%

Mormon
12.1%

Other
7%

The colors red and white were popular in the Pacific long
before the arrival of Europeans. The Tonga constitution (Nov.
4, 1875) established the flag, which was created by King
George Tupou I with the advice of a missionary. The cross
was chosen as a symbol of the widespread Christian religion,
and the color red was related to the blood of Jesus.

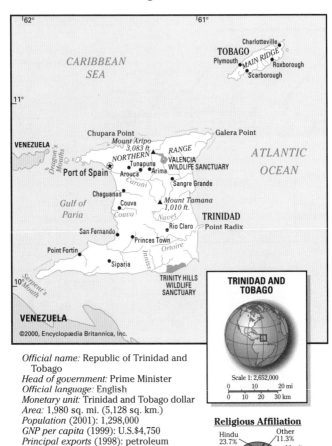

Official name: Republic of Trinidad and Tobago
Head of government: Prime Minister
Official language: English
Monetary unit: Trinidad and Tobago dollar
Area: 1,980 sq. mi. (5,128 sq. km.)
Population (2001): 1,298,000
GNP per capita (1999): U.S.$4,750
Principal exports (1998): petroleum 40.2%; to (1999): U.S. 39.3%; Caricom countries 26.1%, of which Jamaica 8.7%, Barbados 5.3%

Scale 1: 2,652,000
0   10   20 mi
0   10   20   30 km

Religious Affiliation

Hindu 23.7%
Other 11.3%
Muslim 5.9%
Roman Catholic 29.4%
Protestant 29.7%

Hoisted on independence day, Aug. 31, 1962, the flag symbolizes earth, water, and fire as well as past, present, and future. Black also is a symbol of unity, strength, and purpose. White recalls the equality and purity of the people and the sea that unites them. Red is for the sun, the vitality of the people and nation, friendliness, and courage.

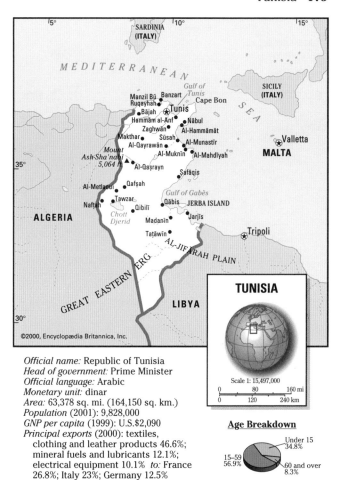

©2000, Encyclopædia Britannica, Inc.

Official name: Republic of Tunisia
Head of government: Prime Minister
Official language: Arabic
Monetary unit: dinar
Area: 63,378 sq. mi. (164,150 sq. km.)
Population (2001): 9,828,000
GNP per capita (1999): U.S.$2,090
Principal exports (2000): textiles,
   clothing and leather products 46.6%;
   mineral fuels and lubricants 12.1%;
   electrical equipment 10.1% *to:* France
   26.8%; Italy 23%; Germany 12.5%

TUNISIA

Scale 1: 15,497,000

0   80   160 mi
0   120   240 km

Age Breakdown

Under 15
34.8%

15–59
56.9%

60 and over
8.3%

The Tunisian flag, established in 1835, contains the crescent and moon, a symbol used by the Ottoman Empire but dating from the ancient Egyptians and Phoenicians. More as a cultural than a religious symbol, the crescent and star came to be associated with Islam because of its widespread adoption in Muslim nations.

Official name: Republic of Turkey
Head of government: Prime Minister
Official language: Turkish
Monetary unit: Turkish lira
Area: 300,948 sq. mi. (779,452 sq. km.)
Population (2001): 66,229,000
GNP per capita (1999): U.S.$2,900
Principal exports (2000): textiles and
   clothing 22.6%; electrical and
   electronic machinery 7.1%
   to: Germany 18.8%; U.S. 11.2%; Russia
   and Eastern Europe 10.8%

Scale 1: 24,576,000

| 0 | 100 | 200 mi |
| 0 | 150 | 300 km |

Religious Affiliation

Sunni Muslim 80%

Other Muslim 20%

In June 1793 the flag was established for the navy, although
its star had eight points instead of the current five (since
about 1844). This design was reconfirmed in 1936 following
the revolution led by Ataturk. Various myths are associated
with the symbolism of the red color and the star and crescent, but none really explains their origins.

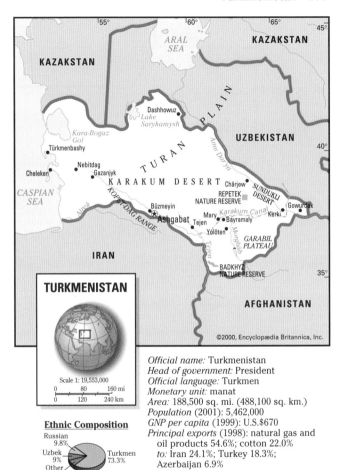

©2000, Encyclopædia Britannica, Inc.

TURKMENISTAN

Scale 1: 19,553,000

| 0 | 80 | 160 mi |
| 0 | 120 | 240 km |

Ethnic Composition

Russian 9.8%
Uzbek 9%
Other 7.9%
Turkmen 73.3%

Official name: Turkmenistan
Head of government: President
Official language: Turkmen
Monetary unit: manat
Area: 188,500 sq. mi. (488,100 sq. km.)
Population (2001): 5,462,000
GNP per capita (1999): U.S.$670
Principal exports (1998): natural gas and
  oil products 54.6%; cotton 22.0%
  to: Iran 24.1%; Turkey 18.3%;
  Azerbaijan 6.9%

The flag was introduced on Feb. 19, 1992. Its stripe contains intricate designs for five Turkmen tribes. Its green background is for Islam, and its crescent symbolizes faith in a bright future. The stars are for the human senses and the states of matter (liquid, solid, gas, crystal, and plasma). On Feb. 19, 1997, an olive wreath was added to the stripe.

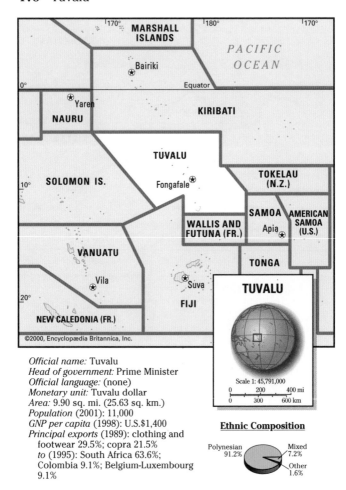

©2000, Encyclopædia Britannica, Inc.

Official name: Tuvalu
Head of government: Prime Minister
Official language: (none)
Monetary unit: Tuvalu dollar
Area: 9.90 sq. mi. (25.63 sq. km.)
Population (2001): 11,000
GNP per capita (1998): U.S.$1,400
Principal exports (1989): clothing and
  footwear 29.5%; copra 21.5%
  to (1995): South Africa 63.6%;
  Colombia 9.1%; Belgium-Luxembourg
  9.1%

TUVALU

Scale 1: 45,791,000

0   200   400 mi
0 300   600 km

Ethnic Composition

Polynesian 91.2%
Mixed 7.2%
Other 1.6%

On Oct. 1, 1978, three years after separating from the Gilbert
Islands, Tuvalu became independent under the current flag.
The stars represent the atolls and islands of the country. The
Union Jack recalls links with Britain and the Commonwealth.
Replaced by supporters of republicanism on Oct. 1, 1995, the
flag was reinstated on April 11, 1997.

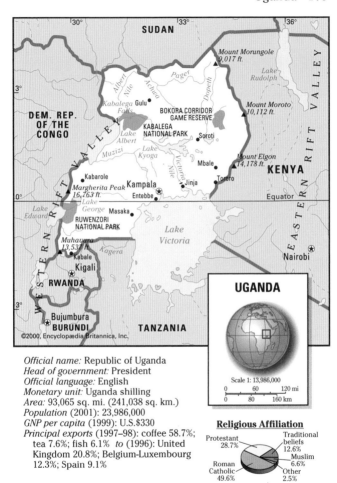

Official name: Republic of Uganda
Head of government: President
Official language: English
Monetary unit: Uganda shilling
Area: 93,065 sq. mi. (241,038 sq. km.)
Population (2001): 23,986,000
GNP per capita (1999): U.S.$330
Principal exports (1997–98): coffee 58.7%;
    tea 7.6%; fish 6.1% *to* (1996): United
    Kingdom 20.8%; Belgium-Luxembourg
    12.3%; Spain 9.1%

Scale 1: 13,986,000

0   60   120 mi
0   80   160 km

Religious Affiliation

Protestant 28.7%
Traditional beliefs 12.6%
Muslim 6.6%
Other 2.5%
Roman Catholic 49.6%

The crested crane symbol was selected by the British for Uganda. The flag, established for independence on Oct. 9, 1962, was based on the flag of the ruling Uganda People's Congress (which has three black-yellow-red stripes), with the addition of the crane in the center. Black stands for the people, yellow for sunshine, and red for brotherhood.

UKRAINE

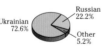

Scale 1: 19,690,000

| 0 | 80 | 160 mi |
| 0 | 120 | 240 km |

©2000, Encyclopædia Britannica, Inc.

Official name: Ukraine
Head of government: Prime Minister
Official language: Ukrainian
Monetary unit: hryvnya
Area: 233,100 sq. mi. (603,700 sq. km.)
Population (2001): 48,767,000
GNP per capita (1999): U.S.$840
Principal exports (1999): ferrous and
   nonferrous metals 39.1%; food and
   raw materials 11.4% *to:* Russia 19.2%;
   China 5.9%; Turkey 5.4%

Ethnic Composition

Ukrainian 72.6%
Russian 22.2%
Other 5.2%

The first national flag of Ukraine, adopted in 1848, had equal
stripes of yellow over blue and was based on the coat of arms
of the city of Lviv. In 1918 the stripes were reversed to reflect
the symbolism of blue skies over golden wheat fields. A red
Soviet banner flew from 1949, but it was replaced by the blue-
yellow bicolor on Jan. 28, 1992.

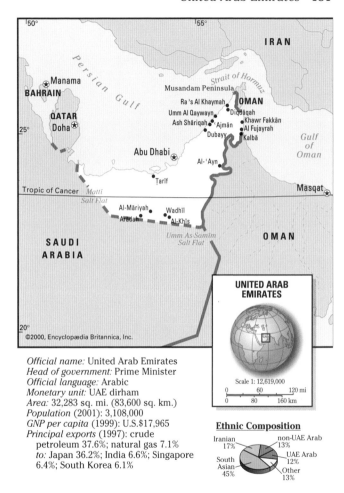

Official name: United Arab Emirates
Head of government: Prime Minister
Official language: Arabic
Monetary unit: UAE dirham
Area: 32,283 sq. mi. (83,600 sq. km.)
Population (2001): 3,108,000
GNP per capita (1999): U.S.$17,965
Principal exports (1997): crude
  petroleum 37.6%; natural gas 7.1%
  to: Japan 36.2%; India 6.6%; Singapore
  6.4%; South Korea 6.1%

UNITED ARAB EMIRATES

Scale 1: 12,619,000

| 0 | | 60 | | 120 mi |
| 0 | 80 | | 160 km | |

Ethnic Composition

Iranian 17%
non-UAE Arab 13%
UAE Arab 12%
Other 13%
South Asian 45%

On Dec. 2, 1971, six small Arab states formed the United Arab Emirates, and a seventh state joined on Feb. 11, 1972. The flag took its colors from the Arab Revolt flag of 1917. The colors are included in a 13th-century poem which speaks of green Arab lands defended in black battles by blood-red swords of Arabs whose deeds are pure white.

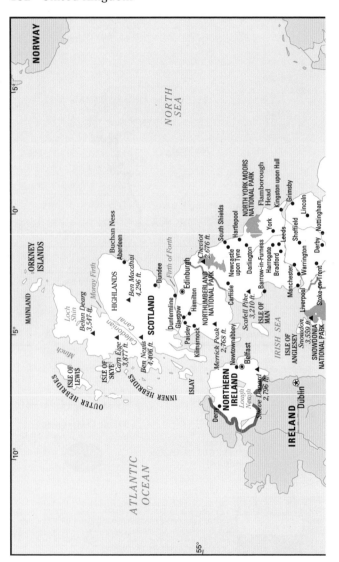

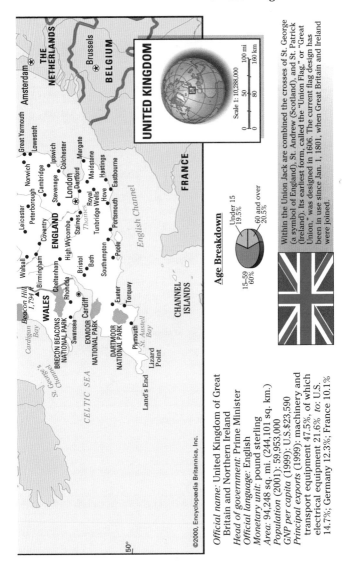

Age Breakdown

Under 15
19.5%

60 and over
20.5%

15–59
60%

Within the Union Jack are combined the crosses of St. George (a symbol of England), St. Andrew (Scotland), and St. Patrick (Ireland). Its earliest form, called the "Union Flag," or "Great Union," was designed in 1606. The current flag design has been in use since Jan. 1, 1801, when Great Britain and Ireland were joined.

Official name: United Kingdom of Great
Britain and Northern Ireland
Head of government: Prime Minister
Official language: English
Monetary unit: pound sterling
Area: 94,248 sq. mi. (244,101 sq. km.)
Population (2001): 59,953,000
GNP per capita (1999): U.S.$23,590
Principal exports (1999): machinery and
transport equipment 47.5%, of which
electrical equipment 21.6% *to:* U.S.
14.7%; Germany 12.3%; France 10.1%

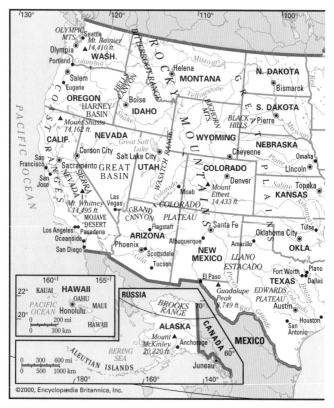

Official name: United States of America
Head of government: President
Official language: (none)
Monetary unit: dollar
Area: 3,675,031 sq. mi. (9,518,323 sq. km.)
Population (2001): 286,067,000
GNP per capita (2000): U.S.$35,040
Principal exports (1999): Machinery and transport equipment 47.1%;
   chemicals, chemical products 8.1%; food 5.3% *to:* Canada 23.9%;
   Mexico 12.2%; Japan 8.3%

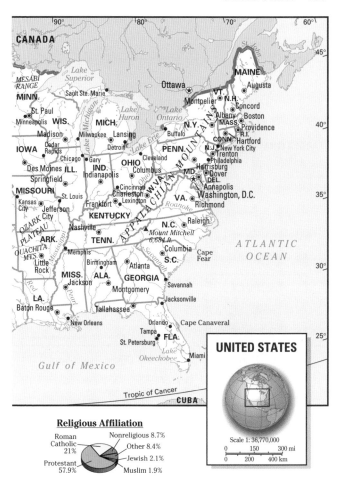

Religious Affiliation

- Roman Catholic 21%
- Protestant 57.9%
- Nonreligious 8.7%
- Other 8.4%
- Jewish 2.1%
- Muslim 1.9%

UNITED STATES

Scale 1: 36,770,000

0   150   300 mi
0   200   400 km

The Stars and Stripes has white stars corresponding to the states of the union (50 since July 4, 1960), as well as stripes for the 13 original states. The first unofficial national flag, hoisted on Jan. 1, 1776, had the British Union flag in the canton. The official flag dates to June 14, 1777; its design was standardized in 1912 and 1934.

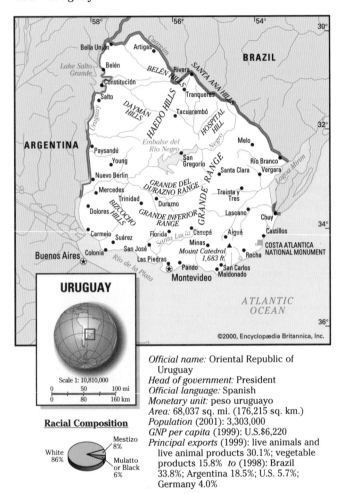

©2000, Encyclopædia Britannica, Inc.

URUGUAY

Scale 1: 10,810,000

| 0 | 50 | 100 mi |
| 0 | 80 | 160 km |

Racial Composition

White 86%

Mestizo 8%

Mulatto or Black 6%

Official name: Oriental Republic of Uruguay
Head of government: President
Official language: Spanish
Monetary unit: peso uruguayo
Area: 68,037 sq. mi. (176,215 sq. km.)
Population (2001): 3,303,000
GNP per capita (1999): U.S.$6,220
Principal exports (1999): live animals and live animal products 30.1%; vegetable products 15.8% *to* (1998): Brazil 33.8%; Argentina 18.5%; U.S. 5.7%; Germany 4.0%

The flag adopted on Dec. 16, 1828, combined symbols of Argentina with the flag pattern of the United States. It was last altered on July 11, 1830. On the canton is the golden "Sun of May," which was seen on May 25, 1810, as a favorable omen for anti-Spanish forces in Buenos Aires, Arg. The stripes are for the original Uruguayan departments.

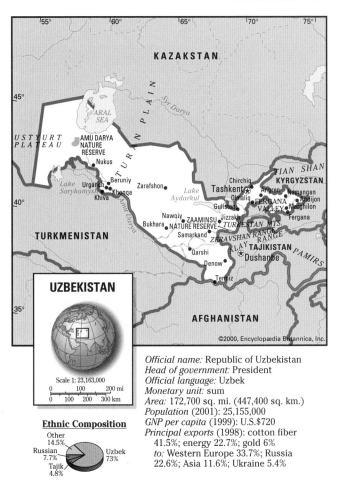

Ethnic Composition

Other 14.5%
Russian 7.7%
Tajik 4.8%
Uzbek 73%

Scale 1: 23,163,000
0   100   200 mi
0 100 200 300 km

Official name: Republic of Uzbekistan
Head of government: President
Official language: Uzbek
Monetary unit: sum
Area: 172,700 sq. mi. (447,400 sq. km.)
Population (2001): 25,155,000
GNP per capita (1999): U.S.$720
Principal exports (1998): cotton fiber 41.5%; energy 22.7%; gold 6%
  to: Western Europe 33.7%; Russia 22.6%; Asia 11.6%; Ukraine 5.4%

The flag of the former Soviet republic was legalized on Nov. 18, 1991. The blue is for water but also recalls the 14th-century ruler Timur. The green is for nature, fertility, and new life. The white is for peace and purity; red is for human life force. The stars are for the months and the Zodiac, while the moon is for the new republic and Islam.

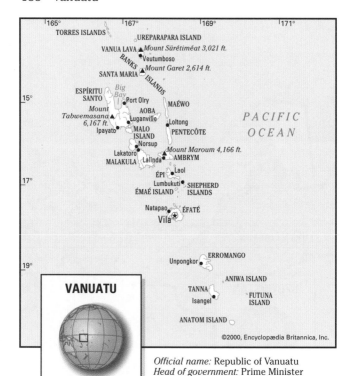

Official name: Republic of Vanuatu
Head of government: Prime Minister
Official languages: Bislama; French;
English
Monetary unit: vatu
Area: 4,707 sq. mi. (12,190 sq. km.)
Population (2001): 195,000
GNP per capita (1999): U.S.$1,180
Principal exports (1997): copra 49.0%;
timber 12.3%; beef 10.2% *to:* European
Union 45.9%; Bangladesh 12.6%;
Japan 10.4%

Religious Affiliation

Roman Catholic 14.5%
Anglican 14%
Seventh-day Adventist 8.2%
Presbyterian 35.8%
Other 27.5%

The flag was hoisted upon independence from France and Britain, on July 30, 1980. Black is for the soil and the people, green for vegetation, and red for local religious traditions such as the sacrifice of pigs. On the triangle are two crossed branches and a full-round pig's tusk, a holy symbol. The horizontal "Y" is for peace and Christianity.

CARIBBEAN SEA

©2000, Encyclopædia Britannica, Inc.

VENEZUELA

Scale 1: 24,004,000

0   100   200 mi

0   150   300 km

Ethnic Composition

White 21%
Mestizo 67%
Black 10%
Indian 2%

Official name: Bolivarean Republic of Venezuela
Head of government: President
Official language: Spanish
Monetary unit: bolivar
Area: 353,841 sq. mi. (916,445 sq. km.)
Population (2001): 24,632,000
GNP per capita (1999): U.S.$3,680
Principal exports (1998): crude petroleum and petroleum products 69.8%; basic and precious metals 6.6% *to:* U.S. 48.5%; Andean Pact countries 11.1%; Canada 2.1%

The Venezuelan flag was adopted on March 18, 1864. Yellow was originally said to stand for the gold of the New World, separated by the blue of the Atlantic Ocean from "bloody Spain," symbolized by red. The stars are for the original seven provinces. In the upper hoist corner, the national arms are added to flags which serve the government.

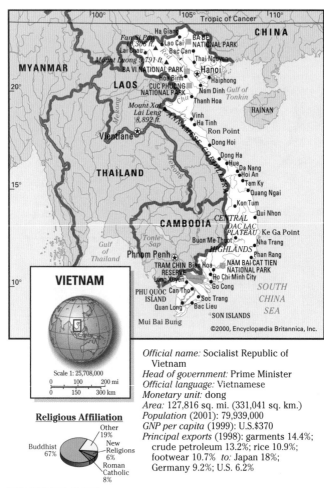

©2000, Encyclopædia Britannica, Inc.

Scale 1: 25,708,000

| 0 | 100 | 200 mi |
| 0 | 150 | 300 km |

Religious Affiliation

Buddhist 67%

Other 19%

New Religions 6%

Roman Catholic 8%

Official name: Socialist Republic of Vietnam
Head of government: Prime Minister
Official language: Vietnamese
Monetary unit: dong
Area: 127,816 sq. mi. (331,041 sq. km.)
Population (2001): 79,939,000
GNP per capita (1999): U.S.$370
Principal exports (1998): garments 14.4%; crude petroleum 13.2%; rice 10.9%; footwear 10.7% *to:* Japan 18%; Germany 9.2%; U.S. 6.2%

On Sept. 29, 1945, Vietnamese communists adopted the red flag in use today. On July 4, 1976, following the defeat of the American-sponsored government in the south, the flag became official throughout the nation. The three points of the star are said to stand for the proletariat, peasantry, military, intellectuals, and petty bourgeoisie.

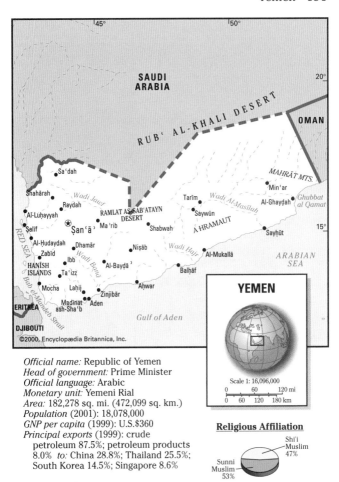

©2000, Encyclopædia Britannica, Inc.

Official name: Republic of Yemen
Head of government: Prime Minister
Official language: Arabic
Monetary unit: Yemeni Rial
Area: 182,278 sq. mi. (472,099 sq. km.)
Population (2001): 18,078,000
GNP per capita (1999): U.S.$360
Principal exports (1999): crude
petroleum 87.5%; petroleum products
8.0% *to:* China 28.8%; Thailand 25.5%;
South Korea 14.5%; Singapore 8.6%

Scale 1: 16,096,000

| 0 | 60 | 120 mi |
| 0 | 60 | 120 | 180 km |

Religious Affiliation

Shi'i
Muslim
47%

Sunni
Muslim
53%

Revolutions broke out in North Yemen in 1962 and in South
Yemen in 1967. In 1990 the two states unified, and that May 23
the tricolor was adopted, its design influenced by the former
United Arab Republic. The black is for the dark days of the
past, white for the bright future, and red for the blood shed
for independence and unity.

©2000, Encyclopædia Britannica, Inc.

Official name: Federal Republic of
Yugoslavia (Serbia and Montenegro)
Head of government: Prime Minister
Official language: Serbian
Monetary unit: Yugoslav dinar
Area: 39,449 sq. mi. (102,173 sq. km.)
Population (2001): 10,677,000
GNP per capita (1999): U.S.$1,742
Principal exports (1998): manufactured
goods 38.5%; machinery and transport
equipment 14.2% *to:* Italy 11.6%;
Macedonia 10.8%; Germany 8.9%;
Russia 8.6%

YUGOSLAVIA

Scale 1: 8,452,000

0   40   80 mi

0   60   120 km

Ethnic Composition

Serb
62.6%

Albanian
16.5%

Other
15.9%

Montenegrin
5%

The Pan-Slavic colors (blue, white, and red) have been in the
flag from Oct. 31, 1918. A central star was introduced after
World War II, under the leadership of Josip Broz Tito. In 1991
the country broke up, leaving only Serbia and Montenegro
united, and the constitution of April 27, 1992, maintained the
tricolor but omitted the star.

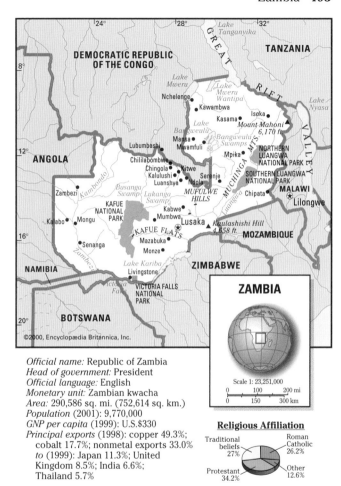

Official name: Republic of Zambia
Head of government: President
Official language: English
Monetary unit: Zambian kwacha
Area: 290,586 sq. mi. (752,614 sq. km.)
Population (2001): 9,770,000
GNP per capita (1999): U.S.$330
Principal exports (1998): copper 49.3%;
  cobalt 17.7%; nonmetal exports 33.0%
  to (1999): Japan 11.3%; United
  Kingdom 8.5%; India 6.6%;
  Thailand 5.7%

ZAMBIA

Scale 1: 23,251,000

0   100   200 mi
0   150   300 km

Religious Affiliation

Traditional beliefs 27%
Roman Catholic 26.2%
Other 12.6%
Protestant 34.2%

Zambia separated from Britain on Oct. 24, 1964. Its flag, based on the flag of the United National Independence Party, has a green background for agriculture, red for the freedom struggle, black for the African people, and orange for copper. The orange eagle appeared in the colonial coat of arms of 1939. It symbolizes freedom and success.

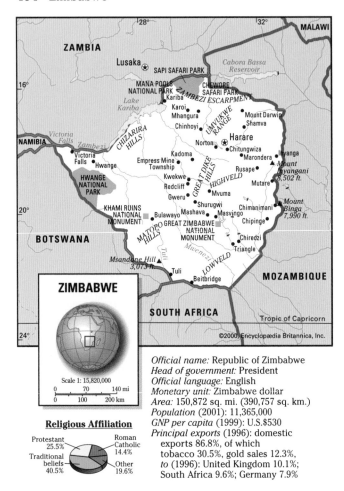

Official name: Republic of Zimbabwe
Head of government: President
Official language: English
Monetary unit: Zimbabwe dollar
Area: 150,872 sq. mi. (390,757 sq. km.)
Population (2001): 11,365,000
GNP per capita (1999): U.S.$530
Principal exports (1996): domestic
  exports 86.8%, of which
  tobacco 30.5%, gold sales 12.3%,
  to (1996): United Kingdom 10.1%;
  South Africa 9.6%; Germany 7.9%

Religious Affiliation

Protestant 25.5%
Roman Catholic 14.4%
Traditional beliefs 40.5%
Other 19.6%

ZIMBABWE
Scale 1: 15,820,000
0   70   140 mi
0   100   200 km

©2000, Encyclopædia Britannica, Inc.

On April 18, 1980, elections brought the black majority to power under the current flag. The black color is for the ethnic majority, while red is for blood, green for agriculture, yellow for mineral wealth, and white for peace and progress. At the hoist is a red star (for socialism) and the ancient "Zimbabwe Bird" from the Great Zimbabwe ruins.

List of
Selected Cities

AFGHANISTAN ....pg. 1

Adraskan	33°39' N,	062°16' E
Almār	35°50' N,	064°32' E
Anār Darreh	32°46' N,	061°39' E
Andkhvoy	36°56' N,	065°08' E
Āqchah	36°56' N,	066°11' E
Baghlān	36°13' N,	068°46' E
Bāghrān	33°04' N,	065°05' E
Bagrām	34°58' N,	069°17' E
Bālā Bolūk	32°38' N,	062°28' E
Bāmīān (Bāmyān)	34°50' N,	067°50' E
Barg-e Matāl	35°40' N,	071°21' E
Bāzār-e Panjvā'i	31°32' N,	065°28' E
Chaghcharān	34°31' N,	065°15' E
Chahār Borjak	30°17' N,	062°03' E
Chakhānsūr	31°10' N,	062°04' E
Delārām	32°11' N,	063°25' E
Do Qal'eh	32°08' N,	061°27' E
Dowlatābād	36°26' N,	064°55' E
Dūrāj	37°56' N,	070°43' E
Eslām Qal'eh	34°40' N,	061°04' E
Farāh (Farrah, Ferah)	32°22' N,	062°07' E
Feyzābād (Faizābād)	37°06' N,	070°34' E
Ghaznī	33°33' N,	068°26' E
Ghūrīān	34°21' N,	061°30' E
Gīzāb	33°23' N,	066°16' E
Golestān	32°37' N,	063°39' E
Golrān	35°06' N,	061°41' E
Gowmal Kalay	32°31' N,	068°51' E
Herāt (Harāt)	34°20' N,	062°12' E
Jabal os Sarāj	35°07' N,	069°14' E
Jalālābād	34°26' N,	070°28' E
Jaldak	31°58' N,	066°43' E
Jawand	35°04' N,	064°09' E
Kabul	34°31' N,	069°12' E
Kajakī	32°16' N,	065°03' E
Kandahār (Qandahār)	31°35' N,	065°45' E
Khadīr	33°55' N,	065°56' E
Khānābād	36°41' N,	069°07' E
Kholm	36°42' N,	067°41' E
Khowst	33°22' N,	069°57' E
Kondūz (Qonduz)	36°45' N,	068°51' E
Koshk	34°57' N,	062°15' E
Kūhestānāt	35°49' N,	065°52' E
Lashkar Gāh (Bust)	31°35' N,	064°21' E
Maḥmūd-e Rāqī	35°01' N,	069°20' E
Mazār-e Sharif	36°42' N,	067°06' E
Nāvor	33°53' N,	067°57' E
Orgūn	32°57' N,	069°11' E
Orūzgān	32°56' N,	066°38' E
Owbeh	34°22' N,	063°10' E
Palālak	30°14' N,	062°54' E
Pol-e 'Alam	33°59' N,	069°02' E
Porchaman	33°08' N,	063°51' E
Qalāt	32°07' N,	066°54' E
Qal'eh-ye Now	34°59' N,	063°08' E
Sar-e Pol	36°14' N,	065°55' E
Sayghān	35°11' N,	067°42' E
Shāh Jūy	32°31' N,	067°25' E
Shahrak	34°06' N,	064°18' E
Shīndand (Sabzevār)	33°18' N,	062°08' E
Shīr Khān	37°11' N,	068°36' E
Yangī Qal'eh	37°28' N,	069°36' E
Zaranj	30°58' N,	061°53' E

ALBANIA ....pg. 2

Berat	40°42' N,	019°57' E
Burrel	41°36' N,	020°01' E
Cërrik	41°02' N,	019°57' E
Çorovodë	40°30' N,	020°13' E
Durrës	41°19' N,	019°26' E
Elbasan	41°06' N,	020°05' E
Ersekë	40°22' N,	020°40' E
Fier	40°43' N,	019°34' E
Gjirokastër	40°05' N,	020°10' E
Gramsh	40°52' N,	020°11' E
Himarë	40°07' N,	019°44' E
Kavajë	41°11' N,	019°33' E
Korçë (Koritsa)	40°37' N,	020°46' E
Krujë	41°30' N,	019°48' E
Kukës	42°05' N,	020°24' E
Laç	41°38' N,	019°43' E
Lezhë	41°47' N,	019°39' E
Librazhd	41°11' N,	020°19' E
Lushnje	40°56' N,	019°42' E
Patos	40°38' N,	019°39' E
Përmet	40°14' N,	020°21' E
Peshkopi	41°41' N,	020°25' E
Pogradec	40°54' N,	020°39' E
Pukë	42°03' N,	019°54' E
Rrëshen	41°47' N,	019°54' E
Sarandë	39°52' N,	020°00' E
Shkodër (Scutari)	42°05' N,	019°30' E
Tepelenë	40°19' N,	020°01' E
Tiranë (Tirana)	41°20' N,	019°50' E
Vlorë	40°27' N,	019°30' E
Vorë	41°23' N,	019°40' E

ALGERIA ....pg. 3

Adrar (Timmi)	27°54' N,	000°17'W
Aïn Beïda (Daoud)	35°48' N,	007°24' E
Algiers (or Al-Jaza'ir)	36°47' N,	003°03' E
Annaba (Bone)	36°54' N,	007°46' E
Batna	35°34' N,	006°11' E
Béchar (Colomb-Bechar)	31°37' N,	002°13' W
Bejaïa (Bougie)	36°45' N,	005°05' E
Beni Abbès	30°08' N,	002°10' W
Biskra (Beskra)	34°51' N,	005°44' E
Bordj Bou Arréridj	36°04' N,	004°47' E

196   List of Selected Cities

Chlef (El-Asnam or
Orleansville) . . . . 36°10' N, 001°20' E
Constantine (Qacentina) . . 36°22' N, 006°37' E
Djelfa . . . . 34°40' N, 003°15' E
El-Oued . . . . 33°20' N, 006°53' E
Ghardaïa . . . . 32°29' N, 003°40' E
In Salah (Aïn Salah) . . . . . . 27°13' N, 002°28' E
Kenadsa . . . . 31°34' N, 002°26' E
Médéa (Lemdiyya) . . . . 36°16' N, 002°45' E
Mostaganem
(Mestghanem) . . . . 35°56' N, 000°05' E
Oran (Wahran) . . . . 35°42' N, 000°38' W
Ouargla (Warqla) . . . . 31°57' N, 005°20' E
Saïda . . . . 34°50' N, 000°09' E
Sétif (Stif) . . . . 36°12' N, 005°24' E
Sidi Bel Abbés . . . . 35°12' N, 000°38' W
Skikda (Philippeville) . . . . . 36°52' N, 006°54' E
Souk-Ahras . . . . 36°17' N, 007°57' E
Tamanrasset
(Fort Laperrine) . . . . 22°47' N, 005°31' W
Tébessa (Tbessa or
Theveste) . . . . 35°24' N, 008°07' E
Tiaret
(Tihert or Tagdempt) . . . 35°22' N, 001°19' E
Tindouf . . . . 27°42' N, 008°09' W
Tlemcen (Tlemsen) . . . . . . 34°52' N, 001°19' W
Touggourt . . . . 33°06' N, 006°04' E

ANDORRA . . . . pg. 4

Andorra la Vella . . . . 42°30' N, 001°30' E
Canillo . . . . 42°34' N, 001°35' E
Encamp . . . . 42°32' N, 001°35' E
La Massana . . . . 42°33' N, 001°31' E
Les Escaldes . . . . 42°30' N, 001°32' E
Ordino . . . . 42°34' N, 001°30' E
Sant Julià de Lòria . . . . 42°28' N, 001°30' E
Soldeu . . . . 42°35' N, 001°40' E

ANGOLA . . . . pg. 5

Benguela (São Félipe
de Benguela) . . . . 12°35' S, 013°24' E
Caála (Robert Williams) . . . 12°51' S, 015°34' E
Cabinda . . . . 05°33' S, 012°12' E
Cacolo . . . . 10°08' S, 019°16' E
Caconda . . . . 13°44' S, 015°04' E
Caluquembe . . . . 13°52' S, 014°26' E
Camacupa (General
Machado) . . . . 12°01' S, 017°29' E
Cangamba . . . . 13°41' S, 019°52' E
Catumbela . . . . 12°26' S, 013°33' E
Cubal . . . . 13°02' S, 014°15' E
Cuchi . . . . 14°39' S, 016°54' E
Damba . . . . 06°41' S, 015°08' E
Gabela . . . . 10°51' S, 014°22' E
Ganda (Mariano
Machado) . . . . 13°01' S, 014°38' E
Huambo (Nova Lisboa) . . . 12°46' S, 015°44' E
Kuito (Silva Porto) . . . . 12°23' S, 016°56' E

Lobito . . . . 12°21' S, 013°33' E
Luanda (São Paulo de
Luanda) . . . . 08°49' S, 013°15' E
Luau . . . . 10°42' S, 022°14' E
Lubango (Sá da Bandeira) . 14°55' S, 013°30' E
Lucapa . . . . 08°25' S, 020°45' E
Luena (Vila Luso) . . . . 11°47' S, 019°55' E
Malanje . . . . 09°32' S, 016°20' E
Mavinga . . . . 15°48' S, 020°21' E
M'banza Congo
(São Salvador) . . . . 06°16' S, 014°15' E
Menongue (Serpa Pinto) . . 14°40' S, 017°42' E
Namibe (Moçâmedes,
or Mossamedes) . . . . 15°10' S, 012°09' E
N'dalatando
(Dalatando, or Salazar) . . 09°18' S, 014°55' E
Negage . . . . 07°46' S, 015°16' E
Nóqui . . . . 05°51' S, 013°26' E
Ondjiva . . . . 17°04' S, 015°44' E
Porto Amboin . . . . 10°44' S, 013°45' E
Quimbele . . . . 06°31' S, 016°13' E
Saurimo
(Henrique de Carvalho) . 09°39' S, 020°24' E
Soyo . . . . 06°08' S, 012°22' E
Sumbe (Novo Redondo) . . . 11°12' S, 013°50' E
Tombua (Porto
Alexandre) . . . . 15°48' S, 011°51' E
Uige (Carmona) . . . . 07°37' S, 015°03' E
Waku Kungo
(Santa Comba) . . . . 11°21' S, 015°07' E

ANTIGUA AND
BARBUDA . . . . pg. 6

Codrington . . . . 17°38' N, 061°50' W
St. John's . . . . 17°06' N, 061°51' W

ARGENTINA . . . . . . pg. 7

Avellaneda . . . . 29°07' S, 059°40' W
Bahía Blanca . . . . 38°43' S, 062°17' W
Buenos Aires . . . . 34°36' S, 058°27' W
Comodoro Rivadavia . . . . . 45°52' S, 067°30' W
Concordia . . . . 31°24' S, 058°02' W
Córdoba . . . . 31°24' S, 064°11' W
Corrientes . . . . 27°28' S, 058°50' W
Formosa . . . . 26°11' S, 058°11' W
La Plata . . . . 34°55' S, 057°57' W
La Rioja . . . . 29°26' S, 066°51' W
Luján . . . . 34°34' S, 059°07' W
Mar del Plata . . . . 38°00' S, 057°33' W
Mercedes . . . . 33°40' S, 065°28' W
Neuquén . . . . 38°57' S, 068°04' W
Paraná . . . . 31°44' S, 060°32' W
Posadas . . . . 27°23' S, 055°53' W
Rawson . . . . 43°18' S, 065°06' W
Resistencia . . . . 27°27' S, 058°59' W
Río Gallegos . . . . 51°38' S, 069°13' W

Salta................... 24°47' S, 065°25' W
San Miguel de Tucumán.. 26°49' S, 065°13' W
San Rafael............. 34°36' S, 068°20' W
Santa Fe.............. 31°38' S, 060°42' W
Santa Rosa............ 36°37' S, 064°17' W
Santiago del Estero...... 27°47' S, 064°16' W
Tandil .... 37°19' S, 059°09' W
Tigre .... 34°25' S, 058°34' W
Ushuaia .... 54°48' S, 068°18' W
Viedma .... 40°48' S, 063°00' W
Villa María............ 32°25' S, 063°15' W

ARMENIA.........pg. 8

Abovyan .... 40°15' N, 044°35' E
Alaverdi.............. 41°08' N, 044°39' E
Ararat .... 39°50' N, 044°42' E
Artashat (Artaxata) ..... 39°57' N, 044°33' E
Artik................. 40°37' N, 043°59' E
Charentsavan .... 40°24' N, 044°38' E
Dilijan .... 40°44' N, 044°52' E
Ejmiadzin (Echmiadzin).. 40°10' N, 044°18' E
Goris (Geryusy) .... 39°30' N, 046°23' E
Gyumri (Kumayri,
   Alexandropol,
   or Leninakan) .... 40°48' N, 043°50' E
Hoktemberyan
   (Oktemberyan) .... 40°09' N, 044°02' E
Hrazdan (Razdan)....... 40°29' N, 044°46' E
Ijevan................ 40°51' N, 045°09' E
Kamo (Nor-Bayazet)..... 40°21' N, 045°08' E
Kapan................ 39°12' N, 046°24' E
Sevan .... 40°32' N, 044°56' E
Spitak................ 40°49' N, 044°16' E
Stepanavan .... 41°01' N, 044°23' E
Vanadzor............. 40°48' N, 044°30' E
Yerevan (Erevan) .... 40°11' N, 044°30' E

AUSTRALIA ......pg. 9

Adelaide .... 34°56' S, 138°36' E
Alice Springs........... 23°42' S, 133°53' E
Bowral............... 34°28' S, 150°25' E
Brisbane .... 27°30' S, 153°01' E
Broken Hill .... 31°57' S, 141°26' E
Bunbury .... 33°20' S, 115°38' E
Bundaberg............ 24°51' S, 152°21' E
Cairns............... 16°55' S, 145°46' E
Canberra............. 35°20' S, 149°10' E
Darwin............... 12°28' S, 130°50' E
Devonport............ 41°10' S, 146°21' E
Geelong.............. 38°09' S, 144°21' E
Geraldton .... 28°46' S, 114°36' E
Gladstone .... 23°51' S, 151°15' E
Gold Coast............ 28°06' S, 153°27' E
Goulburn .... 34°45' S, 149°43' E
Hobart............... 42°55' S, 147°20' E
Kalgoorlie-Boulder ...... 30°45' S, 121°28' E
Lismore .... 28°48' S, 153°16' E
Mackay .... 21°09' S, 149°12' E

Maryborough .... 25°32' S, 152°42' E
Melbourne............. 37°50' S, 145°00' E
Mount Gambier........ 37°50' S, 140°46' E
Mount Isa .... 20°44' S, 139°30' E
Newcastle .... 32°55' S, 151°45' E
Perth .... 31°56' S, 115°50' E
Port Macquarie........ 31°26' S, 152°55' E
Rockingham .... 32°17' S, 115°43' E
Sydney............... 33°53' S, 151°12' E
Toowoomba .... 27°33' S, 151°58' E
Warrnambool .... 38°23' S, 142°29' E
Whyalla .... 33°02' S, 137°35' E
Wollongong........... 34°25' S, 150°54' E

AUSTRIA ....pg. 10

Amstetten .... 48°07' N, 014°52' E
Baden .... 48°01' N, 016°14' E
Branau [am Inn] .... 48°16' N, 013°02' E
Bregenz .... 47°30' N, 009°46' E
Bruck [an der Leitha].... 47°25' N, 015°17' E
Dornbirn .... 47°25' N, 009°44' E
Eisenstadt .... 47°51' N, 016°31' E
Feldkirch .... 47°14' N, 009°36' E
Freistadt .... 48°30' N, 014°30' E
Fürstenfeld .... 47°03' N, 016°05' E
Gmünd............... 48°46' N, 014°59' E
Gmunden .... 47°55' N, 013°48' E
Graz................. 47°04' N, 015°27' E
Hallein .... 47°41' N, 013°06' E
Innsbruck .... 47°16' N, 011°24' E
Kapfenberg .... 47°26' N, 015°18' E
Klagenfurt .... 46°38' N, 014°18' E
Klosterneuburg......... 48°18' N, 016°19' E
Köflach .... 47°04' N, 015°05' E
Krems an der Donau..... 48°25' N, 015°36' E
Kufstein .... 47°35' N, 012°10' E
Laa [an der Thaya]...... 48°43' N, 016°23' E
Landeck.............. 47°08' N, 010°34' E
Leibnitz .... 46°46' N, 015°32' E
Leoben (Donawitz)...... 47°23' N, 015°06' E
Leonding .... 48°16' N, 014°15' E
Liezen .... 47°34' N, 014°14' E
Linz .... 48°18' N, 014°18' E
Neunkirchen .... 47°43' N, 016°05' E
Oberwart............. 47°17' N, 016°12' E
Radenthein .... 46°48' N, 013°43' E
Salzburg.............. 47°48' N, 013°02' E
Sankt Pölten .... 48°12' N, 015°38' E
Schrems.............. 48°47' N, 015°04' E
Steyr .... 48°03' N, 014°25' E
Telfs................. 47°18' N, 011°04' E
Ternitz............... 47°43' N, 016°02' E
Traun................ 48°13' N, 014°14' E
Trofaiach............. 47°25' N, 015°00' E
Vienna (Wien)......... 48°12' N, 016°22' E
Villach .... 46°36' N, 013°50' E
Vöcklabruck .... 48°01' N, 013°39' E
Völkermarkt .... 46°39' N, 014°38' E
Weiner Neustadt....... 47°48' N, 016°15' E
Wolfsberg .... 46°50' N, 014°50' E

AZERBAIJAN ..... pg. 11

Ağcabädi . . . . 40°02' N, 047°28' E
Ağdam . . . . 39°59' N, 046°57' E
Ağstafa. . . . . 41°07' N, 045°27' E
Ağsu. . . . . 40°34' N, 048°24' E
Äli-Bayramli. . . . . 39°55' N, 048°56' E
Astara . . . . 38°26' N, 048°53' E
Baku (Bakı) . . . . 40°23' N, 049°51' E
Balakän . . . . 41°43' N, 046°24' E
Bärdä. . . . . 40°24' N, 047°10' E
Daškäsän . . . . 40°32' N, 046°07' E
Däväçi . . . . 41°12' N, 048°59' E
Füzuli. . . . . 39°36' N, 047°09' E
Gäncä (Gyandzha,
   Gandzha, Kirovabad,
   or Yelizavetpol). . . . . . . 40°41' N, 046°22' E
Göyçay. . . . . 40°39' N, 047°45' E
İmişli . . . . 40°47' N, 048°09' E
İsmayıllı. . . . . 40°47' N, 048°09' E
Kürdämir . . . . 40°21' N, 048°11' E
Länkäran . . . . 38°45' N, 048°50' E
Masallı . . . . 39°03' N, 048°40' E
Mingäçevir (Mingechaur). . 40°45' N, 047°03' E
Nakhichevan (Naxcivan) . . 39°12' N, 045°24' E
Neftçala . . . . 39°23' N, 049°16' E
Ordubad . . . . 38°54' N, 046°01' E
Qäbälä (Kutkashen) . . . . . 40°58' N, 047°52' E
Qax . . . . 41°25' N, 046°55' E
Qazax. . . . . 41°05' N, 045°22' E
Qazimämmäd . . . . 40°03' N, 048°56' E
Şäki (Sheki, Nukha). . . . . . 41°12' N, 047°12' E
Salyan . . . . 39°35' N, 048°59' E
Şamaxı . . . . 40°38' N, 048°39' E
Şämkir . . . . 40°50' N, 046°02' E
Siyäzän . . . . 41°04' N, 049°02' E
Sumqayıt . . . . 40°36' N, 049°38' E
Tovuz. . . . . 40°59' N, 045°36' E
Ucar . . . . 40°31' N, 047°39' E
Xaçmaz . . . . 41°28' N, 048°48' E
Xankändi (Stepanakert) . . . 39°50' N, 046°46' E
Xudat. . . . . 41°38' N, 048°41' E
Yevlax . . . . 40°37' N, 047°09' E
Zaqatala. . . . . 41°38' N, 046°39' E

BAHAMAS, THE . pg. 12

Dunmore Town. . . . . 25°30' N, 076°39' W
Freeport . . . . 26°32' N, 078°42' W
Matthew Town . . . . 20°57' N, 073°40' W
Nassau. . . . . 25°05' N, 077°21' W
Old Bight . . . . 24°15' N, 075°21' W
West End. . . . . 26°41' N, 078°58' W

BAHRAIN . . . . pg. 13

Ad Dūr. . . . . 25°59' N, 050°37' E
Al-Ḥadd . . . . 26°15' N, 050°39' E

Al Jasrah . . . . 26°10' N, 050°27' E
Al Mālikīyah . . . . 37°10' N, 042°08' E
Al-Muharraq . . . . 26°16' N, 050°37' E
Ar-Rifa' . . . . 26°07' N, 050°33' E
Ar-Rifa'ash-Sharqī. . . . . . . 26°07' N, 050°34' E
Ar-Rumaythah. . . . . 25°55' N, 050°33' E
'Awāli. . . . . 26°05' N, 050°33' E
Bārbaār . . . . 26°14' N, 050°29' E
Madīnat Ḥamad. . . . . 26°08' N, 050°30' E
Madīnat 'Īsā . . . . 26°10' N, 050°33' E
Manama. . . . . 26°13' N, 050°35' E

BANGLADESH . . . . pg. 14

Azmiriganj. . . . . 24°33' N, 091°14' E
Bāgerhāt . . . . 22°40' N, 089°48' E
Bājitpur . . . . 24°13' N, 090°57' E
Barisāl . . . . 22°42' N, 090°22' E
Bhairab Bāzār . . . . 24°04' N, 090°58' E
Bogra. . . . . 24°51' N, 089°22' E
Brāhmanbāria. . . . . 23°59' N, 091°07' E
Chālna Port
   (Mongla Port) . . . . 22°28' N, 089°35' E
Chāndpur . . . . 23°13' N, 090°39' E
Chaumuhāni
   (Chowmohani). . . . . 22°56' N, 091°07' E
Chittagong. . . . . 22°20' N, 091°50' E
Chuadānga . . . . 23°38' N, 088°51' E
Comilla (Kumillā) . . . . 23°27' N, 091°12' E
Cox's Bāzār . . . . 21°26' N, 091°59' E
Dhaka (Dacca or Dhakal) . . 23°43' N, 090°25' E
Dinājpur . . . . 25°38' N, 088°38' E
Farīdpur . . . . 23°36' N, 089°50' E
Gopālpur . . . . 24°50' N, 090°06' E
Ishurdi (Ishurda) . . . . 24°08' N, 089°05' E
Jamālpur . . . . 24°55' N, 089°56' E
Jessore . . . . 23°10' N, 089°13' E
Jhenida . . . . 23°33' N, 089°10' E
Khulna . . . . 22°48' N, 089°33' E
Kishorganj. . . . . 24°26' N, 090°46' E
Kurigrām . . . . 25°49' N, 089°39' E
Kushtia . . . . 23°55' N, 089°07' E
Lākshām . . . . 23°14' N, 091°08' E
Lakshmipur . . . . 22°57' N, 090°50' E
Lālmanir Hāt
   (Lalmonirhat) . . . . 25°54' N, 089°27' E
Mādārīpur . . . . 23°10' N, 090°12' E
Mymensingh (Nasirābād). . 24°45' N, 090°24' E
Naogaon . . . . 24°47' N, 088°56' E
Nārāyanganj . . . . 23°37' N, 090°30' E
Narsinghdi (Narsingdi). . . . 23°55' N, 090°43' E
Nawābganj. . . . . 24°36' N, 088°17' E
Noākhāli (Sudhárám) . . . . 22°49' N, 091°06' E
Pābna (Pubna) . . . . 24°00' N, 089°15' E
Patuākhāli . . . . 22°21' N, 090°21' E
Rājshāhi. . . . . 24°22' N, 088°36' E
Rāngāmāti . . . . 22°38' N, 092°12' E
Rangpur. . . . . 25°45' N, 089°15' E
Saidpur . . . . 25°47' N, 088°54' E
Sātkhira . . . . 22°43' N, 089°06' E
Sherpur . . . . 24°41' N, 089°25' E

Sherpur . . . . 25°01' N, 090°01' E
Sirajganj (Seraganj) . . . . . 24°27' N, 089°43' E
Sylhet. . . . . 24°54' N, 091°52' E
Tangail. . . . . 24°15' N, 089°55' E

BARBADOS . . . . . . pg. 15

Bennetts . . . . 13°10' N, 059°36' W
Bridgetown . . . . 13°06' N, 059°37' W
Holetown . . . . 13°11' N, 059°39' W
Marchfield. . . . . 13°07' N, 059°28' W
Massiah . . . . 13°10' N, 059°29' W
Oistins . . . . 13°04' N, 059°32' W
Portland . . . . 13°16' N, 059°36' W
Prospect . . . . 13°08' N, 059°36' W
Speightstown . . . . 13°15' N, 059°39' W
Westmoreland. . . . . 13°13' N, 059°37' W

BELARUS . . . . pg. 16

Baranovichi. . . . . 53°08' N, 026°02' E
Beloözersk
 (Beloozyorsk) . . . . 52°28' N, 025°10' E
Bobruysk. . . . . 53°09' N, 029°14' E
Borisov (Barysaw) . . . . . . 54°15' N, 028°30' E
Braslav . . . . 55°38' N, 027°02' E
Brest (Brest-Litovsk) . . . . 52°06' N, 023°42' E
Bykhov . . . . 53°31' N, 030°15' E
Chashniki . . . . 54°52' N, 029°10' E
Cherikov . . . . 53°34' N, 031°23' E
Cherven . . . . 53°42' N, 028°26' E
Dobrush . . . . 52°25' N, 031°19' E
Dokshitsy . . . . 54°54' N, 027°46' E
Drogichin. . . . . 52°11' N, 025°09' E
Dyatlovo . . . . 53°28' N, 025°24' E
Dzerzhinsk . . . . 53°41' N, 027°08' E
Gantsevichi . . . . 52°45' N, 026°26' E
Glubokoye . . . . 55°08' N, 027°41' E
Gorki . . . . 54°17' N, 030°59' E
Gorodok . . . . 55°28' N, 029°59' E
Grodno (Hrodna) . . . . 53°41' N, 023°50' E
Homyel' (Gomel). . . . . 52°25' N, 031°00' E
Kletsk. . . . . 53°04' N, 026°38' E
Klimovichi . . . . 53°37' N, 031°58' E
Kobrin . . . . 52°13' N, 024°21' E
Kossovo. . . . . 52°45' N, 025°09' E
Kostyukovichi. . . . . 53°20' N, 032°03' E
Lepel . . . . 54°53' N, 028°42' E
Lida . . . . 53°53' N, 025°18' E
Luninets . . . . 52°15' N, 026°48' E
Mahilyow
 (Mogilyov, Mahilyou) . . . 53°54' N, 030°21' E
Malorita. . . . . 51°47' N, 024°05' E
Minsk (Mensk) . . . . 53°54' N, 027°34' E
Molodechno
 (Maladzyechna). . . . . . . 54°19' N, 026°51' E
Mosty. . . . . 53°25' N, 024°32' E
Mozyr (Mazyr) . . . . 52°03' N, 029°16' E
Mstislavl . . . . 54°02' N, 031°44' E
Narovlya . . . . 51°48' N, 029°30' E
Nesvizh . . . . 53°13' N, 026°40' E

Novolukomi. . . . . 54°39' N, 029°13' E
Orsha. . . . . 54°31' N, 030°26' E
Oshmyany. . . . . 54°25' N, 025°56' E
Osipovichi. . . . . 53°18' N, 028°38' E
Petrikov. . . . . 52°08' N, 028°30' E
Pinsk . . . . 52°07' N, 026°07' E
Polotsk (Polatsk) . . . . 55°29' N, 028°47' E
Pruzhany . . . . 52°33' N, 024°28' E
Rechitsa (Rechytsa) . . . . . 52°22' N, 030°23' E
Slutsk. . . . . 53°01' N, 027°33' E
Soligorsk (Salihorsk) . . . . 52°48' N, 027°32' E
Starye Dorogi . . . . 53°02' N, 028°16' E
Stolbtsy . . . . 53°29' N, 026°44' E
Stolin . . . . 51°53' N, 026°51' E
Svetlogorsk
 (Svetlahorsk) . . . . 52°38' N, 029°46' E
Verkhnedvinsk . . . . 55°47' N, 027°56' E
Vetka . . . . 52°33' N, 031°10' E
Vileyka. . . . . 54°30' N, 026°55' E
Vitebsk (Vitsyebsk) . . . . . 55°12' N, 030°11' E
Volkovysk . . . . 53°10' N, 024°28' E
Vysokoye. . . . . 52°22' N, 023°22' E
Yelsk . . . . 51°48' N, 029°09' E
Zaslavl . . . . 54°00' N, 027°17' E
Zhitkovichi . . . . 52°14' N, 027°52' E
Zhodino . . . . 54°06' N, 028°21' E

BELGIUM . . . . pg. 17

Aalst (Alost) . . . . 50°56' N, 004°02' E
Aalter. . . . . 51°05' N, 003°27' E
Antwerp (Antwerpen,
 Anvers). . . . . 51°13' N, 004°25' E
Arlon (Aarlen). . . . . 49°41' N, 005°49' E
Ath . . . . 50°38' N, 003°47' E
Athus . . . . 49°34' N, 005°50' E
Bastogne . . . . 50°00' N, 005°43' E
Bouillon . . . . 49°48' N, 005°04' E
Boussu. . . . . 50°26' N, 003°48' E
Braine-l'Alleud. . . . . 50°41' N, 004°22' E
Brecht . . . . 51°21' N, 004°38' E
Bree . . . . 51°08' N, 005°36' E
Brugge (Bruges) . . . . 51°13' N, 003°14' E
Brussels (Brussel,
 Bruxelles). . . . . 50°50' N, 004°20' E
Charleroi . . . . 50°25' N, 004°26' E
Ciney . . . . 50°18' N, 005°06' E
Couvin . . . . 50°03' N, 004°29' E
Dinant . . . . 50°16' N, 004°55' E
Eeklo . . . . 51°11' N, 003°34' E
Enghien (Edingen) . . . . . . 50°42' N, 004°02' E
Eupen . . . . 50°38' N, 006°02' E
Florenville . . . . 49°42' N, 005°18' E
Geel (Gheel) . . . . 51°10' N, 005°00' E
Genk (Genck) . . . . 50°58' N, 005°30' E
Ghent (Gand, Gent) . . . . . 51°03' N, 003°43' E
Hasselt. . . . . 50°56' N, 005°20' E
Ixelles (Elsene) . . . . 50°50' N, 004°22' E
Kapellen . . . . 51°19' N, 004°26' E
Kortrijk (Courtrai) . . . . . . 50°50' N, 003°16' E
La Louviere . . . . 50°28' N, 004°11' E

Liège (Luttich) . . . . 50°38' N, 005°34' E
Louvain (Leuven) . . . . 50°53' N, 004°42' E
Marche-en-Famenne . . . . . 50°12' N, 005°20' E
Mechelen (Malines) . . . . . 51°02' N, 004°28' E
Mons (Bergen) . . . . 50°27' N, 003°56' E
Mouscron (Moeskroen) . . . 50°44' N, 003°13' E
Namur (Namen) . . . . 50°28' N, 004°52' E
Neerpelt . . . . 51°13' N, 005°25' E
Ostend (Oostende) . . . . . . 51°13' N, 002°55' E
Peer . . . . 51°08' N, 005°28' E
Péruwelz . . . . 50°31' N, 003°35' E
Philippeville . . . . 50°12' N, 004°32' E
Riemst . . . . 50°48' N, 005°36' E
Roeselare (Roulers) . . . . . 50°57' N, 003°08' E
Saint-Hubert . . . . 50°01' N, 005°23' E
Schaerbeek
  (Schaarbeek) . . . . 50°51' N, 004°23' E
Seraing . . . . 50°36' N, 005°29' E
Sint-Niklaas . . . . 51°10' N, 004°08' E
Spa . . . . 50°30' N, 005°52' E
Spy . . . . 50°29' N, 004°42' E
Staden . . . . 50°59' N, 003°01' E
Tessenderlo . . . . 51°04' N, 005°05' E
Thuin . . . . 50°20' N, 004°17' E
Tienen . . . . 50°48' N, 004°57' E
Torhout . . . . 51°04' N, 003°06' E
Tournai (Doornik) . . . . . . 50°36' N, 003°23' E
Turnhout . . . . 51°19' N, 004°57' E
Uccle (Ukkel) . . . . 50°48' N, 004°19' E
Verviers . . . . 50°35' N, 005°52' E
Wanze . . . . 50°32' N, 005°13' E
Waremme . . . . 50°41' N, 005°15' E
Waterloo . . . . 50°43' N, 004°23' E
Zwijndrecht . . . . 51°13' N, 004°20' E

BELIZE . . . . pg. 18

Belize City . . . . 17°30' N, 088°12' W
Belmopan . . . . 17°15' N, 088°46' W
Benque Viejo . . . . 17°05' N, 089°08' W
Bermudian Landing . . . . . 17°33' N, 088°31' W
Corozal . . . . 18°24' N, 088°24' W
Dangriga (Stann Creek) . . 16°58' N, 088°13' W
Monkey River . . . . 16°22' N, 088°29' W
Orange Walk . . . . 18°06' N, 088°33' W
Pembroke Hall . . . . 18°17' N, 088°27' W
Punta Gorda . . . . 16°07' N, 088°48' W
San Ignacio (El Cayo) . . . . 17°10' N, 089°04' W

BENIN . . . . pg. 19

Abomey . . . . 07°11' N, 001°59' E
Cotonou . . . . 06°21' N, 002°26' E
Djougou . . . . 09°42' N, 001°40' E
Kandi . . . . 11°08' N, 002°56' E
Natitingou . . . . 10°19' N, 001°22' E
Parakou . . . . 09°21' N, 002°37' E
Porto-Novo . . . . 06°29' N, 002°37' E
Savalou . . . . 07°56' N, 001°58' E
Savé . . . . 08°02' N, 002°29' E

BHUTAN . . . . pg. 20

Bumthang (Byakar or
  Jakar) . . . . 27°32' N, 090°43' E
Chhukha . . . . 27°04' N, 089°35' E
Chima Kothi . . . . 27°03' N, 089°35' E
Chirang . . . . 27°04' N, 090°06' E
Dagana (Taga) . . . . 27°03' N, 089°55' E
Deothang (Dewangiri) . . . 26°52' N, 091°28' E
Domphu (Damphu) . . . . . . 27°01' N, 090°08' E
Gaylegphug (Gelekphu,
  Hatisar or Hatsar) . . . . . 26°51' N, 090°29' E
Ha . . . . 27°22' N, 089°17' E
Kanglung (Kanglum) . . . . . 27°16' N, 091°30' E
Lhuntsi . . . . 27°39' N, 091°09' E
Mongar . . . . 27°15' N, 091°12' E
Paro . . . . 27°26' N, 089°25' E
Pema Gatsel . . . . 26°59' N, 091°26' E
Phuntsholing . . . . 26°52' N, 089°26' E
Punakha . . . . 27°37' N, 089°52' E
Samchi (Tori Bari) . . . . . . 26°53' N, 089°07' E
Samdrup Jongkhar . . . . . . 26°47' N, 091°30' E
Shemgang . . . . 27°12' N, 090°38' E
Shompangkha (Sarbhang) . 26°52' N, 090°16' E
Sibsoo . . . . 27°01' N, 088°55' E
Tashigang . . . . 27°20' N, 091°32' E
Thimphu . . . . 27°28' N, 089°38' E
Tongsa . . . . 27°31' N, 090°30' E
Wangdü Phodrang . . . . . . 27°29' N, 089°54' E

BOLIVIA . . . . pg. 21

Apolo . . . . 14°43' S, 068°31' W
Benavides . . . . 12°38' S, 067°20' W
Bermejo . . . . 22°44' S, 064°21' W
Camargo . . . . 20°39' S, 065°13' W
Camiri . . . . 20°03' S, 063°31' W
Caranavi . . . . 15°46' S, 067°36' W
Chulumani . . . . 16°24' S, 067°31' W
Cobija . . . . 11°02' S, 068°44' W
Cochabamba . . . . 17°24' S, 066°09' W
Concepción . . . . 16°15' S, 062°04' W
Copacabana . . . . 16°10' S, 069°05' W
Corocoro . . . . 17°12' S, 068°29' W
Cuevo . . . . 20°27' S, 063°32' W
El Carmen . . . . 18°49' S, 058°33' W
Fortaleza . . . . 10°37' S, 066°13' W
Guayaramerin . . . . 10°48' S, 065°23' W
Huacaya . . . . 20°45' S, 063°43' W
Huachacalla . . . . 18°45' S, 068°17' W
Ixiamas . . . . 13°45' S, 068°09' W
La Esperanza . . . . 14°34' S, 062°10' W
La Horquilla . . . . 12°34' S, 064°25' W
La Paz . . . . 16°30' S, 068°09' W
Llallagua . . . . 18°25' S, 066°38' W
Llica . . . . 19°52' S, 068°16' W
Loreto . . . . 15°13' S, 064°40' W
Magdalena . . . . 13°20' S, 064°08' W
Monteagudo . . . . 19°49' S, 063°59' W
Montero . . . . 17°20' S, 063°15' W

Oruro. . . . . 17°59′ S, 067°09′ W
Porvenir . . . . 11°15′ S, 068°41′ W
Potosí . . . . 19°35′ S, 065°45′ W
Puerto Acosta . . . . 15°32′ S, 069°15′ W
Puerto Rico . . . . 11°05′ S, 067°38′ W
Punata . . . . 17°33′ S, 065°50′ W
Quetena. . . . . 22°10′ S, 067°25′ W
Quillacollo. . . . . 17°26′ S, 066°17′ W
Reyes . . . . 14°19′ S, 067°23′ W
Riberalta . . . . 10°59′ S, 066°06′ W
Roboré. . . . . 18°20′ S, 059°45′ W
Samaipata . . . . 18°09′ S, 063°52′ W
San Ignacio . . . . 16°23′ S, 060°59′ W
San José. . . . . 17°51′ S, 060°47′ W
San Matías . . . . 16°22′ S, 058°24′ W
San Pablo . . . . 15°41′ S, 063°15′ W
San Ramón . . . . 13°17′ S, 064°43′ W
Santa Cruz. . . . . 17°48′ S, 063°10′ W
Santiago. . . . . 19°22′ S, 060°51′ W
Siglo Veinte . . . . 18°22′ S, 066°38′ W
Sucre. . . . . 19°02′ S, 065°17′ W
Tarabuco. . . . . 19°10′ S, 064°57′ W
Tarija . . . . 21°31′ S, 064°45′ W
Tiahuanaco (Tiwanaku) . . . 16°33′ S, 068°42′ W
Trinidad. . . . . 14°47′ S, 064°47′ W
Tupiza . . . . 21°27′ S, 065°43′ W
Uyuni . . . . 20°28′ S, 066°50′ W
Villazón . . . . 22°06′ S, 065°36′ W
Yacuiba . . . . 22°02′ S, 063°43′ W

BOSNIA AND
HERZEGOVINA . . .pg. 22

Banja Luka. . . . . 44°46′ N, 017°10′ E
Bihać . . . . 44°49′ N, 015°52′ E
Bijeljina . . . . 44°45′ N, 019°13′ E
Bosanska Gradiška . . . . 45°09′ N, 017°15′ E
Bosanski Šamac . . . . 45°04′ N, 018°28′ E
Brčko . . . . 44°52′ N, 018°49′ E
Derventa . . . . 44°59′ N, 017°55′ E
Goražde . . . . 43°40′ N, 018°59′ E
Jablanica . . . . 43°39′ N, 017°45′ E
Jajce . . . . 44°21′ N, 017°17′ E
Kladanj . . . . 44°14′ N, 018°42′ E
Ključ . . . . 44°32′ N, 016°47′ E
Konjic . . . . 43°39′ N, 017°58′ E
Mostar . . . . 43°21′ N, 017°49′ E
Prijedor . . . . 44°59′ N, 016°42′ E
Sanski Most . . . . 44°46′ N, 016°40′ E
Sarajevo. . . . . 43°50′ N, 018°25′ E
Srebrenica. . . . . 44°06′ N, 019°18′ E
Travnik . . . . 44°14′ N, 017°40′ E
Tuzla . . . . 44°33′ N, 018°41′ E
Vareš . . . . 44°10′ N, 018°20′ E
Zenica . . . . 44°13′ N, 017°55′ E

BOTSWANA . . . . . .pg. 23

Francistown . . . . 21°13′ S, 027°31′ E

Gaborone. . . . . 24°40′ S, 025°54′ E
Ghanzi . . . . 21°34′ S, 021°47′ E
Kanye. . . . . 24°59′ S, 025°21′ E
Kasane. . . . . 17°49′ S, 025°09′ E
Letlhakane. . . . . 21°25′ S, 025°35′ E
Lobatse . . . . 25°13′ S, 025°40′ E
Mahalapye. . . . . 23°04′ S, 026°50′ E
Maun . . . . 19°59′ S, 023°25′ E
Mochudi . . . . 24°25′ S, 026°09′ E
Orapa. . . . . 21°17′ S, 025°22′ E
Palapye
  (Palapye Road) . . . . 22°33′ S, 027°08′ E
Ramotswa . . . . 24°52′ S, 025°49′ E
Selebi-Phikwe . . . . 22°01′ S, 027°50′ E
Serowe. . . . . 22°23′ S, 026°43′ E
Shashe. . . . . 21°26′ S, 027°27′ E
Tlokweng. . . . . 24°32′ S, 025°58′ E
Tshabong . . . . 26°03′ S, 022°27′ E
Tshane. . . . . 24°05′ S, 021°54′ E

BRAZIL . . . . .pg. 24

Aracaju . . . . 10°55′ S, 037°04′ W
Belém (Para) . . . . 01°27′ S, 048°29′ W
Belo Horizonte . . . . 19°55′ S, 043°56′ W
Boa Vista . . . . 02°49′ N, 060°30′ W
Brasília . . . . 15°47′ S, 047°55′ W
Campina Grande . . . . 07°13′ S, 035°53′ W
Campo Grande . . . . 20°27′ S, 054°37′ W
Canoas. . . . . 29°56′ S, 051°11′ W
Caxias do Sul . . . . 29°10′ S, 051°11′ W
Curitiba . . . . 25°25′ S, 049°15′ W
Duque de Caxias . . . . 22°47′ S, 043°18′ W
Florianópolis. . . . . 27°35′ S, 048°34′ W
Fortaleza . . . . 03°43′ S, 038°30′ W
Goiânia . . . . 16°40′ S, 049°16′ W
Itabuna . . . . 14°48′ S, 039°16′ W
João Pessoa . . . . 07°07′ S, 034°52′ W
Macapá . . . . 00°02′ N, 051°03′ W
Maceió. . . . . 09°40′ S, 035°43′ W
Manaus . . . . 03°08′ S, 060°01′ W
Natal . . . . 05°47′ S, 035°13′ W
Nova Iguaçu . . . . 22°45′ S, 043°27′ W
Novo Hamburgo . . . . 29°41′ S, 051°08′ W
Passo Fundo . . . . 28°15′ S, 052°24′ W
Pôrto Alegre . . . . 30°04′ S, 051°11′ W
Pôrto Velho. . . . . 08°46′ S, 063°54′ W
Recife. . . . . 08°03′ S, 034°54′ W
Rio Branco . . . . 09°58′ S, 067°48′ W
Rio de Janeiro . . . . 22°54′ S, 043°14′ W
Rio Grande . . . . 32°02′ S, 052°05′ W
Salvador . . . . 12°59′ S, 038°31′ W
Santarém . . . . 02°26′ S, 054°42′ W
Santo André . . . . 23°40′ S, 046°31′ W
São Gonçalo . . . . 22°51′ S, 043°04′ W
São José do Rio Prêto . . . . . 20°48′ S, 049°23′ W
São Luís . . . . 02°31′ S, 044°16′ W
São Paulo. . . . . 23°32′ S, 046°37′ W
Tefé . . . . 03°22′ S, 064°42′ W
Teresina . . . . 05°05′ S, 042°49′ W
Vitória . . . . 20°19′ S, 040°21′ W

BRUNEI . . . . .pg. 25

Badas. . . . . 04°36' N, 114°27' E
Bandar Seri Begawan
  (Brunei) . . . . 04°53' N, 114°56' E
Bangar. . . . . 04°43' N, 115°04' E
Kuala Belait. . . . . 04°36' N, 114°14' E
Labi. . . . . 04°23' N, 114°27' E
Labu. . . . . 04°45' N, 115°11' E
Muara. . . . . 05°02' N, 115°04' E
Seria. . . . . 04°37' N, 114°19' E
Sukang. . . . . 04°19' N, 114°37' E
Tutong. . . . . 04°48' N, 114°39' E

BULGARIA . . . . . . .pg. 26

Balchik. . . . . 43°25' N, 028°10' E
Berkovitsa. . . . . 43°14' N, 023°07' E
Blagoevgrad . . . . 42°01' N, 023°06' E
Burgas . . . . 42°30' N, 027°28' E
Dimitrovgrad. . . . . 42°03' N, 025°36' E
Dobrich (Tolbukhin) . . . . . 43°34' N, 027°50' E
Dulovo. . . . . 43°49' N, 027°09' E
Gabrovo. . . . . 42°52' N, 025°19' E
Grudovo . . . . 42°21' N, 027°10' E
Kazanlŭk. . . . . 42°37' N, 025°24' E
Khaskovo. . . . . 41°56' N, 025°33' E
Kŭrdzhali. . . . . 41°39' N, 025°22' E
Kyustendil . . . . 42°17' N, 022°41' E
Lom . . . . 43°49' N, 023°14' E
Lovech. . . . . 43°08' N, 024°43' E
Montana
  (Mikhaylovgrad) . . . . . . 43°25' N, 023°13' E
Nikopol . . . . 43°42' N, 024°54' E
Pazardzhik. . . . . 42°12' N, 024°20' E
Pernik (Dimitrovo) . . . . . . 42°36' N, 023°02' E
Petrich. . . . . 41°24' N, 023°13' E
Pleven . . . . 43°25' N, 024°37' E
Plovdiv . . . . 42°09' N, 024°45' E
Razgrad. . . . . 43°32' N, 026°31' E
Ruse. . . . . 43°50' N, 025°57' E
Shumen (Kolarovgrad). . . . 43°16' N, 026°55' E
Silistra . . . . 44°07' N, 027°16' E
Sliven. . . . . 42°40' N, 026°19' E
Sofia. . . . . 42°41' N, 023°19' E
Stara Zagora . . . . 42°25' N, 025°38' E
Troyan. . . . . 42°53' N, 024°43' E
Varna. . . . . 43°13' N, 027°55' E
Veliko Tŭrnovo . . . . 43°04' N, 025°39' E
Velingrad. . . . . 42°01' N, 024°00' E
Vidin . . . . 43°59' N, 022°52' E
Vratsa (Vraca) . . . . 43°12' N, 023°33' E
Vrŭv . . . . 44°11' N, 022°44' E
Yambol . . . . 42°29' N, 026°30' E

BURKINA FASO . .pg. 27

Banfora . . . . 10°38' N, 004°46' W
Bobo-Dioulasso. . . . . 11°12' N, 004°18' W

Boulsa . . . . 12°39' N, 000°34' W
Dédougou . . . . 12°28' N, 003°28' W
Diébougou . . . . 10°58' N, 003°15' W
Dori . . . . 14°02' N, 000°02' W
Fada Ngourma. . . . . 12°04' N, 000°21' W
Faramana. . . . . 12°03' N, 004°40' W
Gaoua . . . . 10°20' N, 003°11' W
Kaya. . . . . 13°05' N, 001°05' W
Koudougou . . . . 12°15' N, 002°22' W
Koupéla . . . . 12°11' N, 000°21' W
Léo. . . . . 11°06' N, 002°06' W
Nouna . . . . 12°44' N, 003°52' W
Orodara. . . . . 10°59' N, 004°55' W
Ouagadougou . . . . 12°22' N, 001°31' W
Ouahigouya. . . . . 13°35' N, 002°25' W
Pô. . . . . 11°10' N, 001°09' W
Réo. . . . . 12°19' N, 002°28' W
Tenkodogo . . . . 11°47' N, 000°22' W
Yako. . . . . 12°58' N, 002°16' W

BURUNDI . . . . .pg. 28

Bubanza. . . . . 03°06' S, 029°23' E
Bujumbura . . . . 03°23' S, 029°22' E
Bururi . . . . 03°57' S, 029°37' E
Gitega . . . . 03°26' S, 029°56' E
Muramvya . . . . 03°16' S, 029°37' E
Ngozi . . . . 02°54' S, 029°50' E
Nyanza-Lac . . . . 04°21' S, 029°36' E

CAMBODIA . . . . . .pg. 29

Ânlóng Vêng . . . . 14°14' N, 104°05' E
Bâ Kêv. . . . . 13°42' N, 107°12' E
Battambang
  (Batdâmbâng) . . . . 13°06' N, 103°12' E
Chbar. . . . . 12°46' N, 107°10' E
Chôâm Khsant . . . . 14°13' N, 104°56' E
Chŏng Kal . . . . 13°57' N, 103°35' E
Kâmpóng Cham . . . . 12°00' N, 105°27' E
Kâmpóng Chhnǎng . . . . . . 12°15' N, 104°40' E
Kâmpóng Kdei. . . . . 13°07' N, 104°21' E
Kâmpóng Saôm
  (Sihanoukville) . . . . 10°38' N, 103°30' E
Kâmpóng Spœ . . . . 11°27' N, 104°32' E
Kâmpóng Thum . . . . 12°42' N, 104°54' E
Kampot (Kâmpôt). . . . . . . 10°37' N, 104°11' E
Krâchéh (Kratie). . . . . 12°29' N, 106°01' E
Krâkôr . . . . 12°32' N, 104°12' E
Krŏng Kaôh Kŏng . . . . 11°37' N, 102°59' E
Lumphät (Lomphat). . . . . . 13°30' N, 106°59' E
Mémôt . . . . 11°49' N, 106°11' E
Moŭng Roessei . . . . 12°46' N, 103°27' E
Ŏdôngk . . . . 11°48' N, 104°45' E
Péam Prus . . . . 12°19' N, 103°09' E
Phnom Penh (Phnum Penh
  or Pnom Penh) . . . . 11°33' N, 104°55' E
Phnum Tbêng Méanchey . . 13°49' N, 104°58' E
Phsar Réam (Ream) . . . . . . 10°30' N, 103°37' E

Prey Vêng	11°29′ N,	105°19′ E
Pursat (Poŭthĭsăt)	12°32′ N,	103°55′ E
Rôviĕng Tbong	13°21′ N,	105°07′ E
Sândăn	12°42′ N,	106°01′ E
Senmonorom	12°27′ N,	107°12′ E
Siĕmpang	14°07′ N,	106°23′ E
Siem Reap (Siĕmréab)	13°22′ N,	103°51′ E
Sisŏphŏn	13°35′ N,	102°59′ E
Stoeng Trêng (Stung Treng)	13°31′ N,	105°58′ E
Svay Chék	13°48′ N,	102°58′ E
Takêv (Takéo)	10°59′ N,	104°47′ E
Tăng Krăsăng	12°34′ N,	105°03′ E
Virôchey	13°59′ N,	106°49′ E

CAMEROON . . . . . .pg. 30

Bafang	05°09′ N,	010°11′ E
Bafia	04°45′ N,	011°14′ E
Bafoussam	05°28′ N,	010°25′ E
Bamenda	05°56′ N,	010°10′ E
Banyo	06°45′ N,	011°49′ E
Batibo	05°50′ N,	009°52′ E
Batouri	04°26′ N,	014°22′ E
Bertoua	04°35′ N,	013°41′ E
Bétaré-Oya	05°36′ N,	014°05′ E
Douala	04°03′ N,	009°42′ E
Ebolowa	02°54′ N,	011°09′ E
Edéa	03°48′ N,	010°08′ E
Eséka	03°39′ N,	010°46′ E
Foumban	05°43′ N,	010°55′ E
Garoua	09°18′ N,	013°24′ E
Guider	09°56′ N,	013°57′ E
Kaélé	10°07′ N,	014°27′ E
Kribi	02°57′ N,	009°55′ E
Kumba	04°38′ N,	009°25′ E
Loum	04°43′ N,	009°44′ E
Mamfe	05°46′ N,	009°17′ E
Maroua	10°36′ N,	014°20′ E
Mbalmayo	03°31′ N,	011°30′ E
Meiganga	06°31′ N,	014°18′ E
Mora	11°03′ N,	014°09′ E
Ngaoundéré	07°19′ N,	013°35′ E
Nkambe	06°38′ N,	010°40′ E
Nkongsamba	04°57′ N,	009°56′ E
Obala	04°10′ N,	011°32′ E
Sangmélima	02°56′ N,	011°59′ E
Tcholliré	08°24′ N,	014°10′ E
Tibati	06°28′ N,	012°38′ E
Wum	06°23′ N,	010°24′ E
Yagoua	10°20′ N,	015°14′ E
Yaoundé	03°52′ N,	011°31′ E
Yokadouma	03°31′ N,	015°03′ E

CANADA . . . . .pg. 31

Amos	48°35′ N,	078°07′ W
Arctic Bay	73°02′ N,	085°11′ W
Baie-Comeau	49°13′ N,	068°09′ W
Baker Lake	64°15′ N,	096°00′ W

Banff	51°10′ N,	115°34′ W
Barrie	44°24′ N,	079°40′ W
Battleford	52°44′ N,	108°19′ W
Beauport	46°52′ N,	071°11′ W
Bonavista	48°39′ N,	053°07′ W
Brandon	49°50′ N,	099°57′ W
Bridgewater	44°23′ N,	064°31′ W
Brooks	50°35′ N,	111°53′ W
Buchans	48°49′ N,	056°52′ W
Burlington	43°19′ N,	079°47′ W
Burnaby	49°16′ N,	122°57′ W
Calgary	51°03′ N,	114°05′ W
Cambridge Bay	69°03′ N,	105°05′ W
Camrose	53°01′ N,	112°50′ W
Carbonear	47°44′ N,	053°13′ W
Carmacks	62°05′ N,	136°17′ W
Charlesbourg	46°51′ N,	071°16′ W
Charlottetown	46°14′ N,	063°08′ W
Chatham	42°24′ N,	082°11′ W
Chibougamau	49°55′ N,	074°22′ W
Chicoutimi	48°26′ N,	071°04′ W
Churchill	58°46′ N,	094°10′ W
Churchill Falls	53°33′ N,	064°01′ W
Cranbrook	49°30′ N,	115°46′ W
Dartmouth	44°40′ N,	063°34′ W
Dauphin	51°09′ N,	100°03′ W
Dawson	64°04′ N,	139°26′ W
Dawson Creek	55°46′ N,	120°14′ W
Duck Lake	52°49′ N,	106°14′ W
Edmonton	53°33′ N,	113°28′ W
Elliot Lake	46°23′ N,	082°42′ W
Enderby	50°33′ N,	119°09′ W
Eskimo Point	61°07′ N,	094°03′ W
Esterhazy	50°39′ N,	102°05′ W
Estevan	49°08′ N,	102°59′ W
Faro	62°14′ N,	133°20′ W
Fernie	49°30′ N,	115°04′ W
Flin Flon	54°46′ N,	101°53′ W
Fogo	49°43′ N,	054°17′ W
Fort Liard	60°15′ N,	123°28′ W
Fort MacLeod	49°43′ N,	113°25′ W
Fort McMurray	56°44′ N,	111°23′ W
Fort McPherson	67°27′ N,	134°53′ W
Fort Qu'Appelle	50°46′ N,	103°48′ W
Fort St. John	56°15′ N,	120°51′ W
Fort Smith	60°00′ N,	111°53′ W
Fredericton	45°58′ N,	066°39′ W
Gagnon	51°53′ N,	068°10′ W
Gander	48°57′ N,	054°37′ W
Gaspe	48°50′ N,	064°29′ W
Glace Bay	46°12′ N,	059°57′ W
Granby	45°24′ N,	072°43′ W
Grand Bank	47°06′ N,	055°46′ W
Grande Prairie	55°10′ N,	118°48′ W
Grand Falls	48°56′ N,	055°40′ W
Grimshaw	56°11′ N,	117°36′ W
Grise Fiord	76°25′ N,	082°55′ W
Haines Junction	60°45′ N,	137°30′ W
Halifax	44°39′ N,	063°36′ W
Hamilton	43°15′ N,	079°51′ W
Happy Valley-Goose Bay	53°19′ N,	060°20′ W

Harbour Grace	47°42′ N, 053°13′ W
Hay River	60°49′ N, 115°42′ W
Inuvik	68°21′ N, 133°43′ W
Iqaluit (Frobisher Bay)	63°45′ N, 068°31′ W
Iroquois Falls	48°46′ N, 080°41′ W
Jasper	52°53′ N, 118°05′ W
Joliette	46°01′ N, 073°27′ W
Jonquiere	48°25′ N, 071°13′ W
Kamloops	50°40′ N, 120°19′ W
Kapuskasing	49°25′ N, 082°26′ W
Kelowna	49°53′ N, 119°29′ W
Kenora	49°47′ N, 094°29′ W
Kindersley	51°28′ N, 109°10′ W
Kirkland Lake	48°09′ N, 080°02′ W
Kitchener	43°27′ N, 080°29′ W
Kuujjuaq (Fort-Chimo)	58°06′ N, 068°25′ W
La Baie	48°20′ N, 070°52′ W
Labrador City	52°57′ N, 066°55′ W
La Tuque	47°26′ N, 072°47′ W
Lethbridge	49°42′ N, 112°49′ W
Lewisporte	49°14′ N, 055°03′ W
Liverpool	44°02′ N, 064°43′ W
Lloydminster	53°17′ N, 110°00′ W
London	42°59′ N, 081°14′ W
Longueuil	45°32′ N, 073°30′ W
Lynn Lake	56°51′ N, 101°03′ W
Maple Creek	49°55′ N, 109°29′ W
Marystown	47°10′ N, 055°09′ W
Mayo	63°36′ N, 135°54′ W
Medicine Hat	50°03′ N, 110°40′ W
Mississauga	43°35′ N, 079°39′ W
Moncton	46°07′ N, 064°48′ W
Montmagny	46°59′ N, 070°33′ W
Montreal	45°30′ N, 073°36′ W
Moose Jaw	50°24′ N, 105°32′ W
Mount Pearl	47°31′ N, 052°47′ W
Nanaimo	49°10′ N, 123°56′ W
Nelson	49°30′ N, 117°17′ W
Nepean	45°16′ N, 075°46′ W
New Liskeard	47°30′ N, 079°40′ W
Niagara Falls	43°06′ N, 079°04′ W
Nickel Centre	46°34′ N, 080°49′ W
Nipawin	53°22′ N, 104°00′ W
North Battleford	52°47′ N, 108°17′ W
North Bay	46°19′ N, 079°28′ W
North West River	53°32′ N, 060°08′ W
Old Crow	67°34′ N, 139°50′ W
Oshawa	43°54′ N, 078°51′ W
Ottawa	45°25′ N, 075°42′ W
Pangnirtung	66°08′ N, 065°43′ W
Parry Sound	45°21′ N, 080°02′ W
Peace River	56°14′ N, 117°17′ W
Perce	48°32′ N, 064°13′ W
Peterborough	44°18′ N, 078°19′ W
Pine Point	60°50′ N, 114°28′ W
Portage la Prairie	49°59′ N, 098°18′ W
Port Alberni	49°14′ N, 124°48′ W
Port Hawkesbury	45°37′ N, 061°21′ W
Prince Albert	53°12′ N, 105°46′ W
Prince George	53°55′ N, 122°45′ W
Prince Rupert	54°19′ N, 130°19′ W

Quebec	46°49′ N, 071°14′ W
Quesnel	53°00′ N, 122°30′ W
Rae-Edzo	62°50′ N, 116°03′ W
Rankin Inlet	62°49′ N, 092°05′ W
Red Deer	52°16′ N, 113°48′ W
Regina	50°27′ N, 104°37′ W
Resolute Bay	74°41′ N, 094°54′ W
Revelstoke	50°59′ N, 118°12′ W
Rimouski	48°26′ N, 068°33′ W
Roberval	48°31′ N, 072°13′ W
Ross River	61°59′ N, 132°26′ W
Sachs Harbour	72°00′ N, 125°13′ W
Saint Albert	53°38′ N, 113°38′ W
Sainte-Foy	46°47′ N, 071°17′ W
Saint John	45°16′ N, 066°03′ W
Saint John's	47°34′ N, 052°43′ W
Saskatoon	52°07′ N, 106°38′ W
Sault Ste. Marie	46°31′ N, 084°20′ W
Scarborough	43°47′ N, 079°15′ W
Schefferville	54°48′ N, 066°50′ W
Selkirk	50°09′ N, 096°52′ W
Senneterre	48°23′ N, 077°14′ W
Sept-Îles	50°12′ N, 066°23′ W
Shawinigan	46°33′ N, 072°45′ W
Shelburne	43°46′ N, 065°19′ W
Sherbrooke	45°25′ N, 071°54′ W
Snow Lake	54°53′ N, 100°02′ W
Springdale	49°30′ N, 056°04′ W
Sturgeon Falls	46°22′ N, 079°55′ W
Sudbury	46°30′ N, 081°00′ W
Surrey	49°06′ N, 122°47′ W
Swan River	52°07′ N, 101°16′ W
Sydney	46°09′ N, 060°11′ W
Teslin	60°10′ N, 132°43′ W
The Pas	53°50′ N, 101°15′ W
Thompson	55°45′ N, 097°52′ W
Thunder Bay	48°24′ N, 089°19′ W
Timmins	48°28′ N, 081°20′ W
Toronto	43°39′ N, 079°23′ W
Trois-Rivieres	46°21′ N, 072°33′ W
Truro	45°22′ N, 063°16′ W
Tuktoyaktuk	69°27′ N, 133°02′ W
Val-d'Or	48°06′ N, 077°47′ W
Vancouver	49°15′ N, 123°07′ W
Vernon	50°16′ N, 119°16′ W
Victoria	48°26′ N, 123°22′ W
Wabush	52°55′ N, 066°52′ W
Watson Lake	60°04′ N, 128°42′ W
Weyburn	49°40′ N, 103°51′ W
Whitehorse	60°43′ N, 135°03′ W
Williams Lake	52°08′ N, 122°09′ W
Windsor	42°18′ N, 083°01′ W
Windsor	44°59′ N, 064°08′ W
Winnipeg	49°53′ N, 097°09′ W
Yarmouth	43°50′ N, 066°07′ W
Yellowknife	62°27′ N, 114°22′ W
Yorkton	51°13′ N, 102°28′ W

CAPE VERDE ..... pg. 32

Mindelo	16°53′ N, 025°00′ W

Porto Novo	17°01′ N, 025°04′ W
Praia	14°55′ N, 023°31′ W
São Filipe	14°54′ N, 024°31′ W

CENTRAL AFRICAN REPUBLIC........pg. 33

Alindao	05°02′ N, 021°13′ E
Baboua	05°48′ N, 014°49′ E
Bambari	05°45′ N, 020°40′ E
Bangassou	04°44′ N, 022°49′ E
Bangui	04°22′ N, 018°35′ E
Batangafo	07°18′ N, 018°18′ E
Berbérati	04°16′ N, 015°47′ E
Bimbo	04°18′ N, 018°33′ E
Birao	10°17′ N, 022°47′ E
Boda	04°19′ N, 017°28′ E
Bossangoa	06°29′ N, 017°27′ E
Bossembélé	05°16′ N, 017°39′ E
Bouar	05°57′ N, 015°36′ E
Bouca	06°30′ N, 018°17′ E
Bozoum	06°19′ N, 016°23′ E
Bria	06°32′ N, 021°59′ E
Carnot	04°56′ N, 015°52′ E
Dekóa	06°19′ N, 019°04′ E
Ippy	06°15′ N, 021°12′ E
Kaga Bandoro	06°59′ N, 019°11′ E
Mbaïki	03°53′ N, 018°00′ E
Mobaye	04°19′ N, 021°11′ E
Mouka	07°16′ N, 021°52′ E
Ndélé	08°24′ N, 020°39′ E
Nola	03°32′ N, 016°04′ E
Obo	05°24′ N, 026°30′ E
Ouadda	08°04′ N, 022°24′ E
Ouanda Djallé	08°54′ N, 022°48′ E
Sibut	05°44′ N, 019°05′ E
Zinga	03°43′ N, 018°35′ E

CHAD............pg. 34

Abéché	13°49′ N, 020°49′ E
Adre	13°28′ N, 022°12′ E
Am Dam	12°46′ N, 020°29′ E
Am Timan	11°02′ N, 020°17′ E
Am Zoer	14°13′ N, 021°23′ E
Aozou	21°49′ N, 017°25′ E
Arada	15°01′ N, 020°40′ E
Ati	13°13′ N, 018°20′ E
Biltine	14°32′ N, 020°55′ E
Bol	13°28′ N, 014°43′ E
Bongor	10°17′ N, 015°22′ E
Doba	08°39′ N, 016°51′ E
Gélengdeng	10°56′ N, 015°32′ E
Goré	07°55′ N, 016°38′ E
Goz Beïda	12°13′ N, 021°25′ E
Koro Toro	16°05′ N, 018°30′ E
Laï	09°24′ N, 016°18′ E
Largeau (Faya-Largeau)	17°55′ N, 019°07′ E
Mao	14°07′ N, 015°19′ E

Massenya	11°24′ N, 016°10′ E
Mongo	12°11′ N, 018°42′ E
Moundou	08°34′ N, 016°05′ E
N'Djamena (Fort Lamy)	12°07′ N, 015°03′ E
Pala	09°22′ N, 014°54′ E
Sarh (Fort-Archambault)	09°09′ N, 018°23′ E

CHILE ....pg. 35

Antofagasta	23°39′ S, 070°24′ W
Arica	18°29′ S, 070°20′ W
Castro	42°29′ S, 073°46′ W
Chillán	36°36′ S, 072°07′ W
Chuquicamata	22°19′ S, 068°56′ W
Coihaique	45°34′ S, 072°04′ W
Concepción	36°50′ S, 073°03′ W
Copiapó	27°22′ S, 070°20′ W
Coquimbo	29°58′ S, 071°21′ W
Iquique	20°13′ S, 070°10′ W
La Serena	29°54′ S, 071°16′ W
Porvenir	53°18′ S, 070°22′ W
Potrerillos	26°26′ S, 069°29′ W
Puerto Aisén	45°24′ S, 072°42′ W
Puerto Montt	41°28′ S, 072°57′ W
Punta Arenas	53°09′ S, 070°55′ W
Purranque	40°55′ S, 073°10′ W
San Pedro	33°54′ S, 071°28′ W
Santiago	33°27′ S, 070°40′ W
Talca	35°26′ S, 071°40′ W
Talcahuano	36°43′ S, 073°07′ W
Temuco	38°44′ S, 072°36′ W
Tocopilla	22°05′ S, 070°12′ W
Valdivia	39°48′ S, 073°14′ W
Valparaíso	33°02′ S, 071°38′ W
Viña del Mar	33°02′ S, 071°34′ W

CHINA ....pg. 36-7

Anshan	41°07′ N, 122°57′ E
Beijing	39°56′ N, 116°24′ E
Changchun	43°52′ N, 125°21′ E
Changsha	28°12′ N, 112°58′ E
Chengdu	30°40′ N, 104°04′ E
Chongqing (locally Yuzhou)	29°34′ N, 106°35′ E
Dalian (Lüda)	38°55′ N, 121°39′ E
Fushun	41°52′ N, 123°53′ E
Fuzhou	26°05′ N, 119°18′ E
Guangzhou	23°07′ N, 113°15′ E
Guiyang	26°35′ N, 106°43′ E
Haikou	20°03′ N, 110°19′ E
Hangzhou	30°15′ N, 120°10′ E
Harbin	45°45′ N, 126°39′ E
Hefei	31°51′ N, 117°17′ E
Hohhot	40°47′ N, 111°37′ E
Jinan	36°40′ N, 117°00′ E
Kunming	25°04′ N, 102°41′ E
Lanzhou	36°03′ N, 103°41′ E
Lhasa	29°39′ N, 091°06′ E
Nanchang	28°41′ N, 115°53′ E

Nanjing	32°03' N,	118°47' E
Nanning	22°49' N,	108°19' E
Qingdao	36°04' N,	120°19' E
Shanghai	31°14' N,	121°28' E
Shaoxing	30°00' N,	120°35' E
Shenyang	41°48' N,	123°27' E
Shijiazhuang	38°03' N,	114°29' E
Tai'an	36°12' N,	117°07' E
Taiyuan	37°52' N,	112°33' E
Tianjin	39°08' N,	117°12' E
Ürümqi	43°48' N,	087°35' E
Wuhan	30°35' N,	114°16' E
Xi'an	34°16' N,	108°54' E
Xining	36°37' N,	101°46' E
Yinchuan	38°28' N,	106°19' E
Zhengzhou	34°45' N,	113°40' E

COLOMBIA . . . . pg. 38

Armenia	04°31' N,	075°41' W
Barranquilla	10°59' N,	074°48' W
Bello	06°20' N,	075°33' W
Bisinaca	04°30' N,	069°40' W
Bogotá	04°36' N,	074°05' W
Bolívar	01°50' N,	076°58' W
Bucaramanga	07°08' N,	073°09' W
Buenaventura	03°53' N,	077°04' W
Cali	03°27' N,	076°31' W
Caranacoa	02°25' N,	068°57' W
Cartagena	10°25' N,	075°32' W
Cúcuta	07°54' N,	072°31' W
Duitama	05°50' N,	073°02' W
El Dorado	01°11' N,	071°52' W
El Yopal	05°21' N,	072°23' W
Florencia	01°36' N,	075°36' W
Ibagué	04°27' N,	075°14' W
Macujer	00°24' N,	073°07' W
Magangué	09°14' N,	074°45' W
Manizales	05°05' N,	075°32' W
Matarca	00°30' S,	072°38' W
Medellín	06°15' N,	075°35' W
Mitú	01°08' N,	070°03' W
Montería	08°46' N,	075°53' W
Ocaña	08°15' N,	073°20' W
Palmira	03°32' N,	076°16' W
Pasto	01°13' N,	077°17' W
Pereira	04°49' N,	075°43' W
Popayán	02°27' N,	076°36' W
Puerto Berrío	06°29' N,	074°24' W
Puerto Carreño	06°12' N,	067°22' W
Puerto Inírida	03°51' N,	067°55' W
Quibdó	05°42' N,	076°40' W
Ríohacha	11°33' N,	072°55' W
San José de Guaviare	02°35' N,	072°38' W
San Martín	03°42' N,	073°42' W
Santa Marta	11°15' N,	074°13' W
Sincelejo	09°18' N,	075°24' W
Sogamoso	05°43' N,	072°56' W
Tuluá	04°06' N,	076°11' W
Tumaco	01°49' N,	078°46' W

Tunja	05°31' N,	073°22' W
Urrao	06°20' N,	076°11' W
Valledupar	10°29' N,	073°15' W
Villa Rosario	07°50' N,	072°28' W
Villavicencio	04°09' N,	073°37' W
Zipaquirá	05°02' N,	074°00' W

COMOROS . . . . pg. 39

Fomboni	12°18' S,	043°46' E
Mitsamiouli	11°22' S,	043°21' E
Moroni	11°41' S,	043°16' E
Mutsamudu	12°10' S,	044°25' E

CONGO, DEMOCRATIC REPUBLIC OF THE . . . . pg. 40

Aketi	02°44' N,	023°46' E
Banana	06°01' S,	012°24' E
Bandundu	03°19' S,	017°22' E
Beni	00°30' N,	029°28' E
Boende	00°13' S,	020°52' E
Boma	05°51' S,	013°03' E
Buta	02°48' N,	024°44' E
Butembo	00°09' N,	029°17' E
Gandajika	06°45' S,	023°57' E
Gemena	03°15' N,	019°46' E
Ilebo	04°19' S,	020°35' E
Isiro	02°46' N,	027°37' E
Kabinda	06°08' S,	024°29' E
Kalemi (Albertville)	05°56' S,	029°12' E
Kamina	08°44' S,	025°00' E
Kananga (Luluabourg)	05°54' S,	022°25' E
Kikwit	05°02' S,	018°49' E
Kindu	02°57' S,	025°56' E
Kinshasa (Leopoldville)	04°18' S,	015°18' E
Kisangani (Stanleyville)	00°30' N,	025°12' E
Kolwezi	10°43' S,	025°28' E
Kutu	02°44' S,	018°09' E
Likasi	10°59' S,	026°44' E
Lubumbashi (Elisabethville)	11°40' S,	027°28' E
Manono	07°18' S,	027°25' E
Matadi	05°49' S,	013°27' E
Mbandaka	00°04' N,	018°16' E
Mbanza-Ngungu	05°15' S,	014°52' E
Mbuji-Mayi	06°09' S,	023°36' E
Mwene-Ditu	07°03' S,	023°27' E
Samba	04°38' S,	026°22' E
Tshikapa	06°25' S,	020°48' E
Yangambi	00°47' N,	024°28' E

CONGO, REPUBLIC OF THE ....pg. 41

COSTA RICA .....pg. 42

CROATIA ....pg. 43

CUBA ....pg. 44

CYPRUS ....pg. 45

Kalokhorio. . . . . 34°55' N, 033°32' E
Kouklia . . . . 34°42' N, 032°34' E
Kyrenia . . . . 35°20' N, 033°19' E
Larnaca . . . . 34°55' N, 033°38' E
Laxia . . . . 35°06' N, 033°22' E
Leonarisso. . . . . 35°28' N, 034°08' E
Limassol . . . . 34°40' N, 033°02' E
Livadhia. . . . . 35°24' N, 034°02' E
Liveras. . . . . 35°23' N, 032°57' E
Mari . . . . 34°44' N, 033°18' E
Morphou . . . . 35°12' N, 032°59' E
Nicosia (Lefkosia). . . . . . . 35°10' N, 033°22' E
Ora. . . . . 34°51' N, 033°12' E
Ormidhia . . . . 34°59' N, 033°47' E
Pakhna. . . . . 34°46' N, 032°48' E
Pano Lakatamia . . . . 35°06' N, 033°18' E
Paphos. . . . . 34°45' N, 032°25' E
Paralimni. . . . . 35°02' N, 033°59' E
Patriki . . . . 35°22' N, 033°59' E
Perivolia . . . . 34°49' N, 033°35' E
Pomos . . . . 35°09' N, 032°33' E
Prastio. . . . . 35°10' N, 033°45' E
Trikomo. . . . . 35°17' N, 033°52' E
Tsadha. . . . . 34°50' N, 032°28' E
Varosha. . . . . 35°06' N, 033°57' E
Vroisha . . . . 35°04' N, 032°40' E
Yialoussa. . . . . 35°32' N, 034°11' E

CZECH REPUBLIC
. . . . .pg. 46

Břeclav . . . . 48°46' N, 016°53' E
Brno. . . . . 49°12' N, 016°38' E
Česká Lípa. . . . . 50°41' N, 014°33' E
České Budějovice . . . . 48°59' N, 014°28' E
Český Těšín . . . . 49°45' N, 018°37' E
Cheb . . . . 50°04' N, 012°22' E
Chomutov . . . . 50°27' N, 013°26' E
Děčín . . . . 50°47' N, 014°13' E
Frýdek Místek . . . . 49°41' N, 018°21' E
Havířov . . . . 49°47' N, 018°22' E
Havlíčkův Brod . . . . 49°37' N, 015°35' E
Hodonín. . . . . 48°52' N, 017°08' E
Hradec Králové. . . . . 50°13' N, 015°50' E
Jablonec . . . . 50°43' N, 015°11' E
Jihlava. . . . . 49°24' N, 015°35' E
Karlovy Vary. . . . . 50°13' N, 012°54' E
Karviná . . . . 49°52' N, 018°33' E
Kladno. . . . . 50°09' N, 014°06' E
Kolín. . . . . 50°02' N, 015°12' E
Krnov. . . . . 50°06' N, 017°43' E
Kroměříž . . . . 49°18' N, 017°24' E
Liberec . . . . 50°47' N, 015°03' E
Litvínov. . . . . 50°36' N, 013°37' E
Mladá Boleslav . . . . 50°25' N, 014°54' E
Most. . . . . 50°32' N, 013°39' E
Nový Jičín . . . . 49°36' N, 018°01' E
Olomouc . . . . 49°35' N, 017°15' E
Opava . . . . 49°57' N, 017°55' E
Orlová . . . . 49°51' N, 018°25' E

Ostrava . . . . 49°50' N, 018°17' E
Pardubice . . . . 50°02' N, 015°47' E
Písek . . . . 49°18' N, 014°09' E
Plzeň . . . . 49°45' N, 013°22' E
Prague (Praha) . . . . 50°05' N, 014°28' E
Přerov . . . . 49°27' N, 017°27' E
Příbřam . . . . 49°42' N, 014°01' E
Prostějov. . . . . 49°28' N, 017°07' E
Šumperk . . . . 49°58' N, 016°58' E
Tábor. . . . . 49°25' N, 014°40' E
Teplice. . . . . 50°38' N, 013°50' E
Třebíč . . . . 49°13' N, 015°53' E
Trinec . . . . 49°41' N, 018°39' E
Trutnov . . . . 50°34' N, 015°54' E
Uherské Hradiště . . . . 49°04' N, 017°27' E
Ústí nad Labem. . . . . 50°40' N, 014°02' E
Valašské Meziříči . . . . 49°28' N, 017°58' E
Vsetín . . . . 49°20' N, 018°00' E
Žd'ár nad Sázavou . . . . . . 49°35' N, 015°56' E
Zlín . . . . 49°13' N, 017°40' E
Znojmo . . . . 48°51' N, 016°03' E

DENMARK . . . . . . .pg. 47

Ålborg (Aalborg). . . . . 57°03' N, 009°56' E
Århus (Aarhus). . . . . 56°09' N, 010°13' E
Ärs . . . . 56°48' N, 009°32' E
Brønderslev . . . . 57°16' N, 009°58' E
Brørup. . . . . 55°29' N, 009°01' E
Copenhagen (København). 55°40' N, 012°35' E
Esbjerg . . . . 55°28' N, 008°27' E
Fakse . . . . 55°15' N, 012°08' E
Fredericia . . . . 55°35' N, 009°46' E
Frederiksberg . . . . 55°41' N, 012°32' E
Frederikshavn . . . . 57°26' N, 010°32' E
Gilleleje . . . . 56°07' N, 012°19' E
Give . . . . 55°51' N, 009°15' E
Grenå . . . . 56°25' N, 010°53' E
Hadsund . . . . 56°43' N, 010°07' E
Helsingör . . . . 56°02' N, 012°37' E
Herning . . . . 56°08' N, 008°59' E
Hillerød . . . . 55°56' N, 012°19' E
Hirtshals . . . . 57°35' N, 009°58' E
Hjørring . . . . 57°28' N, 009°59' E
Holstebro . . . . 56°21' N, 008°38' E
Hornslet. . . . . 56°19' N, 010°20' E
Horsens . . . . 55°52' N, 009°52' E
Jyderup . . . . 55°40' N, 011°26' E
Klarup . . . . 57°01' N, 010°03' E
Køge. . . . . 55°27' N, 012°11' E
Kolding . . . . 55°29' N, 009°29' E
Lemvig. . . . . 56°32' N, 008°18' E
Løgstør . . . . 56°58' N, 009°15' E
Næstved . . . . 55°14' N, 011°46' E
Nakskov. . . . . 54°50' N, 011°09' E
Nykøbing . . . . 54°46' N, 011°53' E
Nykøbing . . . . 55°55' N, 011°41' E
Nykøbing . . . . 56°48' N, 008°52' E
Odense . . . . 55°24' N, 010°23' E
Ølgod. . . . . 55°49' N, 008°37' E

Otterup	55°31′ N,	010°24′ E
Padborg	54°49′ N,	009°22′ E
Randers	56°28′ N,	010°03′ E
Ribe	55°21′ N,	008°46′ E
Ringkøbing	56°05′ N,	008°15′ E
Rønne	55°06′ N,	014°42′ E
Roskilde	55°39′ N,	012°05′ E
Rudkøbing	54°56′ N,	010°43′ E
Skagen	57°44′ N,	010°36′ E
Skive	56°34′ N,	009°02′ E
Skjern	55°57′ N,	008°30′ E
Slagelse	55°24′ N,	011°22′ E
Struer	56°29′ N,	008°37′ E
Svendborg	55°03′ N,	010°37′ E
Thisted	56°57′ N,	008°42′ E
Tilst	56°12′ N,	010°07′ E
Toftlund	55°11′ N,	009°04′ E
Tønder	54°56′ N,	008°54′ E
Varde	55°38′ N,	008°29′ E
Vejle	55°42′ N,	009°32′ E
Viborg	56°26′ N,	009°24′ E
Vodskov	57°06′ N,	010°02′ E
Vordingborg	55°01′ N,	011°55′ E

DJIBOUTI . . . . pg. 48

Ali Sabih	11°10′ N,	042°42′ E
Dikhil	11°06′ N,	042°23′ E
Djibouti	11°36′ N,	043°09′ E
Tadjoura	11°47′ N,	042°53′ E

DOMINICA . . . . pg. 49

Castle Bruce	15°26′ N,	061°16′ W
Colihaut	15°30′ N,	061°29′ W
La Plaine	15°20′ N,	061°17′ W
Marigot	15°32′ N,	061°18′ W
Portsmouth	15°35′ N,	061°28′ W
Rosalie	15°22′ N,	061°16′ W
Roseau	15°18′ N,	061°24′ W
Saint Joseph	15°24′ N,	061°26′ W
Salibia	15°29′ N,	061°16′ W
Vieille Case	15°36′ N,	061°24′ W

DOMINICAN REPUBLIC . . . . pg. 50

Azua	18°27′ N,	070°44′ W
Baní	18°17′ N,	070°20′ W
Barahona	18°12′ N,	071°06′ W
Bayaguana	18°58′ N,	069°00′ W
Bonao	18°56′ N,	070°25′ W
Cotuí	19°03′ N,	070°09′ W
Dajabón	19°33′ N,	071°42′ W
Duvergé	18°22′ N,	071°31′ W
El Seibo	18°46′ N,	069°02′ W
Enriquillo	17°54′ N,	071°14′ W

Higüey	18°37′ N,	068°42′ W
Jimaní	18°28′ N,	071°51′ W
La Romana	18°25′ N,	068°58′ W
La Vega	19°13′ N,	070°31′ W
Las Matas	18°52′ N,	071°31′ W
Mao	19°34′ N,	071°05′ W
Miches	18°59′ N,	069°03′ W
Moca	19°24′ N,	070°31′ W
Montecristi	19°52′ N,	071°39′ W
Nagua (Julia Molina)	19°23′ N,	069°50′ W
Neiba	18°28′ N,	071°25′ W
Pedernales	18°02′ N,	071°45′ W
Puerto Plata	19°48′ N,	070°41′ W
Sabaneta	19°28′ N,	071°20′ W
Salcedo	19°23′ N,	070°25′ W
Samaná	19°13′ N,	069°19′ W
San Cristóbal	18°25′ N,	070°06′ W
San Juan	18°48′ N,	071°14′ W
San Pedro de Macorís	18°27′ N,	069°18′ W
Sánchez	19°14′ N,	069°36′ W
Santiago	19°27′ N,	070°42′ W
Santo Domingo	18°28′ N,	069°54′ W

EAST TIMOR . . . . . pg. 51

Dili	08°33′ S,	125°35′ E

ECUADOR . . . . pg. 52

Ambato	01°15′ S,	078°37′ W
Azogues	02°44′ S,	078°50′ W
Babahoyo	01°49′ S,	079°31′ W
Cuenca	02°53′ S,	078°59′ W
Esmeraldas	00°59′ N,	079°42′ W
General Leonidas Plaza Gutiérrez	02°58′ S,	078°25′ W
Girón	03°10′ S,	079°08′ W
Guayaquil	02°10′ S,	079°54′ W
Huaquillas	03°29′ S,	080°14′ W
Ibarra	00°21′ N,	078°07′ W
Jipijapa	01°20′ S,	080°35′ W
Latacunga	00°56′ S,	078°37′ W
Loja	04°00′ S,	079°13′ W
Macará	04°23′ S,	079°57′ W
Macas	02°19′ S,	078°07′ W
Machala	03°16′ S,	079°58′ W
Manta	00°57′ S,	080°44′ W
Milagro	02°07′ S,	079°36′ W
Muisne	00°36′ N,	080°02′ W
Naranjal	02°40′ S,	079°37′ W
Pasaje	03°20′ S,	079°49′ W
Piñas	03°40′ S,	079°39′ W
Portoviejo	01°03′ S,	080°27′ W
Puerto Francisco de Orellana (Coca)	00°28′ S,	076°58′ W
Puyo	01°28′ S,	077°59′ W
Quevedo	01°02′ S,	079°27′ W
Quito	00°13′ S,	078°30′ W
Riobamba	01°40′ S,	078°38′ W
Salinas	02°13′ S,	080°58′ W

San Gabriel . . . . 00°36' N, 077°49' W
San Lorenzo . . . . 01°17' N, 078°50' W
Santo Domingo de los
   Colorados (Santo
   Domingo) . . . . 00°15' S, 079°09' W
Tena . . . . 00°59' S, 077°49' W
Tulcán . . . . 00°48' N, 077°43' W
Valdez . . . . 01°15' N, 079°00' W
Yantzaza . . . . 03°51' S, 078°45' W
Zamora . . . . 04°04' S, 078°58' W
Zaruma . . . . 03°41' S, 079°37' W

EGYPT . . . . pg. 53

Akhmīm . . . . 26°34' N, 031°44' E
Al-'Arish . . . . 31°08' N, 033°48' E
Alexandria
   (Al-Iskandariyah) . . . . . . 31°12' N, 029°54' E
Al-Fayyūm . . . . 29°19' N, 030°50' E
Al-Khārijah . . . . 25°26' N, 030°33' E
Al-Maḥallah Al-Kubrā . . . . 30°58' N, 031°10' E
Al-Manṣūrah . . . . 31°03' N, 031°23' E
Al-Ma'ṣarah . . . . 25°30' N, 029°04' E
Al-Minyā . . . . 28°06' N, 030°45' E
Aswān . . . . 24°05' N, 032°53' E
Asyut . . . . 27°11' N, 031°11' E
Aṭ-Ṭur . . . . 28°14' N, 033°37' E
Az-Zāqaziq . . . . 30°35' N, 031°31' E
Banhā . . . . 30°28' N, 031°11' E
Bani Suwayf . . . . 29°05' N, 031°05' E
Cairo (Al-Qahirah) . . . . . . 30°03' N, 031°15' E
Damanhūr . . . . 31°02' N, 030°28' E
Damietta (Dumyāṭ) . . . . . . 31°25' N, 031°48' E
Giza (Al-Jīzah) . . . . 30°01' N, 031°13' E
Jirjā . . . . 26°20' N, 031°53' E
Luxor (Al-Uqsur) . . . . 25°41' N, 032°39' E
Mallawī . . . . 27°44' N, 030°50' E
Matruh . . . . 31°21' N, 027°14' E
Port Said (Bur Sa'id) . . . . . 31°16' N, 032°18' E
Qinā . . . . 26°10' N, 032°43' E
Sawhāj . . . . 26°33' N, 031°42' E
Shibīn al-Kawm . . . . 30°33' N, 031°01' E
Suez (As-Suways) . . . . 29°58' N, 032°33' E
Ṭanṭā . . . . 30°47' N, 031°00' E

EL SALVADOR . . . pg. 54

Acajutla . . . . 13°35' N, 089°50' W
Chalatenango . . . . 14°02' N, 088°56' W
Chalchuapa . . . . 13°59' N, 089°41' W
Cojutepeque . . . . 13°43' N, 088°56' W
Ilobasco . . . . 13°51' N, 088°51' W
Izalco . . . . 13°45' N, 089°40' W
La Unión . . . . 13°20' N, 087°51' W
Nueva San Salvador
   (Santa Tecla) . . . . 13°41' N, 089°17' W
San Francisco
   (San Francisco Gotera) . . 13°42' N, 088°06' W
San Miguel . . . . 13°29' N, 088°11' W

San Salvador . . . . 13°42' N, 089°12' W
Santa Ana . . . . 13°59' N, 089°34' W
San Vincente . . . . 13°38' N, 088°48' W
Sensuntepeque . . . . 13°52' N, 088°38' W
Sonsonate . . . . 13°43' N, 089°44' W
Usulatán . . . . 13°21' N, 088°27' W
Zacatecoluca . . . . 13°20' N, 088°52' W

EQUATORIAL
GUINEA . . . . pg. 55

Bata . . . . 01°51' N, 009°45' E
Kogo . . . . 01°05' N, 009°42' E
Malabo (Santa Isabel) . . . . . 03°21' N, 008°40' E
Mbini . . . . 01°34' N, 009°37' E
Mikomeseng . . . . 02°08' N, 010°37' E
Niefang . . . . 01°51' N, 010°15' E
San Antonio de Ureca . . . . 03°16' N, 008°32' E

ERITREA . . . . pg. 56

Akordat . . . . 15°33' N, 037°53' E
Aseb (Àssab) . . . . 13°00' N, 042°44' E
Asmara (Asmera) . . . . 15°20' N, 038°56' E
Keren . . . . 15°47' N, 038°28' E
Massawa (Mitsiwa) . . . . . . 15°36' N, 039°28' E
Nakfa . . . . 16°40' N, 038°29' E

ESTONIA . . . . pg. 57

Abja-Paluoja . . . . 58°08' N, 025°21' E
Ambla . . . . 59°11' N, 025°51' E
Antsla . . . . 57°50' N, 026°32' E
Haapsalu . . . . 58°56' N, 023°33' E
Järva-Jaani . . . . 59°02' N, 025°53' E
Järvakandi . . . . 58°47' N, 024°49' E
Jõgeva . . . . 58°45' N, 026°24' E
Käina . . . . 58°50' N, 022°47' E
Kallaste . . . . 58°39' N, 027°09' E
Kärdla . . . . 59°00' N, 022°45' E
Kehra . . . . 59°20' N, 025°20' E
Keila . . . . 59°18' N, 024°25' E
Kilingi-Nõmme . . . . 58°09' N, 024°58' E
Kiviõli . . . . 59°21' N, 026°57' E
Kohtla-Järve . . . . 59°24' N, 027°15' E
Kunda . . . . 59°29' N, 026°32' E
Kuressaare (Kingissepa) . . 58°15' N, 022°28' E
Lavassaare . . . . 58°31' N, 024°22' E
Līhula (Lihula) . . . . 58°41' N, 023°50' E
Loksa . . . . 59°35' N, 025°42' E
Maardu . . . . 59°25' N, 024°59' E
Märjamaa . . . . 58°54' N, 024°26' E
Mõisaküla . . . . 58°06' N, 025°11' E
Mustla . . . . 58°14' N, 025°52' E
Narva . . . . 59°23' N, 028°12' E
Nuia . . . . 58°06' N, 025°33' E
Orissaare . . . . 58°34' N, 023°05' E

Otepää	58°03' N,	026°30' E
Paide	58°54' N,	025°33' E
Paldiski	59°20' N,	024°06' E
Pärnu	58°24' N,	024°32' E
Põlva	58°03' N,	027°03' E
Püssi	59°22' N,	027°03' E
Rakvere	59°22' N,	026°20' E
Räpina	58°06' N,	027°27' E
Rapla	59°01' N,	024°47' E
Saue	59°18' N,	024°34' E
Sindi	58°24' N,	024°40' E
Suure-Jaani	58°33' N,	025°28' E
Tallinn	59°25' N,	024°45' E
Tapa	59°16' N,	025°58' E
Tartu	58°23' N,	026°43' E
Tootsi	58°34' N,	024°49' E
Tõrva	58°00' N,	025°56' E
Türi	58°48' N,	025°26' E
Valga	57°47' N,	026°02' E
Viivikonna	59°19' N,	027°42' E
Viljandi	58°24' N,	025°36' E
Võsu	59°35' N,	025°58' E

ETHIOPIA ....pg. 58

Addis Ababa (Adis Abeba)	09°02' N,	038°42' E
Adigrat	14°17' N,	039°28' E
Adwa (Adowa or Aduwa)	14°10' N,	038°54' E
Agaro	07°51' N,	036°39' E
Akaki	09°05' N,	039°00' E
Aksum	14°08' N,	038°43' E
Alamata	12°25' N,	039°33' E
Arba Minch (Arba Mench)	06°02' N,	037°33' E
Bahir Dar	11°36' N,	037°23' E
Debre Markos	10°21' N,	037°44' E
Debre Zeyit	08°45' N,	038°59' E
Dembidollo	08°32' N,	038°48' E
Dese (Dase)	11°08' N,	039°38' E
Dire Dawa	09°35' N,	041°52' E
Finchaa	09°33' N,	037°21' E
Gonder	12°36' N,	037°28' E
Gore	08°09' N,	035°32' E
Harer (Harar)	09°19' N,	042°07' E
Jijiga	09°21' N,	042°48' E
Jima (Jimma)	07°40' N,	036°50' E
Kembolcha (Kombolcha)	11°05' N,	039°44' E
Kibre Mengist	05°53' N,	038°59' E
Lalibela	12°02' N,	039°02' E
Mekele	13°30' N,	039°28' E
Metu	08°18' N,	035°35' E
Nazret	08°33' N,	039°16' E
Nekemte	09°05' N,	036°33' E
Sodo	06°54' N,	037°45' E
Weldya	11°50' N,	039°41' E
Yirga Alem	06°45' N,	038°25' E

FIJI ....pg. 59

Ba	17°33' S,	177°41' E

Lami	18°07' S,	178°25' E
Lautoka	17°37' S,	177°28' E
Nadi	17°48' S,	177°25' E
Suva	18°08' S,	178°25' E

FINLAND ....pg. 60

Espoo (Esbo)	60°13' N,	024°40' E
Forssa	60°49' N,	023°38' E
Hämeenlinna (Tavastehus)	61°00' N,	024°27' E
Hanko	59°50' N,	022°57' E
Haukipudas	65°11' N,	025°21' E
Heinola	61°13' N,	026°02' E
Helsinki	60°10' N,	024°58' E
Ilmajoki	62°44' N,	022°34' E
Ivalo	68°39' N,	027°36' E
Jämsä	61°52' N,	025°12' E
Joensuu	62°36' N,	029°46' E
Jyväskylä	62°14' N,	025°44' E
Kangasala	61°28' N,	024°05' E
Kaskinen	62°23' N,	021°13' E
Kemi	65°44' N,	024°34' E
Kittilä	67°40' N,	024°54' E
Kotka	60°28' N,	026°55' E
Kouvola	60°52' N,	026°42' E
Kuhmo	64°08' N,	029°31' E
Kuopio	62°54' N,	027°41' E
Lahti	60°58' N,	025°40' E
Lappeenranta (Villmanstrand)	61°04' N,	028°11' E
Lapua	62°57' N,	023°00' E
Lohja	60°15' N,	024°05' E
Mariehamn (Maarianhamina)	60°06' N,	019°57' E
Mikkeli (Sankt Michel)	61°41' N,	027°15' E
Nivala	63°55' N,	024°58' E
Nurmes	63°33' N,	029°07' E
Oulu (Uleåborg)	65°01' N,	025°28' E
Pello	66°47' N,	023°55' E
Pietarsaari	63°40' N,	022°42' E
Pori (Björneborg)	61°29' N,	021°47' E
Posio	66°06' N,	028°09' E
Raahe	64°41' N,	024°29' E
Rauma	61°08' N,	021°30' E
Rovaniemi	66°30' N,	025°43' E
Salla	66°50' N,	028°40' E
Salo	60°23' N,	023°08' E
Sotkamo	64°08' N,	028°25' E
Tampere (Tammerfors)	61°30' N,	023°45' E
Turku (Åbo)	60°27' N,	022°17' E
Vaasa (Vasa)	63°06' N,	021°36' E
Vantaa (Vanda)	60°18' N,	024°51' E

FRANCE ....pg. 61

Ajaccio	41°55' N,	008°44' E
Amiens	49°54' N,	002°18' E
Angers	47°28' N,	000°33' W

Annecy	45°54' N,	006°07' E
Auch	43°39' N,	000°35' E
Aurillac	44°55' N,	002°27' E
Auxerre	47°48' N,	003°34' E
Avignon	43°57' N,	004°49' E
Bar-le-Duc	48°47' N,	005°10' E
Bastia	42°42' N,	009°27' E
Beauvais	49°26' N,	002°05' E
Belfort	47°38' N,	006°52' E
Bonifacio	41°23' N,	009°09' E
Bordeaux	44°50' N,	000°34' W
Bourges	47°05' N,	002°24' E
Brest	48°24' N,	004°29' W
Caen	49°11' N,	000°21' W
Cahors	44°26' N,	001°26' E
Calais	50°57' N,	001°50' E
Charleville-Mézières	49°46' N,	004°43' E
Chartres	48°27' N,	001°30' E
Clermont-Ferrand	45°47' N,	003°05' E
Colmar	48°05' N,	007°22' E
Dijon	47°19' N,	005°01' E
Dunkirk (Dunkerque)	51°03' N,	002°22' E
Épinal	48°11' N,	006°27' E
Grenoble	45°10' N,	005°43' E
Guéret	46°10' N,	001°52' E
La Rochelle	46°10' N,	001°09' W
Le Havre	49°30' N,	000°08' E
Le Mans	48°00' N,	000°12' E
Lille	50°38' N,	003°04' E
Limoges	45°45' N,	001°20' E
Lyon	45°45' N,	004°51' E
Marseille	43°18' N,	005°24' E
Metz	49°08' N,	006°10' E
Mont-de-Marsan	43°53' N,	000°30' W
Moulins	46°34' N,	003°20' E
Nancy	48°41' N,	006°12' E
Nantes	47°13' N,	001°33' W
Nevers	46°59' N,	003°10' E
Nice	43°42' N,	007°15' E
Nîmes	43°50' N,	004°21' E
Niort	46°19' N,	000°28' W
Orléans	47°55' N,	001°54' E
Paris	48°52' N,	002°20' E
Pau	43°18' N,	000°22' W
Périgueux	45°11' N,	000°43' E
Perpignan	42°41' N,	002°53' E
Poitiers	46°35' N,	000°20' E
Quimper	48°00' N,	004°06' W
Rennes	48°05' N,	001°41' W
Saint-Brieuc	48°31' N,	002°47' W
Strasbourg	48°35' N,	007°45' E
Tarbes	43°14' N,	000°05' E
Toulon	43°07' N,	005°56' E
Toulouse	43°36' N,	001°26' E
Tours	47°23' N,	000°41' E
Troyes	48°18' N,	004°05' E
Tulle	45°16' N,	001°46' E
Valence	44°56' N,	004°54' E
Vannes	47°40' N,	002°45' W
Versailles	48°48' N,	002°08' E
Vesoul	47°38' N,	006°10' E

GABON . . . . .pg. 62

Bitam	02°05' N,	011°29' E
Booué	00°06' S,	011°56' E
Fougamou	01°13' S,	010°36' E
Franceville	01°38' S,	013°35' E
Kango	00°09' N,	010°08' E
Koula-Moutou	01°08' S,	012°29' E
Lambaréné	00°42' S,	010°13' E
Lastoursville	00°49' S,	012°42' E
Léconi	01°35' S,	014°14' E
Libreville	00°23' N,	009°27' E
Makokou	00°34' N,	012°52' E
Mayumba	03°25' S,	010°39' E
Mekambo	01°01' N,	013°56' E
Mimongo	01°38' S,	011°39' E
Minvoul	02°09' N,	012°08' E
Mitzic	00°47' N,	011°34' E
Mouila	01°52' S,	011°01' E
Ndjolé	00°11' S,	010°45' E
Okondja	00°41' S,	013°47' E
Omboué	01°34' S,	009°15' E
Ovendo	00°17' N,	009°30' E
Oyem	01°37' N,	011°35' E
Port-Gentil	00°43' S,	008°47' E
Setté Cama	02°32' S,	009°45' E
Tchibanga	02°51' S,	011°02' E

GAMBIA, THE . . . .pg. 63

Banjul	13°27' N,	016°35' W
Basse Santa Su	13°19' N,	014°13' W
Brikama	13°16' N,	016°39' W
Georgetown	13°32' N,	014°46' W
Mansa Konko	13°28' N,	015°33' W
Serekunda	13°26' N,	016°34' W
Yundum	13°20' N,	016°41' W

GEORGIA . . . . .pg. 64

Akhalk'alak'i	41°24' N,	043°29' E
Batumi	41°38' N,	041°38' E
Chiat'ura	42°19' N,	043°18' E
Gagra	43°20' N,	040°15' E
Gardabani	41°28' N,	045°05' E
Gori	41°58' N,	044°07' E
Gudaut'a	43°06' N,	040°38' E
Khashuri	41°59' N,	043°36' E
K'obulet'i	41°50' N,	041°45' E
Kutaisi	42°15' N,	042°40' E
Marneuli	41°27' N,	044°48' E
Och'amch'ire	42°43' N,	041°28' E
Pot'i	42°09' N,	041°40' E
Rustari	41°33' N,	045°03' E
Samtredia	42°11' N,	042°20' E
Sokhumi	43°00' N,	041°02' E
Tbilisi (Tiflis)	41°42' N,	044°45' E
T'elavi	41°55' N,	045°28' E

Tqibuli . . . . 42°22' N, 042°59' E
Tqvarch'eli (Tkvarchely) . . 42°51' N, 041°41' E
Ts'khinvali (Staliniri) . . . . . 42°14' N, 043°58' E
Tsqaltubo . . . . 42°20' N, 042°34' E
Zugdidi . . . . 42°30' N, 041°53' E

GERMANY . . . . .pg. 65

Aachen . . . . 50°46' N, 006°06' E
Augsburg . . . . 48°22' N, 010°53' E
Aurich . . . . 53°28' N, 007°29' E
Baden-Baden . . . . 48°45' N, 008°15' E
Berlin . . . . 52°30' N, 013°22' E
Bielefeld. . . . . 52°02' N, 008°32' E
Bonn . . . . 50°44' N, 007°06' E
Brandenburg . . . . 52°25' N, 012°33' E
Bremen . . . . 53°05' N, 008°48' E
Bremerhaven . . . . 53°33' N, 008°35' E
Chemnitz
   (Karl-Marx-Stadt) . . . . 50°50' N, 012°55' E
Cologne (Köln) . . . . 50°56' N, 006°57' E
Cottbus . . . . 51°46' N, 014°20' E
Dessau . . . . 51°50' N, 012°15' E
Dortmund . . . . 51°31' N, 007°27' E
Dresden . . . . 51°03' N, 013°45' E
Duisburg . . . . 51°26' N, 006°45' E
Düsseldorf. . . . . 51°13' N, 006°46' E
Erfurt . . . . 50°59' N, 011°02' E
Erlangen . . . . 49°36' N, 011°01' E
Essen . . . . 51°27' N, 007°01' E
Frankfurt am Main . . . . 50°07' N, 008°41' E
Freiburg. . . . . 48°00' N, 007°51' E
Göttingen. . . . . 51°32' N, 009°56' E
Halle. . . . . 51°30' N, 012°00' E
Hamburg . . . . 53°33' N, 010°00' E
Hannover. . . . . 52°22' N, 009°43' E
Heidelberg. . . . . 49°25' N, 008°42' E
Jena . . . . 50°56' N, 011°35' E
Kassel . . . . 51°19' N, 009°30' E
Kiel. . . . . 54°20' N, 010°08' E
Leipzig. . . . . 51°18' N, 012°20' E
Lübeck. . . . . 53°52' N, 010°42' E
Magdeburg . . . . 52°10' N, 011°40' E
Mainz . . . . 50°00' N, 008°15' E
Mannheim . . . . 49°29' N, 008°28' E
Munich . . . . 48°09' N, 011°35' E
Nürnberg (Nuremberg) . . . . 49°27' N, 011°05' E
Oldenburg . . . . 54°18' N, 010°53' E
Osnabrück. . . . . 52°16' N, 008°03' E
Potsdam . . . . 52°24' N, 013°04' E
Regensburg . . . . 49°01' N, 012°06' E
Rostock . . . . 54°05' N, 012°08' E
Saarbrücken . . . . 49°14' N, 007°00' E
Schwerin . . . . 53°38' N, 011°23' E
Siegen . . . . 50°52' N, 008°02' E
Stuttgart . . . . 48°46' N, 009°11' E
Ulm . . . . 48°24' N, 010°00' E
Wiesbaden . . . . 50°05' N, 008°15' E
Würzburg . . . . 49°48' N, 009°56' E
Zwickau . . . . 50°44' N, 012°30' E

GHANA . . . . .pg. 66

Accra . . . . 05°33' N, 000°13' E
Anloga . . . . 05°48' N, 000°54' E
Awaso . . . . 06°14' N, 002°16' W
Axim . . . . 04°52' N, 002°14' W
Bawku . . . . 11°03' N, 000°15' W
Bolgatanga . . . . 10°47' N, 000°51' W
Cape Coast . . . . 05°06' N, 001°15' W
Damongo . . . . 09°05' N, 001°49' W
Dunkwa . . . . 05°58' N, 001°47' W
Koforidua . . . . 05°14' N, 001°20' W
Kumasi. . . . . 06°41' N, 001°37' W
Mampong . . . . 07°04' N, 001°24' W
Obuasi . . . . 06°12' N, 001°40' W
Prestea . . . . 05°26' N, 002°09' W
Salaga . . . . 08°33' N, 000°31' W
Sekondi-Takoradi . . . . 04°53' N, 001°45' W
Sunyani . . . . 07°20' N, 002°20' W
Swedru . . . . 05°32' N, 000°42' W
Tamale. . . . . 09°24' N, 000°50' W
Tarkwa . . . . 05°18' N, 001°59' W
Tema . . . . 05°37' N, 000°01' W
Wa . . . . 10°03' N, 002°29' W
Yendi . . . . 09°26' N, 000°01' W

GREECE . . . . .pg. 67

Alexandroúpolis
   (Alexandhroupolis) . . . . . 40°51' N, 025°52' E
Ándros. . . . . 37°50' N, 024°56' E
Árgos . . . . 37°38' N, 022°44' E
Árta . . . . 39°09' N, 020°59' E
Áyios Nikólaos . . . . 35°11' N, 025°43' E
Drama . . . . 41°09' N, 024°09' E
Edessa (Edhessa) . . . . 40°48' N, 022°03' E
Ermoúpolis
   (Hermoúpolis) . . . . 37°27' N, 024°56' E
Flórina . . . . 40°47' N, 021°24' E
Hydra (Ídhra) . . . . 37°21' N, 023°28' E
Igoumenítsa. . . . . 39°30' N, 020°16' E
Ioánnina (Yannina) . . . . . . 39°40' N, 020°50' E
Ios . . . . 36°44' N, 025°17' E
Iráklion
   (Candia or Heraklion) . . . 35°20' N, 025°08' E
Kalamariá . . . . 40°35' N, 022°58' E
Kalamata (Kalámai) . . . . . . 37°02' N, 022°07' E
Kálimnos . . . . 36°57' N, 026°59' E
Karditsa. . . . . 39°22' N, 021°55' E
Kariaí. . . . . 40°15' N, 024°15' E
Karpenísion . . . . 38°55' N, 021°47' E
Kateríni . . . . 40°16' N, 022°30' E
Kavála
   (Kaválla or Neapolis) . . . 40°56' N, 024°25' E
Kéa. . . . . 37°38' N, 024°21' E
Kérkira . . . . 39°36' N, 019°55' E
Khalkís (Chalcis) . . . . 38°28' N, 023°36' E
Khaniá (Canea) . . . . 35°31' N, 024°02' E
Khíos (Chios) . . . . 38°22' N, 026°08' E

Kilkís . . . . 41°00' N, 022°52' E
Komotiní . . . . 41°07' N, 025°24' E
Lamía . . . . 38°54' N, 022°26' E
Larissa (Lárisa) . . . . 39°38' N, 022°25' E
Laurium (Lávrion) . . . . . . 37°43' N, 024°03' E
Mégara . . . . 38°00' N, 023°21' E
Mesolóngion
 (Missolonghi) . . . . 38°22' N, 021°26' E
Mitilíni (Mytilene) . . . . . . 39°06' N, 026°33' E
Monemvasía . . . . 36°41' N, 023°03' E
Náuplia(Navplion) . . . . . . 37°34' N, 022°48' E
Náxos . . . . 37°06' N, 025°23' E
Néa Ionía . . . . 38°02' N, 023°45' E
Pátrai . . . . 38°15' N, 021°44' E
Piraeus (Piraievs) . . . . . . 37°57' N, 028°38' E
Préveza . . . . 38°57' N, 020°45' E
Pylos (Pílos) . . . . 36°55' N, 021°42' E
Pyrgos (Pírgos) . . . . 37°41' N, 021°27' E
Réthimnon . . . . 35°22' N, 024°28' E
Rhodes (Ródhos) . . . . . . 36°26' N, 028°13' E
Sámos . . . . 37°45' N, 026°58' E
Samothráki . . . . 40°29' N, 025°31' E
Sérrai . . . . 41°05' N, 023°33' E
Sparta (Spárti) . . . . 37°05' N, 022°26' E
Thásos . . . . 40°47' N, 024°43' E
Thebes (Thívai) . . . . 38°19' N, 023°19' E
Thessaloníki (Salonika) . . 40°38' N, 022°56' E
Tríkala . . . . 39°33' N, 021°46' E
Trípolis . . . . 37°31' N, 022°22' E
Vólos . . . . 39°22' N, 022°57' E
Yithion (Githion) . . . . 36°45' N, 022°34' E
Xánthi . . . . 41°08' N, 024°53' E
Zákinthos . . . . 37°47' N, 020°54' E

GRENADA . . . . pg. 68

Birch Grove . . . . 12°07' N, 061°40' W
Concord . . . . 12°07' N, 061°44' W
Corinth . . . . 12°02' N, 061°40' W
Gouyave . . . . 12°10' N, 061°44' W
Grand Anse . . . . 12°01' N, 061°45' W
Grenville . . . . 12°07' N, 061°37' W
Hillsborough . . . . 12°29' N, 061°28' W
La Poterie . . . . 12°10' N, 061°36' W
Rose Hill . . . . 12°12' N, 061°37' W
St. George's . . . . 12°03' N, 061°45' W
Sauteurs . . . . 12°14' N, 061°38' W
Victoria . . . . 12°12' N, 061°42' W

GUATEMALA . . . . . pg. 69

Amatitlán . . . . 14°29' N, 090°37' W
Antigua Guatemala
 (Antigua) . . . . 14°34' N, 090°44' W
Champerico . . . . 14°18' N, 091°55' W
Coatepeque . . . . 14°42' N, 091°52' W
Cobán . . . . 15°29' N, 090°22' W
Cuilapa (Cuajiniquilapa) . . 14°17' N, 090°18' W

El Estor . . . . 15°32' N, 089°21' W
Escuintla . . . . 14°18' N, 090°47' W
Esquipulas . . . . 14°34' N, 089°21' W
Flores . . . . 16°56' N, 089°53' W
Gualán . . . . 15°08' N, 089°22' W
Guatemala City
 (Guatemala) . . . . 14°38' N, 090°31' W
Huehuetenango . . . . 15°20' N, 091°28' W
Jalapa . . . . 14°38' N, 089°59' W
Jutiapa . . . . 14°17' N, 089°54' W
Mazatenango . . . . 14°32' N, 091°30' W
Poptún . . . . 16°21' N, 089°26' W
Pueblo Nuevo Tiquisate . . 14°17' N, 091°22' W
Puerto Barrios . . . . 15°43' N, 088°36' W
Puerto San José . . . . 13°55' N, 090°49' W
Quezaltenango . . . . 14°50' N, 091°31' W
Salamá . . . . 15°06' N, 090°16' W
San Benito . . . . 16°55' N, 089°54' W
San Cristóbal Verapaz . . . 15°23' N, 090°24' W
Santa Cruz del Quiché . . . 15°02' N, 091°08' W
Sololá . . . . 14°46' N, 091°11' W
Todos Santos
 Cuchumatán . . . . 15°31' N, 091°37' W
Villa Nueva . . . . 14°31' N, 090°35' W
Zacapa . . . . 14°58' N, 089°32' W
Zunil . . . . 14°47' N, 091°29' W

GUINEA . . . . pg. 70

Beyla . . . . 08°41' N, 008°38' W
Boffa . . . . 10°10' N, 014°02' W
Boké . . . . 10°56' N, 014°18' W
Conakry . . . . 09°31' N, 013°43' W
Dabola . . . . 10°45' N, 011°07' W
Dalaba . . . . 10°42' N, 012°15' W
Dinguiraye . . . . 11°18' N, 010°43' W
Faranah . . . . 10°02' N, 010°44' W
Forécariah . . . . 09°26' N, 013°06' W
Fria . . . . 10°27' N, 013°32' W
Gaoual . . . . 11°45' N, 013°12' W
Guéckédou . . . . 08°33' N, 010°09' W
Kankan . . . . 10°23' N, 009°18' W
Kérouané . . . . 09°16' N, 009°01' W
Kindia . . . . 10°04' N, 012°51' W
Kissidougou . . . . 09°11' N, 010°06' W
Kouroussa . . . . 10°39' N, 009°53' W
Labé . . . . 11°19' N, 012°17' W
Macenta . . . . 08°33' N, 009°28' W
Mamou . . . . 10°23' N, 012°05' W
Nzérékoré . . . . 07°45' N, 008°49' W
Pita . . . . 11°05' N, 012°24' W
Siguiri . . . . 11°25' N, 009°10' W
Télimélé . . . . 10°54' N, 013°02' W
Tougué . . . . 11°27' N, 011°41' W

GUINEA-BISSAU . . pg. 71

Bafatá . . . . 12°10' N, 014°40' W
Bambadinca . . . . 12°02' N, 014°52' W
Bedanda . . . . 11°21' N, 015°07' W

Béli . . . . 11°51' N, 013°56' W
Bissau . . . . 11°51' N, 015°35' W
Bissorã . . . . 12°03' N, 015°26' W
Bolama . . . . 11°35' N, 015°28' W
Buba . . . . 11°35' N, 015°00' W
Bula . . . . 12°07' N, 015°43' W
Buruntuma . . . . 12°26' N, 013°39' W
Cacheu . . . . 12°16' N, 016°10' W
Catió . . . . 11°17' N, 015°15' W
Empada . . . . 11°33' N, 015°14' W
Farim . . . . 12°29' N, 015°13' W
Fulacunda . . . . 11°46' N, 015°10' W
Gabú (Nova Lamego) . . . . . 12°17' N, 014°13' W
Galomaro . . . . 11°57' N, 014°38' W
Jolmete . . . . 12°13' N, 015°52' W
Madina do Boé . . . . 11°45' N, 014°13' W
Mansôa . . . . 12°04' N, 015°19' W
Nhacra . . . . 11°58' N, 015°33' W
Piche . . . . 12°20' N, 013°57' W
Pirada . . . . 12°40' N, 014°10' W
Quebo . . . . 11°20' N, 014°56' W
Quinhámel . . . . 11°53' N, 015°51' W
Safīm . . . . 11°57' N, 015°39' W
Sangonhá . . . . 11°10' N, 014°53' W
São Domingos . . . . 12°24' N, 016°12' W
Teixeira Pinto . . . . 12°04' N, 016°02' W
Tite . . . . 11°47' N, 015°24' W
Xitole . . . . 11°44' N, 014°49' W

GUYANA . . . . pg. 72

Apoteri . . . . 04°02' N, 058°34' W
Bartica . . . . 06°24' N, 058°37' W
Charity . . . . 07°24' N, 058°36' W
Corriverton . . . . 05°52' N, 057°10' W
Georgetown . . . . 06°48' N, 058°10' W
Isherton . . . . 02°19' N, 059°22' W
Ituni . . . . 05°30' N, 058°14' W
Karasabai . . . . 04°02' N, 059°32' W
Karmuda Village . . . . . . 05°38' N, 060°18' W
Lethem . . . . 03°23' N, 059°48' W
Linden . . . . 06°00' N, 058°18' W
Mabaruma . . . . 08°12' N, 059°47' W
Mahaicony Village . . . . . 06°36' N, 057°48' W
Matthews Ridge . . . . 07°30' N, 060°10' W
New Amsterdam . . . . 06°15' N, 057°31' W
Orinduik . . . . 04°42' N, 060°01' W
Parika . . . . 06°52' N, 058°25' W
Port Kaituma . . . . 07°44' N, 059°53' W
Rose Hall . . . . 06°16' N, 057°21' W
Suddie . . . . 07°07' N, 058°29' W
Vreed en Hoop . . . . 06°48' N, 058°11' W

HAITI . . . . pg. 73

Anse-d'Hainault . . . . 18°30' N, 074°27' W
Cap-Haïtien . . . . 19°45' N, 072°12' W
Desdunes . . . . 19°17' N, 072°39' W
Gonaïves . . . . 19°27' N, 072°41' W
Grand Goâve . . . . 18°26' N, 072°46' W

Hinche . . . . 19°09' N, 072°01' W
Jean Rabel . . . . 18°15' N, 072°40' W
Lascahobas . . . . 18°50' N, 071°56' W
Léogâne . . . . 18°31' N, 072°38' W
Limbé . . . . 19°42' N, 072°24' W
Miragoâne . . . . 18°27' N, 073°06' W
Mirebalais . . . . 18°55' N, 072°06' W
Môle Saint-Nicolas . . . . . 19°48' N, 073°23' W
Ouanaminthe . . . . 19°33' N, 071°44' W
Pètionville . . . . 18°31' N, 072°17' W
Petite Rivière de
    l'Artibonite . . . . 19°08' N, 072°29' W
Port-au-Prince . . . . 18°32' N, 072°20' W
Roseaux . . . . 18°36' N, 074°01' W
Saint-Louis du Nord . . . . . 19°56' N, 072°43' W
Saint-Michel de l'Atalaye . . 19°22' N, 072°20' W
Thomasique . . . . 19°05' N, 071°50' W
Trou du Nord . . . . 19°38' N, 072°01' W
Verrettes . . . . 19°03' N, 072°28' W

HONDURAS . . . . . . pg. 74

Amapala . . . . 13°17' N, 087°39' W
Catacamas . . . . 14°48' N, 085°54' W
Choloma . . . . 15°37' N, 087°57' W
Choluteca . . . . 13°18' N, 087°12' W
Comayagua . . . . 14°27' N, 087°38' W
Danlí . . . . 14°02' N, 086°35' W
El Paraíso . . . . 15°01' N, 088°59' W
El Progreso . . . . 15°24' N, 087°48' W
Gracias . . . . 14°35' N, 088°35' W
Guaimaca . . . . 14°32' N, 086°49' W
Intibucá . . . . 14°19' N, 088°10' W
Juticalpa . . . . 14°39' N, 086°12' W
La Ceiba . . . . 15°47' N, 086°48' W
La Esperanza . . . . 14°18' N, 088°11' W
La Lima . . . . 15°26' N, 087°55' W
La Paz . . . . 14°19' N, 087°41' W
Morazán . . . . 15°19' N, 087°36' W
Nacaome . . . . 13°32' N, 087°29' W
Olanchito . . . . 15°30' N, 086°34' W
Puerto Cortés . . . . 15°50' N, 087°50' W
Puerto Lempira . . . . 15°16' N, 083°46' W
San Lorenzo . . . . 13°25' N, 087°27' W
San Marcos de Colón . . . . 13°26' N, 086°48' W
San Pedro Sula . . . . 15°30' N, 088°02' W
Santa Bárbara . . . . 14°55' N, 088°14' W
Santa Rita . . . . 15°12' N, 087°53' W
Signatapeque . . . . 14°36' N, 087°57' W
Talanga . . . . 14°24' N, 087°05' W
Tegucigalpa . . . . 14°06' N, 087°13' W
Trujillo . . . . 15°55' N, 86°00' W
Yoro . . . . 15°08' N, 087°08' W
Yuscarán . . . . 13°56' N, 086°51' W

HUNGARY . . . . pg. 75

Baja . . . . 46°11' N, 018°58' E
Balmazújváros . . . . 47°37' N, 021°21' E
Barcs . . . . 45°58' N, 017°28' E

ICELAND . . . . pg. 76

INDIA . . . . pg. 77

Shiliguri (Siliguri) . . . . 26°42' N, 088°26' E
Sholapur (Solapur) . . . . 17°41' N, 075°55' E
Sibsāgar . . . . 26°59' N, 094°38' E
Srinagar . . . . 34°05' N, 074°49' E
Surat . . . . 21°10' N, 072°50' E
Thanjavur (Tanjore) . . . . . . 10°48' N, 079°09' E
Tiruppur (Tirupper) . . . . . . 11°06' N, 077°21' E
Vadodara (Baroda) . . . . 22°18' N, 073°12' E
Vārānasi (Banāras,
   Benares) . . . . 25°20' N, 083°00' E
Vishākhapatnam
   (Visākhāpatam) . . . . 17°42' N, 083°18' E

INDONESIA . . . . . . pg. 78

Ambon . . . . 03°43' S, 128°12' E
Balikpapan . . . . 01°17' S, 116°50' E
Banda Aceh (Kuta Raja) . . 05°34' N, 095°20' E
Bandung . . . . 06°54' S, 107°36' E
Banjarmasin . . . . 03°20' S, 114°35' E
Cilacap . . . . 07°44' S, 109°00' E
Jakarta . . . . 06°10' S, 106°48' E
Jambi . . . . 01°36' S, 103°37' E
Kendari . . . . 03°57' S, 122°35' E
Kupang . . . . 10°10' S, 123°35' E
Malang . . . . 07°59' S, 112°37' E
Manado . . . . 01°29' N, 124°51' E
Mataram . . . . 08°35' S, 116°07' E
Medan . . . . 03°35' N, 098°40' E
Padang . . . . 00°57' S, 100°21' E
Palembang . . . . 02°55' S, 104°45' E
Palu . . . . 00°53' S, 119°53' E
Samarinda . . . . 00°30' S, 117°09' E
Semarang . . . . 06°58' S, 110°25' E
Surabaya . . . . 07°15' S, 112°45' E
Ujungpandang . . . . 05°07' S, 119°24' E

IRAN . . . . pg. 79

Ahvāz . . . . 31°19' N, 048°42' E
Āmol . . . . 36°28' N, 052°21' E
Arāk . . . . 34°05' N, 049°41' E
Ardabīl . . . . 38°15' N, 048°18' E
Bakhtarān . . . . 34°19' N, 047°04' E
Bandar 'Abbās . . . . 27°11' N, 056°17' E
Behbahān . . . . 30°35' N, 050°14' E
Bīrjand . . . . 32°53' N, 059°13' E
Būshehr . . . . 28°59' N, 050°50' E
Dārāb . . . . 28°45' N, 054°34' E
Dezfūl . . . . 32°23' N, 048°24' E
Eṣfahān . . . . 32°40' N, 051°38' E
Gorgān . . . . 36°50' N, 054°29' E
Hamadān . . . . 34°48' N, 048°30' E
Kāshān . . . . 33°59' N, 051°29' E
Kāzerūn . . . . 29°37' N, 051°38' E
Kermān . . . . 30°17' N, 057°05' E
Khorramābād . . . . 33°30' N, 048°20' E
Khvoy . . . . 38°33' N, 044°58' E
Mahābād . . . . 36°45' N, 045°43' E
Mashhad . . . . 36°18' N, 059°36' E

Orūmīyeh . . . . 37°33' N, 045°04' E
Qā'en . . . . 33°44' N, 059°11' E
Qom . . . . 34°39' N, 050°54' E
Quchan . . . . 37°06' N, 058°30' E
Rafsanjān . . . . 30°24' N, 056°00' E
Rasht . . . . 37°16' N, 049°36' E
Sanandaj . . . . 35°19' N, 047°00' E
Shīrāz . . . . 29°36' N, 052°32' E
Tabrīz . . . . 38°05' N, 046°18' E
Tehran . . . . 35°40' N, 051°26' E
Yazd . . . . 31°53' N, 054°22' E
Zāhedān . . . . 29°30' N, 060°52' E
Zanjān . . . . 36°40' N, 048°29' E

IRAQ . . . . pg. 80

Ad-Diwaniyah . . . . 31°59' N, 044°56' E
Al-'Amarah . . . . 31°50' N, 047°09' E
Al-Gharrāf . . . . 31°21' N, 046°17' E
Al-Hillah . . . . 32°29' N, 044°25' E
Al-Khāliṣ . . . . 33°49' N, 044°32' E
Al-Kūt . . . . 32°30' N, 045°49' E
Al-Maḥmūdiya . . . . 33°03' N, 044°21' E
Al-Majarr al-Kabir . . . . . . 31°34' N, 047°00' E
'Ānah . . . . 34°28' N, 041°56' E
An-Najaf . . . . 31°59' N, 044°20' E
An-Nashwah . . . . 30°49' N, 047°36' E
An-Nasiriyah . . . . 31°02' N, 046°16' E
Ar-Ramādī . . . . 33°25' N, 043°17' E
Ar-Ruṭbah . . . . 33°02' N, 040°17' E
As-Samawah . . . . 31°18' N, 045°17' E
As-Sulaymaniyah . . . . 35°33' N, 045°26' E
Aṣ-Ṣuwayrah . . . . 32°55' N, 044°47' E
Baghdad . . . . 33°21' N, 044°25' E
Ba'qubah . . . . 33°45' N, 044°38' E
Barzān . . . . 36°55' N, 044°03' E
Basra (Al-Basrah) . . . . 30°30' N, 047°47' E
Dibs . . . . 35°40' N, 044°04' E
Hīt . . . . 33°38' N, 042°49' E
Irbil
   (Arbela, Arbil, or Erbil) . . 36°11' N, 044°01' E
Jalūlā' . . . . 34°16' N, 045°10' E
Karbala' . . . . 32°36' N, 044°02' E
Khānaqin . . . . 34°21' N, 045°22' E
Kirkuk . . . . 35°28' N, 044°23' E
Mosul (Al-Mawsil) . . . . . . 36°20' N, 043°08' E
Qal'at Dizah . . . . 36°11' N, 045°07' E
Sinjār . . . . 36°19' N, 041°52' E
Tall Kayf . . . . 36°29' N, 043°08' E
Tikrīt . . . . 34°36' N, 043°42' E
Ṭūz Khurmātū
   (Touz Hourmato) . . . . . . 34°53' N, 044°38' E
Zummār . . . . 36°47' N, 042°38' E

IRELAND . . . . pg. 81

Arklow
   (An tinbhear Mor) . . . . . . 52°48' N, 006°09' W
Athlone . . . . 53°26' N, 007°57' W
Ballina . . . . 54°07' N, 009°10' W

Ballycastle . . . . 54°17′ N, 009°22′ W
Ballycotton . . . . 51°50′ N, 008°01′ W
Ballymote . . . . 54°05′ N, 008°31′ W
Ballyvaghan . . . . 53°07′ N, 009°09′ W
Bandon
  (Droichead na Bandan) . . 51°45′ N, 008°44′ W
Bantry . . . . 51°41′ N, 009°27′ W
Belmullet . . . . 54°13′ N, 010°00′ W
Blarney . . . . 51°56′ N, 008°34′ W
Boyle . . . . 53°58′ N, 008°18′ W
Bray (Bre) . . . . 53°12′ N, 006°06′ W
Buncrana . . . . 55°08′ N, 007°27′ W
Carlow (Ceatharlach) . . . . . 52°50′ N, 006°56′ W
Carndonagh . . . . 55°15′ N, 007°16′ W
Carrick on Shannon . . . . . 53°57′ N, 008°05′ W
Castlebar . . . . 53°51′ N, 009°18′ W
Castletownbere . . . . 51°39′ N, 009°55′ W
Cavan (Cabhan, An) . . . . . 54°00′ N, 007°22′ W
Charleville (Rath Luirc) . . . 52°21′ N, 008°41′ W
Clifden . . . . 53°29′ N, 010°01′ W
Clonakilty . . . . 51°37′ N, 008°53′ W
Clonmel (Cluain Meala) . . . 52°21′ N, 007°42′ W
Cobh . . . . 51°51′ N, 008°17′ W
Cork (Corcaigh) . . . . 51°54′ N, 008°28′ W
Dingle . . . . 52°08′ N, 010°15′ W
Donegal . . . . 54°39′ N, 008°07′ W
Drogheda
  (Droichead Atha) . . . . . . 53°43′ N, 006°21′ W
Dublin . . . . 53°20′ N, 006°15′ W
Dundalk (Dun Dealgan) . . 54°00′ N, 006°25′ W
Dungarvan . . . . 52°05′ N, 007°37′ W
Ennis (Inis) . . . . 52°51′ N, 008°59′ W
Enniscorthy . . . . 52°30′ N, 006°34′ W
Ennistimon . . . . 52°56′ N, 009°18′ W
Galway (Gaillimh) . . . . . . 53°17′ N, 009°03′ W
Gort . . . . 53°04′ N, 008°49′ W
Kenmare . . . . 51°53′ N, 009°35′ W
Kilkee . . . . 52°41′ N, 009°38′ W
Kilkenny
  (Cill Chainnigh) . . . . . . 52°39′ N, 007°15′ W
Killarney (Cill Airne) . . . . . 52°03′ N, 009°31′ W
Letterkenny . . . . 54°57′ N, 007°44′ W
Lifford . . . . 54°50′ N, 007°29′ W
Limerick (Luimneach) . . . . 52°40′ N, 008°37′ W
Listowel . . . . 52°27′ N, 009°29′ W
Longford . . . . 53°44′ N, 007°48′ W
Loughrea . . . . 53°12′ N, 008°34′ W
Mallow . . . . 52°08′ N, 008°38′ W
Monaghan . . . . 54°15′ N, 006°58′ W
Naas (Nas, An) . . . . 53°13′ N, 006°40′ W
New Ross (Ros Mhic
  Thriuin) . . . . 52°23′ N, 006°56′ W
Portlaoise (Maryborough,
  Portlaoighise) . . . . 53°02′ N, 007°18′ W
Portumna . . . . 53°05′ N, 008°13′ W
Roscommon . . . . 53°38′ N, 008°11′ W
Rosslare . . . . 52°17′ N, 006°23′ W
Shannon . . . . 52°42′ N, 008°52′ W
Sligo . . . . 54°16′ N, 008°29′ W
Swords . . . . 53°27′ N, 006°13′ W
Tralee . . . . 52°16′ N, 009°43′ W

Trim . . . . 53°33′ N, 006°48′ W
Tullamore . . . . 53°16′ N, 007°29′ W
Waterford (Port Lairge) . . . 52°15′ N, 007°06′ W
Westport . . . . 53°48′ N, 009°31′ W
Wexford (Loch Garman) . . . 52°20′ N, 006°28′ W
Wicklow (Cill Mhantain) . . . 52°59′ N, 006°03′ W
Youghal . . . . 51°57′ N, 007°51′ W

ISRAEL . . . . .pg. 82

'Arad . . . . 31°15′ N, 035°13′ E
Ashdod . . . . 31°49′ N, 034°39′ E
Ashqelon . . . . 31°40′ N, 034°35′ E
Bat Yam . . . . 32°01′ N, 034°45′ E
Beersheba
  (Be'er Sheva') . . . . 31°14′ N, 034°47′ E
Bet She'an . . . . 32°30′ N, 035°30′ E
Bet Shemesh . . . . 31°45′ N, 035°00′ E
Dimona . . . . 31°04′ N, 035°02′ E
Elat. . . . . 29°33′ N, 034°57′ E
'En Yahav . . . . 30°38′ N, 035°11′ E
Hadera . . . . 32°26′ N, 034°55′ E
Haifa (Hefa) . . . . 32°50′ N, 035°00′ E
Hazeva . . . . 30°48′ N, 035°15′ E
Herzliyya . . . . 32°10′ N, 034°51′ E
Holon . . . . 32°01′ N, 034°46′ E
Jerusalem
  (Yerushalayim) . . . . 31°46′ N, 035°14′ E
Karmi'el . . . . 32°55′ N, 035°18′ E
Nazareth (Nazerat) . . . . . . 32°42′ N, 035°18′ E
Netanya . . . . 32°20′ N, 034°51′ E
Nir Yizhaq . . . . 31°14′ N, 034°22′ E
Petah Tiqwa . . . . 32°05′ N, 034°53′ E
Qiryat Ata . . . . 32°48′ N, 035°06′ E
Qiryat Shemona . . . . 33°13′ N, 035°34′ E
Rama . . . . 32°56′ N, 035°22′ E
Rehovot . . . . 31°54′ N, 034°49′ E
Tel Aviv-Yafo . . . . 32°04′ N, 034°46′ E

ITALY . . . . .pg. 83

Agrigento (Girgenti) . . . . . 37°19′ N, 013°34′ E
Ancona . . . . 43°38′ N, 013°30′ E
Aosta . . . . 45°44′ N, 007°20′ E
Arezzo . . . . 43°25′ N, 011°53′ E
Bari . . . . 41°08′ N, 016°51′ E
Bologna . . . . 44°29′ N, 011°20′ E
Bolzano . . . . 46°31′ N, 011°22′ E
Brescia . . . . 45°33′ N, 010°15′ E
Cagliari . . . . 39°13′ N, 009°07′ E
Catania . . . . 37°30′ N, 015°06′ E
Catanzaro . . . . 38°54′ N, 016°35′ E
Crotone . . . . 39°05′ N, 017°08′ E
Cuneo (Coni) . . . . 44°23′ N, 007°32′ E
Fermo . . . . 43°09′ N, 013°43′ E
Florence (Firenze or
  Firenza) . . . . 43°46′ N, 011°15′ E
Foggia . . . . 41°27′ N, 015°34′ E
Genoa (Genova) . . . . 44°25′ N, 008°57′ E
Grosseto . . . . 42°46′ N, 011°08′ E

Iglesias	39°19' N,	008°32' E
Latina	41°28' N,	012°52' E
Manfredonia	41°38' N,	015°55' E
Marsala	37°48' N,	012°26' E
Milan (Milano)	45°28' N,	009°12' E
Naples (Napoli or		
Neapolis)	40°50' N,	014°15' E
Oristano	39°54' N,	008°36' E
Padua (Padova)	45°25' N,	011°53' E
Palermo	38°07' N,	013°22' E
Perugia (Perusia)	43°08' N,	012°22' E
Pescara	42°28' N,	014°13' E
Piombino	42°55' N,	010°32' E
Pisa	43°43' N,	010°23' E
Porto Torres	40°50' N,	008°24' E
Potenza	40°38' N,	015°48' E
Ragusa	36°55' N,	014°44' E
Ravenna	44°25' N,	012°12' E
Rome (Roma)	41°54' N,	012°29' E
Salerno	40°41' N,	014°47' E
San Remo	43°49' N,	007°46' E
Sassari	40°43' N,	008°34' E
Siena	43°19' N,	011°21' E
Syracuse (Siracusa)	37°04' N,	015°18' E
Taranto (Taras or		
Tarentum)	40°28' N,	017°14' E
Trapani	38°01' N,	012°29' E
Trento	46°04' N,	011°08' E
Trieste	45°40' N,	013°46' E
Turin (Torino)	45°03' N,	007°40' E
Udine	46°03' N,	013°14' E
Venice (Venezia)	45°27' N,	012°21' E
Verona	45°27' N,	011°00' E

IVORY COAST . . . .pg. 84

Abengourou	06°44' N,	003°29' W
Abidjan	05°19' N,	004°02' W
Aboisso	05°28' N,	003°12' W
Adzopé	06°06' N,	003°52' W
Agboville	05°56' N,	004°13' W
Anyama	05°30' N,	004°03' W
Arrah	06°40' N,	003°58' W
Biankouma	07°44' N,	007°37' W
Bondoukou	08°02' N,	002°48' W
Bouaflé	06°59' N,	005°45' W
Bouaké	07°41' N,	005°02' W
Bouna	09°16' N,	003°00' W
Boundiali	09°31' N,	006°29' W
Daloa	06°53' N,	006°27' W
Daoukro	07°03' N,	003°58' W
Dimbokro	06°39' N,	004°42' W
Divo	05°50' N,	005°22' W
Duékoué	06°45' N,	007°21' W
Ferkéssédougou	09°36' N,	005°12' W
Gagnoa	06°08' N,	005°56' W
Grand-Bassam	05°12' N,	003°44' W
Guiglo	06°33' N,	007°29' W
Katiola	08°08' N,	005°06' W
Kong	09°09' N,	004°37' W
Korhogo	09°27' N,	005°38' W

Lakota	05°51' N,	005°41' W
Man	07°24' N,	007°33' W
Odienné	09°30' N,	007°34' W
Oumé	06°23' N,	005°25' W
San-Pédro	04°44' N,	006°37' W
Sassandra	04°57' N,	006°05' W
Séguéla	07°57' N,	006°40' W
Sinfra	06°37' N,	005°55' W
Tabou	04°25' N,	007°21' W
Tengréla	10°26' N,	006°20' W
Tortiya	08°46' N,	005°41' W
Yamoussoukro	06°49' N,	005°17' W

JAMAICA . . . . .pg. 85

Annotto Bay	18°16' N,	076°46' W
Kingston	17°58' N,	076°48' W
Lucea	18°27' N,	078°10' W
Mandeville	18°02' N,	077°30' W
May Pen	17°58' N,	077°14' W
Montego Bay	18°28' N,	077°55' W
Port Antonio	18°11' N,	076°28' W
St. Ann's Bay	18°26' N,	077°08' W
Savanna-la-Mar	18°13' N,	078°08' W
Spanish Town	17°59' N,	076°57' W

JAPAN . . . . .pg. 86-87

Akita	39°43' N,	140°07' E
Aomori	40°49' N,	140°45' E
Asahikawa	43°46' N,	142°22' E
Chiba	35°36' N,	140°07' E
Fukui	36°04' N,	136°13' E
Fukuoka	33°35' N,	130°24' E
Fukushima	37°45' N,	140°28' E
Funabashi	35°42' N,	139°59' E
Gifu	35°25' N,	136°45' E
Hachinohe	40°30' N,	141°29' E
Hakodate	41°45' N,	140°43' E
Hiroshima	34°24' N,	132°27' E
Hofu	34°03' N,	131°34' E
Iwaki	37°05' N,	140°50' E
Kagoshima	31°36' N,	130°33' E
Kanazawa	36°34' N,	136°39' E
Kawasaki	35°32' N,	139°43' E
Kita-Kyushu	33°50' N,	130°50' E
Kōbe	34°41' N,	135°10' E
Kōchi	33°33' N,	133°33' E
Kumamoto	32°48' N,	130°43' E
Kushiro	42°58' N,	144°23' E
Kutchan	42°54' N,	140°45' E
Kyōto	35°00' N,	135°45' E
Matsue	35°28' N,	133°04' E
Matsuyama	33°50' N,	132°45' E
Mito	36°22' N,	140°28' E
Miyazaki	31°52' N,	131°25' E
Morioka	39°42' N,	141°09' E
Muroran	42°18' N,	140°59' E
Nagano	36°39' N,	138°11' E
Nagasaki	32°48' N,	129°55' E

Nagoya . . . . 35°10′ N, 136°55′ E
Naha . . . . 26°13′ N, 127°40′ E
Niigata . . . . 37°55′ N, 139°03′ E
Obihiro . . . . 42°55′ N, 143°12′ E
Okayama . . . . 34°39′ N, 133°55′ E
Ōsaka . . . . 34°40′ N, 135°30′ E
Otaru . . . . 43°13′ N, 141°00′ E
Sakai . . . . 34°35′ N, 135°28′ E
Sapporo . . . . 43°03′ N, 141°21′ E
Sendai . . . . 31°49′ N, 130°18′ E
Shizuoka . . . . 34°58′ N, 138°23′ E
Tokyo . . . . 35°42′ N, 139°46′ E
Tomakomai . . . . 42°38′ N, 141°36′ E
Tottori . . . . 35°30′ N, 134°14′ E
Toyama . . . . 36°41′ N, 137°13′ E
Utsunomiya . . . . 36°33′ N, 139°52′ E
Wakayama . . . . 34°13′ N, 135°11′ E
Wakkanai . . . . 45°25′ N, 141°40′ E
Yaizu . . . . 34°52′ N, 138°20′ E
Yamagata . . . . 38°15′ N, 140°20′ E
Yokohama . . . . 35°27′ N, 139°39′ E

JORDAN . . . . pg. 88

Adir . . . . 31°12′ N, 035°46′ E
Al-ʿAqabah . . . . 29°31′ N, 035°00′ E
Al-Faydah . . . . 32°35′ N, 038°13′ E
Al-Ḥiṣn . . . . 32°29′ N, 035°53′ E
Al-Karak . . . . 31°11′ N, 035°42′ E
Al-Mafraq . . . . 32°21′ N, 036°12′ E
Al-Mazraʿah . . . . 31°16′ N, 035°31′ E
Al-Mudawwarah . . . . 29°19′ N, 035°59′ E
Al-Qaṭrānah . . . . 31°15′ N, 036°03′ E
Amman (ʿAmmān) . . . . 31°57′ N, 035°56′ E
Ar-Ramthā . . . . 32°34′ N, 036°00′ E
Ash-Shawbak . . . . 30°32′ N, 035°34′ E
Aṣ Ṣalt . . . . 32°03′ N, 035°44′ E
At-Ṭafilah . . . . 30°50′ N, .035°36′ E
Az-Zarqāʾ . . . . 32°05′ N, 036°06′ E
Bāʾir . . . . 30°46′ N, 036°41′ E
Dhāt Raʾs . . . . 31°00′ N, 035°46′ E
Irbid . . . . 32°33′ N, 035°51′ E
Maʿān . . . . 30°12′ N, 035°44′ E
Maʾdabā . . . . 31°43′ N, 035°48′ E
Maḥaṭṭat al-Ḥafif . . . . 32°12′ N, 037°08′ E
Maḥaṭṭat al-Jufūr . . . . 32°30′ N, 038°12′ E
Ṣuwayliḥ . . . . 32°02′ N, 035°50′ E

KAZAKSTAN . . . . . pg. 89

Almaty (Alma-Ata) . . . . 43°15′ N, 076°57′ E
Aqtau (Aktau, or
  Shevchenko) . . . . 43°39′ N, 051°12′ E
Aqtöbe (Aktyubinsk) . . . . . 50°17′ N, 057°10′ E
Arqalyq . . . . 50°13′ N, 066°50′ E
Astana (Akmola,
  Akmolinsk, Aqmola,
  or Tselinograd) . . . . 51°10′ N, 071°30′ E
Atyraū (Atenau, Gurjev, or
  Guryev) . . . . 47°07′ N, 051°53′ E

Ayaguz . . . . 47°56′ N, 080°23′ E
Balqash (Balkhash or
  Balchas) . . . . 46°49′ N, 075°00′ E
Dzhezkazgan . . . . 47°47′ N, 067°46′ E
Kokchetav . . . . 53°17′ N, 069°30′ E
Leningor (Leninogorsk
  or Ridder) . . . . 50°22′ N, 083°32′ E
Oral (Uralsk) . . . . 51°14′ N, 051°22′ E
Öskemen
  (Ust-Kamenogorsk) . . . . . 49°58′ N, 082°40′ E
Panfilov (Zharkent) . . . . . . 44°10′ N, 080°01′ E
Pavlodar . . . . 52°18′ N, 076°57′ E
Petropavl
  (Petropavlovsk) . . . . 54°52′ N, 069°06′ E
Qaraghandy
  (Karaganda) . . . . 49°50′ N, 073°10′ E
Qostanay (Kustanay) . . . . . 53°10′ N, 063°35′ E
Qyzylorda(Kzyl-Orda) . . . . 44°48′ N, 065°28′ E
Rūdnyy (Rudny) . . . . 52°57′ N, 063°07′ E
Semey (Semipalatinsk . . . . 50°28′ N, 080°13′ E
Shchūchinsk . . . . 52°56′ N, 070°12′ E
Shymkent (Chimkent or
  Cimkent) . . . . 42°18′ N, 069°36′ E
Taldyqorghan (Taldy
  -Kurgan) . . . . 45°00′ N, 078°24′ E
Talghar . . . . 43°19′ N, 077°15′ E
Termirtaū
  (Samarkand) . . . . 50°05′ N, 072°56′ E
Türkistan . . . . 43°20′ N, 068°15′ E
Tyuratam (Turaram or
  Leninsk) . . . . 45°40′ N, 063°20′ E
Zhambyl (Dzhambul) . . . . . 42°54′ N, 071°22′ E
Zhangatas . . . . 43°34′ N, 069°45′ E
Zhetiqara . . . . 52°11′ N, 061°12′ E
Zhezqazghan . . . . 47°47′ N, 067°46′ E
Zyryan . . . . 49°43′ N, 084°20′ E

KENYA . . . . pg. 90

Bungoma . . . . 00°34′ N, 034°34′ E
Busia . . . . 00°28′ N, 034°06′ E
Eldoret . . . . 00°31′ N, 035°17′ E
Embu . . . . 00°32′ S, 037°27′ E
Garissa . . . . 00°28′ S, 039°38′ E
Isiolo . . . . 00°21′ N, 037°35′ E
Kisii . . . . 00°41′ S, 034°46′ E
Kisumu . . . . 00°06′ S, 034°45′ E
Lamu . . . . 02°16′ S, 040°54′ E
Lodwar . . . . 03°07′ N, 035°36′ E
Machakos . . . . 01°31′ S, 037°16′ E
Malindi . . . . 03°13′ S, 040°07′ E
Mandera . . . . 03°56′ N, 041°52′ E
Maralal . . . . 01°06′ N, 036°42′ E
Marsabit . . . . 02°20′ N, 037°59′ E
Meru . . . . 00°03′ N, 037°39′ E
Mombasa . . . . 04°03′ N, 039°40′ E
Murang'a . . . . 00°43′ N, 037°09′ E
Nairobi . . . . 01°17′ S, 036°49′ E
Nakuru . . . . 00°17′ S, 036°04′ E
Nanyuki . . . . 00°01′ N, 037°04′ E

Wajir . . . . 01°45' N, 040°04' E

KIRIBATI . . . . .pg. 91

Bairiki . . . . 01°20' N, 173°01' E

KUWAIT . . . . .pg. 92

Al-Aḥmadī . . . . 29°05' N, 048°04' E
Al-Jahrah . . . . 29°20' N, 047°40' E
Ash-Shu'aybah . . . . 29°03' N, 048°08' E
Ḥawallī . . . . 29°19' N, 048°02' E
Kuwait . . . . 29°20' N, 047°59' E
Umm Qasar . . . . 30°02' N, 047°55' E

KYRGYZSTAN . . . .pg. 93

Bishkek (Frunze) . . . . 42°54' N, 074°36' E
Dzhalal-Abad . . . . 40°56' N, 073°00' E
Irkeshtam . . . . 39°41' N, 073°55' E
Kara-Balta . . . . 42°50' N, 073°52' E
Karakol (Przhevalsk) . . . . 42°33' N, 078°18' E
Kök-Janggak . . . . 41°02' N, 073°12' E
Kyzyl-Kyya . . . . 40°16' N, 072°08' E
Mayly-Say . . . . 41°17' N, 072°24' E
Naryn . . . . 41°26' N, 075°58' E
Osh . . . . 40°32' N, 072°48' E
Sülüktü . . . . 39°56' N, 069°34' E
Talas . . . . 42°32' N, 072°14' E
Tash-Kömür . . . . 41°21' N, 072°14' E
Tokmok . . . . 42°52' N, 075°18' E
Ysyk-Kül (Rybachye) . . . . 42°26' N, 076°12' E

LAOS . . . . .pg. 94

Attapu . . . . 14°48' N, 106°50' E
Ban Houayxay . . . . 20°18' N, 100°26' E
Champasak . . . . 14°53' N, 105°52' E
Louang Namtha . . . . 20°57' N, 101°25' E
Louangphrabang . . . . 19°52' N, 102°08' E
Muang Khammouan
   (Muang Thakhek) . . . . . 17°24' N, 104°48' E
Muang Pek . . . . 19°35' N, 103°19' E
Muang Xaignabouri
   (Sayaboury) . . . . 19°15' N, 101°45' E
Muang Xay . . . . 20°42' N, 101°59' E
Pakxé . . . . 15°07' N, 105°47' E
Phôngsali . . . . 21°41' N, 102°06' E
Saravan . . . . 15°43' N, 106°25' E
Savannakhêt . . . . 16°33' N, 104°45' E
Vientiane
   (Viangchan) . . . . 17°58' N, 102°36' E
Xam Nua . . . . 20°25' N, 104°02' E

LATVIA . . . . .pg. 95

Aizpute . . . . 56°43' N, 021°36' E

Alūksne . . . . 57°25' N, 027°03' E
Auce . . . . 56°28' N, 022°53' E
Balvi . . . . 57°08' N, 027°15' E
Bauska . . . . 56°24' N, 024°11' E
Cēsis . . . . 57°18' N, 025°15' E
Daugavpils . . . . 55°53' N, 026°32' E
Dobele . . . . 56°37' N, 023°16' E
Gulbene . . . . 57°11' N, 026°45' E
Ilūkste . . . . 55°58' N, 026°18' E
Jaunjelgava . . . . 56°37' N, 025°05' E
Jēkabpils . . . . 56°29' N, 025°51' E
Jelgava . . . . 56°39' N, 023°42' E
Jūrmala . . . . 56°58' N, 023°34' E
Kandava . . . . 57°02' N, 022°46' E
Kārsava . . . . 56°47' N, 027°40' E
Ķegums . . . . 56°44' N, 024°43' E
Krāslava . . . . 55°54' N, 027°10' E
Liepāja . . . . 56°31' N, 021°01' E
Limbaži . . . . 57°31' N, 024°42' E
Ludza . . . . 56°33' N, 027°43' E
Malta . . . . 56°23' N, 027°07' E
Mazsalace . . . . 57°52' N, 025°03' E
Ogre . . . . 56°49' N, 024°36' E
Piltene . . . . 57°13' N, 021°40' E
Preili . . . . 56°18' N, 026°43' E
Priekule . . . . 55°33' N, 021°19' E
Rēzekne . . . . 56°30' N, 027°19' E
Riga (Rīga) . . . . 56°57' N, 024°06' E
Rujiena . . . . 57°54' N, 025°19' E
Sabile . . . . 57°03' N, 022°35' E
Salacgrīva . . . . 57°45' N, 024°21' E
Saldus . . . . 56°40' N, 022°30' E
Sigulda . . . . 57°09' N, 024°51' E
Stučka . . . . 56°35' N, 025°12' E
Talsi . . . . 57°15' N, 022°36' E
Valdemārpils . . . . 57°22' N, 022°35' E
Valmiera . . . . 57°33' N, 025°24' E
Ventspils . . . . 57°24' N, 021°31' E
Viesīte . . . . 56°21' N, 025°33' E
Viļaka . . . . 57°11' N, 027°41' E
Viļāni . . . . 56°33' N, 026°57' E
Zilupe . . . . 56°23' N, 028°07' E

LEBANON . . . . . . .pg. 96

Ad-Dāmūr . . . . 33°44' N, 035°27' E
Al-'Abdah . . . . 34°31' N, 035°58' E
Al-Batrūn . . . . 34°15' N, 035°39' E
Al-Hirmīl . . . . 34°23' N, 036°23' E
Al-Labwah . . . . 34°12' N, 036°21' E
Al-Qubayyāt . . . . 34°34' N, 036°17' E
Amyūn . . . . 34°18' N, 035°49' E
An-Nabaṭīyah at-Taḥtā . . 33°23' N, 035°29' E
Aṣ-Ṣarafand . . . . 33°27' N, 035°18' E
Baalbek (Ba'labakk) . . . . 34°00' N, 036°12' E
B'aqlīn . . . . 33°41' N, 035°33' E
Beirut (Bayrut) . . . . 33°53' N, 035°30' E
Bḥamdūn . . . . 33°48' N, 035°39' E
Bint Jubayl . . . . 33°07' N, 035°26' E
Bsharri . . . . 34°15' N, 036°01' E

En-Nāqūrah . . . . 33°07′ N, 035°08′ E
Ghazir . . . . 34°01′ N, 035°40′ E
Ghazzah . . . . 33°40′ N, 035°49′ E
Ghūmāh . . . . 34°13′ N, 035°42′ E
Halbā . . . . 34°33′ N, 036°05′ E
Ḥaṣbayya . . . . 33°24′ N, 035°41′ E
Ḥimlāyā . . . . 33°56′ N, 035°42′ E
Ihdin . . . . 34°17′ N, 035°58′ E
Jubayl (Byblos) . . . . 34°07′ N, 035°39′ E
Jubb Jannin . . . . 33°37′ N, 035°47′ E
Jūniyah . . . . 33°59′ N, 035°58′ E
Jwayyā . . . . 33°14′ N, 035°19′ E
Khaldah . . . . 33°47′ N, 035°29′ E
Marj ‘Uyūn . . . . 33°22′ N, 035°35′ E
Shḥim . . . . 33°37′ N, 035°29′ E
Shikkā . . . . 34°20′ N, 035°44′ E
Sidon (Sayda) . . . . 33°33′ N, 035°22′ E
Tripoli (Tarabulus) . . . . 34°26′ N, 035°51′ E
Tyre (Ṣūr) . . . . 33°16′ N, 035°11′ E
Zaḥlah . . . . 33°51′ N, 035°53′ E
Zghartā . . . . 34°24′ N, 035°54′ E

LESOTHO . . . . pg. 97

Butha-Butha . . . . 28°45′ S, 028°15′ E
Libono . . . . 28°38′ S, 028°35′ E
Mafeteng . . . . 29°49′ S, 027°15′ E
Maseru . . . . 29°19′ S, 027°29′ E
Mohales Hoek . . . . 30°09′ S, 027°28′ E
Mokhotlong . . . . 29°22′ S, 029°02′ E
Qacha's Nek . . . . 30°08′ S, 028°41′ E
Quthing . . . . 30°24′ S, 027°43′ E
Roma . . . . 29°27′ S, 027°42′ E
Teyateyaneng . . . . 29°09′ S, 027°44′ E

LIBERIA . . . . pg. 98

Bentol . . . . 06°26′ N, 010°36′ W
Bopolu . . . . 06°54′ N, 010°46′ W
Buchanan
  (Grand Bassa) . . . . 05°53′ N, 010°03′ W
Careysburg . . . . 06°24′ N, 010°33′ W
Gbarnga . . . . 07°00′ N, 009°29′ W
Grand Cess
  (Grand Sesters) . . . . 04°34′ N, 008°13′ W
Greenville (Sino) . . . . 05°00′ N, 009°02′ W
Harbel . . . . 06°16′ N, 010°21′ W
Harper . . . . 04°22′ N, 007°23′ W
Kle . . . . 06°42′ N, 010°53′ W
Monrovia . . . . 06°19′ N, 010°48′ W
Robertsport . . . . 06°45′ N, 011°22′ W
Saniquellie
  (Sangbui) . . . . 07°22′ N, 008°43′ W
Tubmanburg
  (Vaitown) . . . . 06°52′ N, 010°49′ W
Voinjama . . . . 08°25′ N, 009°45′ W
Yekepa . . . . 07°35′ N, 008°32′ W
Zorzor . . . . 07°47′ N, 009°26′ W
Zwedru (Tchien) . . . . 06°04′ N, 008°08′ W

LIBYA . . . . pg. 99

Al-Bayḍā (Baida or
  Zāwiyat al-Bayḍā) . . . . . 32°46′ N, 021°43′ E
Al-Kufrah . . . . 24°10′ N, 023°15′ E
Al-Marj (Barce) . . . . 32°30′ N, 020°50′ E
Al-‘Uwaynāt
  (Sardalas) . . . . 25°48′ N, 010°33′ E
As-Sidrah (Es-Sidre) . . . . . . 30°39′ N, 018°22′ E
Awbāri (Ubari) . . . . 26°35′ N, 012°46′ E
Az-Zuwaytinah . . . . 30°58′ N, 020°07′ E
Benghazi (Banghazi or
  Bengasi) . . . . 32°07′ N, 020°04′ E
Dahra . . . . 29°30′ N, 017°50′ E
Darnah (Dērna) . . . . 32°46′ N, 022°39′ E
Ghadāmis (Ghadāmes) . . . . 30°08′ N, 009°30′ E
Ghaddūwah (Goddua) . . . . . 26°26′ N, 014°18′ E
Gharyān (Garian) . . . . 32°10′ N, 013°01′ E
Ghāt . . . . 24°58′ N, 010°11′ E
Marādah . . . . 29°14′ N, 019°13′ E
Miṣrātah (Misurata) . . . . . . 32°23′ N, 015°06′ E
Murzuq . . . . 25°55′ N, 013°55′ E
Sabhā (Sebha) . . . . 27°02′ N, 014°26′ E
Sarīr . . . . 27°30′ N, 022°30′ E
Surt (Sirte) . . . . 31°13′ N, 016°35′ E
Tarabulus, see Tripoli
Tāzirbū . . . . 25°45′ N, 021°00′ E
Tobruk (Ṭubruq) . . . . 32°05′ N, 023°59′ E
Tripoli (Ṭarābulus) . . . . 32°54′ N, 013°11′ E
Waddān . . . . 29°10′ N, 016°08′ E
Wāw al-Kabīr . . . . 25°20′ N, 016°43′ E
Zalṭan (Zelten) . . . . 32°57′ N, 011°52′ E
Zlīṭan (Zliten) . . . . 32°28′ N, 014°34′ E
Zuwārah (Zuāra) . . . . 32°56′ N, 012°06′ E

LIECHTENSTEIN pg. 100

Balzers . . . . 47°04′ N, 009°32′ E
Eschen . . . . 47°13′ N, 009°32′ E
Mauren . . . . 47°13′ N, 009°33′ E
Schaan . . . . 47°10′ N, 009°31′ E
Triesen . . . . 47°07′ N, 009°32′ E
Vaduz . . . . 47°09′ N, 009°31′ E

LITHUANIA . . . . . . pg. 101

Alytus . . . . 54°24′ N, 024°03′ E
Anykščiai . . . . 55°32′ N, 025°06′ E
Birštonas . . . . 54°37′ N, 024°02′ E
Biržai . . . . 56°12′ N, 024°45′ E
Druskininkai . . . . 54°01′ N, 023°58′ E
Gargždai . . . . 55°43′ N, 021°24′ E
Ignalina . . . . 55°21′ N, 026°10′ E
Jonava . . . . 55°05′ N, 024°17′ E
Joniškis . . . . 56°14′ N, 023°37′ E
Jurbarkas . . . . 55°04′ N, 022°46′ E
Kaunas . . . . 54°54′ N, 023°54′ E
Kazlų Rūda . . . . 54°46′ N, 023°30′ E
Kėdainiai . . . . 55°17′ N, 023°58′ E

Kelmė. . . . . 55°38' N, 022°56' E
Klaipėda. . . . . 55°43' N, 021°07' E
Kuršėnai . . . . 56°00' N, 022°56' E
Lazdijai . . . . 54°14' N, 023°31' E
Marijampolė (Kapsukas) . . 54°34' N, 023°21' E
Mažeikiai . . . . 56°19' N, 022°20' E
Naujoji Akmenė. . . . . 56°19' N, 022°54' E
Neringa . . . . 55°22' N, 021°04' E
Pagėgiai. . . . . 55°09' N, 021°54' E
Pakruojis . . . . 58°58' N, 023°52' E
Palanga . . . . 55°55' N, 021°03' E
Pandėlys . . . . 56°01' N, 025°13' E
Panevėžys . . . . 55°44' N, 024°21' E
Pasvalys . . . . 56°04' N, 024°24' E
Plungė . . . . 55°55' N, 021°51' E
Priekulė . . . . 55°33' N, 021°19' E
Radviliškis . . . . 55°49' N, 023°32' E
Ramygala . . . . 55°31' N, 024°18' E
Raseiniai . . . . 55°22' N, 023°07' E
Rokiškis . . . . 55°58' N, 025°35' E
Šalčininkai . . . . 54°18' N, 025°23' E
Šiauliai . . . . 55°56' N, 023°19' E
Šilalė . . . . 55°28' N, 022°12' E
Šilutė . . . . 55°21' N, 021°29' E
Širvintos . . . . 55°03' N, 024°57' E
Skuodas . . . . 56°16' N, 021°32' E
Tauragė . . . . 55°15' N, 022°17' E
Telšiai . . . . 55°59' N, 022°15' E
Trakai . . . . 54°38' N, 024°56' E
Utena . . . . 55°30' N, 025°36' E
Varėna . . . . 54°13' N, 024°34' E
Vilkaviškis . . . . 54°39' N, 023°02' E
Vilkija . . . . 55°03' N, 023°35' E
Vilnius . . . . 54°41' N, 025°19' E
Zarasai. . . . . 55°44' N, 026°15' E

LUXEMBOURG . .pg. 102

Bains (Modorf-les-Bains) . . 49°30' N, 006°17' E
Bettembourg. . . . . 49°31' N, 006°06' E
Capellen. . . . . 49°39' N, 005°59' E
Clervaux . . . . 50°03' N, 006°02' E
Diekirch. . . . . 49°52' N, 006°10' E
Differdange . . . . 49°31' N, 005°53' E
Dudelange . . . . 49°28' N, 006°06' E
Echternach . . . . 49°49' N, 006°25' E
Esch-sur-Alzette . . . . 49°30' N, 005°59' E
Ettelbruck . . . . 49°51' N, 006°07' E
Grevenmacher . . . . 49°41' N, 006°27' E
Hesperange . . . . 49°34' N, 006°09' E
Junglinster. . . . . 49°43' N, 006°15' E
Lorentzweiler . . . . 49°42' N, 006°09' E
Luxembourg . . . . 49°36' N, 006°08' E
Mamer . . . . 49°38' N, 006°02' E
Mersch . . . . 49°45' N, 006°06' E
Niederanven . . . . 49°39' N, 006°15' E
Pétange . . . . 49°33' N, 005°53' E
Rambrouch . . . . 49°50' N, 005°51' E
Redange. . . . . 49°46' N, 005°53' E

Remich . . . . 49°32' N, 006°22' E
Sanem . . . . 49°33' N, 005°56' E
Schifflange. . . . . 49°30' N, 006°01' E
Vianden . . . . 49°56' N, 006°13' E
Walfedange . . . . 49°39' N, 006°08' E
Wiltz . . . . 49°58' N, 005°56' E
Wincrange . . . . 50°03' N, 005°55' E
Wormeldange . . . . 49°37' N, 006°25' E

MACEDONIA . . . .pg. 103

Bitola . . . . 41°02' N, 021°20' E
Gostivar. . . . . 41°48' N, 020°54' E
Kavadarci . . . . 41°26' N, 022°00' E
Kičevo . . . . 41°31' N, 020°57' E
Kočani . . . . 41°55' N, 022°25' E
Kruševo . . . . 41°22' N, 021°15' E
Kumanovo . . . . 42°08' N, 021°43' E
Ohrid . . . . 41°07' N, 020°48' E
Prilep . . . . 41°21' N, 021°34' E
Skopje (Skoplje) . . . . 42°00' N, 021°29' E
Štip . . . . 41°44' N, 022°12' E
Strumica . . . . 41°26' N, 022°39' E
Tetovo . . . . 42°01' N, 020°59' E
Tito Veles . . . . 41°42' N, 021°48' E

MADAGASCAR . .pg. 104

Ambanja . . . . 13°41' S, 048°27' E
Ambatondrazaka. . . . . 17°50' S, 048°25' E
Andapa . . . . 14°39' S, 049°39' E
Ankarana (Sosumav) . . . . 13°05' S, 048°55' E
Antalaha . . . . 14°53' S, 050°17' E
Antananarivo
(Tananarive) . . . . 18°55' S, 047°31' E
Antsirabe. . . . . 19°51' S, 047°02' E
Antsirañana
(Diégo-Suarez). . . . . 12°16' S, 049°17' E
Antsohihy . . . . 14°52' S, 047°59' E
Fianarantsoa . . . . 21°26' S, 047°05' E
Ihosy . . . . 22°24' S, 046°07' E
Maevatanana . . . . 16°57' S, 046°50' E
Mahabo . . . . 20°23' S, 044°40' E
Mahajanga (Majunga). . . . 15°43' S, 046°19' E
Mahanoro . . . . 19°54' S, 048°48' E
Mananjary . . . . 21°13' S, 048°20' E
Maroantsetra . . . . 15°26' S, 049°44' E
Marovoay . . . . 16°06' S, 046°38' E
Morombe. . . . . 21°44' S, 043°21' E
Morondava . . . . 20°17' S, 044°17' E
Port-Bergé (Boriziny) . . . . 15°33' S, 047°40' E
Toamasina
(Tamatave) . . . . 18°10' S, 049°23' E
Tôlañaro (Faradofay,
Fort-Dauphin or
Taolanaro). . . . . 25°02' S, 047°00' E
Toliara
(Toliary or Tulear) . . . . 23°21' S, 043°40' E
Vangaindrano . . . . 23°21' S, 047°36' E
Vatomandry . . . . 19°20' S, 048°59' E

MALAWI . . . . .pg. 105

Balaka	14°59' S,	034°57' E
Blantyre	15°47' S,	035°00' E
Chikwawa	16°03' S,	034°48' E
Cholo (Thyolo)	16°04' S,	035°08' E
Dedza	14°22' S,	034°20' E
Dowa	13°39' S,	033°56' E
Karonga	09°56' S,	033°56' E
Kasungu	13°02' S,	033°29' E
Lilongwe	13°59' S,	033°47' E
Mangoche		
(Fort Johnson)	14°28' S,	035°16' E
Mchinji (Fort Manning) . .	13°48' S,	032°54' E
Monkey Bay	14°05' S,	034°55' E
Mzimba	11°54' S,	033°36' E
Mzuzu	11°27' S,	033°55' E
Nkhata Bay	11°36' S,	034°18' E
Nkhota Kota		
(Kota Kota)	12°55' S,	034°18' E
Nsanje (Port Herald)	16°55' S,	035°16' E
Salima	13°47' S,	034°26' E
Zomba	15°23' S,	035°20' E

MALAYSIA . . . . . . .pg. 106

Alor Setar	06°07' N,	100°22' E
Batu Pahat	01°51' N,	102°56' E
Bau	01°25' N,	110°09' E
Bentong	03°32' N,	101°55' E
Bintulu	03°10' N,	113°02' E
Butterworth	05°25' N,	100°24' E
George Town (Pinang)	05°25' N,	100°20' E
Ipoh	04°35' N,	101°05' E
Johor Baharu	01°28' N,	103°45' E
Kangar	06°26' N,	100°12' E
Kelang (Klang)	03°02' N,	101°27' E
Keluang	02°02' N,	103°19' E
Kota Baharu	06°08' N,	102°15' E
Kota Kinabalu		
(Jesselton)	05°59' N,	116°04' E
Kota Tinggi	01°44' N,	103°54' E
Kuala Dungun (Dungun) . .	04°47' N,	103°26' E
Kuala Lumpur	03°10' N,	101°42' E
Kuala Terengganu	05°20' N,	103°08' E
Kuantan	03°48' N,	103°20' E
Kuching	01°33' N,	110°20' E
Lundu	01°40' N,	109°51' E
Melaka (Malacca)	02°12' N,	102°15' E
Miri	04°23' N,	113°59' E
Muar		
(Bandar Maharani)	02°02' N,	102°34' E
Petaling Jaya	03°05' N,	101°39' E
Sandakan	05°50' N,	118°07' E
Sarikei	02°07' N,	111°31' E
Seremban	02°43' N,	101°56' E
Sibu	02°18' N,	111°49' E
Song	02°01' N,	112°33' E
Sri Aman (Simanggang) . . .	01°15' N,	111°26' E

Taiping	04°51' N,	100°44' E
Tawau	04°15' N,	117°54' E
Teluk Intan		
(Telok Anson)	04°02' N,	101°01' E
Victoria (Labuan)	05°17' N,	115°15' E

MALDIVES . . . . . . .pg. 107

Male	04°10' N,	073°30' E

MALI . . . . .pg. 108

Ansongo	15°40' N,	000°30' E
Bafoulabé	13°48' N,	010°50' W
Bamako	12°39' N,	008°00' W
Diamou	14°05' N,	011°16' W
Diré	16°16' N,	003°24' W
Gao	16°16' N,	000°03' W
Goundam	16°25' N,	003°40' W
Kalana	10°47' N,	008°12' W
Kangaba	11°56' N,	008°25' W
Kayes	14°27' N,	011°26' W
Kolokani	13°35' N,	008°02' W
Koro	14°04' N,	003°05' W
Labbezanga	14°57' N,	000°42' E
Ménaka	15°55' N,	002°24' E
Mopti	14°30' N,	004°12' W
Nara	15°10' N,	007°17' W
Niafounké	15°56' N,	004°00' W
Nioro Du Sahel	15°14' N,	009°35' W
San	13°18' N,	004°54' W
Ségou	13°27' N,	006°16' W
Sikasso	11°19' N,	005°40' W
Taoudenni	22°40' N,	003°59' W
Timbuktu	16°46' N,	003°01' W

MALTA . . . . .pg. 109

Birkirkara	35°54' N,	014°28' E
Hamrun	35°53' N,	014°29' E
Mosta	35°55' N,	014°26' E
Rabat	35°53' N,	014°24' E
Valletta (Valetta)	35°54' N,	014°31' E
Żabbar	35°52' N,	014°32' E
Żebbug	35°52' N,	014°26' E
Żejtun	35°51' N,	014°32' E

MARSHALL ISLANDS . . . . .pg. 110

Majuro	07°09' N,	171°12' E

MAURITANIA . . . .pg. 111

Akjoujt	19°45' N,	014°23' W
Aleg	17°03' N,	013°55' W
Atar	20°31' N,	013°03' W

Ayoûn el 'Atroûs.........	16°40' N, 009°37' W
Bir Mogrein............	25°14' N, 011°35' W
Bogué (Boghé)	16°35' N, 014°16' W
Boutilimit	17°33' N, 014°42' W
Chinguetti	20°27' N, 012°22' W
Fdérik	22°41' N, 012°43' W
Guérou................	16°48' N, 011°50' W
Kaédi	16°09' N, 013°30' W
Kiffa	16°37' N, 011°24' W
Maghama..............	15°31' N, 012°51' W
M'Bout...............	16°02' N, 012°35' W
Mederdra..............	16°55' N, 015°39' W
Néma	16°37' N, 007°15' W
Nouadhibou	20°54' N, 017°04' W
Nouakchott	18°06' N, 015°57' W
Rosso................	16°30' N, 015°49' W
Sélibaby..............	15°10' N, 012°11' W
Tichit................	18°28' N, 009°30' W
Tidjikdja	18°33' N, 011°25' W
Timbédra	16°15' N, 008°10' W
Zouirât...............	22°42' N, 012°30' W

MEXICO .... pg. 112

Acapulco..............	16°51' N, 099°55' W
Aguascalientes	21°53' N, 102°18' W
Caborca...............	30°37' N, 112°06' W
Campeche	19°51' N, 090°32' W
Cananea..............	30°57' N, 110°18' W
Cancún	21°05' N, 086°46' W
Carmen	18°38' N, 091°50' W
Casas Grandes	30°22' N, 107°57' W
Chetumal.............	18°30' N, 088°18' W
Chihuahua............	28°38' N, 106°05' W
Ciudad Acuña (Las Vacas).	29°18' N, 100°55' W
Ciudad Juárez..........	31°44' N, 106°29' W
Ciudad Obregón	27°29' N, 109°56' W
Ciudad Victoria.........	23°44' N, 099°08' W
Colima	19°14' N, 103°43' W
Culiacán..............	24°48' N, 107°24' W
Durango..............	24°02' N, 104°40' W
Guadalajara............	20°40' N, 103°20' W
Guadalupe............	25°41' N, 100°15' W
Guaymas	27°56' N, 110°54' W
Hermosillo............	29°04' N, 110°58' W
Jiménez	27°08' N, 104°55' W
Juchitán..............	16°26' N, 095°01' W
La Paz	24°10' N, 110°18' W
León.................	21°07' N, 101°40' W
Matamoros	25°53' N, 097°30' W
Matehuala	23°39' N, 100°39' W
Mazatlán.............	23°13' N, 106°25' W
Mérida...............	20°58' N, 089°37' W
Mexicali..............	32°40' N, 115°29' W
Mexico City	
(Ciudad de Mexico)	19°24' N, 099°09' W
Minatitlán.............	17°59' N, 094°31' W
Monterrey	25°40' N, 100°19' W
Morelia	19°42' N, 101°07' W
Nuevo Laredo	27°30' N, 099°31' W

Oaxaca................	17°03' N, 096°43' W
Poza Rica..............	20°33' N, 097°27' W
Puebla	19°03' N, 098°12' W
Saltillo	25°25' N, 101°00' W
San Felipe	31°00' N, 114°52' W
San Ignacio	27°27' N, 112°51' W
Tampico	22°13' N, 097°51' W
Tijuana	32°32' N, 117°01' W
Torreón	25°33' N, 103°26' W
Tuxtla	16°45' N, 093°07' W
Veracruz..............	19°12' N, 096°08' W
Villahermosa...........	17°59' N, 092°55' W
Zapopan..............	20°43' N, 103°24' W

MICRONESIA, FEDERATED STATES OF .... pg. 113

Colonia	09°31' N, 138°08' E
Kosrae	05°19' N, 162°59' E
Palikir	06°59' N, 158°08' E
Weno	07°26' N, 151°52' E

MOLDOVA ...... pg. 114

Bălți.................	47°46' N, 027°56' E
Calaras...............	47°16' N, 028°19' E
Căuşeni	46°38' N, 029°25' E
Chişinău	47°00' N, 028°50' E
Ciadăr-Lunga..........	46°03' N, 028°50' E
Comrat (Komrat)	46°18' N, 028°39' E
Drochia	48°02' N, 027°48' E
Dubăsari	47°07' N, 029°10' E
Fălești (Faleshty)	47°34' N, 027°42' E
Florești	47°53' N, 028°17' E
Hânceşti (Kotovsk).......	46°50' N, 028°36' E
Kagul	45°54' N, 028°11' E
Leova (Leovo)..........	46°28' N, 028°15' E
Orhei (Orgeyev)	47°22' N, 028°49' E
Rābnita	47°45' N, 029°00' E
Rezina	47°45' N, 028°58' E
Soroca (Soroki)	48°09' N, 028°18' E
Tighina	46°49' N, 029°29' E
Tiraspol..............	46°50' N, 029°37' E
Ungheni	47°12' N, 027°48' E

MONGOLIA ...... pg. 115

Altay	46°20' N, 096°18' E
Arvayheer	46°15' N, 102°48' E
Baruun-Urt	46°42' N, 113°15' E
Bulgan	48°45' N, 103°34' E
Choybalsan (Bayan	
Tumen)	48°04' N, 114°30' E
Choyr................	46°20' N, 108°20' E
Dalandzadgad	43°34' N, 104°25' E
Darhan...............	49°29' N, 105°55' E

Dariganga . . . . 45°18' N, 113°52' E
Dzüünharaa . . . . 48°52' N, 106°28' E
Erdenet . . . . 49°02' N, 104°05' E
Ereen . . . . 49°15' N, 112°29' E
Hanh . . . . 51°30' N, 100°40' E
Hatgal . . . . 50°26' N, 100°09' E
Hovd (Jirgalanta) . . . . 48°01' N, 091°38' E
Mörön . . . . 49°38' N, 100°10' E
Öndörhaan (Tsetsen
  Khan) . . . . 47°19' N, 110°39' E
Saynshand . . . . 44°52' N, 110°09' E
Sühbaatar . . . . 50°15' N, 106°12' E
Tes . . . . 49°41' N, 095°48' E
Tosontsengel . . . . 48°47' N, 098°15' E
Tsetserleg . . . . 47°30' N, 101°27' E
Tümentsogt . . . . 47°27' N, 112°15' E
Ulaanbaatar . . . . 47°55' N, 106°53' E
Uliastay . . . . 47°45' N, 096°49' E

MOROCCO . . . . . . pg. 116

Agadir . . . . 30°24' N, 009°36' W
Asilah (Arzila or Arcila) . . 35°28' N, 006°02' W
Beni Mellal . . . . 32°20' N, 006°21' W
Berkane . . . . 34°56' N, 002°20' W
Boudenib . . . . 31°57' N, 003°36' W
Boulemane . . . . 33°22' N, 004°45' W
Casablanca
  (Ad-Dār al-Bayḍāʾ
  or Dar el-Beida) . . . . 33°37' N, 007°35' W
El Jadida (Mazagan) . . . . . 33°15' N, 008°30' W
El-Kelaa des Srarhna . . . . . 32°03' N, 007°24' W
Er-Rachidia
  (Ksar es-Souk) . . . . 31°56' N, 004°26' W
Fès (Fez) . . . . 34°02' N, 004°59' W
Figuig . . . . 32°06' N, 001°14' W
Guelmim (Goulimine) . . . . 28°56' N, 010°04' W
Kenitra (Mina Hassan Tani
  or Port-Lyautey) . . . . . . 34°16' N, 006°36' W
Khouribga . . . . 32°53' N, 006°54' W
Larache (El-Araish) . . . . . . 35°12' N, 006°09' W
Marrakech . . . . 31°38' N, 008°00' W
Meknès . . . . 33°54' N, 005°33' W
Mohammedia (Fedala) . . . . 33°42' N, 007°24' W
Nador . . . . 35°11' N, 002°56' W
Ouarzazate . . . . 30°55' N, 006°55' W
Oued Zem . . . . 32°52' N, 006°34' W
Oujda . . . . 34°40' N, 001°54' W
Rabat (Ribat) . . . . 34°02' N, 006°50' W
Safi (Asfi) . . . . 32°18' N, 009°14' W
Salé (Sla) . . . . 34°04' N, 006°48' W
Settat . . . . 33°00' N, 007°37' W
Tangier (Tanger) . . . . 35°48' N, 005°48' W
Tan-Tan . . . . 28°26' N, 011°06' W
Taounate . . . . 34°33' N, 004°39' W
Tarfaya . . . . 27°57' N, 012°55' W
Tata . . . . 29°45' N, 007°59' W
Taza . . . . 34°13' N, 004°01' W
Tétouan (Tetuan) . . . . 35°34' N, 005°22' W
Zagora . . . . 30°19' N, 005°50' W

MOZAMBIQUE . .pg. 117

Angoche . . . . 16°15' S, 039°54' E
Beira . . . . 19°50' S, 034°52' E
Chimoio (Vila Pery) . . . . . . 19°08' S, 033°29' E
Chokwe . . . . 24°32' S, 032°59' E
Inhambane . . . . 23°52' S, 035°23' E
Lichinga . . . . 13°18' S, 035°14' E
Maputo (Lourenço
  Marques) . . . . 25°58' S, 032°34' E
Massinga . . . . 23°20' S, 035°22' E
Memba . . . . 14°12' S, 040°32' E
Moçambique
  (Mozambique) . . . . 15°03' S, 040°45' E
Mocubúri . . . . 14°39' S, 038°54' E
Mopeia Velha . . . . 17°59' S, 035°43' E
Morrumbene . . . . 23°39' S, 035°20' E
Nacala . . . . 14°33' S, 040°40' E
Namapa . . . . 13°43' S, 039°50' E
Nampula . . . . 15°09' S, 039°18' E
Panda . . . . 24°03' S, 034°43' E
Pemba . . . . 12°57' S, 040°30' E
Quelimane . . . . 17°51' S, 036°52' E
Quissico . . . . 24°43' S, 034°45' E
Tete . . . . 16°10' S, 033°36' E
Vila de Manhiça . . . . 25°24' S, 032°48' E
Vila da Mocimboa
  da Praia . . . . 11°20' S, 040°21' E
Vila do Chinde (Chinde) . . 18°34' S, 036°27' E
Xai Xai (Joaõ Belo) . . . . . . 25°04' S, 033°39' E

MYANMAR . . . . . . pg. 118

Allanmyo . . . . 19°22' N, 095°13' E
Bassein (Pathein) . . . . 16°47' N, 094°44' E
Bhamo . . . . 24°16' N, 097°14' E
Chauk . . . . 20°53' N, 094°49' E
Henzada . . . . 17°38' N, 095°28' E
Homalin . . . . 24°52' N, 094°55' E
Kale . . . . 16°05' N, 097°54' E
Katha . . . . 24°11' N, 096°21' E
Kawthaung . . . . 09°59' N, 098°33' E
Kēng Tung . . . . 21°17' N, 099°36' E
Kyaikkami . . . . 16°04' N, 097°34' E
Kyaukpyu (Ramree) . . . . . . 19°05' N, 093°52' E
Labutta . . . . 16°09' N, 094°46' E
Loi-kaw . . . . 19°41' N, 097°13' E
Magwe (Magwa) . . . . 20°09' N, 094°55' E
Mandalay . . . . 22°00' N, 096°05' E
Mergui . . . . 12°26' N, 098°36' E
Minbu . . . . 20°11' N, 094°53' E
Monywa . . . . 22°07' N, 095°08' E
Moulmein (Mawlamyine) . . 16°30' N, 097°38' E
Myitkyina . . . . 25°23' N, 097°24' E
Palaw . . . . 12°58' N, 098°39' E
Pegu (Bago) . . . . 17°20' N, 096°29' E
Prome (Pye) . . . . 18°49' N, 095°13' E
Putao . . . . 27°21' N, 097°24' E

Sagaing	21°52' N, 095°59' E
Shwebo	22°34' N, 095°42' E
Sittwe (Akyab)	20°09' N, 092°54' E
Syriam	16°46' N, 096°15' E
Taunggyi	20°47' N, 097°02' E
Tavoy (Dawei)	14°05' N, 098°12' E
Tenasserim	12°05' N, 099°01' E
Thaton	16°55' N, 097°22' E
Tonzang	23°36' N, 093°42' E
Toungoo	18°56' N, 096°26' E
Yangon (Rangoon)	16°47' N, 096°10' E

NAMIBIA ....pg. 119

Aranos	24°08' S, 019°07' E
Bagani	18°07' S, 021°38' E
Gobabis	22°27' S, 018°58' E
Grootfontein	19°34' S, 018°07' E
Karasburg	28°01' S, 018°45' E
Karibib	21°56' S, 015°50' E
Keetmanshoop	26°35' S, 018°08' E
Khorixas	20°22' S, 014°58' E
Lüderitz	26°38' S, 015°09' E
Maltahöhe	24°50' S, 016°59' E
Mariental	24°38' S, 017°58' E
Okahandja	21°59' S, 016°55' E
Omaruru	21°26' S, 015°56' E
Ondangwa (Ondangua)	17°55' S, 015°57' E
Opuwo	18°04' S, 013°51' E
Oranjemund	28°33' S, 016°26' E
Oshakati	17°47' S, 015°41' E
Otjimbingwe	22°21' S, 016°08' E
Otjiwarongo	20°27' S, 016°39' E
Outjo	20°07' S, 016°09' E
Rehoboth	23°19' S, 017°05' E
Rundu	17°56' S, 019°46' E
Swakopmund	22°41' S, 014°32' E
Tsumeb	19°14' S, 017°43' E
Usakos	22°00' S, 015°36' E
Walvis Bay	22°57' S, 014°30' E
Warmbad	28°27' S, 018°44' E
Windhoek	22°35' S, 017°05' E

NEPAL ....pg. 120

Bāglūṅg	28°16' N, 083°36' E
Banepa	27°38' N, 085°31' E
Bhairahawā	27°30' N, 083°27' E
Bhaktapur (Bhadgaon)	27°41' N, 085°25' E
Bhojpūr	27°10' N, 087°03' E
Biratnagar	26°29' N, 087°17' E
Birendranagar	28°46' N, 081°38' E
Birganj	27°00' N, 084°52' E
Dailekh	28°50' N, 081°44' E
Dandeldhūrā	29°18' N, 080°35' E
Ilām	26°54' N, 087°56' E
Jājarkot	28°42' N, 082°12' E
Jaléswar	26°38' N, 085°48' E
Jomosom	28°47' N, 083°44' E
Jumlā	29°17' N, 082°10' E

Kathmandu	27°43' N, 085°19' E
Lahān	26°43' N, 086°29' E
Lalitpur (Patan)	27°40' N, 085°20' E
Lumbini (Rummin-dei)	27°29' N, 083°17' E
Mahendranagar	28°55' N, 080°20' E
Mustāng	29°11' N, 083°58' E
Nepālganj	28°03' N, 081°37' E
Pokharā	28°14' N, 083°59' E
Sallyān	28°22' N, 082°10' E
Simikot	29°58' N, 081°50' E
Taplejūṅg	27°21' N, 087°40' E

NETHERLANDS, THE ....pg. 121

Alkmaar	52°38' N, 004°45' E
Almelo	52°21' N, 006°40' E
Amersfoort	52°09' N, 005°23' E
Amstelveen	52°18' N, 004°52' E
Amsterdam	52°21' N, 004°55' E
Apeldoorn	52°13' N, 005°58' E
Arnhem	51°59' N, 005°55' E
Assen	53°00' N, 006°33' E
Bergen op Zoom	51°30' N, 004°18' E
Breda	51°34' N, 004°48' E
Delft	52°00' N, 004°22' E
Den Helder	52°58' N, 004°46' E
Deventer	52°15' N, 006°12' E
Dordrecht (Dort or Dordt)	51°48' N, 004°40' E
Drachten	53°06' N, 006°06' E
Ede	52°02' N, 005°40' E
Eindhoven	51°27' N, 005°28' E
Emmen	52°47' N, 006°54' E
Enschede	52°13' N, 006°54' E
Geleen	50°58' N, 005°50' E
Gendringen	51°52' N, 006°23' E
Groningen	53°13' N, 006°33' E
Haarlem	52°22' N, 004°39' E
Heerenveen	52°57' N, 005°56' E
Heerlen	50°54' N, 005°59' E
Helmond	51°29' N, 005°40' E
Hengelo	52°16' N, 006°48' E
Hilversum	52°14' N, 005°11' E
Hoofddorp (Haarlemmermeer)	52°18' N, 004°42' E
Hoorn	52°39' N, 005°04' E
IJmuiden	52°28' N, 004°36' E
Langedijk	52°42' N, 004°49' E
Leeuwarden (Ljouwert)	53°12' N, 005°47' E
Leiden (Leyden)	52°09' N, 004°30' E
Lelystad	52°31' N, 005°29' E
Maastricht	50°51' N, 005°41' E
Meppel	52°42' N, 006°12' E
Middelburg	51°30' N, 003°37' E
Nieuwegein	52°02' N, 005°06' E
Nijmegen (Nimwegen)	51°50' N, 005°52' E
Ommen	52°31' N, 006°26' E
Oostburg	51°20' N, 003°30' E
Oss	51°46' N, 005°32' E

Purmerend . . . . 52°31' N, 004°57' E
Ridderkerk . . . . 51°52' N, 004°36' E
Roermond . . . . 51°12' N, 006°00' E
Roosendaal . . . . 51°32' N, 004°28' E
Rosmalen . . . . 51°43' N, 005°22' E
Rotterdam . . . . 51°55' N, 004°30' E
Schiedam . . . . 51°55' N, 004°24' E
's-Hertogenbosch (Den
  Bosch or Bois-le-Duc) . . . 51°42' N, 005°19' E
Sneek (Snits) . . . . 53°02' N, 005°40' E
Soest . . . . 52°11' N, 005°18' E
Steenwijk . . . . 52°47' N, 006°07' E
Stein . . . . 50°58' N, 005°46' E
Terneuzen . . . . 51°20' N, 003°50' E
The Hague ('s-Gravenhage,
  Den Haag, or La Haye) . . 52°05' N, 004°18' E
Tholen . . . . 51°32' N, 004°13' E
Tilburg . . . . 51°33' N, 005°07' E
Utrecht . . . . 52°05' N, 005°08' E
Veenendaal . . . . 52°02' N, 005°33' E
Venlo . . . . 51°22' N, 006°10' E
Vlaardingen . . . . 51°55' N, 004°21' E
Vlissingen (Flushing) . . . . . 51°27' N, 003°35' E
Zaanstad . . . . 52°27' N, 004°50' E
Zoetermeer . . . . 52°03' N, 004°30' E
Zwolle . . . . 52°30' N, 006°05' E

NEW ZEALAND . . pg. 122

Auckland . . . . 36°52' S, 174°46' E
Blenheim . . . . 41°31' S, 173°57' E
Cheviot . . . . 42°49' S, 173°16' E
Christchurch . . . . 43°32' S, 172°39' E
Dunedin . . . . 45°53' S, 170°29' E
East Coast Bays . . . . 36°45' S, 174°45' E
Gisborne . . . . 38°39' S, 178°01' E
Greymouth . . . . 42°27' S, 171°12' E
Hamilton . . . . 37°47' S, 175°16' E
Hastings . . . . 39°39' S, 176°50' E
Invercargill . . . . 46°25' S, 168°22' E
Lower Hutt . . . . 41°13' S, 174°56' E
Manukau . . . . 36°57' S, 174°56' E
Milford Sound . . . . 44°41' S, 167°55' E
Napier . . . . 39°31' S, 176°54' E
Nelson . . . . 41°17' S, 173°17' E
New Plymouth . . . . 39°04' S, 174°04' E
Oamaru . . . . 45°06' S, 170°58' E
Paeroa . . . . 37°23' S, 175°40' E
Palmerston North . . . . 40°21' S, 175°37' E
Porirua . . . . 41°08' S, 174°51' E
Rotorua . . . . 38°10' S, 176°14' E
Takapuna . . . . 36°47' S, 174°45' E
Tauranga . . . . 37°42' S, 176°08' E
Timaru . . . . 44°24' S, 171°14' E
Upper Hutt . . . . 41°08' S, 175°03' E
Waihi . . . . 37°24' S, 175°56' E
Wanganui . . . . 39°56' S, 175°02' E
Wellington . . . . 41°18' S, 174°47' E
Westport . . . . 41°45' S, 171°36' E
Whangarei . . . . 35°43' S, 174°20' E

NICARAGUA . . . . . pg. 123

Bluefields . . . . 12°00' N, 083°45' W
Chinandega . . . . 12°37' N, 087°09' W
Esquipulas . . . . 12°40' N, 085°47' W
Estelí . . . . 13°05' N, 086°21' W
Granada . . . . 11°56' N, 085°57' W
Juigalpa . . . . 12°05' N, 085°24' W
León . . . . 12°26' N, 086°53' W
Managua . . . . 12°09' N, 086°17' W
Masaya . . . . 11°58' N, 086°06' W
Matagalpa . . . . 12°55' N, 085°55' W
Nandaime . . . . 11°45' N, 086°03' W
Ocotal . . . . 13°38' N, 086°29' W
Puerto Cabezas . . . . 14°02' N, 083°23' W
San Carlos . . . . 11°07' N, 084°47' W
San Juan del Norte
  (Greytown) . . . . 10°55' N, 083°42' W
San Juan del Sur . . . . 11°15' N, 085°52' W
Somoto . . . . 13°29' N, 086°35' W
Waspam . . . . 14°44' N, 083°58' W

NIGER . . . . pg. 124

Agadez . . . . 16°58' N, 007°59' E
Ayorou . . . . 14°44' N, 000°55' E
Bilma . . . . 18°41' N, 012°56' E
Dakoro . . . . 14°31' N, 006°46' E
Diffa . . . . 13°19' N, 012°37' E
Dogondoutchi . . . . 13°38' N, 004°02' E
Dosso . . . . 13°03' N, 003°12' E
Filingué . . . . 14°21' N, 003°19' E
Gaya . . . . 11°53' N, 003°27' E
Gouré . . . . 13°58' N, 010°18' E
I-n-Gall . . . . 16°47' N, 006°56' E
Keïta . . . . 14°46' N, 005°46' E
Kolo . . . . 13°19' N, 002°20' E
Madaoua . . . . 14°06' N, 006°26' E
Magaria . . . . 13°00' N, 008°54' E
Maradi . . . . 13°29' N, 007°06' E
Mayahi . . . . 13°58' N, 007°40' E
Nguigmi . . . . 14°15' N, 013°07' E
Niamey . . . . 13°31' N, 002°07' E
Tahoua . . . . 14°54' N, 005°16' E
Tānout . . . . 14°58' N, 008°53' E
Zinder . . . . 13°48' N, 008°59' E

NIGERIA . . . . pg. 125

Aba . . . . 05°07' N, 007°22' E
Abuja . . . . 09°15' N, 006°56' E
Ado-Ekiti . . . . 07°38' N, 005°13' E
Asari . . . . 10°31' N, 012°18' E
Awka . . . . 06°13' N, 007°05' E
Azare . . . . 11°41' N, 010°12' E
Bauchi . . . . 10°19' N, 009°50' E
Benin City . . . . 06°20' N, 005°38' E
Bida . . . . 09°05' N, 006°01' E
Birnin Kebbi . . . . 12°28' N, 004°12' E

Biu	10°37' N,	012°12' E
Calabar	04°57' N,	008°19' E
Deba Habe	10°13' N,	011°23' E
Dikwa	12°02' N,	013°55' E
Dukku	10°49' N,	010°46' E
Ede	07°44' N,	004°26' E
Enugu	06°26' N,	007°29' E
Funtua	11°32' N,	007°19' E
Garko	11°39' N,	008°48' E
Gashua	12°52' N,	011°03' E
Gboko	07°19' N,	009°00' E
Gombe	10°17' N,	011°10' E
Gumel	12°38' N,	009°23' E
Gusau	12°10' N,	006°40' E
Ibadan	07°23' N,	003°54' E
Ibi	08°11' N,	009°45' E
Idah	07°06' N,	006°44' E
Ife	07°28' N,	004°34' E
Ifon	06°55' N,	005°46' E
Ikerre	07°30' N,	005°14' E
Ila	08°01' N,	004°54' E
Ilorin	08°30' N,	004°33' E
Iwo	07°38' N,	004°11' E
Jega	12°13' N,	004°23' E
Jimeta	09°17' N,	012°28' E
Jos	09°55' N,	008°54' E
Kaduna	10°31' N,	007°26' E
Kano	12°00' N,	008°31' E
Katsina	13°00' N,	007°36' E
Kaura Namoda	12°36' N,	006°35' E
Keffi	08°51' N,	007°52' E
Kishi	09°05' N,	003°51' E
Kumo	10°03' N,	011°13' E
Lafia	08°29' N,	008°31' E
Lafiagi	08°52' N,	005°25' E
Lagos	06°27' N,	003°23' E
Lere	09°43' N,	009°21' E
Mada	12°09' N,	006°56' E
Maiduguri	11°51' N,	013°09' E
Makurdi	07°44' N,	008°32' E
Minna	09°37' N,	006°33' E
Mubi	10°16' N,	013°16' E
Mushin	06°32' N,	003°22' E
Ngurtuwa	13°05' N,	013°34' E
Nguru	12°53' N,	010°28' E
Nsukka	06°52' N,	007°23' E
Ogbomosho	08°08' N,	004°16' E
Omoko	05°21' N,	006°39' E
Onitsha	06°10' N,	006°47' E
Opobo Town	04°31' N,	007°32' E
Oron	04°50' N,	008°14' E
Oshogbo	07°46' N,	004°34' E
Oyo	07°51' N,	003°56' E
Pindiga	09°59' N,	010°54' E
Port Harcourt	04°46' N,	007°01' E
Potiskum	11°43' N,	011°04' E
Sapele	05°55' N,	005°42' E
Shaki	08°40' N,	003°23' E
Sokoto	13°04' N,	005°15' E
Ugep	05°48' N,	008°05' E
Umuahia	05°32' N,	007°29' E

Uyo	05°03' N,	007°56' E
Warri	05°31' N,	005°45' E
Wukari	07°51' N,	009°47' E
Zaria	11°04' N,	007°42' E

NORTH KOREA. .pg. 126

Anju	39°36' N,	125°40' E
Ch'ŏngjin	41°46' N,	129°49' E
Cho'san	40°50' N,	125°48' E
Haeju	38°02' N,	125°42' E
Hamhŭng	39°54' N,	127°32' E
Hŭichŏn	40°10' N,	126°17' E
Hyangsan	40°03' N,	126°10' E
Hyesan	41°24' N,	128°10' E
Ich'ŏn	38°29' N,	126°53' E
Kaesŏng	37°58' N,	126°33' E
Kanggye	40°58' N,	126°36' E
Kimch'aek (Songjin)	40°41' N,	129°12' E
Kŭmch'ŏn	38°09' N,	126°29' E
Kusŏng	39°59' N,	125°15' E
Kyŏngwŏn	42°49' N,	130°09' E
Manp'o	41°09' N,	126°17' E
Myŏngch'ŏn	41°04' N,	129°26' E
Najin	42°15' N,	130°18' E
Namp'o	38°44' N,	125°24' E
P'anmunjŏm	37°57' N,	126°40' E
Puryŏng	42°04' N,	129°43' E
P'yŏngsŏng	39°15' N,	125°52' E
P'yŏngyang	39°01' N,	125°45' E
Sariwŏn	38°30' N,	125°45' E
Sinp'o	40°02' N,	128°12' E
Sinŭiju	40°06' N,	124°24' E
Songnim	38°44' N,	125°38' E
Taegwan	40°13' N,	125°12' E
Tanch'ŏn	40°28' N,	128°55' E
Tŏkch'ŏn	39°45' N,	126°18' E
T'ongch'ŏn	38°57' N,	127°52' E
Unggi	42°20' N,	130°24' E
Wŏnsan	39°10' N,	127°26' E

NORWAY . . . . . . .pg. 127

Ålesund	62°28' N,	006°09' E
Alta	69°58' N,	023°15' E
Båtsfjord	70°38' N,	029°44' E
Bergen	60°23' N,	005°20' E
Bodø	67°17' N,	014°23' E
Brønnøysund	65°28' N,	012°13' E
Drammen	59°44' N,	010°15' E
Elverum	60°53' N,	011°34' E
Evje	58°36' N,	007°51' E
Fauske	67°15' N,	015°24' E
Finnsnes	69°14' N,	017°59' E
Flekkefjord	58°17' N,	006°41' E
Hamar	60°48' N,	011°06' E
Hammerfest	70°40' N,	023°42' E
Hareid	62°22' N,	006°02' E
Harstad	68°47' N,	016°33' E
Haugesund	59°25' N,	005°18' E

OMAN . . . . .pg. 128

PAKISTAN . . . . . . .pg. 129

PALAU . . . . .pg. 130

PANAMA . . . . . . .pg. 131

Las Cumbres	09°05' N, 079°32' W
Las Lajas	08°15' N, 081°52' W
Las Tablas	07°46' N, 080°17' W
Ocú	07°57' N, 080°47' W
Panama City (Panama)	08°58' N, 079°32' W
Pedregal	09°04' N, 079°26' W
Penonomé	08°31' N, 080°22' W
Portobelo (Puerto Bello)	09°33' N, 079°39' W
Puerto Armuelles	08°17' N, 082°52' W
San Miguelito	09°02' N, 079°30' E
Santiago	08°06' N, 080°59' W
Soná	08°01' N, 081°19' W
Yaviza (Yavisa)	08°11' N, 077°41' W

PAPUA NEW GUINEA . . . . .pg. 132

Aitape	03°08' S, 142°21' E
Alotau	10°20' S, 150°25' E
Ambunti	04°14' S, 142°50' E
Arawa	06°13' S, 155°33' E
Baimuru	07°30' S, 144°49' E
Balimo	08°03' S, 142°57' E
Bogia	04°16' S, 144°54' E
Buin	06°50' S, 155°44' E
Bulolo	07°12' S, 146°39' E
Bwagaoia	10°42' S, 152°50' E
Daru	09°05' S, 143°12' E
Finschhafen	06°36' S, 147°51' E
Goroka	06°05' S, 145°23' E
Kandrian	06°13' S, 149°33' E
Kavieng	02°34' S, 150°48' E
Kerema	07°58' S, 145°46' E
Kikori	07°25' S, 144°15' E
Kimbe	05°33' S, 150°09' E
Kiunga	06°07' S, 141°18' E
Kupiano	10°05' S, 148°11' E
Lae	06°44' S, 147°00' E
Lorengau	02°01' S, 147°16' E
Losuia	08°32' S, 151°04' E
Madang	05°13' S, 145°48' E
Mt. Hagen	05°52' S, 144°13' E
Namatanai	03°40' S, 152°27' E
Popondetta	08°46' S, 148°14' E
Port Moresby	09°29' S, 147°11' E
Rabaul	04°12' S, 152°11' E
Saidor	05°38' S, 146°28' E
Samarai	10°37' S, 150°40' E
Tari	05°42' S, 142°57' E
Vanimo	02°41' S, 141°18' E
Wewak	03°33' S, 143°38' E

PARAGUAY . . . . . .pg. 133

Asunción	25°16' S, 057°40' W
Caacupé	25°23' S, 057°09' W
Caaguazú	25°26' S, 056°02' W
Caazapá	26°09' S, 056°24' W
Capitán Pablo Lagerenza	19°55' S, 060°47' W

Ciudad del Este (Puerto Presidente Stroessner)	25°31' S, 054°37' W
Concepción	23°25' S, 057°17' W
Encarnación	27°20' S, 055°54' W
Filadelfia	22°21' S, 060°02' W
Fuerto Olimpo	21°02' S, 057°54' W
General Eugenio A. Garay	20°31' S, 062°08' W
Luque	25°16' S, 057°34' W
Mariscal Estigarribia	22°02' S, 060°38' W
Paraguarí	25°38' S, 057°09' W
Pedro Juan Caballero	22°34' S, 055°37' W
Pilar	26°52' S, 058°23' W
Pozo Colorado	23°26' S, 058°58' W
Salto del Guairá	24°05' S, 054°20' W
San Juan Bautista	26°38' S, 057°10' W
San Lázaro	22°10' S, 057°58' W
Villarica	25°45' S, 056°26' W

PERU . . . . .pg. 134

Abancay	13°35' S, 072°55' W
Acomayo	13°55' S, 071°41' W
Arequipa	16°24' S, 071°33' W
Ayabaca	04°38' S, 079°43' W
Ayacucho	13°07' S, 074°13' W
Ayaviri	14°52' S, 070°35' W
Bagua	05°40' S, 078°31' W
Barranca	10°45' S, 077°46' W
Cajamarca	07°10' S, 078°31' W
Callao	12°04' S, 077°09' W
Castilla	05°12' S, 080°38' W
Cerro de Pasco	10°41' S, 076°16' W
Chiclayo	06°46' S, 079°51' W
Chimbote	09°05' S, 078°36' W
Contamana	07°15' S, 074°54' W
Cuzco	13°31' S, 071°59' W
Espinar	14°47' S, 071°29' W
Huacho	11°07' S, 077°37' W
Huancayo	12°04' S, 075°14' W
Huánuco	09°55' S, 076°14' W
Huaraz	09°32' S, 077°32' W
Huarmey	10°04' S, 078°10' W
Ica	14°04' S, 075°42' W
Iñapari	10°57' S, 069°35' W
Iquitos	03°46' S, 073°15' W
Juliaca	15°30' S, 070°08' W
Lagunas	05°14' S, 075°38' W
Lima	12°03' S, 077°03' W
Macusani	14°05' S, 070°26' W
Miraflores	12°07' S, 077°02' W
Moquegua	17°12' S, 070°56' W
Moyobamba	06°03' S, 076°58' W
Nauta	04°32' S, 073°33' W
Pampas	12°24' S, 074°54' W
Pisco	13°42' S, 076°13' W
Piura	05°12' S, 080°38' W
Pucallpa	08°23' S, 074°32' W
Puerto Maldonado	12°36' S, 069°11' W
Puno	15°50' S, 070°02' W
Requena	04°58' S, 073°50' W

San Juan . . . . 15°21' S, 075°10' W
Tacna . . . . 18°01' S, 070°15' W
Tarapoto . . . . 06°30' S, 076°25' W
Trujillo . . . . 08°07' S, 079°02' W
Tumbes . . . . 03°34' S, 080°28' W

PHILIPPINES . . . . . pg. 135

Angeles . . . . 15°09' N, 120°35' E
Aparri . . . . 18°22' N, 121°39' E
Bacolod . . . . 10°40' N, 122°56' E
Balabac . . . . 07°59' N, 117°04' E
Batangas . . . . 13°45' N, 121°03' E
Bayombong . . . . 16°29' N, 121°09' E
Borongan . . . . 11°37' N, 125°26' E
Butuan . . . . 08°54' N, 125°35' E
Cagayan de Oro . . . . 08°29' N, 124°39' E
Caloocan . . . . 14°39' N, 120°58' E
Cavite . . . . 14°29' N, 120°55' E
Cebu . . . . 10°18' N, 123°54' E
Daet . . . . 14°05' N, 122°55' E
Dagupan . . . . 16°03' N, 120°20' E
Dipolog . . . . 08°35' N, 123°20' E
Dumaguete . . . . 09°18' N, 123°18' E
General Santos . . . . 06°07' N, 125°10' E
Iligan . . . . 08°14' N, 124°14' E
Iloilo City . . . . 10°42' N, 122°33' E
Isabela . . . . 06°42' N, 121°58' E
Jolo . . . . 06°03' N, 121°00' E
Laoag . . . . 12°34' N, 125°00' E
Lucena . . . . 13°56' N, 121°37' E
Manila . . . . 14°35' N, 121°00' E
Masbate . . . . 12°22' N, 123°36' E
Mati . . . . 06°57' N, 126°13' E
Naga (Nueva Caceres) . . . . 13°37' N, 123°11' E
Ormoc . . . . 11°00' N, 124°37' E
Ozamiz . . . . 08°08' N, 123°50' E
Pandan . . . . 14°03' N, 124°10' E
Puerto Princesa . . . . 09°44' N, 118°44' E
Quezon City . . . . 14°38' N, 121°00' E
Romblon . . . . 12°35' N, 122°15' E
Roxas (Capiz) . . . . 11°35' N, 122°45' E
Surigao . . . . 09°45' N, 125°30' E
Tagbilaran . . . . 09°39' N, 123°51' E
Tuguegarao . . . . 17°37' N, 121°44' E
Zamboanga . . . . 06°54' N, 122°04' E

POLAND . . . . pg. 136

Biała Podlaska . . . . 52°02' N, 023°08' E
Białystok . . . . 53°08' N, 023°09' E
Bielsko-Biała . . . . 49°49' N, 019°02' E
Bydgoszcz . . . . 53°09' N, 018°00' E
Ciechanów . . . . 52°53' N, 020°37' E
Częstochowa . . . . 50°48' N, 019°07' E
Dąbrova Górnicza . . . . 50°20' N, 019°12' E
Elbląg . . . . 54°10' N, 019°23' E
Gdańsk (Danzig) . . . . 54°21' N, 018°40' E
Gdynia . . . . 54°30' N, 018°33' E
Gorzów Wielkopolski . . . . 52°44' N, 015°14' E

Grudziądz . . . . 53°29' N, 018°46' E
Iława . . . . 53°36' N, 019°34' E
Inowrocław . . . . 52°48' N, 018°16' E
Kalisz . . . . 51°45' N, 018°05' E
Katowice . . . . 50°16' N, 019°01' E
Kielce . . . . 50°50' N, 020°40' E
Konin . . . . 52°13' N, 018°16' E
Koszalin . . . . 54°12' N, 016°11' E
Kraków . . . . 50°05' N, 019°55' E
Krosno . . . . 49°41' N, 021°47' E
Legnica . . . . 51°12' N, 016°12' E
Leszno . . . . 51°51' N, 016°35' E
Łódź . . . . 51°45' N, 019°28' E
Łomża . . . . 53°11' N, 022°05' E
Lublin . . . . 51°15' N, 022°34' E
Malbork . . . . 54°02' N, 019°03' E
Mogilno . . . . 52°40' N, 017°58' E
Nidzica . . . . 53°22' N, 020°26' E
Nowy Sącz . . . . 49°38' N, 020°43' E
Olsztyn . . . . 53°47' N, 020°29' E
Opole . . . . 50°40' N, 017°57' E
Ostrołęka . . . . 53°05' N, 021°34' E
Piła . . . . 53°09' N, 016°45' E
Pińczów . . . . 50°32' N, 020°32' E
Piotrków Trybunalski . . . . 51°24' N, 019°41' E
Pisz . . . . 53°38' N, 021°48' E
Poznań . . . . 52°25' N, 016°58' E
Radom . . . . 51°25' N, 021°09' E
Rybnik . . . . 50°07' N, 018°32' E
Rzeszów . . . . 50°03' N, 022°00' E
Siedlce . . . . 52°10' N, 022°18' E
Słupsk . . . . 54°27' N, 017°02' E
Suwałki . . . . 54°06' N, 022°56' E
Szczecin (Stettin) . . . . 53°25' N, 014°35' E
Tarnobrzeg . . . . 50°35' N, 021°41' E
Tarnów . . . . 50°01' N, 020°59' E
Tczew . . . . 54°06' N, 018°48' E
Tomaszów Mazowiecki . . . 51°32' N, 020°01' E
Toruń . . . . 53°02' N, 018°36' E
Tuchola . . . . 53°35' N, 017°51' E
Tychy . . . . 50°08' N, 018°59' E
Wałbrzych . . . . 50°46' N, 016°17' E
Warsaw (Warszawa) . . . . . 52°15' N, 021°00' E
Włocławek . . . . 52°39' N, 019°05' E
Wrocław (Breslau) . . . . 51°06' N, 017°02' E
Zabrze . . . . 50°19' N, 018°47' E
Zamość . . . . 50°43' N, 023°15' E
Zielona Góra . . . . 51°56' N, 015°30' E

PORTUGAL . . . . . . pg. 137

Alcobaça . . . . 39°33' N, 008°59' W
Almada . . . . 38°41' N, 009°09' W
Amadora . . . . 38°45' N, 009°14' W
Aveiro . . . . 40°38' N, 008°39' W
Barreiro . . . . 38°40' N, 009°04' W
Batalha . . . . 39°39' N, 008°50' W
Beja . . . . 38°01' N, 007°52' W
Braga . . . . 41°33' N, 008°26' W
Bragança . . . . 41°49' N, 006°45' W
Castelo Branco . . . . 39°49' N, 007°30' W

Chaves. . . . . 41°44' N, 007°28' W
Coimbra. . . . . 40°12' N, 008°25' W
Elvas . . . . 38°53' N, 007°10' W
Évora . . . . 38°34' N, 007°54' W
Faro . . . . 37°01' N, 007°56' W
Fátima . . . . 39°37' N, 008°39' W
Figueira da Foz . . . . 40°09' N, 008°52' W
Guarda . . . . 40°32' N, 007°16' W
Guimarães. . . . . 41°27' N, 008°18' W
Leiria . . . . 39°45' N, 008°48' W
Lisbon (Lisboa). . . . . 38°43' N, 009°08' W
Nazaré . . . . 39°36' N, 009°04' W
Odivelas . . . . 38°47' N, 009°11' W
Oeiras . . . . 38°41' N, 009°19' W
Portalegre . . . . 39°17' N, 007°26' W
Portimão (Vila Nova de
   Portimão). . . . . 37°08' N, 008°32' W
Porto (Oporto) . . . . 41°09' N, 008°37' W
Póvoa de Varzim. . . . . . . 41°23' N, 008°46' W
Queluz. . . . . 38°45' N, 009°15' W
Santarém . . . . 39°14' N, 008°41' W
Setúbal. . . . . 38°32' N, 008°54' W
Sines . . . . 37°57' N, 008°52' W
Tomar . . . . 39°36' N, 008°25' W
Torres Vedras. . . . . 39°06' N, 009°16' W
Urgeiriça . . . . 40°30' N, 007°53' W
Viana do Castelo . . . . 41°42' N, 008°50' W
Vila do Conde . . . . 41°21' N, 008°45' W
Vila Franca de Xira . . . . . 38°57' N, 008°59' W
Vila Nova de Gaia . . . . . . 41°08' N, 008°37' W
Vila Real . . . . 41°18' N, 007°45' W
Viseu . . . . 40°39' N, 007°55' W

QATAR . . . . .pg. 138

Al-Wakrah . . . . 25°10' N, 051°36' E
Ar Rayyān . . . . 25°18' N, 051°27' E
Ar-Ruways. . . . . 26°08' N, 051°13' E
Doha (ad-Dawhah) . . . . . . 25°17' N, 051°32' E
Dukhān . . . . 25°25' N, 050°47' E
Musay'id . . . . 25°00' N, 051°33' E
Umm Bāb. . . . . 25°09' N, 050°50' E

ROMANIA . . . . . .pg. 139

Alba Iulia
   (Gyulafehérvár). . . . . . . 46°04' N, 023°35' E
Alexandria. . . . . 43°59' N, 025°20' E
Arad. . . . . 46°11' N, 021°19' E
Bacău. . . . . 46°34' N, 026°54' E
Baia Mare . . . . 47°40' N, 023°35' E
Bârlad . . . . 46°14' N, 027°40' E
Bistrița. . . . . 47°08' N, 024°29' E
Botoșani . . . . 47°45' N, 026°40' E
Brăila . . . . 45°16' N, 027°59' E
Brașov (Orașul Stalin) . . . 45°38' N, 025°35' E
Bucharest . . . . 44°26' N, 026°06' E
Buzău. . . . . 45°09' N, 026°50' E
Calafat . . . . 43°59' N, 022°56' E
Călărași . . . . 44°12' N, 027°20' E

Cluj-Napoca. . . . . 46°46' N, 023°36' E
Constanța . . . . 44°11' N, 028°39' E
Craiova . . . . 44°19' N, 023°48' E
Dej . . . . 47°09' N, 023°52' E
Deva. . . . . 45°53' N, 022°54' E
Drobeta-Turnu Severin. . . . 44°38' N, 022°40' E
Focșani . . . . 45°42' N, 027°11' E
Galați (Galatz). . . . . 45°27' N, 028°03' E
Giurgiu. . . . . 43°53' N, 025°58' E
Hunedoara. . . . . 45°45' N, 022°54' E
Iași (Jassy) . . . . 47°10' N, 027°36' E
Lugoj . . . . 45°41' N, 021°55' E
Mangalia . . . . 43°48' N, 028°35' E
Medgidia . . . . 44°15' N, 028°17' E
Mediaș. . . . . 46°10' N, 024°21' E
Mizil. . . . . 45°01' N, 026°27' E
Onești (Gheorghe
   Gheorghiu Dej) . . . . . . 46°15' N, 026°45' E
Oradea (Nagyvarad). . . . . . 47°04' N, 021°56' E
Petroșani . . . . 45°25' N, 023°22' E
Piatra-Neamț. . . . . 46°56' N, 026°20' E
Pitești . . . . 44°51' N, 024°52' E
Ploiești (Ploești) . . . . 44°57' N, 026°01' E
Reșița. . . . . 45°18' N, 021°55' E
Roman . . . . 46°55' N, 026°55' E
Satu Mare . . . . 47°48' N, 022°53' E
Sebeș . . . . 45°58' N, 023°34' E
Slatina . . . . 44°26' N, 024°22' E
Suceava . . . . 47°38' N, 026°15' E
Țăndărei . . . . 44°39' N, 027°40' E
Târgoviște . . . . 44°56' N, 025°27' E
Targu Jiu . . . . 45°03' N, 023°17' E
Târgu Mureș . . . . 46°33' N, 024°34' E
Tecuci . . . . 45°52' N, 027°25' E
Timișoara . . . . 45°45' N, 021°13' E
Tulcea . . . . 45°10' N, 028°48' E
Turda. . . . . 46°34' N, 023°47' E
Vaslui. . . . . 46°38' N, 027°44' E
Zalau . . . . 47°12' N, 023°03' E

RUSSIA . . . . .pg. 140-1

Abakan . . . . 53°43' N, 091°26' E
Aginskoye . . . . 51°06' N, 114°32' E
Anadyr
   (Novo-Mariinsk) . . . . . . 64°45' N, 177°29' E
Angarsk. . . . . 52°34' N, 103°54' E
Birobidzhan . . . . 48°48' N, 132°57' E
Biysk (Biisk) . . . . 52°34' N, 085°15' E
Cheboksary. . . . . 56°09' N, 047°15' E
Chelyabinsk. . . . . 55°10' N, 061°24' E
Cherepovets . . . . 59°08' N, 037°54' E
Chita . . . . 52°03' N, 113°30' E
Dudinka. . . . . 69°25' N, 086°15' E
Gorno-Altaysk (Ulala, or
   Oyrot-Tura) . . . . 51°58' N, 085°58' E
Grozny. . . . . 43°20' N, 045°42' E
Izhevsk (Ustinov) . . . . 56°51' N, 053°14' E
Kaluga . . . . 54°31' N, 036°16' E
Kazan. . . . . 55°45' N, 049°08' E

Khanty-Mansiysk
(Ostyako-Vogulsk)...... 61°00' N, 069°06' E
Kirovsk .... 67°37' N, 033°40' E
Komsomol'sk-na-Amure ... 50°35' N, 137°02' E
Krasnoyarsk .... 56°01' N, 092°50' E
Kudymkar .... 59°01' N, 054°39' E
Kurgan................ 55°26' N, 065°18' E
Kyzyl (Khem-Beldyr) .... 51°42' N, 094°27' E
Magadan .... 59°34' N, 150°48' E
Makhachkala........... 42°58' N, 047°30' E
Maykop (Maikop)........ 44°35' N, 040°10' E
Moscow (Moskva) ...... 55°45' N, 037°35' E
Murmansk .... 68°58' N, 033°05' E
Nal'chik .... 43°29' N, 043°37' E
Nar'yan-Mar............ 67°39' N, 053°00' E
Nizhnekamsk........... 55°36' N, 051°47' E
Nizhny Novgorod
(Gorky)............. 56°20' N, 044°00' E
Novgorod .... 58°31' N, 031°17' E
Novokuznetsk
(Kuznetsk,
or Stalinsk) .... 53°45' N, 087°06' E
Novosibirsk........... 55°02' N, 082°55' E
Omsk................. 55°00' N, 073°24' E
Orenburg (Chkalov) .... 51°45' N, 055°06' E
Orsk................. 51°12' N, 058°34' E
Palana .... 59°07' N, 159°58' E
Penza................ 53°13' N, 045°00' E
Perm' (Molotov) .... 58°00' N, 056°15' E
Petropavlovsk-
Kamchatsky.......... 53°01' N, 158°39' E
Petrozavodsk .... 61°49' N, 034°20' E
Rostov-na-Donu
(Rostov-on-Don) .... 47°14' N, 039°42' E
St. Petersburg
(Leningrad,
or Sankt Peterburg)..... 59°55' N, 030°15' E
Salavat .... 53°21' N, 055°55' E
Salekhard .... 66°33' N, 066°40' E
Samara (Kuybyshev) .... 53°12' N, 050°09' E
Saransk .... 54°11' N, 045°11' E
Saratov .... 51°34' N, 046°02' E
Smolensk .... 54°47' N, 032°03' E
Syktyvkar............. 61°40' N, 050°48' E
Tomsk .... 56°30' N, 084°58' E
Tver' (Kalinin)......... 56°52' N, 035°55' E
Tyumen'.............. 57°09' N, 065°26' E
Ufa .... 55°45' N, 055°56' E
Ulan-Ude .... 51°50' N, 107°37' E
Ussuriysk............. 43°48' N, 131°59' E
Ust'-Ordinsky .... 52°48' N, 104°45' E
Vladimir.............. 56°10' N, 040°25' E
Vladivostok........... 43°08' N, 131°54' E
Volgograd (Stalingrad,
or Tsaritsyn) .... 48°45' N, 044°25' E
Vologda .... 59°13' N, 039°54' E
Voronezh............. 51°38' N, 039°12' E
Yakutsk .... 62°00' N, 129°40' E
Yaroslavl .... 57°37' N, 039°52' E
Yekaterinburg
(Sverdlovsk) .... 56°51' N, 060°36' E

Yuzhno-Sakhalinsk .... 46°57' N, 142°44' E

RWANDA ....pg. 142

Butare .... 02°36' S, 029°44' E
Gisenyi................. 01°42' S, 029°15' E
Kigali .... 01°57' S, 030°04' E
Ruhengeri .... 01°30' S, 029°38' E

SAINT KITTS AND NEVIS .....pg. 143

Basseterre.............. 17°18' N, 062°43' W
Brown Hill .... 17°08' N, 062°33' W
Cayon .... 17°22' N, 062°43' W
Challengers .... 17°18' N, 062°47' W
Charlestown .... 17°08' N, 062°37' W
Cotton Ground .... 17°11' N, 062°36' W
Half Way Tree .... 17°20' N, 062°49' W
Mansion................ 17°22' N, 062°46' W
Monkey Hill Village...... 17°19' N, 062°43' W
Newcastle .... 17°13' N, 062°34' W
New River .... 17°09' N, 062°32' W
Newton Ground .... 17°23' N, 062°51' W
Old Road Town......... 17°19' N, 062°48' W
Sadlers................. 17°24' N, 062°49' W
Saint Paul's .... 17°24' N, 062°49' W
Sandy Point Town....... 17°22' N, 062°50' W
Verchild's .... 17°20' N, 062°48' W
Zetlands................ 17°08' N, 062°34' W

SAINT LUCIA ....pg. 144

Anse La Raye........... 13°57' N, 061°03' W
Canaries .... 13°55' N, 061°04' W
Castries .... 14°01' N, 061°00' W
Dauphin............... 14°03' N, 060°55' W
Dennery .... 13°55' N, 060°54' W
Grande Anse .... 14°01' N, 061°45' W
Gros Islet............. 14°05' N, 060°58' W
Laborie .... 13°45' N, 061°00' W
Micoud .... 13°50' N, 060°54' W
Praslin................ 13°53' N, 060°54' W
Sans Soucis .... 13°59' N, 061°01' W
Soufrière .... 13°52' N, 061°04' W

SAINT VINCENT AND THE GRENADINES ....pg. 145

Ashton................. 12°36' N, 061°27' W
Barrouallie .... 13°14' N, 061°17' W
Calliaqua .... 13°08' N, 061°12' W
Chateaubelaír .... 13°17' N, 061°15' W
Georgetown............ 13°16' N, 061°08' W
Kingstown .... 13°09' N, 061°14' W

SAMOA . . . . .pg. 146

Apia	13°50′ S,	171°44′ W
Fa'aala	13°45′ S,	172°16′ W
Faleasi'u	13°48′ S,	171°54′ W
Le'auva'a	13°48′ S,	171°51′ W
Lotofaga	13°59′ S,	171°50′ W
Matavai (Asau)	13°28′ S,	172°35′ W
Safotu	13°27′ S,	172°24′ W
Sagone	13°39′ S,	172°35′ W
Samatau	13°54′ S,	172°02′ W
Sili	13°43′ S,	172°21′ W
Si'umu	14°01′ S,	171°47′ W
Solosolo	13°51′ S,	171°36′ W

SAN MARINO . . . .pg. 147

San Marino	43°56′ N,	012°25′ E

SÃO TOMÉ AND PRÍNCIPE . .pg. 148

Infante Don Henrique	01°34′ N,	007°25′ E
Neves	00°22′ N,	006°33′ E
Porto Alegre	00°02′ N,	006°32′ E
Santana	00°16′ N,	006°45′ E
Santo Amaro	00°22′ N,	006°42′ E
Santo António	01°39′ N,	007°25′ E
São Tomé	00°20′ N,	006°44′ E
Trindade	00°15′ N,	006°40′ E

SAUDI ARABIA . .pg. 149

Abhā	18°13′ N,	042°30′ E
Abqaiq (Buqayq)	25°56′ N,	049°40′ E
Ad-Dammām	26°26′ N,	050°07′ E
'Afif	23°55′ N,	042°56′ E
Al-Bāhah	20°01′ N,	041°28′ E
Al-Badī'	22°02′ N,	046°34′ E
Al-Bātin Hafar	28°27′ N,	045°58′ E
Al-Bi'ār	22°39′ N,	039°40′ E
Al-Hā'ir	24°23′ N,	046°50′ E
Al-Hufūf	25°22′ N,	049°34′ E
Al-Ju'aydah	19°40′ N,	041°34′ E
Al-Jubayl	27°01′ N,	049°40′ E
Al-Khubar	26°17′ N,	050°12′ E
Al-Mish'āb	28°12′ N,	048°36′ E
Al-Mubarraz	25°25′ N,	049°35′ E
Al-Qaṭīf	26°33′ N,	050°00′ E
Al-Qunfudhah	19°08′ N,	041°05′ E
Al-Ulā	26°38′ N,	037°55′ E
Ar'ar	30°59′ N,	041°02′ E
As-Ṣafrā'	24°02′ N,	038°56′ E
As-Sulayyil	20°27′ N,	045°34′ E
At-Ta'if	21°16′ N,	040°25′ E
Az-Zilfī	26°18′ N,	044°48′ E
Badanah	30°59′ N,	040°58′ E
Birkah	23°48′ N,	038°50′ E

Buraydah	26°20′ N,	043°59′ E
Buraykah	22°21′ N,	039°20′ E
Hā'il	27°33′ N,	041°42′ E
Halabān	23°29′ N,	044°23′ E
Harajah	17°56′ N,	043°21′ E
Jidda (Jiddah)	21°29′ N,	039°12′ E
Jizān (Qizān)	16°54′ N,	042°32′ E
Khamīs Mushayṭ	18°18′ N,	042°44′ E
Khawsh	18°59′ N,	041°53′ E
Laylā	22°17′ N,	046°45′ E
Madā'in Sālih	26°48′ N,	037°57′ E
Mecca (Makkah)	21°27′ N,	039°49′ E
Medina (al-Madinah; Yathrib)	24°28′ N,	039°36′ E
Miskah	24°49′ N,	042°56′ E
Muṣābih	18°42′ N,	042°01′ E
Na'jān	24°05′ N,	047°10′ E
Najrān	17°26′ N,	044°15′ E
Qanā	27°47′ N,	041°25′ E
Rābigh	22°48′ N,	039°02′ E
Rafhā'	29°38′ N,	043°30′ E
Ras Tanura	26°42′ N,	050°06′ E
Riyadh (ar-Riyad)	24°38′ N,	046°43′ E
Sahwah	19°19′ N,	042°06′ E
Sakākah	29°59′ N,	040°12′ E
Shidād	21°19′ N,	040°03′ E
Tabūk	28°23′ N,	036°35′ E
Taymā'	27°38′ N,	038°29′ E
Turayf	31°41′ N,	038°39′ E
'Usfan	21°55′ N,	039°22′ E
Yanbu'	24°05′ N,	038°03′ E
Zahrān	17°40′ N,	043°30′ E
Zalim	22°43′ N,	042°10′ E

SENEGAL . . . . . . .pg. 150

Bakel	14°54′ N,	012°27′ W
Bignona	12°49′ N,	016°14′ W
Dagana	16°31′ N,	015°30′ W
Dakar	14°40′ N,	017°26′ W
Diourbel	14°40′ N,	016°15′ W
Fatick	14°20′ N,	016°25′ W
Joal	14°10′ N,	016°51′ W
Kaffrine	14°06′ N,	015°33′ W
Kaolack	14°09′ N,	016°04′ W
Kédougou	12°33′ N,	012°11′ W
Kolda	12°53′ N,	014°57′ W
Koungheul	13°59′ N,	014°48′ W
Linguère	15°24′ N,	015°07′ W
Louga	15°37′ N,	016°13′ W
Mbacké	14°48′ N,	015°55′ W
Mbour	14°24′ N,	016°58′ W
Mékhé	15°07′ N,	016°38′ W
Podor	16°40′ N,	014°57′ W
Richard-Toll	16°28′ N,	015°41′ W
Saint Louis	16°02′ N,	016°30′ W
Sédhiou	12°44′ N,	015°33′ W
Tambacounda	13°47′ N,	013°40′ W
Thiès	14°48′ N,	016°56′ W
Tivaouane	14°57′ N,	016°49′ W

Vélingara . . . . 13°09' N, 014°07' W
Ziguinchor . . . . 12°35' N, 016°16' W

SEYCHELLES . . . .pg. 151

Victoria . . . . 04°37' S, 055°27' E

SIERRA LEONE . .pg. 152

Bo . . . . 07°58' N, 011°45' W
Bonthe . . . . 07°32' N, 012°30' W
Freetown . . . . 08°30' N, 013°15' W
Kabala . . . . 09°35' N, 011°33' W
Kailahun . . . . 08°17' N, 010°34' W
Kambia . . . . 09°07' N, 012°55' W
Kenema . . . . 07°52' N, 011°12' W
Koidu-New Sembehun . . . . 08°38' N, 010°59' W
Lunsar . . . . 08°41' N, 012°32' W
Magburaka . . . . 08°43' N, 011°57' W
Makeni . . . . 08°53' N, 012°03' W
Mongeri . . . . 08°19' N, 011°44' W
Moyamba . . . . 08°10' N, 012°26' W
Pepel . . . . 08°35' N, 013°03' W
Port Loko . . . . 08°46' N, 012°47' W
Pujehun . . . . 07°21' N, 011°42' W
Sulima . . . . 06°58' N, 011°35' W

SINGAPORE . . . . .pg. 153

Singapore . . . . 01°16' N, 103°50' E

SLOVAKIA . . . . . . .pg. 154

Banská Bystrica . . . . 48°44' N, 019°09' E
Bardejov . . . . 49°17' N, 021°17' E
Bratislava . . . . 48°09' N, 017°07' E
Čadca . . . . 49°26' N, 018°47' E
Fil'akovo . . . . 48°16' N, 019°50' E
Humenné . . . . 48°56' N, 021°55' E
Komárno . . . . 47°46' N, 018°08' E
Košice . . . . 48°42' N, 021°15' E
Levice . . . . 48°13' N, 018°36' E
Liptovský Mikuláš . . . . . . 49°05' N, 019°37' E
Lučenec . . . . 48°20' N, 019°40' E
Martin . . . . 49°04' N, 018°56' E
Michalovce . . . . 48°45' N, 021°56' E
Nitra . . . . 48°19' N, 018°05' E
Nové Zámky . . . . 47°59' N, 018°10' E
Partizánske . . . . 48°38' N, 018°23' E
Piešťany . . . . 48°36' N, 017°50' E
Poprad . . . . 49°03' N, 020°18' E
Považská Bystrica . . . . 49°07' N, 018°27' E
Prešov . . . . 49°00' N, 021°15' E
Prievidza . . . . 48°46' N, 018°38' E
Rimavská Sobota . . . . 48°23' N, 020°02' E
Rožňava . . . . 48°40' N, 020°32' E
Skalica . . . . 48°51' N, 017°14' E
Spišská Nová Ves . . . . 48°57' N, 020°34' E

Topol'čany . . . . 48°34' N, 018°11' E
Trebišov . . . . 48°38' N, 021°43' E
Trenčín . . . . 48°54' N, 018°02' E
Trnava . . . . 48°22' N, 017°36' E
Žilina . . . . 49°13' N, 018°44' E
Zvolen . . . . 48°35' N, 019°08' E

SLOVENIA . . . . . .pg. 155

Celje . . . . 46°14' N, 015°16' E
Hrastnik . . . . 46°09' N, 015°06' E
Idrija . . . . 46°00' N, 014°02' E
Javornik . . . . 46°14' N, 014°18' E
Jesenice . . . . 46°27' N, 014°04' E
Kočevje . . . . 45°39' N, 014°51' E
Koper . . . . 45°33' N, 013°44' E
Kranj . . . . 46°14' N, 014°22' E
Krško . . . . 45°58' N, 015°29' E
Ljubljana . . . . 46°02' N, 014°30' E
Maribor . . . . 46°33' N, 015°39' E
Murska Sobota . . . . 46°40' N, 016°10' E
Novo Mesto . . . . 45°48' N, 015°10' E
Postojna . . . . 45°47' N, 014°14' E
Ptuj . . . . 46°25' N, 015°52' E
Trbovlje . . . . 46°10' N, 015°03' E
Velenje . . . . 46°22' N, 015°07' E
Zagorje . . . . 46°08' N, 015°00' E

SOLOMON ISLANDS . . . . .pg. 156

Buala . . . . 08°08' S, 159°35' E
Honiara . . . . 09°26' S, 159°57' E
Kirakira . . . . 10°27' S, 161°55' E
Lata . . . . 10°44' S, 165°54' E
Maravovo . . . . 09°17' S, 159°38' E
Munda . . . . 08°19' S, 157°15' E
Sahalu . . . . 09°44' S, 160°31' E
Sasamungga . . . . 07°02' S, 156°47' E
Takwa . . . . 08°22' S, 160°48' E

SOMALIA . . . . . . .pg. 157

Baardheere (Bardera) . . . . 02°20' N, 042°17' E
Baraawe (Brava) . . . . 01°06' N, 044°03' E
Baydhabo (Baidoa) . . . . . . 03°07' N, 043°39' E
Beledweyne (Belet Uen) . . 04°45' N, 045°12' E
Berbera . . . . 10°25' N, 045°02' E
Boosaaso
(Bender Cassim) . . . . 11°17' N, 049°11' E
Burao (Burco) . . . . 09°31' N, 045°32' E
Buulobarde (Bulo Burti) . . 03°51' N, 045°34' E
Eyl . . . . 07°59' N, 049°49' E
Hargeysa . . . . 09°35' N, 044°04' E
Hobyo (Obbia) . . . . 05°21' N, 048°32' E
Jamaame (Giamama or
Jamame or Margherita) . 00°04' N, 042°45' E

Jawhar (Giohar) . . . . 02°46′ N, 045°31′ E
Kismaayo (Chisimayu) . . . . 00°22′ S, 042°32′ E
Marka (Merca) . . . . 01°43′ N, 044°53′ E
Mogadishu (Mogadiscio
  or Mogadisho) . . . . 02°04′ N, 045°22′ E
Seylac (Zeila) . . . . 11°21′ N, 043°29′ E
Xaafun . . . . 10°25′ N, 051°16′ E

SOUTH AFRICA . . pg. 158

Bellville . . . . 33°54′ S, 018°38′ E
Bisho . . . . 32°53′ S, 027°24′ E
Bloemfontein. . . . . 29°08′ S, 026°10′ E
Calvinia . . . . 31°28′ S, 019°47′ E
Cape Town (Kaapstad) . . . . 33°55′ S, 018°25′ E
Durban (Port Natal) . . . . . . 29°51′ S, 031°01′ E
East London . . . . 33°02′ S, 027°55′ E
George . . . . 33°58′ S, 022°27′ E
Germiston . . . . 26°13′ S, 028°11′ E
Hopefield . . . . 33°04′ S, 018°21′ E
Johannesburg . . . . 26°12′ S, 028°05′ E
Kimberley . . . . 28°45′ S, 024°46′ E
Klerksdorp . . . . 26°52′ S, 026°40′ E
Krugersdorp . . . . 26°06′ S, 027°46′ E
Kuruman . . . . 27°28′ S, 023°26′ E
Ladysmith . . . . 28°33′ S, 029°47′ E
Margate . . . . 30°51′ S, 030°22′ E
Newcastle . . . . 27°45′ S, 029°56′ E
Oudtshoorn. . . . . 33°35′ S, 022°12′ E
Pietermaritzburg. . . . . 29°37′ S, 030°23′ E
Port Elizabeth . . . . 33°58′ S, 025°35′ E
Port Nolloth . . . . 29°15′ S, 016°52′ E
Pretoria . . . . 25°45′ S, 028°10′ E
Queenstown . . . . 31°54′ S, 026°53′ E
Rustenburg . . . . 25°40′ S, 027°15′ E
Seshego . . . . 23°51′ S, 029°23′ E
Soweto. . . . . 26°16′ S, 027°52′ E
Stellenbosch . . . . 33°56′ S, 018°51′ E
Uitenhage . . . . 33°46′ S, 025°24′ E
Upington . . . . 28°27′ S, 021°15′ E
Vanderbijlpark . . . . 26°42′ S, 027°49′ E
Welkom . . . . 27°59′ S, 026°42′ E
Worcester . . . . 33°39′ S, 019°26′ E

SOUTH KOREA . . pg. 159

Andong . . . . 36°34′ N, 128°44′ E
Anyang . . . . 37°23′ N, 126°55′ E
Ch'ang won . . . . 35°16′ N, 128°37′ E
Cheju . . . . 33°31′ N, 126°32′ E
Chŏngju. . . . . 36°38′ N, 127°30′ E
Chŏnju . . . . 35°49′ N, 127°09′ E
Ch'unch'ŏn . . . . 37°52′ N, 127°44′ E
Inch'ŏn . . . . 37°28′ N, 126°38′ E
Iri . . . . 35°56′ N, 126°57′ E
Kumi . . . . 36°08′ N, 128°20′ E
Kunsan . . . . 35°59′ N, 126°43′ E
Kwangju. . . . . 35°10′ N, 126°55′ E
Kyŏngju. . . . . 35°50′ N, 129°13′ E
Masan . . . . 35°11′ N, 128°34′ E

Mokp'o. . . . . 34°47′ N, 126°23′ E
P'ohang . . . . 36°02′ N, 129°22′ E
Pusan . . . . 35°06′ N, 129°03′ E
Samch'ŏnp'o . . . . 34°55′ N, 128°04′ E
Seoul (Soul). . . . . 37°34′ N, 127°00′ E
Sŏsan . . . . 36°47′ N, 126°27′ E
Sunch'ŏn . . . . 34°57′ N, 127°29′ E
Suwŏn . . . . 37°16′ N, 127°01′ E
T'aebaek . . . . 37°10′ N, 128°59′ E
Taech'ŏn . . . . 36°21′ N, 126°36′ E
Taegu
  (Daegu or Taiku) . . . . . . 35°52′ N, 128°36′ E
Taejon . . . . 36°20′ N, 127°26′ E
Uijŏngbu . . . . 37°44′ N, 127°02′ E
Ulsan . . . . 35°33′ N, 129°19′ E
Wŏnju . . . . 37°21′ N, 127°58′ E

SPAIN . . . . pg. 160

Albacete . . . . 38°59′ N, 001°51′ W
Alcalá de Henares. . . . . . . 40°29′ N, 003°22′ W
Algeciras . . . . 36°08′ N, 005°30′ W
Alicante (Alacant). . . . . . . 38°21′ N, 000°29′ W
Avilés. . . . . 43°33′ N, 005°55′ W
Badajoz . . . . 38°53′ N, 006°58′ W
Barcelona . . . . 41°23′ N, 002°11′ E
Bilbao . . . . 43°15′ N, 002°58′ W
Burgos . . . . 42°21′ N, 003°42′ W
Cáceres . . . . 39°29′ N, 006°22′ W
Cádiz (Cadiz) . . . . 36°32′ N, 006°18′ W
Cartagena . . . . 37°36′ N, 000°59′ W
Castellón de la Plana . . . . . 39°59′ N, 000°02′ W
Ciudad Real . . . . 38°59′ N, 003°56′ W
Cordova (Córdoba) . . . . . . 37°53′ N, 004°46′ W
Cuenca . . . . 40°04′ N, 002°08′ W
Elche (Elx). . . . . 38°15′ N, 000°42′ W
Ferrol (El Ferrol del
  Caudillo) . . . . 43°29′ N, 008°14′ W
Gernika-Lumo
  (Guernica y Luno) . . . . 43°19′ N, 002°41′ W
Getafe . . . . 40°18′ N, 003°43′ W
Gijón . . . . 43°32′ N, 005°40′ W
Granada . . . . 37°11′ N, 003°36′ W
Huelva . . . . 37°16′ N, 006°57′ W
Jaén . . . . 37°46′ N, 003°47′ W
La Coruña (A Coruña) . . . . 43°22′ N, 008°23′ W
León . . . . 42°36′ N, 005°34′ W
Lérida (Lleida) . . . . 41°37′ N, 000°37′ E
L'Hospitalet
  de Llobregat . . . . 41°22′ N, 002°08′ E
Logroño. . . . . 42°28′ N, 002°27′ W
Lugo. . . . . 43°00′ N, 007°34′ W
Madrid . . . . 40°24′ N, 003°41′ W
Málaga. . . . . 36°43′ N, 004°25′ W
Mérida . . . . 38°55′ N, 006°20′ W
Murcia . . . . 37°59′ N, 001°07′ W
Palencia. . . . . 42°01′ N, 004°32′ W
Pamplona (Iruña) . . . . 42°49′ N, 001°38′ W
Salamanca . . . . 40°58′ N, 005°39′ W
San Fernando . . . . 36°28′ N, 006°12′ W
Santander . . . . 43°28′ N, 003°48′ W

Santiago
de Compostela . . . . 42°53′ N, 008°33′ W
Saragossa (Zaragoza) . . . . . 41°38′ N, 000°53′ W
Segovia . . . . 40°57′ N, 004°07′ W
Seville (Sevilla) . . . . 37°23′ N, 005°59′ W
Soria . . . . 41°46′ N, 002°28′ W
Tarragona . . . . 41°07′ N, 001°15′ E
Terrassa (Tarrasa) . . . . 41°34′ N, 002°01′ E
Teruel . . . . 40°21′ N, 001°06′ W
Toledo . . . . 39°52′ N, 004°01′ W
Valencia . . . . 39°28′ N, 000°22′ W
Valladolid . . . . 41°39′ N, 004°43′ W
Vigo . . . . 42°14′ N, 008°43′ W
Vitoria (Gasteiz) . . . . 42°51′ N, 002°40′ W

SRI LANKA . . . . . . pg. 161

Ambalangoda . . . . 06°14′ N, 080°03′ E
Anuradhapura . . . . 08°21′ N, 080°23′ E
Badulla . . . . 06°59′ N, 081°03′ E
Batticaloa . . . . 07°43′ N, 081°42′ E
Beruwala . . . . 06°29′ N, 079°59′ E
Chavakachcheri . . . . 09°39′ N, 080°09′ E
Colombo . . . . 06°56′ N, 079°51′ E
Dehiwala-
Mount Lavinia . . . . 06°51′ N, 079°52′ E
Eravur . . . . 07°46′ N, 081°36′ E
Galle . . . . 06°02′ N, 080°13′ E
Gampola . . . . 07°10′ N, 080°34′ E
Hambantota . . . . 06°07′ N, 081°07′ E
Jaffna . . . . 09°40′ N, 080°00′ E
Kalutara . . . . 06°35′ N, 079°58′ E
Kandy . . . . 07°18′ N, 080°38′ E
Kankesanturai . . . . 09°49′ N, 080°02′ E
Kegalla . . . . 07°15′ N, 080°21′ E
Kilinochchi . . . . 09°24′ N, 080°24′ E
Kotte . . . . 06°54′ N, 079°54′ E
Kurunegala . . . . 07°29′ N, 080°22′ E
Madampe . . . . 07°30′ N, 079°50′ E
Mannar . . . . 08°59′ N, 079°54′ E
Moratuwa . . . . 06°46′ N, 079°53′ E
Mullaittivu . . . . 09°16′ N, 080°49′ E
Mutur . . . . 08°27′ N, 081°16′ E
Negombo . . . . 07°13′ N, 079°50′ E
Nuwara Eliya . . . . 06°58′ N, 080°46′ E
Point Pedro . . . . 09°50′ N, 080°14′ E
Polonnaruwa . . . . 07°56′ N, 081°00′ E
Puttalam . . . . 08°02′ N, 079°49′ E
Ratnapura . . . . 06°41′ N, 080°24′ E
Tangalla . . . . 06°01′ N, 080°48′ E
Trincomalee . . . . 08°34′ N, 081°14′ E
Vavuniya . . . . 08°45′ N, 080°30′ E
Watugedara . . . . 06°15′ N, 080°03′ E
Weligama . . . . 05°58′ N, 080°25′ E
Yala . . . . 06°22′ N, 081°31′ E

SUDAN . . . . pg. 162

Ad-Damazin
(Ed–Damazin) . . . . 11°46′ N, 034°21′ E

Ad-Dāmir . . . . 17°35′ N, 033°58′ E
Ad-Duwaym
(Ed-Dueim) . . . . 14°00′ N, 032°19′ E
Al-Fūlah . . . . 11°48′ N, 028°24′ E
Al-Fashir (El Fasher) . . . . . 13°38′ N, 025°21′ E
Al-Junaynah (Geneina) . . . 13°27′ N, 022°27′ E
Al-Mijlad . . . . 11°02′ N, 027°44′ E
Al-Qadārif (Gedaref) . . . . . 14°02′ N, 035°24′ E
Al-Ubbayid (El-Obeid) . . . 13°11′ N, 030°13′ E
An-Nuhūd (An-Nahūd) . . . 12°42′ N, 028°26′ E
'Atbarah . . . . 17°42′ N, 033°59′ E
Bor . . . . 06°12′ N, 031°33′ E
Dunqulah (Dongola) . . . . . 19°10′ N, 030°29′ E
Juba . . . . 04°51′ N, 031°37′ E
Kāduqlī . . . . 11°01′ N, 029°43′ E
Kas . . . . 12°30′ N, 024°17′ E
Kassalā . . . . 15°28′ N, 036°24′ E
Khartoum . . . . 15°36′ N, 032°32′ E
Khartoum North . . . . 15°38′ N, 032°33′ E
Kūstī . . . . 13°10′ N, 032°40′ E
Malakāl . . . . 09°31′ N, 031°39′ E
Marawi . . . . 18°29′ N, 031°49′ E
Nagichot . . . . 04°16′ N, 033°34′ E
Nāsir . . . . 08°36′ N, 033°04′ E
Nyala . . . . 12°03′ N, 024°53′ E
Omdurman . . . . 15°38′ N, 032°30′ E
Port Sudan . . . . 19°37′ N, 037°14′ E
Rumbek . . . . 06°48′ N, 029°41′ E
Sannār . . . . 13°33′ N, 033°38′ E
Sawākin . . . . 19°07′ N, 037°20′ E
Shandi . . . . 16°42′ N, 033°26′ E
Wadi Halfa' . . . . 21°48′ N, 031°21′ E
Wad Madanī . . . . 14°24′ N, 033°32′ E
Wāw (Wau) . . . . 07°42′ N, 028°00′ E

SURINAME . . . . . . pg. 163

Albina . . . . 05°30′ N, 054°03′ W
Benzdorp . . . . 03°41′ N, 054°05′ W
Bitagron . . . . 05°10′ N, 056°06′ W
Brokopondo . . . . 05°04′ N, 054°58′ W
Brownsweg . . . . 05°01′ N, 055°10′ W
Goddo . . . . 04°01′ N, 055°28′ W
Groningen . . . . 05°48′ N, 055°28′ W
Meerzorg . . . . 05°49′ N, 055°09′ W
Nieuw Amsterdam . . . . . . 05°53′ N, 055°05′ W
Nieuw Nickerie . . . . 05°57′ N, 056°59′ W
Onverwacht . . . . 05°36′ N, 055°12′ W
Paramaribo . . . . 05°50′ N, 055°10′ W
Totness . . . . 05°53′ N, 056°19′ W
Zanderij . . . . 05°27′ N, 055°12′ W

SWAZILAND . . . . pg. 164

Hlatikulu . . . . 26°58′ S, 031°19′ E
Kadake . . . . 26°13′ S, 031°02′ E
Manzini (Bremersdorp) . . . 26°29′ S, 031°22′ E
Mbabane . . . . 26°19′ S, 031°08′ E
Nhlangono . . . . 27°07′ S, 031°12′ E
Piggs Peak . . . . 25°58′ S, 031°15′ E

Siteki (Stegi) . . . . 26°27´ S, 031°57´ E

SWEDEN . . . . .pg. 165

Älvsbyn . . . . 65°40´ N, 021°00´ E
Falun . . . . 60°36´ N, 015°38´ E
Gävle . . . . 60°40´ N, 017°10´ E
Göteborg . . . . 57°43´ N, 011°58´ E
Halmstad . . . . 56°39´ N, 012°50´ E
Haparanda . . . . 65°50´ N, 024°10´ E
Hudiksvall . . . . 61°44´ N, 017°07´ E
Jönköping . . . . 57°47´ N, 014°11´ E
Karlskrona . . . . 56°10´ N, 015°35´ E
Karlstad . . . . 59°22´ N, 013°30´ E
Kiruna . . . . 67°51´ N, 020°13´ E
Kristianstad . . . . 56°02´ N, 014°08´ E
Linköping . . . . 58°25´ N, 015°37´ E
Luleå . . . . 65°34´ N, 022°10´ E
Lycksele . . . . 64°36´ N, 018°40´ E
Malmberget . . . . 67°10´ N, 020°40´ E
Malmö . . . . 55°36´ N, 013°00´ E
Mariestad . . . . 58°43´ N, 013°51´ E
Mora . . . . 61°00´ N, 014°33´ E
Örebro . . . . 59°17´ N, 015°13´ E
Örnsköldsvik . . . . 63°18´ N, 018°43´ E
Östersund . . . . 63°11´ N, 014°39´ E
Piteå . . . . 65°20´ N, 021°30´ E
Skellefteå . . . . 64°46´ N, 020°57´ E
Söderhamn . . . . 61°18´ N, 017°03´ E
Stockholm . . . . 59°20´ N, 018°03´ E
Strömsund . . . . 63°51´ N, 015°35´ E
Sundsvall . . . . 62°23´ N, 017°18´ E
Umea . . . . 63°50´ N, 020°15´ E
Uppsala . . . . 59°52´ N, 017°38´ E
Vänersborg . . . . 58°22´ N, 012°19´ E
Västerås . . . . 59°37´ N, 016°33´ E
Växjö . . . . 56°53´ N, 014°49´ E
Vetalnda . . . . 57°26´ N, 015°04´ E
Visby . . . . 57°38´ N, 018°18´ E
Ystad . . . . 55°25´ N, 013°49´ E

SWITZERLAND . .pg. 166

Aarau . . . . 47°23´ N, 008°03´ E
Altdorf . . . . 46°53´ N, 008°39´ E
Arbon . . . . 47°31´ N, 009°26´ E
Appenzell . . . . 47°20´ N, 009°24´ E
Arosa . . . . 46°47´ N, 009°40´ E
Baden . . . . 47°28´ N, 008°18´ E
Basel . . . . 47°35´ N, 007°32´ E
Bellinzona . . . . 46°12´ N, 009°01´ E
Bern . . . . 46°55´ N, 007°28´ E
Biel (Bienne) . . . . 47°10´ N, 007°15´ E
Chur (Coire) . . . . 46°51´ N, 009°30´ E
Davos . . . . 46°49´ N, 009°50´ E
Delémont . . . . 47°22´ N, 007°20´ E
Frauenfeld . . . . 47°33´ N, 008°54´ E
Fribourg (Freiburg) . . . . . . 46°48´ N, 007°09´ E
Geneva . . . . 46°12´ N, 006°10´ E
Glarus . . . . 47°02´ N, 009°04´ E

Grindelwald . . . . 46°37´ N, 008°03´ E
Gstaad . . . . 46°28´ N, 007°17´ E
Herisau . . . . 47°24´ N, 009°16´ E
Interlaken . . . . 46°41´ N, 007°51´ E
La Chaux-de-Fonds . . . . . . 47°08´ N, 006°51´ E
Lausanne . . . . 46°32´ N, 006°40´ E
Liestal . . . . 47°28´ N, 007°44´ E
Locarno (Luggarus) . . . . . . 46°10´ N, 008°48´ E
Lucerne (Luzern) . . . . 47°05´ N, 008°16´ E
Lugano (Lauis) . . . . 46°00´ N, 008°58´ E
Montreux . . . . 46°26´ N, 006°55´ E
Neuchatel (Neuenburg) . . . 47°00´ N, 006°58´ E
Saint Gall
  (Sankt Gallen) . . . . 47°28´ N, 009°24´ E
Saint Moritz
  (San Murezzan,
  Saint-Moritz,
  or Sankt Moritz) . . . . . . 46°30´ N, 009°50´ E
Sarnen . . . . 46°54´ N, 008°14´ E
Schaffhausen . . . . 47°42´ N, 008°38´ E
Sion (Sitten) . . . . 46°14´ N, 007°21´ E
Solothurn (Soleure) . . . . . . 47°14´ N, 007°31´ E
Stans . . . . 46°58´ N, 008°21´ E
Thun (Thoune) . . . . 46°45´ N, 007°37´ E
Vevey . . . . 46°27´ N, 006°51´ E
Winterthur . . . . 47°30´ N, 008°45´ E
Zermatt . . . . 46°01´ N, 007°45´ E
Zug . . . . 47°10´ N, 008°31´ E
Zürich . . . . 47°22´ N, 008°33´ E

SYRIA . . . . .pg. 167

Al-Bāb . . . . 36°22´ N, 037°31´ E
Al-Hasakah . . . . 36°29´ N, 040°45´ E
Al-Mayādin . . . . 35°01´ N, 040°27´ E
Al-Qāmishli
  (Al-Kamishly) . . . . 37°02´ N, 041°14´ E
Aleppo (Ḥalab) . . . . 36°12´ N, 037°10´ E
Ar-Raqqah (Rakka) . . . . . . 35°57´ N, 039°01´ E
As-Safirah . . . . 36°04´ N, 037°22´ E
As-Suwaydā´ . . . . 32°42´ N, 036°34´ E
A´zāz (I´zaz) . . . . 36°35´ N, 037°03´ E
Damascus . . . . 33°30´ N, 036°18´ E
Dar´ā . . . . 32°37´ N, 036°06´ E
Dayr az-Zawr . . . . 35°20´ N, 040°09´ E
Dūmā (Douma) . . . . 33°35´ N, 036°24´ E
Hamāh (Hama) . . . . 35°08´ N, 036°45´ E
Ḥimṣ (Homs) . . . . 34°44´ N, 036°43´ E
Idlib . . . . 35°55´ N, 036°38´ E
Jablah (Jableh) . . . . 35°21´ N, 035°55´ E
Jarābulus . . . . 36°49´ N, 038°01´ E
Latakia (Al-Lādhiqīyah) . . . 35°31´ N, 035°47´ E
Ma´arrat an-Nu´mān . . . . . 35°38´ N, 036°40´ E
Ma´lūlā . . . . 33°50´ N, 036°33´ E
Manbij (Manbej) . . . . 36°31´ N, 037°57´ E
Mukharram al-Fawqāni . . . . 34°49´ N, 037°05´ E
Ra´s al-´Ayn . . . . 36°51´ N, 040°04´ E
Salamīyah . . . . 35°01´ N, 037°03´ E
Tadmur . . . . 34°33´ N, 038°17´ E
Ṭarṭūs . . . . 34°53´ N, 035°53´ E

TAIWAN ....pg. 168

Chang-hua	24°05' N, 120°32' E
Ch'ao-chou	22°33' N, 120°32' E
Ch'e-ch'eng	22°05' N, 120°42' E
Chia-i	23°29' N, 120°27' E
Ch'ih-shang	23°07' N, 121°12' E
Chi-lung	25°08' N, 121°44' E
Chung-hsing Hsin-ts'un	23°57' N, 120°41' E
Chu-tung	24°44' N, 121°05' E
Erh-lin	23°54' N, 120°22' E
Feng-lin	23°45' N, 121°26' E
Feng-shan	22°38' N, 120°21' E
Feng-yüan	24°15' N, 120°43' E
Hsin-chu	24°48' N, 120°58' E
Hsin-ying	23°18' N, 120°19' E
Hua-lien	23°59' N, 121°36' E
I-lan	24°46' N, 121°45' E
Kang-shan	22°48' N, 120°17' E
Kao-hsiung	22°38' N, 120°17' E
Lan-yü	22°02' N, 121°33' E
Lo-tung	24°41' N, 121°46' E
Lu-kang	24°03' N, 120°25' E
Lü-tao	22°40' N, 121°28' E
Miao-li	24°34' N, 120°49' E
Nan-t'ou	23°55' N, 120°41' E
Pan-ch'iao	25°01' N, 121°27' E
P'ing-tung	22°40' N, 120°29' E
San-ch'ung	25°04' N, 121°30' E
Su-ao	24°36' N, 121°51' E
T'ai-chung	24°09' N, 120°41' E
T'ai-nan	23°00' N, 120°12' E
Taipei (T'ai-pei)	25°03' N, 121°30' E
T'ai-tung	22°45' N, 121°09' E
T'ao-yüan	25°00' N, 121°18' E
Tung-ho	22°58' N, 121°18' E
Yüan-lin	23°58' N, 120°34' E
Yung-k'ang	23°02' N, 120°15' E

TAJIKISTAN .....pg. 169

Dushanbe	38°33' N, 068°48' E
Kalininobod	37°52' N, 068°55' E
Khorugh	37°30' N, 071°36' E
Khujand (Leninabad, or Khojand)	40°17' N, 069°37' E
Kofarniqon (Ordzhonikidzeābad)	38°34' N, 069°01' E
Külob	37°55' N, 069°46' E
Norak	38°23' N, 069°21' E
Qayroqqum	40°16' N, 069°49' E
Qŭrghonteppa	37°50' N, 068°47' E
Uroteppa	39°55' N, 069°01' E

TANZANIA .....pg. 170

Arusha	03°22' S, 036°41' E
Bagamoyo	06°26' S, 038°54' E
Bukoba	01°20' S, 031°49' E

Chake Chake	05°15' S, 039°46' E
Dar es Salaam	06°48' S, 039°17' E
Dodoma	06°11' S, 035°45' E
Ifakara	08°08' S, 036°41' E
Iringa	07°46' S, 035°42' E
Kigoma	04°52' S, 029°38' E
Korogwe	05°09' S, 038°29' E
Lindi	10°00' S, 039°43' E
Mbeya	08°54' S, 033°27' E
Mkoani	05°22' S, 039°39' E
Morogoro	06°49' S, 037°40' E
Moshi	03°21' S, 037°20' E
Mpwapwa	06°21' S, 036°29' E
Mtwara	10°16' S, 040°11' E
Musoma	01°30' S, 033°48' E
Mwanza	02°31' S, 032°54' E
Newala	10°56' S, 039°18' E
Pangani	09°32' S, 035°31' E
Shinyanga	03°40' S, 033°26' E
Singida	04°49' S, 034°45' E
Songea	10°41' S, 035°39' E
Sumbawanga	07°58' S, 031°37' E
Tabora	05°01' S, 032°48' E
Tanga	05°04' S, 039°06' E
Tunduru	11°07' S, 037°21' E
Wete	05°04' S, 039°43' E
Zanzibar	06°10' S, 039°11' E

THAILAND .....pg. 171

Bangkok (Krung Thep)	13°45' N, 100°31' E
Chanthaburi (Chantabun)	12°36' N, 102°09' E
Chiang Mai (Chiengmai)	18°47' N, 098°59' E
Chon Buri	13°22' N, 100°59' E
Hat Yai (Haad Yai)	07°01' N, 100°28' E
Khon Kaen	16°26' N, 102°50' E
Mae Sot	16°43' N, 098°34' E
Nakhhon Phanom	17°24' N, 104°47' E
Nakhon Ratchasima (Khorat)	14°58' N, 102°07' E
Nakhon Sawan	15°41' N, 100°07' E
Nakhon Si Thammarat	08°26' N, 099°58' E
Nan	18°47' N, 100°47' E
Nong Khai	17°52' N, 102°44' E
Nonthaburi	13°50' N, 100°29' E
Pathum Thani	14°01' N, 100°32' E
Pattaya	12°54' N, 100°51' E
Phichit	16°26' N, 100°22' E
Phitsanulok	16°50' N, 100°15' E
Phra Nakhon Si Ayutthaya (Ayutthaya)	14°21' N, 100°33' E
Phuket	07°53' N, 098°24' E
Roi Et	16°03' N, 103°40' E
Sakon Nakhon	17°10' N, 104°09' E
Samut Prakan	13°36' N, 100°36' E
Samut Sakhon (Samut Sakorn)	13°32' N, 100°17' E
Sara Buri	14°32' N, 100°55' E
Trang	07°33' N, 099°36' E
Trat	12°14' N, 102°30' E

Ubon Ratchathani........ 15°14′ N, 104°54′ E
Udon Thani............. 17°26′ N, 102°46′ E
Uthai Thani............ 15°22′ N, 100°03′ E
Yala.................. 06°33′ N, 101°18′ E

TOGO ....pg. 172

Aného .... 06°14′ N, 001°36′ E
Atakpamé .... 07°32′ N, 001°08′ E
Bassar .... 09°15′ N, 000°47′ E
Blitta .... 08°19′ N, 000°59′ E
Dapaong .... 10°52′ N, 000°12′ E
Kara (Lama Kara)....... 09°33′ N, 001°12′ E
Lomé .... 06°08′ N, 001°13′ E
Palimé .... 09°21′ N, 002°37′ E
Sokodé................ 08°59′ N, 001°08′ E
Tsévié .... 06°25′ N, 001°13′ E

TONGA ....pg. 173

Nuku'alofa............. 21°08′ N, 175°12′ E

TRINIDAD AND TOBAGO ....pg. 174

Arima................. 10°38′ N, 061°17′ W
Arouca................ 10°38′ N, 061°20′ W
Chaguanas............. 10°31′ N, 061°25′ W
Charlotteville .... 11°19′ N, 060°33′ W
Couva .... 10°25′ N, 061°27′ W
Point Fortin........... 10°11′ N, 061°41′ W
Port of Spain.......... 10°39′ N, 061°31′ W
Princes Town .... 10°16′ N, 061°23′ W
Rio Claro .... 10°18′ N, 061°11′ W
Roxborough .... 11°15′ N, 060°35′ W
San Fernando .... 10°17′ N, 061°28′ W
Sangre Grande .... 10°35′ N, 061°07′ W
Scarborough .... 11°11′ N, 060°44′ W
Siparia .... 10°08′ N, 061°30′ W
Tunapuna .... 10°38′ N, 061°23′ W

TUNISIA ....pg. 175

Al-Ḥammāmāt
  (Hammamet) .... 36°24′ N, 010°37′ E
Al-Mahdīyah (Mahdia) .... 35°30′ N, 011°04′ E
Al-Metlaoui .... 34°20′ N, 008°24′ E
Al-Muknīn (Moknine) ..... 35°38′ N, 010°54′ E
Al-Munastīr (Monastir or
  Ruspina)............. 35°47′ N, 010°50′ E
Al-Qaṣrayn (Kasserine) ... 35°11′ N, 008°48′ E
Al-Qayrawān (Kairouan
  or Qairouan) .... 35°41′ N, 010°07′ E
Bājah (Béja) .... 36°44′ N, 009°11′ E
Banzart (Bizerte) .... 37°17′ N, 009°52′ E
Ḥammām al-Anf
  (Hammam-lif)......... 36°44′ N, 010°20′ E
Jarjīs (Zarzis) .... 33°30′ N, 011°07′ E

Madanīn (Medenine) ..... 33°21′ N, 010°30′ E
Makthar............... 35°51′ N, 009°12′ E
Manzil Bū Ruqaybah
  (Ferryville or Menzel-
  Bourguiba)........... 37°10′ N, 009°48′ E
Nābul (Nabeul or
  Neapolis) .... 36°27′ N, 010°44′ E
Naftah (Nefta) .... 33°52′ N, 007°53′ E
Qābis
  (Gabes or Tacape) ..... 33°53′ N, 010°07′ E
Qafṣah (Gafsa) .... 34°25′ N, 008°48′ E
Qibilī (Kebili) .... 33°42′ N, 008°58′ E
Safāqis (Sfax) .... 34°44′ N, 010°46′ E
Sūsah
  (Sousa or Sousse) ...... 35°49′ N, 010°38′ E
Tawzar (Tozeur)........ 33°55′ N, 008°08′ E
Tunis (Tunis) .... 36°48′ N, 010°11′ E
Zaghwān (Zaghouan) ..... 36°24′ N, 010°09′ E

TURKEY ....pg. 176

Adana .... 37°01′ N, 035°18′ E
Afyon .... 38°45′ N, 030°33′ E
Amasya .... 40°39′ N, 035°51′ E
Ankara (Angora)........ 39°56′ N, 032°52′ E
Antakya (Antioch) ...... 36°14′ N, 036°07′ E
Antalya
  (Attalia or Hatay) ..... 36°53′ N, 030°42′ E
Artvin................ 41°11′ N, 041°49′ E
Aydın .... 37°51′ N, 027°51′ E
Balıkesir............. 39°39′ N, 027°53′ E
Bandırma (Panderma) .... 40°20′ N, 027°58′ E
Batman .... 37°52′ N, 041°07′ E
Bursa (Brusa) .... 40°11′ N, 029°04′ E
Çorum .... 40°33′ N, 034°58′ E
Denizli .... 37°46′ N, 029°06′ E
Diyarbakır (Amida)...... 37°55′ N, 040°14′ E
Elâziğ .... 38°41′ N, 039°14′ E
Erzincan .... 39°44′ N, 039°29′ E
Erzurum............... 39°55′ N, 041°17′ E
Eskisehir .... 39°46′ N, 030°32′ E
Gaziantep .... 37°05′ N, 037°22′ E
Iğdır .... 39°56′ N, 044°02′ E
İskenderun
  (Alexandretta)........ 36°35′ N, 036°10′ E
Isparta (Hamid-Abad).... 37°46′ N, 030°33′ E
Istanbul
  (Constantinople)...... 41°01′ N, 028°58′ E
İzmir (Smyrna) .... 38°25′ N, 027°09′ E
İzmit................. 40°46′ N, 029°55′ E
Kahramanmaraş
  (Maraş) .... 37°36′ N, 036°55′ E
Karabük............... 41°12′ N, 032°37′ E
Karaman .... 37°11′ N, 033°14′ E
Kars.................. 40°37′ N, 043°05′ E
Kayseri (Caesarea) ..... 38°43′ N, 035°30′ E
Kırıkkale .... 39°50′ N, 033°31′ E
Konya (Iconium)........ 37°52′ N, 032°31′ E
Kütahya............... 39°25′ N, 029°59′ E
Manisa .... 38°36′ N, 027°26′ E
Mardin................ 37°18′ N, 040°44′ E

Mersin	36°48′ N,	034°38′ E
Muğla	37°12′ N,	028°22′ E
Nevşehir	38°38′ N,	034°43′ E
Niğde	37°59′ N,	034°42′ E
Ordu	41°00′ N,	037°53′ E
Samsun (Amisus)	41°17′ N,	036°20′ E
Sinop	42°01′ N,	035°09′ E
Sivas (Sebastia)	39°45′ N,	037°02′ E
Trabzon (Trapezus or Trebizond)	41°00′ N,	039°43′ E
Urfa	37°08′ N,	038°46′ E
Uşak (Ushak)	38°41′ N,	029°25′ E
Van	38°30′ N,	043°23′ E
Yalova	40°39′ N,	029°15′ E
Yozgat	39°50′ N,	034°48′ E
Zonguldak	41°27′ N,	031°49′ E

TURKMENISTAN pg. 177

Ashgabat (Ashkhabad)	37°57′ N,	058°23′ E
Bayramaly	37°37′ N,	062°10′ E
Büzmeyin	38°05′ N,	058°12′ E
Chärjew	39°06′ N,	063°34′ E
Cheleken	39°26′ N,	053°07′ E
Chirchiq	41°29′ N,	069°35′ E
Dashhowuz	41°50′ N,	059°58′ E
Gowurdak	37°50′ N,	066°04′ E
Kerki	37°50′ N,	065°12′ E
Mary (Merv)	37°36′ N,	061°50′ E
Nebitdag	39°30′ N,	054°22′ E
Türkmenbashy (Krasnovodsk)	40°00′ N,	053°00′ E
Yolöten	37°18′ N,	062°21′ E

TUVALU ....pg. 178

Fongafale	08°31′ S,	179°13′ E

UGANDA ......pg. 179

Entebbe	00°04′ N,	032°28′ E
Gulu	02°47′ N,	032°18′ E
Jinja	00°26′ N,	033°12′ E
Kabarole	00°39′ N,	030°16′ E
Kampala	00°19′ N,	032°35′ E
Masaka	00°20′ S,	031°44′ E
Mbale	01°05′ N,	034°10′ E
Soroti	01°43′ N,	033°37′ E
Tororo	00°42′ N,	034°11′ E

UKRAINE ......pg. 180

Alchevsk	48°30′ N,	038°47′ E
Berdyansk	46°45′ N,	036°47′ E
Berdychiv	49°54′ N,	028°35′ E
Bila Tserkva	49°47′ N,	030°07′ E
Cherkasy	49°26′ N,	032°04′ E

Chernihiv	51°30′ N,	031°18′ E
Chernivtsi	48°18′ N,	025°56′ E
Chornobyl (Chernobyl)	51°16′ N,	030°14′ E
Dnipropetrovs′k	48°27′ N,	034°59′ E
Donetsk	48°00′ N,	037°48′ E
Kerch	45°21′ N,	036°28′ E
Kharkiv	50°00′ N,	036°15′ E
Khmelnytskyy	49°25′ N,	027°00′ E
Kiev (Kyyiv)	50°26′ N,	030°31′ E
Korosten	50°57′ N,	028°39′ E
Kovel	51°13′ N,	024°43′ E
Krasny Luch	48°08′ N,	038°56′ E
Kryvyy Rih	47°55′ N,	033°21′ E
Luhansk	48°34′ N,	039°20′ E
Lutsk	50°45′ N,	025°20′ E
Lviv	49°50′ N,	024°00′ E
Makiyivka	48°02′ N,	037°58′ E
Marhanets	47°38′ N,	034°38′ E
Mariupol	47°06′ N,	037°33′ E
Melitopol	46°50′ N,	035°22′ E
Mykolayiv	46°58′ N,	032°00′ E
Myrhorod	49°58′ N,	033°36′ E
Novhorod-Siverskyy	52°00′ N,	033°16′ E
Odessa	46°28′ N,	030°44′ E
Pavlograd	48°31′ N,	035°52′ E
Poitava	49°35′ N,	034°34′ E
Pryluky	50°36′ N,	032°24′ E
Rivne	50°37′ N,	026°15′ E
Rubizhne	49°01′ N,	038°23′ E
Sevastopol	44°36′ N,	033°32′ E
Shostka	51°52′ N,	033°29′ E
Simferopol	44°57′ N,	034°06′ E
Sumy	50°54′ N,	034°48′ E
Syeverodonets′k	48°58′ N,	038°26′ E
Uzhhorod	48°37′ N,	022°18′ E
Vinnytsya	49°14′ N,	028°29′ E
Voznesensk	47°33′ N,	031°20′ E
Yevpatoriya	45°12′ N,	033°22′ E
Zaporizhzhya	47°49′ N,	035°11′ E
Zhytomyr	50°15′ N,	028°40′ E

UNITED ARAB EMIRATES ......pg. 181

Abu Dhabi	24°28′ N,	054°22′ E
′Ajmān	25°25′ N,	055°27′ E
Al-′Ayn	24°13′ N,	055°46′ E
Al-Fujayrah	25°08′ N,	056°21′ E
Al-Khīs	23°00′ N,	054°12′ E
Al-Māriyah	23°08′ N,	053°44′ E
′Arādah	22°59′ N,	053°26′ E
Ash-Shāriqah	25°22′ N,	055°23′ E
Diqdāqah	25°40′ N,	055°58′ E
Dubayy	25°16′ N,	055°18′ E
Kalbā	025°05′ N,	056°22′ E
Khawr Fakkān	25°21′ N,	056°22′ E
Ra's Al-Khaymah	25°47′ N,	055°57′ E
Tarīf	24°03′ N,	053°46′ E
Umm Al-Qaywayn	25°35′ N,	055°34′ E
Wadhīl	23°03′ N,	054°08′ E

UNITED KINGDOM ......pg. 182-3

Aberdeen. . . . . 57°09' N, 002°08' W
Barrow-in-Furness. . . . . . . 54°07' N, 003°14' W
Bath . . . . 51°23' N, 002°22' W
Belfast . . . . 54°35' N, 005°56' W
Birmingham. . . . . 52°29' N, 001°51' W
Bradford . . . . 53°47' N, 001°45' W
Bristol . . . . 51°26' N, 002°35' W
Cambridge. . . . . 52°12' N, 000°09' E
Cardiff . . . . 51°29' N, 003°11' W
Carlisle . . . . 54°53' N, 002°57' W
Cheltenham. . . . . 51°54' N, 002°05' W
Colchester. . . . . 51°54' N, 000°54' E
Coventry . . . . 52°24' N, 001°31' W
Darlington . . . . 54°32' N, 001°34' W
Dartford. . . . . 51°26' N, 000°12' W
Derby. . . . . 52°55' N, 001°28' W
Derry (Londonderry) . . . . . 55°00' N, 007°20' W
Dundee . . . . 56°29' N, 003°02' W
Dunfermline . . . . 56°04' N, 003°26' W
Eastbourne . . . . 50°47' N, 000°16' E
Edinburgh . . . . 55°57' N, 003°10' W
Exeter . . . . 50°43' N, 003°31' W
Glasgow. . . . . 55°52' N, 004°15' W
Great Yarmouth . . . . 52°36' N, 001°44' E
Grimsby. . . . . 53°34' N, 000°05' W
Hamilton . . . . 55°47' N, 004°02' W
Harrogate . . . . 54°00' N, 001°32' W
Hartlepool . . . . 54°41' N, 001°13' W
Hastings . . . . 50°52' N, 000°35' E
High Wycombe . . . . 51°38' N, 000°45' W
Hove . . . . 50°50' N, 000°11' W
Ipswich . . . . 52°03' N, 001°09' E
Kilmarnock . . . . 55°36' N, 004°30' W
King's Lynn . . . . 52°45' N, 000°24' E
Kingston upon Hull. . . . . . . 53°45' N, 000°20' W
Leeds . . . . 53°48' N, 001°32' W
Leicester . . . . 52°38' N, 001°08' W
Lincoln. . . . . 53°14' N, 000°32' W
Liverpool. . . . . 53°25' N, 002°57' W
London . . . . 51°30' N, 000°07' W
Lowestoft . . . . 52°28' N, 001°45' E
Maidstone . . . . 51°16' N, 000°32' E
Manchester . . . . 53°29' N, 002°15' W
Margate . . . . 51°23' N, 001°23' E
Newcastle upon Tyne. . . . . 54°58' N, 001°36' W
Newtownabbey . . . . 54°40' N, 005°57' W
Norwich. . . . . 52°38' N, 001°18' E
Nottingham . . . . 52°58' N, 001°10' W
Paisley . . . . 55°50' N, 004°25' W
Peterborough . . . . 52°35' N, 000°14' W
Plymouth. . . . . 50°23' N, 004°09' W
Poole . . . . 50°43' N, 001°59' W
Portsmouth . . . . 50°49' N, 001°04' W
Rhondda . . . . 51°39' N, 003°29' W
Royal Tunbridge Wells . . . . 51°08' N, 000°16' E
Sheffield. . . . . 53°23' N, 001°28' W
South Shields . . . . 54°59' N, 001°26' W

Southampton . . . . 50°55' N, 001°24' W
Staines. . . . . 51°26' N, 000°30' W
Stevenage . . . . 51°54' N, 000°12' W
Stoke-on-Trent . . . . 53°01' N, 002°11' W
Swansea. . . . . 51°38' N, 003°58' W
Torquay. . . . . 50°29' N, 003°32' W
Walsall. . . . . 52°35' N, 001°59' W
Warrington . . . . 53°24' N, 002°36' W
York. . . . . 53°57' N, 001°06' W

UNITED STATES
......pg. 184-5

Aberdeen, S.D. . . . . 45°28' N, 098°29' W
Aberdeen, Wash.. . . . . 46°59' N, 123°50' W
Abilene, Kan. . . . . 38°55' N, 097°13' W
Abilene, Tex. . . . . 32°28' N, 099°43' W
Ada, Okla. . . . . 34°46' N, 096°41' W
Akron, Ohio. . . . . 41°05' N, 081°31' W
Alamogordo, N.M.. . . . . . . 32°54' N, 105°57' W
Alamosa, Colo. . . . . 37°28' N, 105°52' W
Albany, Ga. . . . . 31°35' N, 084°10' W
Albany, N.Y. . . . . 42°39' N, 073°45' W
Albuquerque, N.M. . . . . . . 35°05' N, 106°39' W
Alexandria, La. . . . . 31°18' N, 092°27' W
Alexandria, Va. . . . . 38°48' N, 077°03' W
Alliance, Neb. . . . . 42°06' N, 102°52' W
Alpena, Mich. . . . . 45°04' N, 083°27' W
Alton, Ill. . . . . 38°53' N, 090°11' W
Alturas, Calif. . . . . 41°29' N, 120°32' W
Altus, Okla. . . . . 34°38' N, 099°20' W
Amarillo, Tex. . . . . 35°13' N, 101°50' W
Americus, Ga. . . . . 32°04' N, 084°14' W
Anaconda, Mont. . . . . 46°08' N, 112°57' W
Anchorage, Alaska . . . . 61°13' N, 149°54' W
Andalusia, Ala. . . . . 31°18' N, 086°29' W
Ann Arbor, Mich. . . . . 42°17' N, 083°45' W
Annapolis, Md. . . . . 38°59' N, 076°30' W
Appleton, Wis.. . . . . 44°16' N, 088°25' W
Arcata, Calif. . . . . 40°52' N, 124°05' W
Arlington, Tex. . . . . 32°44' N, 097°07' W
Arlington, Va. . . . . 38°53' N, 077°07' W
Asheville, N.C. . . . . 35°36' N, 082°33' W
Ashland, Ky. . . . . 38°28' N, 082°38' W
Ashland, Wis. . . . . 46°35' N, 090°53' W
Aspen, Colo. . . . . 39°11' N, 106°49' W
Astoria, Ore. . . . . 46°11' N, 123°50' W
Athens, Ga. . . . . 33°57' N, 083°23' W
Atlanta, Ga. . . . . 33°45' N, 084°23' W
Atlantic City, N.J. . . . . 39°21' N, 074°27' W
Augusta, Ga. . . . . 33°28' N, 081°58' W
Augusta, Me. . . . . 44°19' N, 069°47' W
Aurora, Colo. . . . . 39°43' N, 104°49' W
Austin, Minn.. . . . . 43°40' N, 092°58' W
Austin, Tex.. . . . . 30°17' N, 097°45' W
Baker, Mont. . . . . 46°22' N, 104°17' W
Baker, Ore. . . . . 44°47' N, 117°50' W
Bakersfield, Calif. . . . . 35°23' N, 119°01' W
Baltimore, Md. . . . . 39°17' N, 076°37' W
Bangor, Me.. . . . . 44°48' N, 068°46' W

Bar Harbor, Me.	44°23′ N, 068°13′ W
Barrow, Alaska	71°18′ N, 156°47′ W
Bartlesville, Okla.	36°45′ N, 095°59′ W
Baton Rouge, La.	30°27′ N, 091°11′ W
Bay City, Mich.	43°36′ N, 083°54′ W
Beaumont, Tex.	30°05′ N, 094°06′ W
Bellingham, Wash.	48°46′ N, 122°29′ W
Beloit, Wis.	42°31′ N, 089°01′ W
Bemidji, Minn.	47°28′ N, 094°52′ W
Bend, Ore.	44°04′ N, 121°19′ W
Berlin, N.H.	44°28′ N, 071°11′ W
Bethel, Alaska	60°48′ N, 161°45′ W
Beulah, N.D.	47°15′ N, 101°46′ W
Billings, Mont.	45°47′ N, 108°30′ W
Biloxi, Miss.	30°24′ N, 088°53′ W
Birmingham, Ala.	33°31′ N, 086°48′ W
Bismarck, N.D.	46°48′ N, 100°47′ W
Bloomington, Ind.	39°10′ N, 086°32′ W
Blythe, Calif.	33°37′ N, 114°36′ W
Boca Raton, Fla.	26°21′ N, 080°05′ W
Bogalusa, La.	30°47′ N, 089°52′ W
Boise, Idaho	43°37′ N, 116°13′ W
Boston, Mass.	42°22′ N, 071°04′ W
Boulder, Colo.	40°01′ N, 105°17′ W
Bowling Green, Ky.	36°59′ N, 086°27′ W
Bozeman, Mont.	45°41′ N, 111°02′ W
Bradenton, Fla.	27°30′ N, 082°34′ W
Brady, Tex.	31°09′ N, 099°20′ W
Brainerd, Minn.	46°22′ N, 094°12′ W
Bremerton, Wash.	47°34′ N, 122°38′ W
Brigham City, Utah	41°31′ N, 112°01′ W
Brookings, S.D.	44°19′ N, 096°48′ W
Brownsville, Tex.	25°54′ N, 097°30′ W
Brunswick, Ga.	31°10′ N, 081°30′ W
Bryan, Tex.	30°40′ N, 096°22′ W
Buffalo, N.Y.	42°53′ N, 078°53′ W
Buffalo, Tex.	31°28′ N, 096°04′ W
Burlington, Ia.	40°48′ N, 091°06′ W
Burlington, Vt.	44°29′ N, 073°12′ W
Burns, Ore.	43°35′ N, 119°03′ W
Butte, Mont.	46°00′ N, 112°32′ W
Cairo, Ill.	37°00′ N, 089°11′ W
Caldwell, Idaho	43°40′ N, 116°41′ W
Canton, Ohio	40°48′ N, 081°23′ W
Cape Girardeau, Mo.	37°19′ N, 089°32′ W
Carbondale, Ill.	37°44′ N, 089°13′ W
Carlsbad, N.M.	32°25′ N, 104°14′ W
Carson City, Nev.	39°10′ N, 119°46′ W
Casa Grande, Ariz.	32°53′ N, 111°45′ W
Casper, Wyo.	42°51′ N, 106°19′ W
Cedar City, Utah	37°41′ N, 113°04′ W
Cedar Rapids, Ia.	41°59′ N, 091°40′ W
Chadron, Neb.	42°50′ N, 103°00′ W
Champaign, Ill.	40°07′ N, 088°15′ W
Charleston, S.C.	32°46′ N, 079°56′ W
Charleston, W.Va.	38°21′ N, 081°39′ W
Charlotte, N.C.	35°13′ N, 080°51′ W
Chattanooga, Tenn.	35°03′ N, 085°19′ W
Chesapeake, Va.	36°50′ N, 076°17′ W
Cheyenne, Wyo.	41°08′ N, 104°49′ W
Chicago, Ill.	41°53′ N, 087°38′ W

Chico, Calif.	39°44′ N, 121°50′ W
Chula Vista, Calif.	32°38′ N, 117°05′ W
Cincinnati, Ohio	39°06′ N, 084°31′ W
Clarksdale, Miss.	34°12′ N, 090°35′ W
Clayton, N.M.	36°27′ N, 103°11′ W
Clearwater, Fla.	27°58′ N, 082°48′ W
Cleveland, Ohio	41°30′ N, 081°42′ W
Clinton, Okla.	35°31′ N, 098°58′ W
Clovis, N.M.	34°24′ N, 103°12′ W
Cody, Wyo.	44°32′ N, 109°03′ W
Coeur d'Alene, Idaho	47°41′ N, 116°46′ W
College Station, Tex.	30°37′ N, 096°21′ W
Colorado Springs, Colo.	38°50′ N, 104°49′ W
Columbia, S.C.	34°00′ N, 081°03′ W
Columbus, Ga.	32°29′ N, 084°59′ W
Columbus, Miss.	33°30′ N, 088°25′ W
Columbus, Ohio	39°58′ N, 083°00′ W
Concord, N.H.	43°12′ N, 071°32′ W
Coos Bay, Ore.	43°22′ N, 124°12′ W
Coral Gables, Fla.	25°45′ N, 080°16′ W
Cordele, Ga.	31°58′ N, 083°47′ W
Cordova, Alaska	60°33′ N, 145°45′ W
Corinth, Miss.	34°56′ N, 088°31′ W
Corpus Christi, Tex.	27°47′ N, 097°24′ W
Corsicana, Tex.	32°06′ N, 096°28′ W
Corvallis, Ore.	44°34′ N, 123°16′ W
Council Bluffs, Ia.	41°16′ N, 095°52′ W
Covington, Ky.	39°05′ N, 084°31′ W
Crescent City, Calif.	41°45′ N, 124°12′ W
Crystal City, Tex.	28°41′ N, 099°50′ W
Dalhart, Tex.	36°04′ N, 102°31′ W
Dallas, Tex.	32°47′ N, 096°49′ W
Dalton, Ga.	34°46′ N, 084°58′ W
Danville, Va.	36°36′ N, 079°23′ W
Davenport, Ia.	41°32′ N, 090°35′ W
Davis, Calif.	38°33′ N, 121°44′ W
Dayton, Ohio	39°45′ N, 084°12′ W
Daytona Beach, Fla.	29°13′ N, 081°01′ W
Decorah, Ia.	43°18′ N, 091°48′ W
Denver, Colo.	39°44′ N, 104°59′ W
Des Moines, Ia.	41°35′ N, 093°37′ W
Detroit, Mich.	42°20′ N, 083°03′ W
Dickinson, N.D.	46°53′ N, 102°47′ W
Dillingham, Alaska	59°03′ N, 158°28′ W
Dillon, Mont.	45°13′ N, 112°38′ W
Dodge City, Kan.	37°45′ N, 100°00′ W
Dothan, Ala.	31°13′ N, 085°24′ W
Dover, Del.	39°10′ N, 075°32′ W
Dover, N.H.	43°12′ N, 070°53′ W
Dubuque, Ia.	42°30′ N, 090°41′ W
Duluth, Minn.	46°47′ N, 092°07′ W
Duncan, Okla.	34°30′ N, 097°57′ W
Durango, Colo.	37°17′ N, 107°53′ W
Durham, N.C.	36°00′ N, 078°54′ W
Dutch Harbor, Alaska	53°53′ N, 166°32′ W
East St. Louis, Ill.	38°37′ N, 090°09′ W
Eau Claire, Wis.	44°49′ N, 091°30′ W
El Cajon, Calif.	32°48′ N, 116°58′ W
El Dorado, Ark.	33°12′ N, 092°40′ W
El Paso, Tex.	31°45′ N, 106°29′ W
Elko, Nev.	40°50′ N, 115°46′ W

Kingsville, Tex.	27°31' N, 097°52' W
Kirksville, Mo.	40°12' N, 092°35' W
Klamath Falls, Ore.	42°12' N, 121°46' W
Knoxville, Tenn.	35°58' N, 083°55' W
Kodiak, Alaska	57°47' N, 152°24' W
Kokomo, Ind.	40°30' N, 086°08' W
La Crosse, Wis.	43°48' N, 091°15' W
Lafayette, La.	30°14' N, 092°01' W
La Junta, Colo.	37°59' N, 103°33' W
Lake Charles, La.	30°14' N, 093°13' W
Lake Havasu City, Ariz. . . .	34°29' N, 114°19' W
Lakeland, Fla.	28°03' N, 081°57' W
Lansing, Mich.	42°44' N, 084°33' W
Laramie, Wyo.	41°19' N, 105°35' W
Laredo, Tex.	27°30' N, 099°30' W
Las Cruces, N.M.	32°19' N, 106°47' W
Las Vegas, Nev.	36°01' N, 115°09' W
Las Vegas, N.M.	35°36' N, 105°13' W
Laurel, Miss.	31°41' N, 089°08' W
Lawton, Okla.	34°37' N, 098°25' W
Lebanon, N.H.	43°39' N, 072°15' W
Lewiston, Idaho	46°25' N, 117°01' W
Lewiston, Me.	44°06' N, 070°13' W
Lewiston, Mont.	47°03' N, 109°25' W
Lexington, Ky.	38°01' N, 084°30' W
Liberal, Kan.	37°02' N, 100°55' W
Lihue, Hawaii	21°59' N, 159°23' W
Lima, Ohio.	40°44' N, 084°06' W
Lincoln, Me.	45°22' N, 068°30' W
Lincoln, Neb.	40°50' N, 096°41' W
Little Rock, Ark.	34°45' N, 092°17' W
Logan, Utah	41°44' N, 111°50' W
Long Beach, Calif.	33°47' N, 118°11' W
Los Alamos, N.M.	35°53' N, 106°19' W
Los Angeles, Calif.	34°04' N, 118°15' W
Louisville, Ky.	38°15' N, 085°46' W
Lowell, Mass.	42°38' N, 071°19' W
Lubbock, Tex.	33°35' N, 101°51' W
Lynchburg, Va.	37°25' N, 079°09' W
Macomb, Ill.	40°27' N, 090°40' W
Macon, Ga.	32°51' N, 083°38' W
Madison, Wis.	43°04' N, 089°24' W
Manchester, N.H.	43°00' N, 071°28' W
Mandan, N.D.	46°50' N, 100°54' W
Mankato, Minn.	44°10' N, 094°00' W
Marietta, Ohio.	39°25' N, 081°27' W
Marinette, Wis.	45°06' N, 087°38' W
Marion, Ind.	40°32' N, 085°40' W
Marquette, Mich.	46°33' N, 087°24' W
Massillon, Ohio.	40°48' N, 081°32' W
McAllen, Tex.	26°12' N, 098°14' W
McCall, Idaho	44°55' N, 116°06' W
McCook, Neb.	40°12' N, 100°38' W
Medford, Ore.	42°19' N, 122°52' W
Meeker, Colo.	40°02' N, 107°55' W
Melbourne, Fla.	28°05' N, 080°37' W
Memphis, Tenn.	35°08' N, 090°03' W
Meridian, Miss.	32°22' N, 088°42' W
Mesa, Ariz.	33°25' N, 111°49' W
Miami, Fla.	25°47' N, 080°11' W
Midland, Mich.	43°36' N, 084°14' W
Midland, Tex.	32°00' N, 102°05' W
Miles City, Mont.	46°25' N, 105°51' W
Milledgeville, Ga.	33°05' N, 083°14' W
Milwaukee, Wis.	43°02' N, 087°55' W
Minneapolis, Minn.	44°59' N, 093°16' W
Minot, N.D.	48°14' N, 101°18' W
Missoula, Mont.	46°52' N, 114°01' W
Mitchell, S.D.	43°43' N, 098°02' W
Moab, Utah	38°35' N, 109°33' W
Mobile, Ala.	30°41' N, 088°03' W
Moline, Ill.	41°30' N, 090°31' W
Monterey, Calif.	36°37' N, 121°55' W
Montgomery, Ala.	32°23' N, 086°19' W
Montpelier, Vt.	44°16' N, 072°35' W
Montrose, Colo.	38°29' N, 107°53' W
Morehead City, N.C.	34°43' N, 076°43' W
Morgan City, La.	29°42' N, 091°12' W
Morgantown, W.Va.	39°38' N, 079°57' W
Moscow, Idaho	46°44' N, 117°00' W
Mount Vernon, Ill.	38°19' N, 088°55' W
Murfreesboro, Ark.	34°04' N, 093°41' W
Murfreesboro, Tenn.	35°50' N, 086°23' W
Muskogee, Okla.	35°45' N, 095°22' W
Myrtle Beach, S.C.	33°42' N, 078°53' W
Naples, Fla.	26°08' N, 081°48' W
Nashville, Tenn.	36°10' N, 086°47' W
Natchez, Miss.	31°34' N, 091°24' W
Needles, Calif.	34°51' N, 114°37' W
Nevada, Mo.	37°51' N, 094°22' W
New Albany, Ind.	38°18' N, 085°49' W
Newark, N.J.	40°44' N, 074°10' W
New Bedford, Mass.	41°38' N, 070°56' W
New Bern, N.C.	35°07' N, 077°03' W
Newcastle, Wyo.	43°50' N, 104°11' W
New Haven, Conn.	41°18' N, 072°55' W
New Madrid, Mo.	36°36' N, 089°32' W
New Orleans, La.	29°58' N, 090°04' W
Newport, Ore.	44°39' N, 124°03' W
Newport, R.I.	41°29' N, 071°18' W
Newport News, Va.	36°59' N, 076°25' W
New York City, N.Y.	40°43' N, 074°00' W
Niagara Falls, N.Y.	43°06' N, 079°03' W
Nogales, Ariz.	31°20' N, 110°56' W
Nome, Alaska	64°30' N, 165°25' W
Norfolk, Va.	36°51' N, 076°17' W
Norman, Okla.	35°13' N, 097°26' W
North Augusta, S.C.	33°30' N, 081°59' W
North Platte, Neb.	41°08' N, 100°46' W
Oakland, Calif.	37°49' N, 122°16' W
Ocala, Fla.	29°11' N, 082°08' W
Oceanside, Calif.	33°12' N, 117°23' W
Odessa, Tex.	31°51' N, 102°23' W
Ogallala, Neb.	41°08' N, 101°43' W
Ogden, Utah	41°13' N, 111°58' W
Oklahoma City, Okla.	35°30' N, 097°30' W
Olympia, Wash.	47°03' N, 122°53' W
Omaha, Neb.	41°17' N, 096°01' W
O'Neill, Neb.	42°27' N, 098°39' W
Orem, Utah	40°18' N, 111°42' W
Orlando, Fla.	28°33' N, 081°23' W
Oshkosh, Wis.	44°01' N, 088°33' W

Ottawa, Ill.	41°20' N, 088°50' W
Ottumwa, Ia.	41°01' N, 092°25' W
Overton, Nev.	36°33' N, 114°27' W
Owensboro, Ky.	37°46' N, 087°07' W
Paducah, Ky.	37°05' N, 088°37' W
Pahala, Hawaii.	19°12' N, 155°29' W
Palm Springs, Calif.	33°50' N, 116°33' W
Palo Alto, Calif.	37°27' N, 122°10' W
Panama City, Fla.	30°10' N, 085°40' W
Paris, Tex.	33°40' N, 095°33' W
Parsons, Kan.	37°20' N, 095°16' W
Pasadena, Calif.	34°09' N, 118°09' W
Pasadena, Tex.	29°43' N, 095°13' W
Pascagoula, Miss.	30°21' N, 088°33' W
Paterson, N.J.	40°55' N, 074°11' W
Pecos, Tex.	31°26' N, 103°30' W
Pendleton, Ore.	45°40' N, 118°47' W
Pensacola, Fla.	30°25' N, 087°13' W
Peoria, Ill.	40°42' N, 089°36' W
Petoskey, Mich.	45°22' N, 084°57' W
Philadelphia, Pa.	39°57' N, 075°10' W
Phoenix, Ariz.	33°27' N, 112°04' W
Pierre, S.D.	44°22' N, 100°21' W
Pine Bluff, Ark.	34°13' N, 092°01' W
Pittsburgh, Pa.	40°26' N, 080°01' W
Plano, Tex.	33°01' N, 096°41' W
Plattsburgh, N.Y.	44°42' N, 073°27' W
Pocatello, Idaho	42°52' N, 112°27' W
Point Hope, Alaska	68°21' N, 166°41' W
Port Gibson, Miss.	31°58' N, 090°59' W
Port Lavaca, Tex.	28°37' N, 096°38' W
Port Royal, S.C.	32°23' N, 080°42' W
Portland, Me.	43°39' N, 070°16' W
Portland, Ore.	45°32' N, 122°37' W
Prescott, Ariz.	34°33' N, 112°28' W
Presque Isle, Me.	46°41' N, 068°01' W
Providence, R.I.	41°49' N, 071°24' W
Provo, Utah	40°14' N, 111°39' W
Pueblo, Colo.	38°15' N, 104°36' W
Pullman, Wash.	46°44' N, 117°10' W
Racine, Wis.	42°44' N, 087°48' W
Raleigh, N.C.	35°46' N, 078°38' W
Rapid City, S.D.	44°05' N, 103°14' W
Red Bluff, Calif.	40°11' N, 122°15' W
Redding, Calif.	40°35' N, 122°24' W
Redfield, S.D.	44°53' N, 098°31' W
Reno, Nev.	39°31' N, 119°48' W
Rice Lake, Wis.	45°30' N, 091°44' W
Richfield, Utah	38°46' N, 112°05' W
Richmond, Ind.	39°50' N, 084°54' W
Richmond, Va.	37°33' N, 077°27' W
Riverside, Calif.	33°59' N, 117°22' W
Riverton, Wyo.	43°02' N, 108°23' W
Roanoke, Va.	37°16' N, 079°56' W
Rochester, Minn.	44°01' N, 092°28' W
Rochester, N.Y.	43°10' N, 077°37' W
Rock Hill, S.C.	34°56' N, 081°01' W
Rock Island, Ill.	41°30' N, 090°34' W
Rock Springs, Wyo.	41°35' N, 109°12' W
Rockford, Ill.	42°16' N, 089°06' W
Rolla, Mo.	37°57' N, 091°46' W
Rome, Ga.	34°15' N, 085°09' W
Roseburg, Ore.	43°13' N, 123°20' W
Roswell, N.M.	33°24' N, 104°32' W
Sacramento, Calif.	38°35' N, 121°29' W
Saginaw, Mich.	43°26' N, 083°56' W
Salem, Ore.	44°56' N, 123°02' W
Salina, Kan.	38°50' N, 097°37' W
Salinas, Calif.	36°40' N, 121°39' W
Salmon, Idaho	45°11' N, 113°54' W
Salt Lake City, Utah	40°45' N, 111°53' W
San Angelo, Tex.	31°28' N, 100°26' W
San Antonio, Tex.	29°25' N, 098°30' W
San Bernardino, Calif.	34°07' N, 117°19' W
San Diego, Calif.	32°43' N, 117°09' W
San Francisco, Calif.	37°47' N, 122°25' W
San Jose, Calif.	37°20' N, 121°53' W
San Luis Obispo, Calif.	35°17' N, 120°40' W
Sanderson, Tex.	30°09' N, 102°24' W
Santa Ana, Calif.	33°46' N, 117°52' W
Santa Barbara, Calif.	34°25' N, 119°42' W
Santa Fe, N.M.	35°41' N, 105°57' W
Santa Maria, Calif.	34°57' N, 120°26' W
Sarasota, Fla.	27°20' N, 082°32' W
Sault Ste. Marie, Mich.	46°30' N, 084°21' W
Savannah, Ga.	32°05' N, 081°06' W
Scott City, Kan.	38°29' N, 100°54' W
Scottsbluff, Neb.	41°52' N, 103°40' W
Scottsdale, Ariz.	33°29' N, 111°56' W
Searcy, Ark.	35°15' N, 091°44' W
Seattle, Wash.	47°36' N, 122°20' W
Sebring, Fla.	27°30' N, 081°27' W
Seguin, Tex.	29°34' N, 097°58' W
Selawik, Alaska	66°36' N, 160°00' W
Seldovia, Alaska	59°26' N, 151°43' W
Selma, Ala.	32°25' N, 087°01' W
Sharpsburg, Md.	39°28' N, 077°45' W
Sheboygan, Wis.	43°45' N, 087°42' W
Sheridan, Wyo.	44°48' N, 106°58' W
Show Low, Ariz.	34°15' N, 110°02' W
Shreveport, La.	32°31' N, 093°45' W
Sierra Vista, Ariz.	31°33' N, 110°18' W
Silver City, N.M.	32°46' N, 108°17' W
Sioux City, Ia.	42°30' N, 096°24' W
Sioux Falls, S.D.	43°33' N, 096°44' W
Skagway, Alaska	59°28' N, 135°19' W
Snyder, Tex.	32°44' N, 100°55' W
Socorro, N.M.	34°04' N, 106°54' W
Somerset, Ky.	37°05' N, 084°36' W
South Bend, Ind.	41°41' N, 086°15' W
Sparks, Nev.	39°32' N, 119°45' W
Spencer, Ia.	43°09' N, 095°10' W
Spokane, Wash.	47°40' N, 117°24' W
Springfield, Ill.	39°48' N, 089°38' W
Springfield, Mo.	37°13' N, 093°17' W
St. Augustine, Fla.	29°54' N, 081°19' W
St. Cloud, Minn.	45°34' N, 094°10' W
St. George, Utah	37°06' N, 113°35' W
St. Joseph, Mo.	39°46' N, 094°50' W
St. Louis, Mo.	38°37' N, 090°11' W
St. Maries, Idaho.	47°19' N, 116°35' W
St. Paul, Minn.	44°57' N, 093°06' W

St. Petersburg, Fla.	27°46′ N, 082°39′ W
State College, Pa.	40°48′ N, 077°52′ W
Ste. Genevieve, Mo.	37°59′ N, 090°03′ W
Steamboat Springs, Colo.	40°29′ N, 106°50′ W
Stillwater, Minn.	45°03′ N, 092°49′ W
Sumter, S.C.	33°55′ N, 080°21′ W
Sun Valley, Idaho	43°42′ N, 114°21′ W
Superior, Wis.	46°44′ N, 092°06′ W
Syracuse, N.Y.	43°03′ N, 076°09′ W
Tacoma, Wash.	47°14′ N, 122°26′ W
Tallahassee, Fla.	30°27′ N, 084°17′ W
Tampa, Fla.	27°57′ N, 082°27′ W
Tempe, Ariz.	33°25′ N, 111°56′ W
Temple, Tex.	31°06′ N, 097°21′ W
Terre Haute, Ind.	39°28′ N, 087°25′ W
Texarkana, Ark.	33°26′ N, 094°03′ W
Thief River Falls, Minn.	48°07′ N, 096°10′ W
Tifton, Ga.	31°27′ N, 083°31′ W
Titusville, Fla.	28°37′ N, 080°49′ W
Toledo, Ohio	41°39′ N, 083°33′ W
Tonopah, Nev.	38°04′ N, 117°14′ W
Topeka, Kan.	39°03′ N, 095°40′ W
Traverse City, Mich.	44°46′ N, 085°38′ W
Trenton, N.J.	40°14′ N, 074°46′ W
Trinidad, Colo.	37°10′ N, 104°31′ W
Troy, Ala.	31°48′ N, 085°58′ W
Troy, N.Y.	42°44′ N, 073°41′ W
Tucson, Ariz.	32°13′ N, 110°58′ W
Tulsa, Okla.	36°10′ N, 095°55′ W
Tupelo, Miss.	34°16′ N, 088°43′ W
Tuscaloosa, Ala.	33°12′ N, 087°34′ W
Twin Falls, Idaho.	42°34′ N, 114°28′ W
Tyler, Tex.	32°21′ N, 095°18′ W
Ukiah, Calif.	39°09′ N, 123°12′ W
Utica, N.Y.	43°06′ N, 075°14′ W
Uvalde, Tex.	29°13′ N, 099°47′ W
Valdez, Alaska.	61°07′ N, 146°16′ W
Valdosta, Ga.	30°50′ N, 083°17′ W
Valentine, Neb.	42°52′ N, 100°33′ W
Vero Beach, Fla.	27°38′ N, 080°24′ W
Vicksburg, Miss.	32°21′ N, 090°53′ W
Victoria, Tex.	28°48′ N, 097°00′ W
Vincennes, Ind.	38°41′ N, 087°32′ W
Virginia Beach, Va.	36°51′ N, 075°59′ W
Waco, Tex.	31°33′ N, 097°09′ W
Wahpeton, N.D.	46°15′ N, 096°36′ W
Wailuku, Hawaii	20°53′ N, 156°30′ W
Walla Walla, Wash.	46°04′ N, 118°20′ W
Warren, Pa.	41°51′ N, 079°08′ W
Washington, D.C.	38°54′ N, 077°02′ W
Waterloo, Ia.	42°30′ N, 092°21′ W
Watertown, N.Y.	43°59′ N, 075°55′ W
Waycross, Ga.	31°13′ N, 082°21′ W
Wayne, Neb.	42°14′ N, 097°01′ W
Weiser, Idaho	44°45′ N, 116°58′ W
West Palm Beach, Fla.	26°43′ N, 080°03′ W
Wheeling, W.Va.	40°04′ N, 080°43′ W
Wichita, Kan.	37°42′ N, 097°20′ W
Wichita Falls, Tex.	33°54′ N, 098°30′ W
Williamsport, Pa.	41°15′ N, 077°00′ W
Wilmington, N.C.	34°14′ N, 077°55′ W

Winfield, Kan.	37°15′ N, 096°59′ W
Winnemucca, Nev.	40°58′ N, 117°44′ W
Winslow, Ariz.	35°02′ N, 110°42′ W
Winston-Salem, N.C.	36°06′ N, 080°14′ W
Worcester, Mass.	42°16′ N, 071°48′ W
Worthington, Minn.	43°37′ N, 095°36′ W
Wrangell, Alaska.	56°28′ N, 132°23′ W
Yakima, Wash.	46°36′ N, 120°31′ W
Yankton, S.D.	42°53′ N, 097°23′ W
Yazoo City, Miss.	32°51′ N, 090°25′ W
Youngstown, Ohio	41°06′ N, 080°39′ W
Yuba City, Calif.	39°08′ N, 121°37′ W
Yuma, Ariz.	32°43′ N, 114°37′ W
Zanesville, Ohio	39°56′ N, 082°01′ W

URUGUAY ......pg. 186

Aiguá	34°12′ S, 054°45′ W
Artigas	30°24′ S, 056°28′ W
Belén	30°47′ S, 057°47′ W
Bella Unión	30°15′ S, 057°35′ W
Carmelo	34°00′ S, 058°17′ W
Castillos	34°12′ S, 053°50′ W
Casupá	34°07′ S, 055°39′ W
Chuy	33°41′ S, 053°27′ W
Colonia	34°28′ S, 057°51′ W
Constitución	31°05′ S, 057°50′ W
Dolores	33°33′ S, 058°13′ W
Durazno	33°22′ S, 056°31′ W
Florida	34°06′ S, 056°13′ W
Lascano	33°40′ S, 054°12′W
Las Piedras	34°44′ S, 056°13′ W
Maldonado	34°54′ S, 054°57′ W
Melo	32°22′ S, 054°11′ W
Mercedes	33°16′ S, 058°01′ W
Minas	34°23′ S, 055°14′ W
Montevideo	34°53′ S, 056°11′ W
Nuevo Berlín	32°59′ S, 058°03′ W
Pando	34°43′ S, 055°57′ W
Paysandú	32°19′ S, 058°05′ W
Rio Branco	32°34′ S, 053°25′ W
Rivera	30°54′ S, 055°31′ W
Rocha	34°29′ S, 054°20′ W
Salto	31°23′ S, 057°58′ W
San Carlos	34°48′ S, 054°55′ W
San Gregorio	32°37′ S, 055°40′ W
San José	34°20′ S, 056°42′ W
Santa Clara	32°55′ S, 054°58′ W
Suárez (Tarariras)	34°17′ S, 057°37′ W
Tacuarembó (San Fructuoso)	31°44′ S, 055°59′ W
Tranqueras	31°12′ S, 055°45′ W
Treinta y Tres	33°14′ S, 054°23′ W
Trinidad	33°32′ S, 056°54′ W
Vergara	32°56′ S, 053°57′ W
Young	32°41′ S, 057°38′ W

UZBEKISTAN ....pg. 187

Andijon	40°45′ N, 072°22′ E

Angren . . . . 41°01' N, 070°12' E
Bekobod . . . . 40°13' N, 069°14' E
Beruniy (Biruni) . . . . 41°42' N, 060°44' E
Bukhara (Bokhoro) . . . . . . 39°48' N, 064°25' E
Chirchiq . . . . 41°29' N, 069°35' E
Denow . . . . 38°16' N, 067°54' E
Fergana (Farghona) . . . . . 40°23' N, 071°46' E
Guliston . . . . 40°29' N, 068°46' E
Jizzakh . . . . 40°06' N, 067°50' E
Kattaqŭrghon . . . . 39°55' N, 066°15' E
Khiva (Khiwa) . . . . 41°24' N, 060°22' E
Khonqa . . . . 41°28' N, 060°47' E
Kogon . . . . 39°43' N, 064°33' E
Marghilon . . . . 40°27' N, 071°42' E
Namangan . . . . 41°00' N, 071°40' E
Nawoiy . . . . 40°09' N, 065°22' E
Nukus . . . . 42°29' N, 059°38' E
Olmaliq . . . . 40°50' N, 069°35' E
Qarshi . . . . 38°53' N, 065°48' E
Qŭqon . . . . 40°30' N, 070°57' E
Samarkand . . . . 39°40' N, 066°58' E
Tashkent (Toshkent) . . . . . 41°20' N, 069°18' E
Termiz . . . . 37°14' N, 067°16' E
Urganch . . . . 41°33' N, 060°38' E
Zarafshon . . . . 41°31' N, 064°15' E

VANUATU . . . . . . .pg. 188

Ipayato . . . . 15°38' S, 166°52' E
Isangel . . . . 19°33' S, 169°16' E
Lakatoro . . . . 16°07' S, 167°25' E
Lalinda . . . . 16°21' S, 168°03' E
Laol . . . . 16°41' S, 168°16' E
Loltong . . . . 15°33' S, 168°09' E
Luganville . . . . 15°32' S, 167°10' E
Lumbukuti . . . . 16°55' S, 168°32' E
Natapao . . . . 17°37' S, 168°13' E
Norsup . . . . 16°04' S, 167°23' E
Port Olry . . . . 15°03' S, 167°04' E
Unpongkor . . . . 18°49' S, 169°01' E
Veutumboso . . . . 13°54' S, 167°27' E
Vila (Port-Vila) . . . . 17°44' S, 168°18' E

VENEZUELA . . . . .pg. 189

Barcelona . . . . 10°08' N, 064°42' W
Barinas . . . . 08°38' N, 070°12' W
Barquisimeto . . . . 10°04' N, 069°19' W
Cabimas . . . . 10°23' N, 071°28' W
Caicara (Caicara de
  Orinoco) . . . . 07°37' N, 066°10' W
Caicara . . . . 09°49' N, 063°36' W
Caracas . . . . 10°30' N, 066°55' W
Ciudad Bolívar . . . . 08°08' N, 063°33' W
Ciudad Guayana
  (San Felix) . . . . 08°23' N, 062°40' W
Coro . . . . 11°25' N, 069°41' W
Cumaná . . . . 10°28' N, 064°10' W
Guasdualito . . . . 07°15' N, 070°44' W
La Asunción . . . . 11°02' N, 063°53' W

Maracaibo . . . . 10°40' N, 071°37' W
Maracay . . . . 10°15' N, 067°36' W
Maturín . . . . 09°45' N, 063°11' W
Mérida . . . . 08°36' N, 071°08' W
Pariaguán . . . . 08°51' N, 064°43' W
Petare . . . . 10°29' N, 066°49' W
Puerto Ayacucho . . . . 05°40' N, 067°35' W
Punto Fijo . . . . 11°42' N, 070°13' W
San Carlos de
  Río Negro . . . . 01°55' N, 067°04' W
San Cristóbal . . . . 07°46' N, 072°14' W
San Fernando de Apure . . . 07°54' N, 067°28' W
San Fernando
  de Atabapo . . . . 04°03' N, 067°42' W
Santa Elena . . . . 04°37' N, 061°08' W
Tucupita . . . . 09°04' N, 062°03' W
Upata . . . . 08°01' N, 062°24' W
Valencia . . . . 10°11' N, 068°00' W
Valera . . . . 09°19' N, 070°37' W

VIETNAM . . . . . . .pg. 190

Bac Can . . . . 22°08' N, 105°50' E
Bac Giang . . . . 21°16' N, 106°12' E
Bac Lieu . . . . 09°17' N, 105°43' E
Bien Hoa . . . . 10°57' N, 106°49' E
Buon Me Thuot
  (Lac Giao) . . . . 12°40' N, 108°03' E
Ca Mau . . . . 09°11' N, 105°08' E
Cam Pha . . . . 21°01' N, 107°19' E
Cam Ranh . . . . 11°54' N, 109°13' E
Can Tho . . . . 10°02' N, 105°47' E
Chau Doc . . . . 10°42' N, 105°07' E
Da Lat . . . . 11°56' N, 108°25' E
Da Nang (Tourane) . . . . . . 16°04' N, 108°13' E
Dong Ha . . . . 16°49' N, 107°08' E
Dong Hoi . . . . 17°29' N, 106°36' E
Go Cong . . . . 10°22' N, 106°40' E
Ha Giang . . . . 22°50' N, 104°59' E
Hai Duong . . . . 20°56' N, 106°19' E
Haiphong (Hai Phong) . . . . 20°52' N, 106°41' E
Hanoi (Ha Noi) . . . . 21°02' N, 105°51' E
Ha Tinh . . . . 18°20' N, 105°54' E
Hoa Binh . . . . 20°50' N, 105°20' E
Ho Chi Minh City
  (Saigon) . . . . 10°45' N, 106°40' E
Hoi An . . . . 15°52' N, 108°19' E
Hong Gai (Hon Gai) . . . . . 20°57' N, 107°05' E
Hue . . . . 16°28' N, 107°36' E
Kon Tum (Cong Tum or
  Kontun) . . . . 14°21' N, 108°00' E
Lai Chau . . . . 22°04' N, 103°10' E
Lao Caí . . . . 22°30' N, 103°58' E
Long Xuyen . . . . 10°23' N, 105°25' E
Minh Hoa . . . . 17°47' N, 106°01' E
My Tho . . . . 10°21' N, 106°21' E
Nam Dinh . . . . 20°25' N, 106°10' E
Nha Trang . . . . 12°15' N, 109°11' E
Phan Rang . . . . 11°34' N, 108°59' E
Phan Thiet . . . . 10°56' N, 108°06' E
Pleiku (Play Cu) . . . . 13°59' N, 108°00' E

Quan Long	09°11' N,	105°08' E	Kragujevac	44°01' N,	020°55' E
Quang Ngai	15°07' N,	108°48' E	Kraljevo	43°44' N,	020°43' E
Qui Nhon	13°46' N,	109°14' E	Kruševac	43°35' N,	021°20' E
Rach Gia	10°01' N,	105°05' E	Leskovac	42°59' N,	021°57' E
Sa Dec	10°18' N,	105°46' E	Majdanpek	44°25' N,	021°56' E
Soc Trang	09°36' N,	105°58' E	Nikšić	42°46' N,	018°58' E
Son La	21°19' N,	103°54' E	Nis	43°19' N,	021°54' E
Tam Ky	15°34' N,	108°29' E	Novi Beograd	44°49' N,	020°27' E
Tan An	10°32' N,	106°25' E	Novi Pazar	43°08' N,	020°31' E
Thai Binh	20°27' N,	106°20' E	Novi Sad	45°15' N,	019°50' E
Thai Nguyen	21°36' N,	105°50' E	Pancevo	44°52' N,	020°39' E
Thanh Hoa	19°48' N,	105°46' E	Pirot	43°09' N,	022°36' E
Tuy Hoa	13°05' N,	109°18' E	Podgorica (Titograd)	42°26' N,	019°16' E
Viet Tri	21°18' N,	105°26' E	Priboj	43°35' N,	019°32' E
Vinh	18°40' N,	105°40' E	Priština	42°40' N,	021°10' E
Vung Tau	10°21' N,	107°04' E	Prizren	42°13' N,	020°45' E
Yen Bai	21°42' N,	104°52' E	Sabac	44°45' N,	019°43' E
			Smederevo	44°39' N,	020°56' E

YEMEN . . . . .pg. 191

			Sombor	45°46' N,	019°07' E
			Sremski Karlovci	45°12' N,	019°56' E
Aden ('Adan)	12°46' N,	045°02' E	Subotica	46°06' N,	019°40' E
Aḥwar	13°31' N,	046°42' E	Titovo Užice (Užice)	43°52' N,	019°51' E
Al-Bayḍā'	13°58' N,	045°35' E	Valjevo	44°16' N,	019°53' E
Al-Ghaydah	16°13' N,	052°11' E	Vranje	42°33' N,	021°54' E
Al-Ḥudaydah	14°48' N,	042°57' E	Zrenjanin	45°23' N,	020°23' E
Al-Luḥayyah	15°43' N,	042°42' E			
Al-Mukallā	14°32' N,	049°08' E			
Balḥāf	13°58' N,	048°11' E			
Dhamār	14°33' N,	044°24' E	## ZAMBIA . . . . .pg. 193		
Ibb	13°58' N,	044°11' E			
Laḥij	13°04' N,	044°53' E	Chililabombwe		
Madīnat ash-Sha'b	12°50' N,	044°56' E	(Bancroft)	12°22' S,	027°50' E
Ma'rib	15°25' N,	045°21' E	Chingola	12°32' S,	027°52' E
Min'ar	16°43' N,	051°18' E	Chipata (Fort Jameson)	13°39' S,	032°40' E
Mocha (al-Mukha)	13°19' N,	043°15' E	Isoka	10°08' S,	032°38' E
Niṣāb	14°31' N,	046°30' E	Kabwe (Broken Hill)	14°27' S,	028°27' E
Raydah	15°50' N,	044°03' E	Kalabo	14°58' S,	022°41' E
Sa'dah	16°57' N,	043°46' E	Kalulushi	12°50' S,	028°05' E
Ṣalif	15°18' N,	042°41' E	Kasama	10°13' S,	031°12' E
Ṣan'ā'	15°21' N,	044°12' E	Kawambwa	09°47' S,	029°05' E
Sayḥūt	15°12' N,	051°14' E	Kitwe	12°49' S,	028°13' E
Saywūn (Say'un)	15°56' N,	048°47' E	Livingstone (Maramba)	17°51' S,	025°52' E
Shabwaḥ	15°22' N,	047°01' E	Luanshya	13°08' S,	028°25' E
Shahārah	16°11' N,	043°42' E	Lusaka	15°25' S,	028°17' E
Ta'izz	13°34' N,	044°02' E	Mansa (Fort Rosebery)	11°12' S,	028°53' E
Tarīm	16°03' N,	049°00' E	Mazabuka	15°51' S,	027°46' E
Zabīd	14°12' N,	043°19' E	Mongu	15°17' S,	023°08' E
Zinjibār	13°08' N,	045°23' E	Monze	16°16' S,	027°29' E
			Mpika	11°50' S,	031°27' E
			Mumbwa	14°59' S,	027°04' E

YUGOSLAVIA . . . .pg. 192

			Mwamfuli (Samfya)	11°21' S,	029°33' E
			Nchelenge	09°21' S,	029°44' E
Bar	42°05' N,	019°06' E	Ndola	12°58' S,	028°38' E
Belgrade	44°50' N,	020°30' E	Senanga	16°07' S,	023°16' E
Bor	44°06' N,	022°06' E	Serenje	13°14' S,	030°14' E
Cacak	43°54' N,	020°21' E	Zambezi	13°33' S,	023°07' E
Gornji Milanovac	44°02' N,	020°27' E			
Kikinda	45°50' N,	020°29' E			
Knjaževac	43°34' N,	022°15' E	## ZIMBABWE . . . . . .pg. 194		
Kosovska Mitrovica					
(Titova Mitrovica)	42°53' N,	020°52' E	Beitbridge	22°13' S,	030°00' E
			Bulawayo	20°09' S,	028°35' E

Acronyms for International Organizations

ACP	African, Caribbean, and Pacific Convention
ADB	Asian Development Bank
APEC	Asia-Pacific Economic Cooperation Council
CARICOM	Caribbean Community and Common Market
EEC	European Economic Community
EU	The European Union
FAO	Food and Agriculture Organization
GCC	Gulf Cooperation Council
I-ADB	Inter-American Development Bank
IDB	Islamic Development Bank
ILO	International Labour Organization
IMF	International Monetary Fund
ITU	International Telecommunications Union
OAS	Organization of American States
OAU	Organization of African Unity
OPEC	Organization of Petroleum Exporting Countries
SPC	South Pacific Commission
UNICEF	United Nations Children's Fund
UNESCO	United Nations Educational, Scientific, and Cultural Organization
WHO	World Health Organization
WTO	World Trade Organization (formerly General Agreement on Tariffs and Trade, GATT)

Country	National Capital	Population of National Capital	United Nations (date of admission)	UNICEF	FAO	ILO
Afghanistan	Kābul	700,000	1946	•	•	•
Albania	Tiranë	300,000	1955	•	•	•
Algeria	Algiers	1,507,241	1962	•	•	•
Andorra	Andorra la Vella	22,821	1993			
Angola	Luanda	2,000,000	1976	•	•	•
Antigua and Barbuda	Saint John's	21,514	1981	•	•	•
Argentina	Buenos Aires	2,988,006	1945	•	•	•
Armenia	Yerevan	1,226,000	1992	•	•	•
Australia	Canberra	303,700	1945	•	•	•
Austria	Vienna	1,539,848	1955	•	•	•
Azerbaijan	Baku	1,087,000	1992	•	•	•
Bahamas, The	Nassau	172,196	1973	•	•	•
Bahrain	Manama	140,401	1971	•	•	•
Bangladesh	Dhākā (Dacca)	3,839,000	1974	•	•	•
Barbados	Bridgetown	6,070	1966	•	•	•
Belarus	Minsk	1,700,000	1945	•		•
Belgium	Brussels	136,424	1945	•	•	•
Belize	Belmopan	3,927	1981	•	•	•
Benin	Cotonou (official)	533,212	1960	•	•	•
	Porto-Novo (de facto)	177,660				
Bhutan	Thimphu	30,340	1971	•	•	
Bolivia	La Paz (administrative)	784,976	1945	•	•	•
	Sucre (judicial)	144,994				
Bosnia and Herzegovina	Sarajevo	250,000	1992	•	•	•
Botswana	Gaborone	156,803	1966	•	•	•
Brazil	Brasília	1,492,542	1945	•	•	•
Brunei	Bandar Seri Begawan	21,484	1984			
Bulgaria	Sofia	1,116,823	1955	•	•	•
Burkina Faso	Ouagadougou	690,000	1960	•	•	•
Burundi	Bujumbura	300,000	1962	•	•	•
Cambodia	Phnom Penh	920,000	1955	•	•	•
Cameroon	Yaoundé	800,000	1960	•	•	•
Canada	Ottawa	313,987	1945	•	•	•
Cape Verde	Praia	61,644	1975	•	•	•
Central African Republic	Bangui	524,000	1960	•	•	•
Chad	N'Djamena	530,965	1960	•	•	•
Chile	Santiago	5,076,808	1945	•	•	•
China	Beijing (Peking)	7,000,000	1945	•	•	•
Colombia	Bogotá	5,237,635	1945	•	•	•
Comoros	Moroni	30,000	1975	•	•	•
Congo, Democratic						
Republic of the	Kinshasa	4,655,313	1960	•	•	•
Congo, Republic of the	Brazzaville	937,579	1960	•	•	•
Costa Rica	San José	321,193	1945	•	•	•
Croatia	Zagreb	867,717	1992	•	•	•
Cuba	Havana	2,241,000	1945	•	•	•
Cyprus	Nicosia (Lefkosia)	186,400	1960	•	•	•
Czech Republic	Prague	1,213,299	1993	•	•	•
Denmark	Copenhagen	1,353,333	1945	•	•	•
Djibouti	Djibouti	317,000	1977	•	•	•
Dominica	Roseau	15,853	1978	•	•	•

IMF	ITU	UNESCO	WHO	WTO	Commonwealth of Nations	EU	GCC	OAS	OAU	SPC	ACP	ADB	APEC	CARICOM	EEC	I-ADB	IDB	OPEC	Country
•	•	•	•									•					•		Afghanistan
•	•	•	•	•															Albania
•	•	•	•	•					•								•	•	Algeria
	•	•						•	•										Andorra
•	•	•	•	•					•		•								Angola
•	•	•	•	•	•			•			•			•					Antigua and Barbuda
•	•	•	•	•				•								•			Argentina
•	•	•	•	•															Armenia
•	•	•	•	•	•					•		•	•						Australia
•	•	•	•	•		•						•				•			Austria
•	•	•	•									•					•		Azerbaijan
•	•	•	•		•			•			•			•		•			Bahamas, The
•	•	•	•	•			•										•		Bahrain
•	•	•	•	•	•							•					•		Bangladesh
•	•	•	•	•	•			•			•			•		•			Barbados
•	•	•	•																Belarus
•	•	•	•	•		•						•				•			Belgium
•	•	•	•	•	•			•			•			•		•			Belize
•	•	•	•	•					•		•								Benin
•	•	•	•									•							Bhutan
•	•	•	•	•				•								•			Bolivia
•	•	•	•																Bosnia and Herzegovina
•	•	•	•	•	•				•		•								Botswana
•	•	•	•	•				•								•			Brazil
	•	•	•	•	•								•				•		Brunei
•	•	•	•	•															Bulgaria
•	•	•	•	•					•		•						•		Burkina Faso
•	•	•	•	•					•		•								Burundi
•	•	•	•	•								•							Cambodia
•	•	•	•	•	•				•		•						•		Cameroon
•	•	•	•	•	•			•				•	•			•			Canada
•	•	•	•	•					•		•								Cape Verde
•	•	•	•	•					•		•								Central African Republic
•	•	•	•	•					•		•						•		Chad
•	•	•	•	•				•					•			•			Chile
•	•	•	•									•	•						China
•	•	•	•	•				•								•			Colombia
•	•	•	•						•		•						•		Comoros
•	•	•	•	•					•		•								Congo, Democratic Republic of the
•	•	•	•	•					•		•								Congo, Republic of the
•	•	•	•	•				•								•			Costa Rica
•	•	•	•	•												•			Croatia
	•	•	•	•				•											Cuba
•	•	•	•	•	•											•			Cyprus
•	•	•	•	•															Czech Republic
•	•	•	•	•		•						•			•	•			Denmark
•	•	•	•	•					•		•						•		Djibouti
•	•	•	•	•	•			•			•			•		•			Dominica

Country	National Capital	Population of National Capital	United Nations (date of admission)	UNICEF	FAO	ILO
Dominican Republic	Santo Domingo	2,138,262	1945	●	●	●
Ecuador	Quito	1,444,363	1945	●	●	●
Egypt	Cairo	6,849,000	1945	●	●	●
El Salvador	San Salvador	422,570	1945	●	●	●
Equatorial Guinea	Malabo	58,040	1968	●	●	●
Eritrea	Asmara	367,300	1993	●	●	●
Estonia	Tallinn	434,763	1991	●	●	●
Ethiopia	Addis Ababa	2,316,400	1945	●	●	●
Fiji	Suva	200,000	1970	●	●	●
Finland	Helsinki	525,031	1955	●	●	●
France	Paris	2,175,200	1945	●	●	●
Gabon	Libreville	362,386	1960	●	●	●
Gambia, The	Banjul	42,407	1965	●		
Georgia	Tbilisi	1,279,000	1992	●	●	●
Germany	Berlin	293,072	1973	●	●	●
Ghana	Accra	1,781,100	1957	●	●	●
Greece	Athens	748,110	1945	●	●	●
Grenada	Saint George's	4,621	1974	●	●	●
Guatemala	Guatemala City	823,301	1945	●	●	●
Guinea	Conakry	1,508,000	1958	●	●	●
Guinea-Bissau	Bissau	197,610	1974	●	●	●
Guyana	Georgetown	248,500	1966	●	●	●
Haiti	Port-au-Prince	846,247	1945	●	●	●
Honduras	Tegucigalpa	775,300	1945	●	●	●
Hungary	Budapest	1,909,000	1955	●	●	●
Iceland	Reykjavik	104,276	1946	●	●	●
India	New Delhi	301,297	1945	●	●	●
Indonesia	Jakarta	8,259,266	1950	●	●	●
Iran	Tehrān	11,000,000	1945	●	●	●
Iraq	Baghdad	4,478,000	1945	●	●	●
Ireland	Dublin	478,389	1955	●	●	●
Israel	Jerusalem (Yerushalayim, Al-Quds)	591,400	1949	●	●	●
Italy	Rome (Roma)	2,687,881	1955	●	●	●
Ivory Coast	Yamoussoukro (de jure; administrative)	106,786	1960	●	●	●
Jamaica	Kingston	103,771	1962	●	●	●
Japan	Tokyo	7,966,195	1956	●	●	●
Jordan	Amman	963,490	1955	●	●	●
Kazakstan	Astana	1,150,500	1992	●		
Kenya	Nairobi	2,000,000	1963	●	●	●
Kiribati	Bairki	2,226	1999	●		
Kuwait	Kuwait (Al-Kuwayt)	31,241	1963	●	●	●
Kyrgyzstan	Bishkek (Frunze)	597,000	1992	●	●	●
Laos	Vientiane (Viangchan)	442,000	1955	●	●	●
Latvia	Rīga	839,670	1991	●	●	●
Lebanon	Beirut (Bayrūt)	1,100,000	1945	●	●	●
Lesotho	Maseru	170,000	1966	●	●	●
Liberia	Monrovia	668,000	1945	●	●	●
Libya	Tripoli (Ṭarābulus)	591,062	1955	●	●	●
Liechtenstein	Vaduz	5,067	1990			

IMF	ITU	UNESCO	WHO	WTO	Commonwealth of Nations	EU	GCC	OAS	OAU	SPC	ACP	ADB	APEC	CARICOM	EEC	I-ADB	IDB	OPEC	Country
•	•	•	•	•				•			•			•		•			Dominican Republic
•	•	•	•	•				•								•			Ecuador
•	•	•	•	•					•								•		Egypt
•	•	•	•	•				•								•			El Salvador
•	•	•	•	•					•		•								Equatorial Guinea
•	•	•	•						•										Eritrea
•	•	•	•	•															Estonia
•	•	•	•						•		•								Ethiopia
•	•	•	•	•						•	•	•							Fiji
•	•	•	•	•		•									•	•			Finland
•	•	•	•	•		•				•	•				•	•			France
•	•	•	•	•					•		•						•	•	Gabon
•	•	•	•	•	•				•		•						•		Gambia, The
•	•	•	•																Georgia
•	•	•	•	•		•		•							•	•			Germany
•	•	•	•	•	•				•		•								Ghana
•	•	•	•	•		•									•				Greece
•	•	•	•	•	•			•			•			•					Grenada
•	•	•	•	•				•								•			Guatemala
•	•	•	•	•					•		•						•		Guinea
•	•	•	•	•					•		•						•		Guinea-Bissau
•	•	•	•	•	•			•			•			•		•			Guyana
•	•	•	•	•				•			•			•		•			Haiti
•	•	•	•	•				•								•			Honduras
•	•	•	•	•															Hungary
•	•	•	•	•															Iceland
•	•	•	•	•	•							•							India
•	•	•	•	•								•	•				•	•	Indonesia
•	•	•	•	•													•	•	Iran
•	•	•	•														•	•	Iraq
•	•	•	•	•		•									•				Ireland
•	•	•	•	•												•			Israel
•	•	•	•	•		•									•	•			Italy
•	•	•	•	•					•		•								Ivory Coast
•	•	•	•	•	•			•			•			•		•			Jamaica
•	•	•	•	•								•	•			•			Japan
•	•	•	•	•													•		Jordan
•	•	•	•	•								•					•		Kazakstan
•	•	•	•	•	•				•		•								Kenya
•	•	•	•	•	•					•	•	•							Kiribati
•	•	•	•	•			•										•	•	Kuwait
•	•	•	•	•								•					•		Kyrgyzstan
•	•	•	•									•							Laos
•	•	•	•	•															Latvia
•	•	•	•														•		Lebanon
•	•	•	•	•	•				•		•								Lesotho
•	•	•	•						•		•								Liberia
•	•	•	•						•								•	•	Libya
	•		•	•															Liechtenstein

Country	National Capital	Population of National Capital	United Nations (date of admission)	UNICEF	FAO	ILO
Lithuania	Vilnius	590,100	1991	•	•	•
Luxembourg	Luxembourg	76,446	1945	•	•	•
Macedonia	Skopje (Skopije)	541,280	1993	•	•	•
Madagascar	Antananarivo	1,052,835	1960	•	•	•
Malawi	Lilongwe	395,500	1964	•	•	•
Malaysia	Kuala Lumpur	1,145,075	1957	•	•	•
Maldives	Male'	62,973	1965	•	•	
Mali	Bamako	800,000	1960	•	•	•
Malta	Valletta	9,129	1964	•	•	•
Marshall Islands	Majuro	20,000	1991	•		
Mauritania	Nouakchott	735,000	1961	•	•	•
Mexico	Mexico City	9,815,795	1945	•	•	•
Federated States of Micronesia	Palikir	-	1991	•		
Moldova	Chişinău	662,000	1992	•	•	•
Mongolia	Ulaanbaatar (Ulan Bator)	619,000	1961	•	•	•
Morocco	Rabat	1,220,000	1956	•	•	•
Mozambique	Maputo (Lourenço Marques)	931,591	1975	•	•	
Myanmar	Yangôn (Rangoon)	3,851,000	1948	•	•	•
Namibia	Windhoek	161,000	1990	•	•	•
Nepal	Kāthmāndu	535,000	1955	•	•	•
Netherlands, The	Amsterdam (de jure)	722,245	1945	•	•	•
New Zealand	Wellington	158,275	1945	•	•	•
Nicaragua	Managua	1,195,000	1945	•	•	•
Niger	Niamey	391,876	1960	•	•	•
Nigeria	Abuja	339,100	1960	•	•	•
North Korea	P'yŏngyang	2,355,000	1991	•	•	•
Norway	Oslo	487,908	1945	•	•	•
Oman	Muscat	51,869	1971	•	•	•
Pakistan	Islāmābād	204,364	1947	•	•	•
Palau	Koror	10,500	1994	•		
Panama	Panama City	445,902	1945	•	•	•
Papua New Guinea	Port Moresby	193,242	1975	•	•	•
Paraguay	Asunción	502,426	1945	•	•	•
Peru	Lima	421,570	1945	•	•	•
Philippines	Manila	1,894,667	1945	•	•	•
Poland	Warsaw (Warszawa)	1,640,700	1945	•	•	•
Portugal	Lisbon	677,790	1955	•	•	•
Qatar	Doha	313,639	1971	•	•	•
Romania	Bucharest	2,343,824	1958	•	•	•
Russia	Moscow	8,717,000	1991	•		
Rwanda	Kigali	232,733	1962	•	•	•
St. Kitts and Nevis	Basseterre	15,000	1983	•		
St. Lucia	Castries	13,615	1979	•	•	•
St. Vincent and The Grenadines	Kingstown	15,466	1980	•	•	•
Samoa	Apia	32,859	1976	•	•	•
San Marino	San Marino	2,316	1992	•		
São Tomé and Príncipe	São Tomé	43,420	1975	•	•	•
Saudi Arabia	Riyadh (Ar-Riyadh)	1,800,000	1945	•	•	•

IMF	ITU	UNESCO	WHO	WTO	Commonwealth of Nations	EU	GCC	OAS	OAU	SPC	ACP	ADB	APEC	CARICOM	EEC	I-ADB	IDB	OPEC	Country
•	•	•	•	•		•													Lithuania
•	•	•	•	•		•													Luxembourg
•	•	•	•	•															Macedonia
•	•	•	•	•					•		•								Madagascar
•	•	•	•	•	•				•		•								Malawi
•	•	•	•	•	•						•	•	•				•		Malaysia
•	•	•	•	•	•						•	•					•		Maldives
•	•	•	•	•					•		•						•		Mali
•	•	•	•	•	•										•				Malta
•	•		•							•		•							Marshall Islands
•	•	•	•	•					•		•						•		Mauritania
•	•	•	•	•				•					•			•			Mexico
•	•	•	•							•		•							Federated States of Micronesia
•	•	•	•	•							•								Moldova
•	•	•	•	•								•							Mongolia
•	•	•	•	•													•		Morocco
•	•	•	•	•	•				•		•								Mozambique
•	•	•	•	•								•							Myanmar
•	•	•	•	•					•		•								Namibia
•	•	•	•	•								•							Nepal
•	•	•	•	•		•						•		•	•				Netherlands, The
•	•	•	•	•	•					•			•						New Zealand
•	•	•	•	•				•								•			Nicaragua
•	•	•	•	•					•		•						•		Niger
•	•	•	•	•	•				•		•						•	•	Nigeria
	•	•	•																North Korea
•	•	•	•	•								•				•			Norway
•	•	•	•	•			•										•		Oman
•	•	•	•	•	•							•					•		Pakistan
		•	•							•									Palau
•	•	•	•	•				•								•			Panama
•	•	•	•	•	•					•	•	•	•						Papua New Guinea
•	•	•	•	•				•								•			Paraguay
•	•	•	•	•				•					•			•			Peru
•	•	•	•	•								•	•						Phillipines
•	•	•	•	•															Poland
•	•	•	•	•		•									•	•			Portugal
•	•	•	•	•			•										•	•	Qatar
•	•	•	•	•															Romania
•	•	•	•										•						Russia
•	•	•	•	•					•		•								Rwanda
•	•	•	•	•	•			•			•			•					St. Kitts and Nevis
•	•	•	•	•	•			•			•			•					St. Lucia
•	•	•	•	•	•			•			•			•					St. Vincent and the Grenadines
•	•	•	•		•					•	•	•							Samoa
•	•	•	•																San Marino
•	•	•	•	•					•		•						•	•	São Tomé and Príncipe
•	•	•	•	•			•										•	•	Saudi Arabia

Country	National Capital	Population of National Capital	United Nations (date of admission)	UNICEF	FAO	ILO
Senegal	Dakar	785,071	1960	•	•	•
Seychelles	Victoria	25,000	1976	•	•	•
Sierra Leone	Freetown	669,000	1961	•	•	•
Singapore	Singapore	3,045,000	1965	•	•	•
Slovakia	Bratislava	450,776	1993	•	•	•
Slovenia	Ljubljana	276,119	1992	•	•	•
Solomon Islands	Honiara	43,643	1978	•	•	•
Somalia	Mogadishu	900,000	1960	•	•	•
South Africa	Bloemfontein (judicial)	126,867	1945	•	•	•
	Cape Town (legislative)	854,616				
	Pretoria (executive)	525,583				
South Korea	Seoul (Sŏul)	10,229,262	1991	•	•	•
Spain	Madrid	3,041,101	1955	•	•	•
Sri Lanka	Colombo	615,000	1955	•	•	•
Sudan	Khartoum	924,505	1956	•	•	•
Suriname	Paramaribo	200,970	1975	•	•	•
Swaziland	Mbabane	47,000	1968	•	•	•
Sweden	Stockholm	711,119	1946	•	•	•
Switzerland	Bern (Berne)	128,422	-	•	•	•
Syria	Damascus (Dimashq)	1,549,932	1956	•	•	•
Taiwan	Taipei (T'ai-pei)	2,626,138	-	•	•	•
Tajikistan	Dushanbe	524,000	1992	•	•	•
Tanzania	Dar es Salaam	1,360,850	1961	•	•	•
Thailand	Bangkok	5,584,288	1946	•	•	•
Togo	Lomé	513,000	1960	•	•	•
Tonga	Nuku'alofa	34,000	1999	•	•	
Trinidad and Tobago	Port-of-Spain	52,451	1962	•	•	•
Tunisia	Tunis	674,100	1956	•	•	•
Turkey	Ankara	2,782,200	1945	•	•	•
Turkmenistan	Ashkhabad (Ashgabat)	518,000	1992	•	•	•
Tuvalu	Funafuti	3,839	-	•		
Uganda	Kampala	773,463	1962	•	•	•
Ukraine	Kiev (Kyyiv)	2,630,000	1945	•	•	•
United Arab Emirates	Abu Dhabi (Abū Ẓaby)	363,432	1971	•	•	•
United Kingdom	London	6,967,500	1945	•	•	•
United States	Washington, D.C.	567,094	1945	•	•	•
Uruguay	Montevideo	1,378,707	1945	•	•	•
Uzbekistan	Tashkent	2,106,000	1992	•		•
Vanuatu	Vila	26,100	1981	•	•	
Venezuela	Caracas	1,822,465	1945	•	•	•
Vietnam	Hanoi	2,154,900	1977	•	•	•
Yemen	Ṣan'ā'	503,600	1947	•	•	•
Yugoslavia	Belgrade (Beograd)	1,168,454	1945	•	•	•
Zambia	Lusaka	982,362	1964	•	•	•
Zimbabwe	Harare	1,184,169	1980	•	•	•

IMF	ITU	UNESCO	WHO	WTO	Commonwealth of Nations	EU	GCC	OAS	OAU	SPC	ACP	ADB	APEC	CARICOM	EEC	I-ADB	IDB	OPEC	Country
•	•	•	•	•					•		•						•		Senegal
•	•	•	•	•	•				•		•								Seychelles
•	•	•	•	•	•				•		•					•			Sierra Leone
•	•		•	•	•							•	•						Singapore
•	•	•	•	•															Slovakia
•	•	•	•	•												•			Slovenia
•	•	•	•	•	•					•	•	•							Solomon Islands
•	•	•	•						•		•						•		Somalia
•	•	•	•	•	•				•										South Africa
•	•	•	•	•								•	•						South Korea
•	•	•	•	•		•						•			•	•			Spain
•	•	•	•	•	•							•							Sri Lanka
•	•	•	•						•		•						•		Sudan
•	•	•	•					•			•			•		•			Suriname
•	•	•	•	•	•				•		•								Swaziland
•	•	•	•	•		•						•			•	•			Sweden
•	•	•	•	•								•				•			Switzerland
•	•	•	•														•		Syria
	•	•	•									•	•						Taiwan
•		•	•																Tajikistan
•	•	•	•	•	•				•		•								Tanzania
•	•	•	•	•								•	•						Thailand
•	•	•	•	•					•		•								Togo
•	•	•	•	•	•					•	•	•							Tonga
•	•	•	•	•	•			•			•			•		•			Trinidad and Tobago
•	•	•	•	•					•							•			Tunisia
•	•	•	•	•								•			•		•		Turkey
•	•		•	•													•		Turkmenistan
	•	•	•	•	•					•	•	•							Tuvalu
•	•	•	•	•	•				•		•								Uganda
•	•	•	•	•															Ukraine
•	•	•	•	•			•										•	•	United Arab Emirates
•	•	•	•	•	•	•					•	•			•	•			United Kingdom
•	•	•	•	•				•			•	•	•			•			United States
•	•	•	•	•				•								•			Uruguay
•	•	•	•	•															Uzbekistan
•	•	•	•		•					•	•	•							Vanuatu
•	•	•	•	•				•						•		•		•	Venezuela
•	•	•	•	•								•							Vietnam
•	•	•	•	•													•		Yemen
•	•	•	•	•															Yugoslavia
•	•	•	•	•	•				•		•								Zambia
•	•	•	•	•	•				•		•								Zimbabwe

Country	Airports with scheduled flights (1996)	Persons per Television (1995)	Persons per Telephone (1993)	Mobile Phones per 1000 people (1995)	Computers per 1000 people (1995)
Afghanistan	3	181	770	...	...
Albania	1	11	70	0	...
Algeria	28	14	25	0.2	3
Andorra	0	2.8	2.4	...	...
Angola	17	220	190	0.2	...
Antigua and Barbuda	2	2.3	3.5	...	...
Argentina	43	4.8	8.1	9.9	24.6
Armenia	1	4.7	6.4	0	...
Australia	400	2.3	2.1	127.7	275.8
Austria	6	3	2.2	47.6	124.2
Azerbaijan	1	4.7	11	0.1	...
Bahamas, The	23	5.5	3.3	...	...
Bahrain	1	2.1	4.3	...	...
Bangladesh	8	200	440	0	...
Barbados	1	4.1	3.2	...	...
Belarus	2	3.7	5.7	0.6	...
Belgium	2	2.4	2.3	23.2	138.3
Belize	11	9.4	7.1	...	...
Benin	1	270	260	0.2	...
Bhutan	1	...	400	...	...
Bolivia	14	8.8	33	1	...
Bosnia and Herzegovina	1	3.4	7.3	0	...
Botswana	4	111	32	0	...
Brazil	139	5.2	13	8	13
Brunei	1	3.2	5.1	...	...
Bulgaria	3	2.7	3.8	...	21.4
Burkina Faso	2	244	460	0	0
Burundi	1	1320	390	0.1	...
Cambodia	7	137	1670	1.5	...
Cameroon	5	882	220	0.2	...
Canada	301	1.5	1.7	86.5	192.5
Cape Verde	9	371	26	...	...
Central African Republic	1	419	480	0	...
Chad	4	127	1430	0	0
Chile	18	7.1	9.1	13.8	37.8
China	113	5.3	68	3	2.2
Colombia	63	6.4	8.9	7.1	16.2
Comoros	4	2550	130	...	...
Congo, Democratic Republic of the	12	2000	1110	0.2	...
Congo, Republic of the	5	305	130	0	...
Costa Rica	14	9.8	11	5.5	...
Croatia	5	6	4.5	7.1	20.9
Cuba	14	4.4	31	0.1	...
Cyprus	2	6.3	2	...	...
Czech Republic	2	2.1	5.3	4.7	53.2
Denmark	13	10.2	1.7	157.3	270.5
Djibouti	1	34	78	...	...

Country	Airports with scheduled flights (1996)	Persons per Television (1995)	Persons per Telephone (1993)	Mobile Phones per 1000 people (1995)	Computers per 1000 people (1995)
Dominica	2	14	5.3	...	...
Dominican Republic	4	11	13	...	...
Ecuador	14	13	19	4.6	3.9
Egypt	14	12	24	0.1	3.4
El Salvador	1	12	26	2.5	...
Equatorial Guinea	2	158	290	...	...
Eritrea	2	...	170	0	...
Estonia	3	2.5	4.3	20.5	6.7
Ethiopia	31	367	400	0	...
Fiji	13	59	11	...	...
Finland	24	2.7	1.8	199.2	182.1
France	66	2	1.9	23.8	134.3
Gabon	23	29	41	2.5	4.5
Gambia, The	1	186	63	1.3	...
Georgia	1	...	9.6	0	...
Germany	40	2.7	2.2	42.8	164.9
Ghana	1	66	330	0.4	1.2
Greece	36	4.6	2.2	26.1	33.4
Grenada	2	6.1	4.5	...	...
Guatemala	2	22	43	2.8	2.8
Guinea	2	103	560	0.1	0.2
Guinea-Bissau	2	...	120	0	...
Guyana	1	51	20	...	...
Haiti	2	264	150	0	...
Honduras	8	34	48	0	...
Hungary	1	2.4	6.9	25.9	39.2
Iceland	24	3.5	1.8	...	...
India	66	47	110	0.1	1.3
Indonesia	81	18	110	1.1	3.7
Iran	19	8.8	17	0.1	...
Iraq	...	20	29	0	...
Ireland	9	3.6	3.1	44.1	145
Israel	7	3.6	2.7	153.5	99.8
Italy	31	3.4	2.4	67.4	83.7
Ivory Coast	11	18	140	0	...
Jamaica	5	5.2	9.5	17.9	...
Japan	73	1.3	2.1	81.5	152.5
Jordan	2	17	14	2.6	8
Kazakstan	6	3.5	11	0.3	...
Kenya	13	57	120	0.1	0.7
Kiribati	17	115	43	...	...
Kuwait	1	2.1	4.1	70.7	57.1
Kyrgyzstan	2	5.1	12	0	...
Laos	11	61	530	0.1	...
Latvia	1	2.2	3.7	6	7.9
Lebanon	1	2.7	11	30	12.5
Lesotho	1	8.2	179	0	...

Country	Airports with scheduled flights (1996)	Persons per Television (1995)	Persons per Telephone (1993)	Mobile Phones per 1000 people (1995)	Computers per 1000 people (1995)
Liberia	1	53	590	...	...
Libya	12	9.8	21	0	...
Liechtenstein	0	3	1.6	...	...
Lithuania	3	2.4	4.4	4	6.5
Luxembourg	1	4.1	1.9	...	...
Macedonia	1	5.9	6.8	0	...
Madagascar	19	114	370	0	...
Malawi	4	...	290	0	...
Malaysia	36	6.5	7.9	43.4	39.7
Maldives	5	53	24	...	...
Mali	1	901	670	0	...
Malta	1	2.6	2.3	...	...
Marshall Islands	23	...	23	...	...
Mauritania	10	2070	290	0	...
Mexico	83	6.5	11	7	26.1
Micronesia, Federated States of	4	15	18	...	...
Moldova	1	3.5	8.3	0	2.1
Mongolia	1	17	36	0	0.2
Morocco	12	22	32	1.1	1.7
Mozambique	7	511	270	0	...
Myanmar (Burma)	19	47	560	0	...
Namibia	13	42	22	2.3	...
Nepal	24	80	290	0	...
Netherlands, The	6	2.4	2	33.2	200.5
New Zealand	36	3.2	2.2	108	222.7
Nicaragua	10	21	60	1.1	...
Niger	6	366	830	0	...
Nigeria	12	16	300	0.1	4.1
North Korea	1	12	21	0	...
Norway	50	2.2	1.8	224.4	273
Oman	6	1.4	8.6	3.7	...
Pakistan	34	68	76	0.3	1.2
Palau	1	11	...	...	...
Panama	10	13	9.8	0	...
Papua New Guinea	129	43	100	0	...
Paraguay	5	14	33	3.2	...
Peru	27	12	34	3.1	5.9
Philippines	21	10	76	7.3	11.4
Poland	12	3.9	8.7	1.9	28.5
Portugal	14	5.6	3.2	34.3	60.4
Qatar	1	2.3	4.7	...	...
Romania	12	5.7	8.7	0.4	5.3
Russia	58	2.7	6.3	0.6	17.7
Rwanda	3	...	630	0	...
St. Kitts and Nevis	2	4.2	3.4	...	...
St. Lucia	2	5.7	6.5	...	...
St. Vincent and the Grenadines	4	6.2	6.7	...	...

Country	Airports with scheduled flights (1996)	Persons per Television (1995)	Persons per Telephone (1993)	Mobile Phones per 1000 people (1995)	Computers per 1000 people (1995)
Samoa	2	33	25	...	...
San Marino	0	3	1.6	...	...
São Tomé and Príncipe	2	6.2	52	...	...
Saudi Arabia	25	3.8	11	0.9	25.1
Senegal	7	136	130	0	7.2
Seychelles	2	5.8	6.2	...	...
Sierra Leone	1	180	310	0	...
Singapore	1	4.6	2.3	97.7	172.4
Slovakia	2	4.2	6	2.3	41
Slovenia	1	3.5	3.9	13.6	47.7
Solomon Islands	30	...	65	...	...
Somalia	1	55	560	...	...
South Africa	24	12	11	12.9	26.5
South Korea	14	4.3	2.7	36.6	120.8
Spain	25	2.3	2.7	24.1	81.6
Sri Lanka	1	26	111	2.8	1.1
Sudan	10	112	440	0	...
Suriname	2	10	8.6	...	...
Swaziland	1	73	56	...	...
Sweden	48	2.4	1.5	229.4	192.5
Switzerland	5	2.7	1.6	63.5	348
Syria	5	20	24	0	0.1
Taiwan	13	3	2.6	...	...
Tajikistan	1	6.3	22	0	...
Tanzania	11	351	313	0.1	...
Thailand	25	18	27	18.5	15.3
Togo	1	28	230	0	0
Tonga	6	40	16	...	...
Trinidad and Tobago	2	5.1	6.5	4.3	19.2
Tunisia	5	14	20	0.4	6.7
Turkey	26	5.9	5.4	7	12.5
Turkmenistan	1	5.3	15	0.2	...
Tuvalu	1	...	77	...	...
Uganda	1	162	830	0.1	0.5
Ukraine	20	3	6.7	0.3	5.6
United Arab Emirates	6	13	2.6	54.2	48.4
United Kingdom	50	2.9	2	98	186.2
United States	834	1.2	1.7	128.4	328
Uruguay	1	5.3	5.9	12.6	22
Uzbekistan	9	6.3	15	...	...
Vanuatu	29	80	39	...	...
Venezuela	24	5.9	10	18	16.7
Vietnam	12	30	270	0.2	...
Yemen	11	131	83	0.5	...
Yugoslavia	5	6.4	5.6	0	11.8
Zambia	4	47	110	0.2	...
Zimbabwe	7	82	84	0	3

Name and location	Area	
	(km)	**(sq mi)**
WORLD		
Caspian Sea, *Turkmenistan–Kazakstan–Russia–Azerbaijan-Iran*	387,770	149,000
Superior, *Canada–United States*	82,350	31,700
Victoria, *Kenya–Tanzania–Uganda*	69,725	26,828
Huron, *Canada–United States*	59,600	23,000
Michigan, *United States*	58,000	22,300
Aral Sea, *Kazakstan–Uzbekistan*	33,640	13,000
Tanganyika, *Burundi–Tanzania–Dem. Rep. Congo–Zambia*	33,000	12,7000
Baikal, *Russia*	31,700	12,200
AFRICA		
Victoria, *Kenya-Tanzania–Uganda*	69,725	26,828
Tanganyika, *Burundi–Tanzania-Dem. Rep. Congo–Zambia*	33,000	22,700
Nyasa (Malawi), *Malawi–Mozambique–Tanzania*	29,600	11,430
Chad, *Cameroon–Chad–Niger–Nigeria*	17,870	6,875
Bangweulu, *Zambia*	9,876	3,800
AMERICA, NORTH		
Superior, *Canada–United States*	82,350	31,700
Huron, *Canada–United States*	59,600	23,000
Michigan, *United States*	58,000	22,300
Great Bear, *Northwest Territories, Canada*	31,260	12,028
Great Slave, *Northwest Territories, Canada*	28,500	11,031
AMERICA, SOUTH		
Maracaibo, *Venezuela*	13,260	5,510
Titicaca, *Peru–Bolivia*	8,300	3,200
Poopó, *Bolivia*	2,600	1,000
Buenos Aires (General Carrera), *Chile–Argentina*	2,248	865
Chiquita, *Argentina*	1855	714
ASIA		
Caspian Sea, *Turkmenistan–Kazakstan–Russia–Azerbaijan-Iran*	387,770	149,200
Aral Sea, *Kazakstan–Uzbekistan*	33,640	13,000
Baikal, *Russia*	31,700	12,200
Balkhash, *Kazakstan*	17,280	6,650
Tonle Sap, *Cambodia*	6,562	2,525
EUROPE		
Ladoga, *Russia*	17,700	6,826
Onega, *Russia*	9,700	3,753
Vänern, *Sweden*	6,500	2,156
Iso Saimaa, *Finland*	4,390	1,690
Peipsi, *Estonia–Russia*	3,568	1,373
OCEANIA		
Eyre, *South Australia*	9,355	3,600
Torrens, *South Australia*	6,105	2,230
Gairdner, *South Australia*	4,800	1,845
Frome, *South Australia*	2,339	900

Name	Outflow	Length	
		(km)	**(miles)**
WORLD			
Nile	Mediterranean Sea	6,620	4,132
Amazon–Ucayali–Apurimac	South Alantic Ocean	6,450	4,000
Chang (Yangtze)	East China Sea	6,380	3,915
Mississippi–Missouri–Red Rock	Gulf of Mexico	6,020	3,710
Yenisey–Baikal–Selenga	Kara Sea	5,550	3,442
Huang (Yellow)	Bo Hai (Gulf of Chihli)	5,464	3,395
Ob–Irtysh	Gulf of Ob	5,410	3,362
Paraná	Río de la Plata	4,500	3,032
AFRICA			
Nile	Mediterranean Sea	6,620	4,132
Congo	South Alantic Ocean	4,620	2,900
Niger	Bight of Biafra	4,180	2,600
Zambezi	Mozambique Channel	3,540	2,200
Kasai	Congo River	2,153	1,338
AMERICA, NORTH			
Mississippi–Missouri–Red Rock	Gulf of Mexico	6,020	3,710
Mackenzie–Slave–Peace	Beaufort Sea	4,240	2,635
Missouri–Red Rock	Mississippi River	3,780	2,540
St. Lawrence–Great Lakes	Gulf of St. Lawrence	4,023	2,500
Mississippi	Gulf of Mexico	3,780	2,340
AMERICA, SOUTH			
Amazon–Ucayali–Apurimac	South Alantic Ocean	6,450	4,000
Paraná	Río de la Plata	4,500	3,032
Madeira–Mamoré–Guaporé	Amazon River	3,350	2,082
Jurua	Amazon River	3,283	2,040
Purus	Amazon River	3,210	1,995
ASIA			
Chang (Yangtze)	East China Sea	6,380	3,915
Yenisey–Baikal–Selenga	Kara Sea	5,550	3,442
Huang (Yellow)	Bo Hai (Gulf of Chihli)	5,464	3,395
Ob–Irtysh	Gulf of Ob	5,400	3,362
Amur–Argun	Sea of Okhotsk	4,400	2,761
EUROPE			
Volga	Caspian Sea	3,700	2,193
Danube	Black Sea	2,850	1,770
Ural	Caspian Sea	2,535	1,509
Dnieper	Black Sea	2,200	1,367
Don	Sea of Azov	1,870	1,162
OCEANIA			
Darling	Murray River	3,070	1,702
Murray	Great Australian Bight	2,575	1,609
Murrumbidgee	Murray River	1,690	981
Lachlan	Murrumbidgee River	1,596	992

Name and location	Height	
	(metres)	(feet)
AFRICA		
Kilimanjaro (Kibo Peak), *Tanzania*	5,895	19,340
Mt. Kenya (Batian Peak), *Kenya*	5,199	17,058
Margherita, Ruwenzori Range, *Dem. Rep. Congo–Uganda*	5,119	16,795
Ras Dashen, Simyen Mts., *Ethiopia*	4,620	15,157
AMERICA, NORTH		
McKinley, Alaska Range, *Alaska, U.S.*	6,194	20,320
Logan, St. Elias Mts., *Yukon, Canada*	5,960	19,524
Citlaltépetl (Orizaba), Cordillera Neo-Volcánica, *Mexico*	5,700	18,406
St. Elias, St Elias Mts., *Alaska, U.S.–Canada*	5,489	18,009
AMERICA, SOUTH		
Aconcagua, Andes, *Argentina–Chile*	6,960	22,831
Ojos del Salado, Andes, *Argentina–Chile*	6,893	22,615
Bonete, Andes, *Argentina*	6,872	22,546
Tupungato, Andes, *Argentina–Chile*	6,800	22,310
Pissis, Andes, *Argentina*	6,779	22,241
ANTARCTICA		
Vinson Massif, Sentinel Range, Ellsworth Mts.	4,897	16,066
Tyree, Sentinel Range, Ellsworth Mts.	4,852	15,919
Shinn, Sentinel Range, Ellsworth Mts.	4,800	15,751
Kirkpatrick, Queen Alexandra Range	4,528	15,856
ASIA		
Everest (Chomolungma), Himalayas, *Nepal–Tibet, China*	8,848	29,028
K2 (Godwin Austen), Karakoram Range, *Pakistan–Xinjiang, China*	8,611	28,251
Kanchenjunga I, Himalayas, *Nepal–India*	8,586	28,169
Lhotse I, Himalayas, *Nepal–Tibet, China*	8,516	27,940
EUROPE		
Mont Blanc, Alps, *France–Italy*	4,807	15,771
Dufourspitze (Monte Rosa), Alps, *Switzerland–Italy*	4,634	15,203
Dom (Mischabel), Alps, *Switzerland*	4,545	14,911
Weisshorn, Alps, *Switzerland*	4,505	14,780
OCEANIA		
Jaya (Sukarno, Carstensz), Sudirman Range, *Indonesia*	5,030	16,500
Pilimsit (Idenburg), Sudirman Range, *Indonesia*	4,800	15,750
Trikora (Wilhelmina), Jayawijaya Mts., *Indonesia*	4,750	15,580
Mandala (Juliana), Jayawijaya Mts., *Indonesia*	4,700	15,420
CAUCASUS		
Elbrus, Caucasus, *Russia*	5,642	18,510
Dyhk-Tau, Caucasus, *Russia*	5,396	17,073
Koshtan-Tau, Caucasus, *Russia*	5,151	16,900
Shkhara, Caucasus, *Russia–Georgia*	5,068	16,627